# FOR REFERENCE

**Do Not Take From This Room**

# Battles That Changed
# American History

# Battles That Changed American History

## 100 of the Greatest Victories and Defeats

Spencer C. Tucker

 ABC-CLIO

Santa Barbara, California • Denver, Colorado • Oxford, England

**Library of Congress Cataloging-in-Publication Data**

Tucker, Spencer, 1937–
    Battles that changed American history / Spencer C. Tucker.
        pages cm
    Includes bibliographical references and index.
    ISBN 978-1-4408-2861-4 (hardcover : alk. paper)
    ISBN 978-1-4408-2862-1 (ebook)
    1. United States—History, Military.    2. Battles—United States—History.    I. Title.
    E181.T933 2014
    355.00973—dc23

                                                                    2013016413

ISBN: 978-1-4408-2861-4
EISBN: 978-1-4408-2862-1

18  17  16  15  14        1  2  3  4  5

This book is also available on the World Wide Web as an eBook.
Visit www.abc-clio.com for details.

ABC-CLIO, LLC
130 Cremona Drive, P.O. Box 1911
Santa Barbara, California 93116-1911

This book is printed on acid-free paper ∞
Manufactured in the United States of America

*For Leo E. Cloutier,*
*veteran of World War II*
*and longtime friend*

# Contents

# List of Entries

# Preface

This collection of 100 influential battles in American history follows closely the format of my *Battles That Changed History.* The current collection discusses mostly individual battles but also some campaigns and a few short wars that in my view most impacted American history from colonial times to the present. Each entry lists books for further reading on the subject as well and has a box containing key information. While I have written the majority of the entries, many other military historians have contributed to the project.

It was difficult to decide just which battles to include. I am most grateful to military historians Drs. David Coffey, Jim Piecuch, Jerry Morelock, Malcolm "Kip" Muir Jr., Paul Pierpaoli Jr., Carol Reardon, and Bradford Wineman, all of whom were gracious enough to review my initial list of some 120 battles. While there was general agreement on perhaps half of my selections, there was little consensus on the remainder; strong opinions were expressed, pro and con, regarding some of the selections. While this process was helpful to me, it also made the task of reducing a long list to fit within the number of words allowed by the publisher more difficult.

I hope that the reader will find this book both informative and interesting.

Spencer C. Tucker

# Battles That Changed American History

## Battle of Mabila

| Date | October 18, 1540 | |
|---|---|---|
| Location | Mabila, Alabama, near the confluence of the Alabama and Tombigbee Rivers | |
| Opponents (*winner) | *Spain | Choctaw Native Americans |
| Commander | Hernando de Soto | Chief Tuskaloosa |
| Approx. # Troops | Some 600 | At least 3,000 |
| Importance | Although this is one of the bloodiest battles in North American history, de Soto is able to continue his exploring expedition, one of the most significant events in the 16th century. | |

In May 1539 Spaniard Hernando de Soto led a force of some 600 men from Cuba in what would be a two-year-long exploration of the American Southeast. De Soto proceeded from Florida, during which time he seized Chief Tuskaloosa (Tascalusa) of the Choctaws and held him as a hostage, demanding supplies. Tuskaloosa directed de Soto to one of his towns, Mabila, and sent a messenger on ahead there. On October 18, 1540, the Spaniards arrived at the fortified town of Mabila at the confluence of the Alabama and Tombigbee Rivers in present-day central Alabama.

De Soto's men noticed that the settlement's inhabitants included thousands of warriors armed with bows, spears, and clubs and that there were few women, children, or elderly men. De Soto entered the town accompanied by several dozen followers, whereupon they were ambushed by Choctaw warriors concealed in the town's structures.

The Spaniards managed to cut their way free, but they lost 20 of their number in the immediate fighting. None of the Spanish troops inside the town escaped unscathed, despite armor that proved sufficient to prevent most lethal wounds. During the escape, the Spaniards lost virtually all of their baggage and equipment.

De Soto's men then fought a pitched battle outside Mabila's palisade. In the open, the Spaniards were able to use superior technology and cavalry tactics to powerful effect. In so doing, they slaughtered hundreds of Choctaws. As the Choctaws retreated behind Mabila's wooden walls, de Soto ordered his men to form four squadrons and assault the palisade surrounding the town from every direction. The Spaniards breached the rough-hewn log palisade and then threw torches at the thatched roofs of houses in the town. De Soto kept a mounted patrol on each side of the palisade to kill any Choctaws attempting to escape the inferno.

The defenders repeatedly repulsed the Spaniards but suffered heavy casualties in each assault. After a nine-hour battle, resistance ended, and every Choctaw defender who had survived the fires was cut down. The town was burned to the ground in the fighting, destroying all of the captured Spanish baggage.

By the end of the day's fighting, at least 22 Spaniards were dead and an additional 148 were wounded. Some historians estimate Spanish casualties at 70 dead and hundreds wounded. Most accounts place the Choctaw casualties at between 2,500 and 3,000, although a Spanish witness to the battle claimed that 11,000 Choctaws perished in the fighting and its aftermath in what was certainly the bloodiest battle in North American history to 1862. Tuskaloosa's remains were never found by the Spaniards, but it is likely that he died in the fighting or in the conflagration. In any event, there is no mention of him in any later European account.

Following the battle, de Soto continued his exploration and conquests, despite talk of mutiny among his followers, many of whom wished to abandon the expedition and return to Cuba. If de Soto's expedition was one of the most significant events in 16th-century American history, the Battle of Mabila was its defining moment.

Paul J. Springer

## Further Reading

Duncan, David Ewing. *Hernando de Soto: A Savage Quest in the Americas.* New York: Crown, 1995.

Hudson, Charles. *Knights of Spain, Warriors of the Sun: Hernando de Soto and the South's Ancient Chiefdoms.* Athens: University of Georgia Press, 1997.

## Destruction of Fort Caroline

| Date | September 20, 1565 | |
|---|---|---|
| Location | Near present-day Jacksonville, Florida | |
| Opponents (*winner) | *Spain | France |
| Commander | Pedro Menéndez de Avilés | René Laudonnière |
| Approx. # Troops | 500 | Few troops; several hundred people in all |
| Importance | Effectively ends the French effort to colonize Florida. | |

Although Spanish explorers had visited the coast of Florida and Spaniards had occasionally visited that peninsula to capture Native Americans to work as slaves in their Caribbean colonies, Spain made no effort to establish a permanent settlement until 1521. In that year Juan Ponce de León, who had led an earlier expedition to Florida in 1513, tried to establish a colony on the peninsula but was stopped by food and water shortages and Native American resistance. Pánfilo de Narváez led another expedition to Florida in 1528 but failed to find gold and suffered disaster in a storm during the expedition's return. Another attempt to establish a colony in Florida, led by Hernando de Soto in 1539, was abandoned when de Soto set out across the American Southeast in search of riches.

Frequent warfare between France and Spain from 1521 to 1559 led French king François I to consider challenging Spanish control in America by establishing a

French presence there. However, these intentions produced no results other than the harassment of Spanish shipping in the area by French privateers. Finally in 1562, Charles IX and his chief minister, Gaspard de Coligny, revived the plan.

Coligny, who was a Huguenot Protestant, hoped to strengthen France in relation to Spain and also provide a refuge for his coreligionists by sending them to colonize North America. In May of that year, 50 Huguenots led by Captain Jean Ribault landed at Port Royal, near modern Beaufort, South Carolina, and built a fort there. Ribault returned to France for supplies and reinforcements, but when he did not come back, the colonists built a ship and also returned to France. Learning of the French presence, the Spaniards dispatched a military force there that destroyed the abandoned fort. A year later the Spaniards established the settlement of St. Elena on the site of the wrecked fort, which they considered part of Florida.

The French made a second attempt to colonize Florida in 1564, sending René de Laudonnière along with 300 Huguenots to secure France's claim to the region. Laudonnière landed at the mouth of the St. Johns River, where the French built Fort Caroline (also known as Charlesfort). After a promising start, the French explored the area and established a good relationship with the local Timucuan tribe; however, food shortages caused dissent among the colonists. Some colonists left, and others blamed Laudonnière for the problems and staged an unsuccessful mutiny.

Aware of this threat to their position in Florida, Spanish officials dispatched Pedro Menéndez de Avilés with 1,000 men and four ships to oust the French. Menéndez landed at the site of present-day St. Augustine, 40 miles south of the French colony, in 1565. The Spaniards immediately erected a fort to protect their position. Indeed, Menéndez had arrived just in time to prevent the landing of 600 French reinforcements under Ribault.

With his ships blocking Ribault's access to the St. Johns River, Menéndez set out to destroy Fort Caroline. On September 20, 1565, 500 Spanish soldiers stormed and captured the French fort after a brief struggle. Laudonnière and some 50 people aboard ship managed to escape and eventually returned to France. Upon learning that his prisoners were Protestants, Menéndez executed about 130 men but spared 60 women and children. He then marched back to St. Augustine to deal with Ribault.

While Menéndez attacked Fort Caroline, Ribault sailed along the coast seeking access to the St. Johns River. During his journey a storm wrecked the French ships, and fewer than 400 survivors managed to reach shore. Learning of their location from his Native American allies, Menéndez marched south to find the French. On his way, he encountered and annihilated several small groups of Huguenots before encountering Ribault and his defenseless followers at Matanzas Bay. After fruitless negotiations between the two commanders, Menéndez ordered the execution of the approximately 350 remaining French on October 12.

The capture of Fort Caroline and the destruction of Ribault's expedition put an end to French efforts to colonize Florida. The Spaniards established a settlement at

St. Augustine and occupied Fort Caroline, which they renamed Fort San Mateo. In April 1568 the French avenged Menéndez's massacre when Dominique de Gourgues attacked Florida with more than 150 men, capturing two small Spanish posts and then seizing Fort San Mateo. Gourgues then executed all of his Spanish prisoners and claimed that the Spanish loss equaled the number of French killed three years earlier by Menéndez. Despite this success, the Spanish hold on Florida remained secure.

Jim Piecuch

### Further Reading

Bannon, John Francis. *The Spanish Borderlands Frontier, 1513–1821.* Albuquerque: University of New Mexico Press, 1974.

Lyon, Eugene. *The Enterprise of Florida: Pedro Menéndez de Avilés and the Spanish Conquest of 1565–1568.* Gainesville: University Press of Florida, 1976.

## Battle of Acoma Pueblo

| Date | January 22–24, 1599 | |
|---|---|---|
| Location | Acoma Pueblo, New Mexico | |
| Opponents (*winner) | *Spain | Acoma Native Americans |
| Commander | Vicente de Zaldivar | Unknown |
| Approx. # Troops | 71 | Population of several thousand |
| Importance | Solidifies Spanish control over the region but helps bring about the later Pueblo Revolt. | |

Located on top of a mesa 357 feet above the desert floor west of the Rio Grande Valley, Acoma Pueblo (or Sky City) was home to approximately 6,000 Keresan-speaking Acomas at the end of the 16th century. Irrigated fields of corn and beans encircled the steep slopes of the mesa walls, and residents traveled between town and farmland by using a combination of stairs and hand-and-toe holes carved into the red rock. Prior to the arrival of the Spaniards, Acoma had been inhabited for at least 500 years, making it one of the oldest continuously occupied settlements in North America.

In the early 16th century, the viceroy of New Spain authorized expeditions north of Mexico in hopes of discovering riches rumored to be found among the adobe towns scattered across the landscape. Francisco Vásquez de Coronado, governor of the province of New Galicia in northern Mexico, led the largest of these expeditions from 1540 to 1542. Coronado's captain of artillery, Hernando de Alvarado, visited Acoma with a small force of men on his way back from a foray to Zuni Pueblo in 1540 and noted the pueblo's virtually impregnable position atop the mesa.

Coronado's accounts of his unprofitable expedition dissuaded further ventures into pueblo country for more than half a century. In 1595 Juan de Oñate was charged by the Spanish Crown with leading an expedition up the Rio Grande Valley to spread the Catholic faith, pacify the natives, and establish a permanent colony in the northern provinces of New Spain. In 1598 after a series of delays, Oñate and 500 men, women, and children entered New Mexico near present-day El Paso, Texas. By late May, Oñate had reached the upper Rio Grande and encountered the first of many pueblos that he formally claimed for Spain. In July 1598 Oñate arrived at the confluence of the Chama River and the Rio Grande and established his headquarters at Ohke Pueblo, which he renamed San Juan, the capital of the new colony.

From San Juan, Oñate dispersed friars to the pueblos and personally led a party of colonists and soldiers on a reconnaissance of the province. On October 27, 1598, Oñate arrived at Acoma, ascended the mesa, and entered the city. Residents of the pueblo disagreed on how best to deal with the Spaniards. Ultimately the natives decided to treat Oñate and his party hospitably and gave them and their horses food and water. Before leaving, the governor informed the inhabitants of Acoma that they were now under Spanish rule.

In December 1598 Oñate's nephew, Juan de Zaldivar, arrived at the base of Acoma Pueblo at the head of a column of 30 soldiers en route to a rendezvous with his uncle. Zaldivar demanded food for his hungry men. The Acomas refused to comply with his request. They did, however, agree to trade cornmeal for tools if the Spaniards could wait until they completed the grinding process. After waiting three days for the promised cornmeal, Zaldivar and 16 of his men ascended the mesa and entered the city. What happened next is not entirely clear. Native accounts blame the ensuing violence on the Spaniards' mistreatment of Acoma women and exploitation of the pueblo's hospitality. Spanish survivors claim that the Acomas attacked by design. Either way, Zaldivar and his men were quickly overwhelmed. Only 4 of the 16 men were able to flee to the desert floor and safety. Zaldivar was among the dead.

When Oñate received word that his nephew had been killed, the governor dispatched Juan's brother, Vicente de Zaldivar, along with a force of 70 men, on a mission to punish the pueblo. On January 22, 1599, the Spanish soldiers arrived at Acoma and, under the cover of darkness, managed to scale the steep-sided mesa and haul a cannon to the top. Zaldivar besieged the city for three days. Cannon fire destroyed adobe walls, and soldiers gored villagers fighting to save their homes and families. When the carnage ended, approximately 800 Acoma men, women, and children lay dead; another 580 were taken captive.

Oñate quickly orchestrated a trial, over which he presided, and found the Acomas guilty of treason against Spain. Adolescents were sentenced to 20 years of servitude, and adult men were to have one foot amputated. The mutilation was to be conducted in the plazas of pueblos along the Rio Grande as a lesson to those who might question Spanish authority.

Although King Philip II of Spain recalled Oñate upon learning of the punishments he had meted out, the Acoma Massacre served to solidify Spanish control over the region. The inhabitants of Acoma eventually rebuilt their city, but the bitter memory of the event contributed to the Pueblo Revolt of 1680.

Alan C. Downs

**Further Reading**

Josephy, Alvin M. *500 Nations: An Illustrated History of North American Indians.* New York: Knopf, 1994.

Simmons, Marc. *The Last Conquistador: Juan de Oñate and the Settling of the Far Southwest.* Norman: University of Oklahoma Press, 1991.

## Jamestown Massacre

| Date | March 22, 1622 | |
| --- | --- | --- |
| Location | Vicinity of Jamestown, Virginia | |
| Opponents (*winner) | *English colonists | Powhatan Confederacy of Native Americans |
| Commander | Captain William Tucker; Dr. John Potts | Chief Opechancanough |
| Approx. # Troops | Some 3,000 settlers | Unknown |
| Importance | Permanently changes the attitude of English settlers toward Native Americans, whom English settlers now wish to exterminate or at least make servants or slaves. | |

Hostilities had been simmering between the English and the Powhatans in Virginia since the end of the First Anglo-Powhatan War (1610–1614). The Powhatans were frustrated by English exploration, were concerned that the English were becoming too numerous and taking too much territory, and resented the English demands for food and the way in which the English self-righteously pushed their culture and religion on the Powhatans.

After Chief Powhatan settled that first war without a victory in 1614, his actual power declined. Although Powhatan remained paramount chief until his death in 1618, his younger brother Opechancanough and others hostile to the English dominated Powhatan diplomacy after that time.

For years, Opechancanough lulled the colonists into a sense of security with friendly overtures and by ignoring their abuses. The English saw the period between 1613 and 1622 as a golden age in their relations with the Powhatans. The English traded freely with the natives and frequently welcomed them at their plantations and in their homes. The English thus felt shocked and betrayed when the attack occurred.

While Opechancanough was appeasing the English, he quietly negotiated with the various Powhatan tribes to join in a fight that would eliminate the English threat. More tribes were persuaded to fight after 1617, when tobacco

Seventeenth-century engraving by Theodor de Bry depicting the surprise massacre by the Indians of English residents near Jamestown, Virginia, on March 22, 1622. This began the Second Anglo-Powhatan War (1622–1632). (Library of Congress)

became an extremely profitable crop in Virginia. Between 1617 and 1622, some 3,000 English settlers arrived to take advantage of the tobacco boom. Thus, settlement spread far beyond Jamestown and put unprecedented pressure on the local natives.

What became known as the Indian Massacre of 1622 touched off the Second Virginia-Indian War (1622–1632), also known as the Second Anglo-Powhatan War. It began on March 22, 1622, with a massive surprise assault by the Powhatans on the English settlers near Jamestown. Just before the first assault, 2 Powhatans betrayed Opechancanough's plans to the English. Nonetheless, the native offensive was indeed costly to the colonists. The Powhatans killed 347 settlers that day, about one-fourth of the entire English population in the colony.

Once the colonists regrouped from the devastating March attack, bitter fighting ensued between them and the Powhatans. The English launched raids against Powhatan towns and sniped at any native in range of their firearms. In addition, the English made treaties with the Powhatans only to break them, as in 1623 when the

English brought poisoned wine to a feast to toast a new peace accord, killing some 200 natives.

Still, nearly another quarter of the English population died in the following year from small-scale native raids, starvation, and dysentery and other diseases. The climax of the war came in a large-scale battle at the town of Pamunky in 1624 in which the English were victorious. The native threat to the English diminished greatly after the battle, and peace was finally negotiated in 1632.

The Second Anglo-Powhatan War permanently changed English views toward Native Americans. Prior to 1622, many settlers envisioned living harmoniously among the natives, whom they expected to convert to Christianity and English cultural mores. The English, however, had not recognized how these goals were nearly impossible to achieve. Working against them were deep-seated cultural differences and their desire to settle on allegedly unoccupied native land. As a result of the betrayal that the English suffered by the conflict, they no longer desired to incorporate Powhatans as English subjects. Most English now wanted to rid the land of natives altogether or at the least to keep them as servants or slaves.

Another result of the war is that King James I came to believe that the Virginia Company of London was mismanaging the colony and endangering the lives of the settlers. In 1624 the king declared Virginia a royal colony, which gave the settlers many new rights that they had not enjoyed under company control.

Jennifer Bridges Oast

**Further Reading**

Axtell, James. *After Columbus: Essays in the Ethnohistory of Colonial North America.* New York: Oxford University Press, 1988.

Rountree, Helen C., ed. *Powhatan Foreign Relations, 1500–1722.* Charlottesville: University Press of Virginia, 1993.

Rountree, Helen C., and E. Randolph Turner III. *Before and After Jamestown: Virginia's Powhatans and Their Predecessors.* Gainesville: University Press of Florida, 2002.

## Capture of Quebec

| Date | July 19, 1629 | |
|---|---|---|
| Location | Quebec, Canada | |
| Opponents (*winner) | *English | French |
| Commander | David Kirke | Samuel de Champlain |
| Approx. # Troops | Several hundred men in perhaps a half dozen ships | Fewer than 100 colonists: men, women, and children; only 20 men under arms |
| Importance | Severely sets back the colonization of New France (Canada). | |

In the wake of the Third Huguenot War between England and France, King Louis XIII's chief minister Armand Jean du Plessis, Cardinal Richelieu, prohibited all non-Catholic immigration to New France. Richelieu also reorganized and recapitalized French holdings in North America through the formation of the Compagnie des Cent-Associés (Company of 100 Associates) and named Quebec's founder, Samuel de Champlain, as chief administrator.

Early in 1628, Richelieu amassed a convoy at the port of Dieppe to carry supplies to New France as well as to transport several hundred settlers as the advance element of an accelerated colonization plan. At the same time, however, empowered by a letter of marque from English king Charles I, Huguenot turned London merchant and privateer Gervase Kirke set out to capture Quebec from the French.

Kirke's flotilla, led by his sons David, Lewis, Thomas, John, and James, consisted of three ships carrying in all 200 men. The flotilla set sail for Canada well ahead of Richelieu's convoy. On the way, the Kirkes captured several small French warships and fishing vessels. The expeditionary force then continued up the St. Lawrence River, taking the trading outpost of Tadoussac on July 10, 1628. This they accomplished with the help of local natives and disaffected French traders put off by Champlain's brusque administrative style.

David Kirke then sent several envoys upriver to deliver a surrender demand to Champlain, who responded with defiance. Kirke then informed Champlain that his force would return early the next year. In addition, Kirke said that he would cut off French supplies during the winter, expecting that this would make Champlain amenable to surrender. Departing for the Gulf of St. Lawrence, Kirke's ships then imposed a naval blockade for the remainder of the season, in the process seizing Richelieu's convoy of 11 ships with 600 crewmen and colonists. In the autumn of 1628, with the St. Lawrence River about to freeze over and cut off Quebec from waterborne resupply, Kirke and his men sailed for England.

The winter of 1628–1629 was severe, and Champlain and the inhabitants of Quebec, who numbered fewer than 100 people at the time, avoided death by freezing or starvation only through the charitable actions of France's Native American allies, the Hurons. In the spring as promised, Kirke returned with an enlarged fleet and again blockaded the St. Lawrence. With Quebec having fewer than 20 men under arms, Champlain was forced to capitulate on July 19, 1629. Having ostensibly achieved the conquest of Canada, the Kirkes garrisoned the fort and then took Champlain and the rest of Quebec's inhabitants back to England.

On his arrival in London on October 29, 1629, Champlain sought out the French ambassador, from whom he learned that war between England and France had ended with the Treaty of Susa on April 29, 1629. By December, Champlain was in Paris lobbying Richelieu and Louis XIII for the return of Canada to French control. However, because of diplomatic hurdles following the peace, Quebec was not officially returned to France until the signing of the Treaty of St. Germain-en-Laye on March 29, 1632.

In July 1632 a French ship carrying some 40 settlers as well as the Jesuit priest Paul Le Jeune and the new French governor, Emery de Caen, arrived at Quebec.

After handing the settlement over to de Caen on July 13, the remaining Kirke brothers and their men returned to England, but not before pilfering a large stockpile of beaver pelts as well as furniture, window frames, and anything else they could pry from the ruins. As Le Jeune later noted, all that was left of the nearly 30-year French effort to colonize Canada was a ransacked fort and some dilapidated stone walls.

The 1629 capture of Quebec was highly significant for the future development of North America. French dreams of colonization were set back decades by the destruction wrought by the Kirkes. Although Quebec was returned to France almost as an afterthought, Quebec in French hands proved to be a threat to English America for the remainder of the colonial period. Furthermore, the events of 1629 led Richelieu to replace the Recollect order with the Jesuits as the primary Catholic proselytizing force in North America. This was a development that would deeply affect the course of North American colonial warfare and have far-reaching consequences for native groups and European settlers alike. Finally, the native alliances that had been formed by the English and French were thrown into disarray by Champlain's capitulation, leading to all-out war between New France and the Iroquois Confederation.

Steve Bunn

**Further Reading**

Champlain, Samuel de. *The Works of Samuel de Champlain,* Vol. 6, *1629–1632.* Toronto: Champlain Society, 1936.

Eccles, William J. *The Canadian Frontier, 1534–1760.* Albuquerque: University of New Mexico Press, 1984.

Eccles, William J. *The Ordeal of New France.* Toronto: Hunter Rose, 1979.

Nester, William R. *The Great Frontier War: Britain, France, and the Imperial Struggle for North America, 1607–1755.* Westport, CT: Praeger, 2000.

Trigger, Bruce G. *Natives and Newcomers: Canada's "Heroic Age" Reconsidered.* Kingston, Ontario: McGill-Queen's University Press, 1985.

## Mystic Fort Fight

| Date | May 26, 1637 | |
|---|---|---|
| Location | Mystic, Connecticut | |
| Opponents (*winner) | *English New England colonies | Pequot Native Americans |
| Commander | John Mason and John Underhill | Unknown |
| Approx. # Troops | 90 Connecticut and Massachusetts militiamen and 70 Mohegans | 400–700 total population in the Pequot fort |
| Importance | Decimates the Pequots, who are no longer recognized as a tribe; the English colonists also seize their lands. | |

With the beginning of the Pequot War (1636–1638) following the Endicott Expedition of September 1636, hostilities for the next six months revolved around Pequot

Engraving depicting combat between colonial militiamen and the Pequot during the Mystic Fort Fight of May 26, 1637. The Pequot War of 1636–1637 decimated the Pequot, who ceased to exist as an independent people afterward. (Hulton Archive/Getty Images)

harassment of the English at Fort Saybrook, at the mouth of the Connecticut River. But in late April 1637, Pequot warriors raided Wethersfield, an English settlement farther up the river, killing 6 men, 3 women, and much livestock and capturing 2 girls. A week later on May 1, the General Court of the Connecticut Colony declared "offensive war" on the Pequots and then sent 90 men under Captain John Mason on a retaliatory mission.

Shortly thereafter, Mason's force arrived at Fort Saybrook accompanied by a number of Mohegan warriors under their leader Uncas. There Mason met a smaller group of 20 men under Captain John Underhill, sent out by the colony at Massachusetts.

Mason's original orders specified that he attack the main Native American settlement on the Pequot River. However, after considering the difficulties of such an attack and consulting with other officers and the expedition's cleric, Mason decided to move his force to Narragansett Bay. From there he planned to attack another large fortified Pequot settlement on the Mystic River.

On the evening of May 23, 1637, Mason landed with about 70 men from Connecticut, 19 men from Massachusetts, and some 70 Mohegan warriors. He negotiated with Miantonomo and other Narragansett leaders to pass through their lands and marched his forces westward the following day. The English and the Mohegans then encamped outside and surrounded an Eastern Niantic village, a precaution to ensure that none of the Niantics, who had an antagonistic attitude, alerted the Pequots of their approach.

On the morning of May 25, several hundred Narragansett warriors joined Mason's expedition. The weather was hot, and the march was a difficult one. Many of the Narragansetts abandoned Mason when his forces reached the Pawtucket River, which was their boundary with Pequot land.

The men rested during the night and then around daybreak on May 26, 1637, began their attack on the Pequot palisaded village near the Mystic River in present-day Connecticut. After first surrounding the village, the attackers fired a musket volley, surprising the sleeping Pequots inside. Then the men, divided into two forces, one each under Mason and Underhill, simultaneously assaulted the two entrances in the palisade. The Pequots defended themselves with bows and arrows and in hand-to-hand combat.

Although the original English intention was to kill the inhabitants, the attackers found the struggle difficult in the tight quarters among the Pequot wigwams, leading their commanders to decide to set fire to the village. The conflagration soon engulfed the settlement, with numerous Pequots dying in the blaze and many warriors fighting to the last. Other Pequots fled the village, but almost all of those who attempted to escape were slain by the English or their Native American allies.

Combat did not end with the destruction of the village, however. Mason's men then had to continue on to the Pequot River to rendezvous with their ships. During the march, warriors from the other main Pequot settlement attacked, although the English effectively kept them at bay. Mason's march was slowed by the exhaustion of his men and the need to transport the wounded. The English reached their vessels later that day.

English casualties for the campaign amounted to 2 killed and 20 wounded; casualties among the accompanying Mohegan and Narragansett warriors are unknown. Estimates of Pequots slain at Mystic range from 400 to 700 people. Mason claimed that only 7 were taken captive and 7 escaped. Pequots elsewhere scattered after the assault, with many later hunted down by the English and their native allies. Although these operations did not result in the wholesale slaughter witnessed at Mystic, hundreds of Pequots were forced into servitude by the English or were incorporated into the Narragansett and Mohegan tribes. The Mystic Fort Fight and the ensuing operations virtually wiped out the Pequot tribe. The English also took the Pequot lands.

Matthew S. Muehlbauer

### Further Reading

Cave, Alfred. *The Pequot War.* Amherst: University of Massachusetts Press, 1996.

Hirsch, Adam J. "The Collision of Military Cultures in Seventeenth-Century New England." *Journal of American History* 74 (1988): 1187–1212.

Karr, Ronald Dale. "'Why Should You Be So Furious?': The Violence of the Pequot War." *Journal of American History* 85 (1998): 876–909.

Orr, Charles. *History of the Pequot War: The Contemporary Accounts of Mason, Underhill, Vincent and Gardener.* Cleveland, OH: Helman-Taylor, 1897.

## Great Swamp Fight

| Date | December 19, 1675 | |
|---|---|---|
| Location | Near present-day South Kingston, Rhode Island | |
| Opponents (*winner) | *English Colonies of Massachusetts Bay, Plymouth, and Connecticut | Narragansett Native Americans |
| Commander | Josiah Winslow | Canonchet |
| Approx. # Troops | More than 1,000 militiamen | Some 1,000 men, women, and children |
| Importance | A critical blow to the Narragansetts from which they never really recover, but they are brought into the struggle against the English colonists that is known as King Philip's War. | |

In the autumn of 1675, King Philip (Metacom, Metacomet) of the Wampanoags led attacks on and destroyed numerous colonial towns in southern New England, beginning what is known as King Philip's War (1675–1676). In short order, his forces grew both in confidence and in numbers.

The large and powerful Narragansett tribe, situated in Rhode Island, was officially neutral. However, colonial leaders believed that some Narragansett warriors were secretly joining King Philip's raiding parties and that the tribe itself was harboring wounded warriors. Determined to put an end to such assistance, the commissioners of the New England Confederation (Massachusetts Bay, Connecticut, and Plymouth) recalled most militia units from the western frontier. They also recruited new units, assembling the largest colonial force that America had seen to that point.

The troops, drawn from all three colonies, were placed under the overall command of Plymouth governor Josiah Winslow. Major Samuel Appleton had charge of the Massachusetts forces, Major William Bradford commanded the Plymouth contingent, and Major Robert Trent was in charge of the Connecticut men. On December 9, 1675, Winslow's entire force of more than 1,000 men marched from Massachusetts Bay toward the Rhode Island stronghold of the Narragansetts.

The Narragansetts had decided to winter that year in a large stronghold on the edges of the Great Swamp. The natives felt safe there in their nearly completed fortification, especially since they knew that the English disliked fighting in the thick woods and swampy land that surrounded the fortification.

On December 13, 1675, the majority of the colonial force gathered at Wickford, Rhode Island, on the outskirts of the Great Swamp. From there they spent several days attacking nearby native enclaves. The winter weather had made traversing the land easier for the militiamen, for it had stripped the leaves from the underbrush and frozen the otherwise swampy ground.

In one of these attacks, the colonists captured a warrior named Indian Peter, who promised to lead them to the Narragansett fort. After the delayed arrival of troops from Connecticut, Winslow decided that the time had come for the main attack. By then his force was running low of food, and winter conditions were already taking a toll.

On December 18 the colonial forces, led by Indian Peter, moved into the swamp. They sighted their objective the next afternoon. The fort was constructed of wooden palisades with a mass of brush and timber around the base of the wall and small blockhouses at each corner. A sizable village of huts lay within the walls. At the time of the colonial attack, there were some 1,000 natives in the fort.

Without time to properly plan an attack, the vanguard of the colonial army rushed the fort. With incredible luck, they happened on a gap in the wall, although it was protected by a nearby blockhouse. Two companies rushed the opening and broke through, only to lose their leaders and be forced back. Other troops rushed forward and were able to break into the village and force the Narragansetts to fall back. The fight now became a series of individual battles among the native dwellings.

Winslow, worried about the fierce fighting, gave the order to burn the fort to force the natives into the open. Winslow's aide, Captain Benjamin Church, tried to dissuade him, arguing that the colonials might use the fort for shelter after the battle was won. However, the militiamen began to burn the huts, with men, women, and children still inside. It was a scene reminiscent of the English attack on Mystic Fort during the Pequot War of 1636–1638.

Soon, all was afire. While some warriors escaped into the woods, many more natives—mostly women, children, and the elderly—perished. Contemporary estimates of Native American dead ranged from 600 to as many as 1,000. The colonials lost 20 killed and some 200 wounded, about 20 percent of their force.

The colonials took quick stock and then prepared to move back to their base at Wickford. The weather was getting worse, and now that the fort and its dwellings had been destroyed, there was no place to shelter the men, especially the wounded. Fearing a Narragansett counterattack, the colonists quickly fashioned stretchers and began the overnight march to Wickford. The retreat was difficult, especially for the wounded, and conditions sharply deteriorated with the arrival of a winter storm.

By the time the colonials had reached Wickford early the next morning, a number of the wounded had died. Within a month, the number of dead had risen from 70 to 80. Losses were especially high among the officers. Half of the 14 company commanders perished. While the campaign was considered a success, it came at a heavy price.

In retrospect, it is questionable whether the campaign was actually successful. Before the attack, the Narragansetts were officially neutral. While the colonials had dealt the Narragansetts a terrible blow, the tribe's survivors were determined to exact revenge and now made common cause with King Philip.

Kyle F. Zelner

### Further Reading

Bodge, George Madison. *Soldiers in King Philip's War.* Baltimore: Genealogical Publishing, 1967.

Chet, Guy. *Conquering the American Wilderness: The Triumph of European Warfare in Colonial Northeast.* Amherst: University of Massachusetts Press, 2003.

Leach, Douglas Edward. *Flintlock and Tomahawk: New England in King Philip's War.* East Orleans, MA: Parnassus Imprints, 1992.

Malone, Patrick M. *The Skulking Way of War: Technology and Tactics among the New England Indians.* Baltimore: Johns Hopkins University Press, 1993.

## Pueblo Revolt

| Date | August 10–21, 1680 | |
|---|---|---|
| Location | Present-day New Mexico | |
| Opponents (*winner) | *Pueblo Native Americans | Spanish |
| Commander | Tewa shaman Popé | Governor Don Antonio de Otermín |
| Approx. # Troops | More than 3,000 warriors | Several hundred soldiers |
| Importance | Although short-lived, the revolt results in Pueblo Native Americans securing a measure of freedom and the preservation of their institutions. | |

The Spanish conquest of New Mexico began with Francisco Vásquez de Coronado's 1540–1542 quest for the mythical Seven Golden Cities of Cíbola. Intermittent Spanish forays into New Mexico occurred thereafter, although permanent European settlements were not begun until Don Juan de Oñate y Salazar formally established New Mexico in 1598. Franciscan missionaries, eager to convert the sedentary horticulturalists they called Indios de los pueblos (village Indians), soon took up residence in the scattered pueblos.

Relations between the Spaniards and the Pueblos took a turn for the worse in 1675, when Governor Juan Francisco Treviño imprisoned 47 Native Americans he termed "sorcerers." These men were shamans who were perpetuating their sacred ceremonies. Three of the detainees were executed. Another committed suicide before angry Pueblo warriors forced the zealous governor to release the remaining shamans.

Nearly a century of colonial encroachments, smallpox outbreaks, prolonged drought, forced conversions, demands for tribute, and the suppression of traditional

Photograph of the ruins of the Spanish mission at Pecos Pueblo, seat of the 17th-century Pueblo Revolt in New Mexico. (North Wind Picture Archives)

practices led most Pueblos to desire an end to Spanish rule. Popé, a Tewa shaman from San Juan, made this wish reality after experiencing a powerful vision that had followed his 1675 detention.

The Pueblos' plot to drive out the Spaniards unfolded on August 9, 1680, when runners carried knotted yucca cords and instructions to two dozen villages as far south as Isleta in New Mexico, a distance of some 400 miles. Tribal leaders receiving the cords were instructed to untie one knot each day until none remained. After the last knot was untied, the warriors would attack the Spaniards.

Governor Don Antonio de Otermín learned of the planned uprising from informants. The rebellion was to begin during the night of the new moon and would coincide with the arrival of the triennial Spanish supply caravan dispatched from Mexico City. The governor then ordered the torture of Nicolás Catua and Pedro Omtua, captured runners from Tesuque, for further details. Confident that the uprising would not commence until August 13, 1680, Otermín adopted a strategy of watchful waiting.

After learning that the Spaniards had captured the two runners, Pueblo raiders attacked unsuspecting Spanish outposts on August 10, 1680. Otermín responded by dispatching soldiers to subdue the warriors. He also ordered all Spanish colonists to gather within the safe confines of Santa Fe's defenses.

Spanish settlements in northern New Mexico as far west as the Hopi mesas in present-day Arizona felt the fury of war. The uprising claimed the lives of

19 Franciscan friars and 2 assistants. In all, some 380 Spaniards, including women and children, perished. Alonso García, New Mexico's lieutenant governor residing in Ro Abajo, learned of the events on August 11. Receiving false reports that all Spanish settlements had been destroyed in the attack and that no colonists had survived, García organized the withdrawal of all remaining Spaniards in the region to El Paso del Norte (present-day Juárez) instead of marching north to the settlers' relief.

Governor Otermín, waiting at Santa Fe for reinforcements that never arrived, prepared for a long siege. Nearly 500 Pueblo warriors attacked the capital of New Mexico on August 15, 1680. Within two days, more than 2,500 Pueblos had joined the fight. Otermín, severely wounded in a desperate counterattack, abandoned Santa Fe on August 21 after the attackers cut off the city's water supply. The Spaniards then withdrew down the Rio Grande Valley.

After the Spaniards had departed, Popé and other leaders of the rebellion launched a purification campaign, destroying Catholic churches, statues, and relics. All Pueblos who had received the sacraments were ordered to cleanse themselves by scrubbing their bodies with yucca fibers while bathing in the Rio Grande. Pueblo traditionalists constructed kivas (partially subterranean ceremonial chambers) to replace those destroyed earlier by the Spaniards.

Otermín attempted to reclaim New Mexico for Spain in November 1681, but Pueblo warriors repelled his invading forces. Spain's interest in New Mexico waned until French explorers visited the lower Mississippi River Delta. Eager to secure the Southwest lest it fall to France, Spanish officials dispatched soldiers there in 1688 and 1689. Although unsuccessful, these expeditions revealed fissures in Pueblo civilization. Officials also learned that Ute, Apache, and Navajo raids, combined with drought and famine, had created severe hardship for the Pueblos.

On August 10, 1692, the 12th anniversary of the Pueblo Revolt, Governor Diego José de Vargas vowed to retake New Mexico, and on September 13 a force of 40 Spanish soldiers, 50 Mexican natives, and 2 missionaries reached Santa Fe. Vargas, anxious to assure the defenders that he meant them no harm, pardoned the Pueblo leaders for their past transgressions. Amazingly, the governor eventually entered the city without having to fire a shot. Vargas also visited the outlying pueblos to assure villagers of his desire for peace.

Despite the governor's efforts, violence returned to the region in 1693, when hostile Pueblos recaptured Santa Fe. A furious Vargas retook the city on December 29, 1693, after cutting off the defenders' water supply. The governor's reconquest of New Mexico ended in December 1696, when Vargas secured a lasting peace.

Although the Spanish colonizers and missionaries returned, they had learned an important lesson. After 1696 the villages were allowed to govern themselves, and the missionaries tolerated residents' traditional practices. Thus, the Pueblo Revolt of 1680 had succeeded in ensuring the perpetuation of cherished tribal languages, dances, and ceremonies.

Jon L. Brudvig

**Further Reading**

Beninato, Stephanie. "Popé, Pose-yema, and Naranjo: A New Look at the Leadership in the Pueblo Revolt of 1680." *New Mexico Historical Review* 65 (October 1990): 417–435.

Bowden, Henry Warner. "Spanish Missions, Cultural Conflict, and the Pueblo Revolt of 1680." *Church History* 44 (June 1975): 217–228.

Knaut, Andrew L. *The Pueblo Revolt of 1680: Conquest and Resistance in Seventeenth-Century New Mexico.* Norman: University of Oklahoma Press, 1995.

Roberts, David. *The Pueblo Revolt: The Secret Rebellion That Drove the Spanish Out of the Southwest.* New York: Simon and Schuster, 2004.

# Siege of Port Royal

| Date | September 24–October 15, 1710 | |
|------|------|------|
| Location | Port Royal, Nova Scotia | |
| Opponents (*winner) | *British | French |
| Commander | Commodore George Martin | Governor Daniel d'Auger de Subercase |
| Approx. # Troops | 3,500 men | 300 French soldiers plus some Micmac Native Americans |
| Importance | The English secure Nova Scotia, a major blow to the already tenuous French hold in North America. | |

During 1702–1713, France and England struggled for North America supremacy in Queen Anne's War, part of the wider War of the Spanish Succession (1701–1714). By 1708 it had become apparent to many New England leaders that London did not place a high priority on military events in Canada, particularly with respect to the allocation of military resources. Prior campaigning with purely militia forces had invariably proved unsatisfactory, so in 1708 Governor Joseph Dudley of Massachusetts began agitating for an influx of regular troops and naval vessels to stiffen future endeavors against Canada.

To this end the enterprising merchant Samuel Vetch, a former Scottish military officer, was dispatched to London to confer with governmental authorities on the subject. The ensuing Canadian campaign of 1709 came to naught, but the following year Vetch again visited London and prevailed on the Board of Trade to augment colonial forces through the addition of several Royal Navy warships.

Rather than the conquest of Quebec, Vetch set his sights on the French settlement of Port Royal, Acadia (present-day Nova Scotia). Port Royal was chosen because of its activities as a privateering center and its relatively weak garrison. The British agreed to provide five warships and a contingent of 400 men of the Royal Marines under the command of Colonel Francis Nicholson, another energetic colonial administrator.

A large contingent of British regulars had also been promised but never materialized. Nonetheless, the efforts of Vetch and Nicholson were also greatly abetted by Governor Dudley, who proved instrumental in cobbling together a diverse body of New England militia. The militia included two regiments from Massachusetts and one each from Rhode Island, Connecticut, and New Hampshire. The usually hesitant Yankees, inspired more by profit than patriotism, also responded with a degree of cooperation heretofore rarely seen in the war.

By the autumn of 1710, an amphibious expedition of 3,500 colonial troops and British marines had assembled in Boston under the aegis of Commodore George Martin. They departed on September 18, 1710, confidently anticipating what appeared to be an easy conquest. The fact that the season was far advanced and that ongoing peace negotiations in Europe could end the conflict added impetus to their endeavors.

Port Royal, despite its strategic significance, was poorly garrisoned by a force of just 300 French soldiers and a number of Micmacs. Governor Daniel d'Auger de Subercase had pleaded with superiors for reinforcements when intelligence of the impending invasion was ascertained, but such aid never materialized. Thus, when the first of Nicholson's 3,500 troops disembarked from 31 transports at Port Royal on September 24, 1710, the outcome was a foregone conclusion.

Subercase, lacking manpower and even adequate supplies, was determined to put on as good a show as limited resources would allow. His forces gamely engaged Nicholson's men with what few cannon Subercase possessed. Nicholson and Vetch responded with an unhurried deployment of siege works and batteries, completed by October 6, that took a gradual toll on the French garrison.

On October 15 Subercase was persuaded by his subordinates to submit to terms of surrender and was granted honors of war. The French troops paraded out of the fort with colors flying and boarded several vessels for a return voyage to France. Once home, the governor was tried for neglect but acquitted.

Port Royal, Acadia, was renamed Annapolis Royal, Nova Scotia, in honor of Queen Anne. Considering its strategic significance, this was an impressive little victory by an enterprising New England military establishment.

With Annapolis Royal secured, Nicholson departed for Boston shortly after the surrender formalities ended and left a 500-man garrison in place. Vetch was then appointed the new military governor there, and for the next three years he administered his charge effectively, although with only sullen cooperation from the French and Micmac inhabitants. Worse, the Native Americans, once reinforced by a party of hostile Abenakis, began a concerted guerrilla war against isolated British outposts. Vetch grew disappointed at Nova Scotia's relegation to backwater status by authorities in London, and his command remained small and undersupplied.

By 1712, conditions had deteriorated to the point where Vetch warned superiors that Nova Scotia might have to be abandoned, a revelation that brought about his replacement by Nicholson in 1713. Port Royal was formally transferred to Great Britain under the Treaty of Utrecht in 1713. Indeed, the siege of Port Royal was the only demonstrable success of British and colonial arms during Queen Anne's War. Although Port Royal was small in terms of area, its loss was a serious blow to the already tenuous French foothold on North America, which grew successively weaker in the following two conflicts. Another result was to prompt Nicholson to venture to London, where he convinced the British government to commit even greater resources to the conquest of Canada. Indeed, success at Port Royal proved to be the genesis of the ill-fated expedition against Canada in 1711.

John C. Fredriksen

## Further Reading

Faragher, John M. *A Great and Noble Scheme: The Tragic Story of the Expulsion of the French Acadians from Their American Homeland.* New York: Norton, 2005.

Plank, Geoffrey G. *An Unsettled Conquest: The British Campaign against the Peoples of Acadia.* Philadelphia: University of Pennsylvania Press, 2001.

Reid, John G., ed. *The "Conquest" of Acadia, 1710: Imperial, Colonial, and Aboriginal Constructions.* Toronto: University of Toronto Press, 2004.

Waller, George M. *Samuel Vetch: Colonial Enterpriser.* Chapel Hill: University of North Carolina Press, 1960.

## Quebec Expedition

| Date | June 25–August 23, 1711 | |
|---|---|---|
| Location | Lower St. Lawrence River | |
| Opponents (*winner) | *French | British |
| Commander | | Admiral Sir Hovenden Walker |
| Approx. # Troops | | 11 warships, 60 transports and supply vessels, 4,000 British troops, and several thousand colonial volunteers |
| Importance | The failure of their expedition prevents the English from capturing New France, with untold consequences for the history of North America. | |

In 1711 during Queen Anne's War (1702–1713), the leaders of New England planned both a seaborne assault on Quebec and a simultaneous diversionary attack by colonial forces from Albany against Montreal. Frustrated by the lack of Crown support for a failed 1709 attack on Canada, however, colonial leaders doubted reports that a new British expedition, led by Admiral Sir Hovenden Walker, would join provincial forces in Boston for the seaborne operation. Nonetheless, the colonial governments cautiously made preparations.

Walker duly arrived from Britain on June 25, 1711, with a dozen warships and numerous transports carrying seven regiments of regulars and a marine battalion numbering more than 4,000 men, all under Brigadier John Hill. This impressive force, bolstered by thousands of provincials, held great promise, but neither Walker nor Hill proved to be up to the task.

Walker faced numerous problems. French agents sowed distrust among colonists with rumors that his ultimate purpose was to reassert centralized royal authority. To confuse the French as to the fleet's destination, the Admiralty outfitted Walker's ships with only limited provisions, making colonial support crucial. Unfortunately, Boston already faced a food shortage and had difficulty feeding its populace.

Provisioning several thousand soldiers and sailors seemed out of the question. As a result, profiteering was rife. Lacking adequate specie, Walker's agents tried to negotiate credit, but New England merchants refused to extend credit or demanded exorbitant interest rates. This crisis forced Governor Joseph Dudley of Massachusetts to intervene. Boston also became a haven for more than 200 British deserters hidden by sympathetic Bostonians. Lacking an understanding of colonial society and sensibilities, Walker saw only intransigence.

Despite all these difficulties, Walker departed Boston on July 30, 1711, with 9 warships, 2 bomb ketches, and more than 60 transport and supply vessels. Although Walker commanded more than 12,000 soldiers and sailors—the largest armed force ever seen in the colonies—he had serious doubts about the prospects for success. He feared the coming winter, unpredictable weather, and supply shortages, which had doomed the New Englanders' 1690 campaign. With only a three-month supply of food, Walker could not support a lengthy siege, and he feared being trapped by winter ice. His force would also have to navigate without adequate charts or pilots some 400 miles up the St. Lawrence, a river known for fog, dangerous shoals, winds, and strong currents.

Tragedy struck the expeditionary force on the night of August 23 as the fleet neared Île-aux-Oeufs, some 100 miles from Quebec. Off course and blinded by fog, the ships blundered toward the north shore. Seven transports and a supply vessel foundered, leaving nearly 900 men dead.

Following two days of salvage efforts and even though he still possessed a sizable force, Walker's spirit was broken. He persuaded a council of war to abandon the operation. When the fleet rendezvoused at Cape Breton Island near the mouth of the St. Lawrence, both Walker and Hill rejected suggestions of a more limited operation against Placentia, Newfoundland. While Walker's force returned to England, the provincials sailed for Boston. Without Walker's attack, the campaign crumbled. New France was saved.

Critics on both sides of the Atlantic sought scapegoats. Walker and Hill blamed colonial obstructionists, claiming that New Englanders had sabotaged the campaign to preserve the lucrative wartime trade with New France. Colonial leaders countered that they had raised the necessary forces under difficult circumstances and faulted Walker's inept leadership. Whatever the cause, the failed expedition reinforced the poor relationship between the New England colonies and the Crown.

Stanley J. Adamiak

## Further Reading

Alsop, J. D. "The Age of the Projectors: British Imperial Strategy in the North Atlantic in the War of the Spanish Succession." *Acadiensis* 21(1) (1991): 30–53.

Graham, Gerald S., ed. *The Walker Expedition to Quebec, 1711.* Toronto: Champlain Society, 1953.

Leach, Douglas Edward. *Arms for Empire: A Military History of the British Colonies in North America.* New York: Macmillan, 1973.

Leach, Douglas Edward. *Roots of Conflict: British Armed Forces and Colonial Americans, 1677–1763.* Chapel Hill: University of North Carolina Press, 1986.

## Yamasee War

| Date | April 15, 1715–November 1717 | |
|---|---|---|
| Location | South Carolina | |
| Opponents (*winner) | *South Carolina, North Carolina, and Virginia Militias | Yamasees, Creeks, Cherokees, and other Native Americans |
| Commander | Governor Charles Craven | |
| Approx. # Troops | Unknown | Unknown |
| Importance | Devastates the colony of South Carolina, leading to changes in its government, and brings the near extinction of the Yamasee tribe. | |

The Yamasees, a Muskogean-speaking people inhabiting the southern reaches of Georgia at the time the Spaniards were occupying nearby Florida, enjoyed cordial relations initially and received Franciscan missionaries until 1680, when the Spaniards attempted to deport tribal members to the Caribbean to work as slaves. A war ensued, and the Yamasees migrated northward to the vicinity of St. Helena and present-day Hilton Head Island, where the English colony of South Carolina was developing. Initially, the Yamasees and the British were amicably disposed. The Yamasees were useful to the British, serving as a buffer between them and the Spaniards. The Yamasees also played a prominent role in the essential deerskin trade and actually fought on behalf of the British in the Tuscarora War (1711–1713).

Around this time, however, poorly regulated British traders and native agents engaged in unscrupulous practices with the Yamasees, including appropriating land without payment, wholesale cheating in trade, and demanding immediate payment for tribal debts estimated at £50,000. When the Yamasees were unable to comply, the English usually resorted to seizing wives and children for the slave market. Such systematic abuse propelled the Yamasees to violence against their antagonists, and the Yamasees began consorting with neighboring tribes, such as the Catawbas, Apalachees, and Creeks, to initiate military action.

The ensuing Yamasee War began on April 15, 1715 (Good Friday), when native warriors staged carefully orchestrated attacks against English outposts along

Nineteenth-century woodcut showing Governor Charles Craven of South Carolina leading an attack on Yamasee Native Americans at the Combahee River at the beginning of the Yamasee War of 1715–1717. (The Granger Collection)

the South Carolina frontier. Traders and native agents were especially targeted for revenge, and upwards of 100 colonials were slaughtered at Pocataligo. Other war bands struck at the settlement of St. Bartholomew, between the Edisto River and the Combahee River, burning it and scattering the inhabitants. The ensuing crush of white refugees toward Charles Town (Charleston) greatly swelled the population of that region, which gave it the ability to muster sufficient manpower for a defense.

Governor Charles Craven proved exceptionally able and energetic, and in late April he mounted a limited offensive with 240 men. Near Salkehatchie, they engaged and defeated 500 warriors. At about this same time, a second column under Colonel Alexander Mackay stormed the occupied village of Pocataligo, dispersing a larger force of Yamasees. In an action fought on July 19, 1715, 120 militiamen under Captain George Chicken chased a band of warriors into a swamp, surrounded them, and then attacked, killing 40 and freeing several white captives. Warfare at this time had broken down into large-scale raiding by both sides, with notable actions at New London and Daufuskie Island (adjacent to Hilton Head Island and the Savannah River). The Yamasees and their coalition were unable to withstand the colonial resurgence and began appealing to other tribes for assistance.

Their Creek neighbors agreed to help, providing additional war bands to supplement their original contingent. Thus augmented, the tribesmen were able to resume their destructive raids and in an action near Port Royal on August 1, 1716, killed several defenders. But the South Carolinians, now reinforced by militiamen from North Carolina and Virginia, were able to withstand this new round of native attacks. They soon began driving the Creeks and the Yamasees back into the swamps of Georgia.

By January 1716, the Creeks felt sufficiently threatened to appeal to their traditional enemy, the Cherokees, who constituted the largest tribe in the Southeast. The Cherokees proved coy initially, but in light of their good relations with the English, they announced their decision by slaughtering the Creek emissaries. The combination of colonial militia under Craven's effective leadership and ample Cherokee manpower proved too much for the Creeks and the remnants of the Yamasee coalition. Both were soon driven from the colony. The Creeks moved deeper into Georgia, and the Yamasees withdrew completely into Florida, where they were welcomed by the Spaniards as allies. It was not until November 1717 that the Creeks and the English formally concluded a peace treaty. The Yamasees were never a party to this agreement, and from their Florida enclave they launched sporadic raids for more than a decade.

Despite its relatively brief duration, the Yamasee War was one of the most costly conflicts waged by a European colony. South Carolina, with a population of only 5,500 settlers, took proportionately heavier losses than those incurred by New Englanders during King Philip's War (1675–1676). Many frontier communities lay gutted, and the lucrative fur trade, heretofore a staple of the local economy, was severely disrupted for many years. And despite Craven's able leadership, the proprietary government's response to the crisis was perceived as sluggish. Thus, in 1719 the government was overthrown by the inhabitants and replaced by royal governance.

The Creeks also drew important lessons from the conflict, realizing that they lacked the power to openly confront both the English and the Cherokees and could not readily rely on assistance from either France or Spain. The Creeks thereafter embarked on a course of cautious neutrality, partly to offset half a century of enmity toward the Cherokees. But the biggest losers were the Yamasees. Driven from their homeland and subject to periodic raids from the new English colony of Georgia, they progressively became weaker in terms of numbers. The Yamasees were gradually absorbed by their Creek and Seminole neighbors. The once proud and influential Yamasee tribe had disappeared as an identifiable culture by the end of the 18th century, although it is speculated that the Altamaha Cherokees of present-day Burke County, Georgia, may be their descendants. The Oklawaha band of the Seminoles is also thought to be largely descended from the Yamasees.

John C. Fredriksen

## Further Reading

Haan, Richard L. "'The Trade Does Not Flourish as Formerly': The Ecological Origins of the Yamasee War of 1715." *Ethnohistory* 28 (1982): 341–358.

Johnson, David L. "The Yamasee War." Master's thesis, University of South Carolina, 1980.

Oatis, Steven J. *A Colonial Complex: South Carolina's Frontiers in the Era of the Yamasee War, 1680–1730.* Lincoln: University of Nebraska Press, 2004.

## Bloody Marsh

| Date | July 18, 1742 | |
|---|---|---|
| Location | Saint Simons Island, Georgia | |
| Opponents (*winner) | *Great Britain | Spain |
| Commander | James Oglethorpe | Captain Antonio Barba |
| Approx. # Troops | 650 British soldiers, militiamen, and allied Indians | 150–200 Spaniards |
| Importance | Ends the effort by Spain to conquer Georgia. | |

During the Anglo-Spanish War (War of Jenkins' Ear) of 1739–1748, Spanish authorities decided on an attack against the British Georgia colony to avenge the destruction caused earlier by a British invasion of Florida and to overthrow Georgia.

On June 1, 1742, 10 Spanish ships departed Havana with troops to reinforce the Spanish stronghold of St. Augustine, Florida, and then attack the British outpost of Fort Frederica on St. Simons Island, just south of present-day Savannah. A week later off the Florida coast, the Spaniards encountered the Royal Navy frigate *Flamborough* (20 guns). The *Flamborough* forced three of the Spanish ships ashore before proceeding north to warn British authorities at Charles Town (present-day Charleston, South Carolina). On June 6, meanwhile, 25 other ships sailed from Havana, protected by a 30-gun Spanish frigate. A storm scattered the ships, but they arrived at St. Augustine by June 15.

Leaving at St. Augustine only 300 men, the Spanish governor of Florida, Manuel de Montiano y Luyando, set out on July 1 with 52 vessels and some 2,000 men, including runaway South Carolina slaves and Native American scouts. Heavy contrary winds on July 2 caused 15 ships of Montiano's fleet to shelter in Cumberland Sound. There they came under fire from guns in British Fort Prince William and from the schooner *Walker.* The Spanish vessels then made their way to the north end of the island, where they anchored beyond the range of the British shore batteries. Informed at Frederica of events, Georgia governor James Oglethorpe called up 1,000 militiamen to meet the invasion.

Captain William Horton with a grenadier company and allied Native Americans from nearby Jekyll Island arrived at Cumberland Island on July 4. Oglethorpe followed with two companies of regular troops in three boats, only to encounter four Spanish galleys in St. Andrews Sound. Oglethorpe and two of the British boats made it through, but the third boat turned back on an erroneous report that the British commander had been captured. Reaching Fort St. Andrew, Oglethorpe ordered it abandoned and his men to concentrate at Fort Prince William. The next day the Spanish flotilla departed for St. Augustine before the British could launch an attack. Oglethorpe then returned to St. Simons Island.

On July 10 the main body of 36 Spanish vessels arrived and anchored some 10 miles north of Fort St. Simons. After the wind abated, Montiano attempted a landing on the southeastern side of the island, but a sudden squall forced him to call it off. He then moved his ships to near the entrance of St. Simons Sound and stood in at 4:00 p.m. on July 16. Fort St. Simons opened fire, as did the guns of the schooner *Walker,* the guard sloop *Faulcon,* and the merchant frigate *Success.* Spanish guns sank the *Faulcon,* and the Spaniards reached the mouth of the Frederica River. At 7:00 p.m., some 500 Spanish regulars under Lieutenant Colonel Antonio Salgado began coming ashore about 1.5 miles from Fort St. Simons. Gunfire from the Spanish ships scattered the few Georgia militiamen and their native allies on the beach.

By the morning of July 17, Montiano was himself ashore with 1,500 men. Oglethorpe then abandoned Fort St. Simons and fell back on Frederica, where he concentrated 500 men. At the same time, he ordered his ships to escape to sea. The Spaniards occupied the abandoned Fort St. Simons on July 18, and Montiano then sent 115 men to explore the six-mile-long road to Frederica.

A mile and a half from Frederica, the Spanish reconnaissance force came under attack by Oglethorpe, personally leading Georgia rangers and Highlanders as well as allied Chickasaw, Yamacraw, and Creek warriors. They killed or capture 36 Spaniards, including their commander, Captain Sebastián Sánchez, and his second-in-command.

Leaving his defenders in place, Oglethorpe returned to Frederica to gather more men. At 3:00 p.m., meanwhile, 150–200 Spanish grenadiers under Captain Antonio Barba arrived from Fort St. Simons to cover the withdrawal of the remainder of the scout force, and they engaged in a heated firefight with Oglethorpe's men. Although one company of British regulars broke free and fled, the remainder held firm, forcing Barba's men to retire. The engagement became known as the Battle of Bloody Marsh.

On July 19, additional British forces reached Frederica, increasing Oglethorpe's strength there to as many as 800 men. The Spaniards continued to hold Fort St. Simons, and during the course of the next several days each side probed the other's defenses while avoiding any major confrontation. On July 25, five British ships arrived from South Carolina, prompting Montiano to order a withdrawal. By that evening, the Spaniards had razed Fort St. Simons and were aboard their ships.

Although the Battle of Bloody Marsh ended quickly and with few casualties, the incident had a profound impact on Georgia. Oglethorpe's military success there helped erase memories of his earlier defeat at St. Augustine. More important, Spain's defeat in the battle effectively ended its campaign to overthrow Georgia, a colony that Spain had considered illegal and part of Florida. In one small, short battle, the debate over the southeastern borderlands was ended. Spain gradually accepted the legitimacy of Britain's southernmost North American colony.

Spencer C. Tucker

## Further Reading

Corkran, David H. *The Carolina Indian Frontier.* Columbia: University of South Carolina Press, 1970.

Ivers, Larry E. *British Drums on the Southern Frontier: The Military Colonization of Georgia, 1733–1749.* Chapel Hill: University of North Carolina Press, 1974.

## Battles of Jumonville Glen and Fort Necessity

| Date | May 28 and July 3, 1754 | |
|---|---|---|
| Location | Allegheny foothills near present-day Uniontown, Pennsylvania | |
| Opponents (*winner) | *British colony of Virginia | France |
| Commander | Lieutenant Colonel George Washington | Ensign Joseph Coulon de Villiers de Jumonville; Captain Louis Coulon de Villiers |
| Approx. # Troops | Some 48 Virginia militiamen and allied Mingo native Americans (Jumonville's Glen); 293 Virginians and 100 British regulars (Fort Necessity) | 36 Frenchmen (Jumonville's Glen); 600 Frenchmen and 100 allied Native Americans (Fort Necessity) |
| Importance | These two small engagements lead directly to the French and Indian War (1754–1763). | |

Following the 1748 Treaty of Aix-la-Chapelle, Britain and France attempted to negotiate an end to a border dispute between their North American empires. While the diplomats talked, British traders moved across the Allegheny Mountains into western Pennsylvania, and the French government in Canada attempted to protect its influence in the same area. Minor frontier squabbles gained new importance on April 15, 1754, when French forces evicted English workmen from a nearly completed blockhouse at Forks of the Ohio. The French then completed the blockhouse and expanded the fortifications, which they renamed Fort Duquesne, using it as a base to stop English incursions into the Ohio Country.

On reports that British provincial forces were operating west of the Alleghenies, the commander of Fort Duquesne, Claude-Pierre Pécaudy de Contrecoeur, sent Ensign Joseph Coulon de Villiers de Jumonville and a scouting party of

35 men to discover the whereabouts of the English. The English force in question was 150 Virginia militiamen and some native Mingo allies commanded by Lieutenant Colonel George Washington, whom Virginia lieutenant governor Robert Dinwiddie had ordered to secure the Forks of the Ohio. Dividing his force into smaller scouting parties, Washington and approximately 47 men caught up with Jumonville in the Allegheny foothills on May 28, 1754.

Earlier that morning, Washington had called a council of war that included Mingo leader Tanaghrisson (Half-King), whose scouts had led the Virginians to Jumonville's camp. While the Virginians took up positions around the encampment, Washington's native allies moved to the French rear. The French, meanwhile, prepared their breakfast, probably unaware of the danger around them.

It is impossible from known records to determine who fired first or how the skirmish developed. Within 10 or 15 minutes, however, 1 Virginian was dead and 2 were wounded, while the French had suffered 12 to 14 casualties. A cease-fire was quickly called, and the Virginians prepared to allow the wounded Jumonville to read his orders.

The ensign had little time to explain his summons—still less to discuss it—before Tanaghrisson attacked him. Tanaghrisson said to Jumonville that "You are not yet dead, my father," a reference to the French practice of paternalistic benevolence toward their American Indian allies, and then split open Jumonville's head with a hatchet and washed his hands in the dead man's brain, an old Iroquois custom. The other natives soon followed suit, killing other French soldiers until only 1 injured Frenchman remained alive. The 20 unwounded Canadians remained untouched and soon became Washington's prisoners. Both sides long argued whether the action at Jumonville Glen was a skirmish or a massacre and whether the ensign's death was an assassination by Washington's order or an unfortunate oversight by a novice officer.

After the incident Washington consolidated his forces, withdrew about 10 miles, and began to construct the aptly named Fort Necessity. Meanwhile, an expedition bent on revenge set out from Fort Duquesne under Jumonville's brother, Captain Louis Coulon de Villiers. On July 3 this force of 600 Canadians and 100 native allies caught up with Washington and his men (293 Virginians now reinforced by about 100 British regulars). Fighting ensued, and Washington was forced to surrender. In the engagement, Washington lost 31 killed and 369 captured (including 70 wounded); French losses were 3 killed and 19 wounded.

These two engagements have been called the opening shots of the French and Indian War (1754–1763). Both sides then began mobilizing for large-scale conflict.

Matt Schumann

## Further Reading

Anderson, Fred. *Crucible of War: The Seven Years' War and the Fate of the Empire in British North America, 1754–1766.* New York: Knopf, 2000.

Frégault, Guy. *Canada: The War of the Conquest.* Translated by Margaret M. Cameron. London: Oxford University Press, 1969.

Leduc, Gilbert F. *Washington and "the Murder of Jumonville."* Boston: Société Historique Franco-Americaine, 1943.

## Battle of Monongahela

| Date | July 9, 1755 | |
|---|---|---|
| Location | Near present-day Braddock, Pennsylvania | |
| Opponents (*winner) | *France | Great Britain |
| Commander | Captain Daniel Liénard de Beaujeu | Major General Edward Braddock |
| Approx. # Troops | 900 Frenchmen and allied Native Americans (two-thirds of them Indians) | 1,300 |
| Importance | Releases French forces for employment elsewhere and causes the British to abort their effort to take Fort Niagara. Three years pass before the British effectively take the offensive in North America. | |

When news of the French victory over the Virginia Militia at Fort Necessity (July 3, 1754) arrived in London that September, the British cabinet debated a new course of action in what was now the French and Indian War (1754–1763) and decided to send to North America two Irish regiments (the 44th and 48th) and a commander in chief for American forces.

In November, Major General Edward Braddock was named commander in chief for North America. Before his departure from England on January 13, 1755, Braddock received orders to attack French Fort Duquesne, Niagara, Crown Point, and Fort Beauséjour. It would be left to his discretion, once in America, whether to attack them in succession or all at once.

On arriving in Williamsburg, Virginia, in March, Braddock found that colonial officials had been busy over the winter. Governor William Shirley of Massachusetts had raised an extra 2,000 troops for the Beauséjour operation. Both Shirley and British Indian agent William Johnson proposed that the main British attack be directed against Niagara, but Braddock stuck to his orders to focus on Fort Duquesne. Nevertheless, Braddock exercised his discretion in allowing Shirley and Johnson to attack Niagara and Crown Point, respectively, while Braddock took his own force of 2,200 men to Fort Duquesne. The remainder of colonial forces were to move against Fort Beauséjour.

Braddock envisioned a road-building project through the wilderness, punctuated by a European-style siege. At first he proposed to take a large contingent with supplies for a major siege, but he soon split his force into two parts—one to

Contemporary illustration showing the mortal wounding of British major general Edward Braddock during the British defeat in the Battle of the Monongahela, July 9, 1755. (Library of Congress)

transport the immense train of baggage and artillery and the other, a flying column of about 1,300 men, to scout ahead and prepare for the siege operation.

Alert to the dangers of wilderness warfare, Braddock regularly employed more than a third of his force in screens and patrols. In June and July the army advanced steadily, thwarting attempts of French commander Claude Pierre Pécaudy de Contrecoeur to disrupt its progress. Despite raids on the colonial frontier, Braddock continued forward, increasing the panic at Fort Duquesne.

On July 8 as Braddock forded the Monongahela River, only 10 miles distant Contrecoeur prepared a last desperate attempt by sending about half of Fort Duquesne's garrison against Braddock. With 36 officers, 72 troupes de la marine (French colonial regulars), 146 Canadian militiamen, and 637 American Indian allies under his command, Captain Daniel Liénard de Beaujeu was supposed to attack Braddock's column east of the Monongahela, but Beaujeu's force was dispatched too late. Ultimately, battle was joined just west of the river shortly after noon on July 9.

As he continued his march on Fort Duquesne, Braddock sent forward a vanguard of about 300 men, followed by an independent company and 250 workers. The main body of 500 men followed with the artillery, and another 100 men covered the rear. Unlike past marches, however, Braddock missed a key terrain feature on the morning of July 9—a hill to his right and front from which scouts would have been able to detect Beaujeu's approach and prepare an adequate defense. That morning also, Braddock's screening forces were unusually small and close to the main body, which was split along the road, with only two ranks to either side of the artillery train. This deployment may have reflected Braddock's confidence in his progress but left his force more vulnerable to surprise.

When the French attacked, Braddock's men fought bravely but paid the price for their commander's errors. The opening volleys went well for the British, killing Beaujeu. But the British vanguard, flanked by Beaujeu's native allies, fell back on the main body, which Braddock had ordered to advance. The units became intertwined, and Braddock's regulars, strung out on either side of the baggage train, struggled to form a line of battle. Having fallen victim to an ambush, Braddock was unable to use the light infantry tactics that had served him throughout his march.

To make matters worse for Braddock and his men, the battlefield was a Native American hunting ground, designed to conceal hunters and expose prey. Braddock's men, still trying to form ranks, became targets for American Indian marksmen, with officers on horseback being particularly vulnerable. Although the British and some colonials fought bravely for more than three hours, they were unable to form units larger than a platoon, and most of their fire proved ineffective.

Unaccustomed to the native tactics, the regulars attempted to form companies and fire in volleys, as on a European battlefield. Panic in the British ranks caused several incidents of friendly fire, increasing confusion. Braddock's force also became an increasingly dense mass, providing an easier target.

Discipline crumbled when Braddock was shot from his horse. The workers, rear guard, and most of the provincial troops had already fled, leaving no one available to cover the withdrawal. The constant pressure from Canadians and American Indians turned the retreat into a rout and entirely reversed the previous month of British progress. Virginian George Washington, along as an observer without official status, helped reestablish order. Braddock's force had lost 456 killed and 521 wounded, along with most of its supplies and equipment. French and native losses totaled fewer than 40. The progress made on Braddock's road once promised a steady flow of supplies from Virginia and Maryland to Fort Duquesne; that same road now rendered the British colonies more vulnerable than ever.

The French victory on the Monongahela released forces from Fort Duquesne and rendered abortive Shirley's proposed expedition to Niagara. Although Shirley took over command of colonial forces from the deceased Braddock, his relations with Johnson steadily deteriorated as they squabbled over supplies. In 1756 Major General John Campbell, Earl of Loudoun, replaced Shirley as commander in chief but was militarily ineffective. Only when Major General Jeffery Amherst took over British military operations in 1758 did British forces return to the offensive against Fort Duquesne, this time successfully.

Matt Schumann

## Further Reading

Anderson, Fred. *Crucible of War: The Seven Years' War and the Fate of the Empire in British North America, 1754–1766.* New York: Knopf, 2000.

Frégault, Guy. *Canada: The War of the Conquest.* Translated by Margaret M. Cameron. London: Oxford University Press, 1969.

Pargellis, Stanley. "Braddock's Defeat." *American Historical Review* 41(2) (January 1936): 253–269.

## Battle of the Plains of Abraham

| Date | September 13, 1759 | |
|---|---|---|
| Location | Quebec, Canada | |
| Opponents (*winner) | *Great Britain | France |
| Commander | Major General James Wolfe | Lieutenant General Louis Joseph, Marquis de Montcalm |
| Approx. # Troops | 4,800 British regulars | 4,400 French regulars, colonial militia, and allied Native Americans |
| Importance | Perhaps the most important battle in the history of North America, it virtually ensures British control of Canada. | |

The French stronghold of Quebec was the capital of New France and a long-standing primary British military objective throughout the colonial wars. Situated on a peninsula towering above the northern bank of the St. Lawrence River at a point where the river narrows, Quebec was known as the "Gibraltar of the Americas" for its natural as much as man-made defenses. High cliffs made bombardment from below almost impossible and made a direct amphibious assault suicidal. Subsidiary rivers blocked attacks on either flank, and a landward approach faced strong walls and in any case would be possible only if supporting ships moved upriver and ran a gauntlet of gun batteries. If Montreal to the southwest, farther up the St. Lawrence, remained secure, Quebec could be supplied indefinitely by water. Siege operations were also complicated by the tides and treacherous currents of the St. Lawrence, and winter made the river impassable with ice.

In spite of these obstacles, British prime minister William Pitt recognized that taking Quebec was the key to the defeat of New France. In 1758 during the French and Indian War (1754–1763), British forces seized the fortress of Louisbourg on Cape Breton Island that guarded the mouth of the St. Lawrence, and Pitt approved plans for a strike led by Brigadier James Wolfe, who held a local commission as a major general. Wolfe, the youngest officer to hold that rank in the army, had distinguished himself in the attack on Louisbourg, and in February 1759 he sailed from England for Quebec with naval commander Vice Admiral Sir Charles Saunders. In all, the force earmarked for operations against Quebec included 49 warships, 119 transports, and 9,000 troops.

The British moved up the St. Lawrence toward Quebec to face some 12,000 French forces assisted by local militia and some Native Americans, all under the command of Lieutenant General Louis-Joseph, Marquis de Montcalm. Wolfe established a base near Quebec on Île d'Orléans on June 26, 1759. The following night, the French dispatched fireships in a failed attempt to burn the British ships. Meanwhile, the British sent gunners ashore at Point Lévis, directly across the St. Lawrence from Quebec. They established a battery of six 32-pounder

Painting showing British troops about to engage the French on the Plains of Abraham at Quebec on September 13, 1759, in what was perhaps the most important battle in the history of North America. (North Wind Picture Archives)

cannon and five 13-inch mortars that opened fire on July 12 and battered the city for the next seven weeks.

Wolfe landed troops north of Quebec at Beaupre on July 9 and assaulted Beauport on July 31. Both attacks failed to provide a clear avenue of advance and left Wolfe deeply frustrated. All efforts to draw the defenders out of the fortress proved futile. Throughout August, Wolfe struggled to approach Quebec without success, while his naval officers endeavored to chart the difficult estuary around the city. The stress of command left Wolfe bedridden with kidney stones and rheumatism. Many of his men thought that he was dying.

Wolfe's spirits improved only slightly when Vice Admiral Saunders slipped some ships past Quebec in July and August and began landing light infantry upriver to destroy French farms and supplies. Montcalm reacted by detaching his aide-de-camp, Louis-Antoine de Bougainville, and 3,000 men to patrol the cliffs south of the city. Then Wolfe saw an opening. On September 3 he quickly moved his headquarters and most of his men to the south shore beyond Quebec. He personally scouted a landing place at L'Anse du Foulon, only two miles from the city; sent British naval units upriver; and then ordered them to drift back with the tide to test Bougainville's reaction.

The French shadowed the fleet each time but slowed as they grew tired and suspected that the movement was a ruse. Wolfe also mounted feint assaults to keep the French off balance. On September 10 he learned from deserters that Quebec was short on food, that Montcalm feared that the British would interdict supplies coming from Montreal, and that no landing was expected near the city.

Time was running out for Wolfe, however. With winter only a few weeks away, Saunders feared that his ships would be trapped in winter ice and threatened to depart with them.

Wolfe sent his ships up and down the river again and again to pull Bougainville away from Quebec and tire his men. Taking advantage of intelligence provided by Captain Robert Stobo, a British captain who had earlier been held prisoner in Quebec and knew the city well, Wolfe then ordered an assault just north of the city at 4:00 a.m. on September 13 at Anse du Foulon, where a narrow footpath angled up the steep cliffs.

In a lucky stroke, Wolfe learned from more deserters that this was the same night that the French expected to be resupplied by boats from Montreal, giving the British a perfect cover for their landing. Wolfe sent Saunders to bombard and launch a feint attack on Beauport, then took 4,800 men upriver and drifted back in the darkness. Bougainville did not follow closely. At 2:00 a.m. on September 13, Wolfe led his men in boats across the St. Lawrence. They landed two hours later, scrambled 180 feet up the narrow path to the top of the cliffs, overwhelmed the French sentries there, and captured a nearby French camp.

By 6:00 a.m., the British had approximately 4,800 men deployed in line of battle on the Plains of Abraham above the city. The next move belonged to Montcalm. The French commander discounted reports that the British had successfully landed. Nevertheless, he dutifully rode out with Governor-General Philippe de Rigaud de Vaudreuil to see for himself and was astonished to find Wolfe's men. Montcalm immediately decided to attack.

Montcalm's decision provided endless fodder for historians. Indeed, he advanced without waiting for Bougainville, without most of his provincial troops or militia, without Quebec's garrison, and with only three artillery pieces. Moreover, with winter approaching, Montcalm had excellent reason to play for time. His defenders have argued that Quebec was short of supplies, that artillery above the city could command the lower town, and that the French had to strike before Wolfe was reinforced. But the decision to offer battle outside the city while outnumbered seems so impulsive that it may have had more to do with emotion than anything else. Montcalm sortied with some 4,400 men: 2,600 regulars and 1,800 militia and allied Native Americans.

Whatever Montcalm's motive, the battle of less than half an hour that followed featured no cavalry and very little artillery. It was purely an infantry duel in which British discipline carried the day. Both sides deployed across the Grande Allée, the main road leading toward Quebec's St. Louis bastion. Six British battalions faced five regiments of French regulars in the center on a tabletop battlefield whose sloping sides prevented maneuver. Wolfe had one battalion in a second line, a battalion on each flank, and one battalion in reserve. In contrast, the outnumbered Montcalm placed marines, militiamen, and Native Americans on his flanks and had no second line or reserves of any kind.

The battle began with sniping and skirmishing on the flanks. At 8:00 a.m. Montcalm's artillery opened up with grapeshot. Wolfe ordered his men to lie down to protect themselves until 10:00 a.m., when the French infantry came on at a run. Their hasty advance opened gaps in their lines, and when some units fired early and began to reload, much of their cohesion was lost.

Wolfe had ordered his men to load an extra ball in their muskets and wait until the French were at close range. As the French neared his position, he ordered his men to stand and fire. Legend has it the British unleashed only one volley, which is almost certainly not true. Some British battalions probably fired as the French closed, but at some point there was one great final volley that sent Montcalm and his men into headlong retreat.

French losses were reported as 644 killed or wounded, compared to 658 killed or wounded for the British. Yet the psychological shock for the French was total. Wolfe, already wounded at least once, was mortally struck as the French broke and ran. He died quickly. Death also claimed Montcalm, who was hit by British grapeshot during the retreat and lingered a day before dying.

Surviving French forces under Vaudreuil ran all the way to Beauport, then turned and fled toward Montreal, picking up Bougainville and his men along the way. Quebec surrendered on September 18 and remained in British hands thereafter. French efforts to resupply their forces in Canada were stymied by a British victory in the Battle of Quiberon Bay on November 20. The French did mount an offensive to retake Quebec in April 1760 and defeated British forces under Brigadier General James Murray on the Plains of Abraham after the British commander impulsively gave battle, much as Montcalm had done. But the British fell back into the city and withstood the ensuing siege. Montreal succumbed to the British in 1760, and when the French and Indian War ended in 1763, France relinquished Canada for good.

The Battle of the Plains of Abraham was the most important military engagement in the century-and-a-half struggle between Britain and France for control of North America east of the Mississippi River and was probably the most important battle in the history of colonial North America.

Lance Janda

## Further Reading

Anderson, Fred. *Crucible of War: The Seven Years' War and the Fate of the Empire in British North America, 1754–1763.* New York: Knopf, 2000.

Donaldson, Gordon. *Battle for a Continent: Quebec, 1759.* Garden City, NY: Doubleday, 1973.

Eccles, W. J. "The Battle of Quebec: A Reappraisal." *French Colonial Historical Society Proceedings* 3 (1978): 70–81.

Jennings, Francis. *Empire of Fortune: Crowns, Colonies, and Tribes in the Seven Years' War in America.* New York: Norton, 1990.

La Pierre, Laurer L. *1759: The Battle for Canada.* Toronto: McClelland and Stewart, 1990.

Lloyd, Christopher. *The Capture of Quebec.* New York: Macmillan, 1959.

Parkman, Francis. *Montcalm and Wolfe.* New York: Atheneum, 1984.

Reid, Stuart, and Gerry Embleton. *Quebec 1759: The Battle That Won Canada.* London: Osprey, 2003.

Stacey, C. P., and Donald E. Graves, eds. *Quebec, 1759: The Siege and the Battle.* Revised ed. London: Robin Brass Studio, 2002.

## Battles of Lexington and Concord

| Date | April 19, 1775 | |
| --- | --- | --- |
| Location | Lexington and Concord and the road to Boston, Massachusetts | |
| Opponents (*winner) | *American Patriots | Great Britain |
| Commander | At Lexington, Captain John Parker | At Lexington, Major John Pitcairn |
| Approx. # Troops | Ultimately some 3,800 militiamen | Ultimately some 1,800 British regulars |
| Importance | The opening battle of the American Revolutionary War, this American victory leads many to believe that a militia force alone will be sufficient to defeat the British. | |

By the winter of 1774–1775, British North America has become a powder keg. Commander in North America Lieutenant General Thomas Gage reported to London that the situation was dangerous and that he had insufficient manpower to deal with events if fighting should break out. This gloomy assessment did not deter King George III and his ministers. Convinced that the vast majority of the population was loyal to the Crown, that the agitation was the work of a small minority who would be easily rooted out, and that order would be restored, London took a hard line. In February 1775 Parliament declared Massachusetts to be in rebellion.

Gage disagreed with London's approach. In a report sent to the ministry but kept secret from Parliament, he estimated that if fighting occurred, it would take a year or two and 20,000 men just to pacify New England. If these men could not be supplied, Gage suggested a naval blockade and economic pressure as the best approach. London disagreed. The British ministry held that 10,000 troops, supported by Loyalists, would be sufficient.

Fighting began in Massachusetts on April 19, 1775, when Gage sent troops from Boston to destroy stores of arms that the radicals were stockpiling at Concord. The British had successfully carried out similar operations in the past, but this time the militiamen were alerted. At Lexington, the British advance under Major John Pitcairn met a hastily called-up militia company of 70 men under Captain John Parker.

Someone opened fire (the shot heard 'round the world), and the British soon drove the militia from Lexington Common. The militia lost 8 dead and 10 wounded for only 1 British soldier wounded.

The British then continued their march to Concord and completed their mission. Their withdrawal to Boston became a nightmare, however. The local militia was now out in full force and sniped at the British from cover along the route. Gage sent out additional forces, but before the troops could reach safety in Boston, the operation had claimed 273 British casualties of some 1,800 men engaged (73 killed, 174 wounded, and 26 missing). Ninety-five Americans were casualties (49 killed, 41 wounded, and 5 missing). Massachusetts militia forces then closed around Boston. The American Revolutionary War, also known as the War for American Independence, had begun.

Spencer C. Tucker

**Further Reading**

Coburn, Frank Warren. *The Battle of April 19, 1775: In Lexington, Concord, Lincoln, Arlington, Cambridge, Somerville, and Charlestown, Massachusetts.* Lexington, MA: Lexington Historical Society, 1922.

Dana, Elizabeth Ellery. *The British in Boston: Being the Diary of Lieutenant John Barker of the King's Own Regiment from November 15, 1774 to May 31, 1776.* Cambridge, MA: Harvard University Press, 1924.

Lister, Jeremy. *Concord Fight.* Cambridge, MA: Harvard University Press, 1931.

Tourtellot, Arthur B. *Lexington and Concord.* New York: Norton, 1959.

Ward, Christopher. *The War of the Revolution,* Vol. 1. New York: Macmillan, 1952.

## Capture of Fort Ticonderoga

| Date | May 10, 1775 | |
| --- | --- | --- |
| **Location** | Fort Ticonderoga, Lake Champlain, New York | |
| **Opponents (*winner)** | *American Patriots | British |
| **Commander** | Colonels Ethan Allen and Benedict Arnold | Captain William Delaplace |
| **Approx. # Troops** | 85 Connecticut and Massachusetts militiamen | 49 British regulars |
| **Importance** | The Americans secure 78 serviceable cannon and mortars, many of which are removed to Boston during the winter, and force the British to evacuate that city, bringing to a close the first period of the American Revolutionary War. | |

With the beginning of hostilities in the American Revolutionary War and in order to secure military supplies, two separate small colonial forces—one led by

Connecticut colonel Ethan Allen and the other by Massachusetts colonel Benedict Arnold—totaling several hundred men advanced against the poorly garrisoned British Fort Ticonderoga on Lake Champlain. At Castleton on May 9, Arnold sought overall command, but Allen refused to yield. In the end, the two men agreed only to act in concert.

Early on the morning of May 10, Allen and Arnold crossed Lake Champlain in two boats with 83 men armed only with small arms. Rather than wait for the remainder of their force to cross, Allen and Arnold led a charge of that small force into the fort's main entrance. When a British officer demanded to know on whose authority the colonists were acting, Allen responded "in the name of the Great Jehovah and the Continental Congress."

Threatened with the massacre of every person at Ticonderoga unless he complied, the fort's commander, Captain William Delaplace, surrendered his small force of 3 officers and 46 enlisted men, along with several dozen women and children.

Allen's subordinate, Lieutenant Colonel Seth Warner, then marched some of the colonial force north 10 miles to Crown Point, which they also captured, taking prisoner there another 9 British soldiers and 10 women and children.

Although many of the cannon taken at Fort Ticonderoga and Crown Point were found to be useless, 78 guns ranging in size from 4-pounders to 24-pounders were serviceable. There were also 6 mortars, 3 howitzers, thousands of cannon balls, 9 tons of musket balls, 30,000 flints, and a large quantity of other military supplies. The cannon would be especially useful to the colonial forces besieging Boston if means could be found to get them there.

That winter in a demanding operation, Colonel Henry Knox, commanding the new Continental Army Artillery Regiment, supervised the transport on sledges of 59 of the captured guns. Continental Army commander General George Washington was then ready to challenge the British in Boston, whom he had been unable to starve into submission thanks to the Royal Navy control of the sea. During the night of March 4–5, 1776, the Americans seized Dorchester Heights and placed the guns from Ticonderoga there. With the Americans now able to bombard Boston at will, General William Howe, British commander in chief in North America, decided to evacuate his 12,000 men. Completed on March 17, the evacuation of Boston brought an end to the first period of the American Revolutionary War.

Spencer C. Tucker

### Further Reading

Brooks, Victor. *The Boston Campaign.* Conshohocken, PA: Combined Publishing, 1999.

Chidsey, Donald Barr. *The Siege of Boston.* Boston: Crown, 1966.

French, Allen. *The Siege of Boston.* Spartanburg, SC: Reprint Co., 1969.

Ward, Christopher. *The War of the Revolution,* Vol. 1. New York: Macmillan, 1952.

## Battle of Bunker Hill

| Date | June 17, 1775 | |
|---|---|---|
| **Location** | Charleston Peninsula, Boston, Massachusetts | |
| **Opponents (*winner)** | *Great Britain | American Patriots |
| **Commander** | Major General William Howe | Major General Israel Putnam |
| **Approx. # Troops** | 2,400 regulars, some field artillery, and warships providing gunfire support | 2,500–4,000 militiamen, 6 small cannon |
| **Importance** | A costly British victory, it nonetheless instills confidence on the Patriot side and imposes caution on Howe as subsequent commander of British forces in North America. | |

Learning that British forces in Boston intended to launch attacks on June 18, 1775, to occupy Dorchester Heights, Roxbury, Cambridge, and the Charlestown Peninsula, on June 15, 1775, the Massachusetts Committee of Safety ordered forces to move into Charlestown Peninsula. Colonel William Prescott led three regiments, totaling some 1,200 men. Equipped with entrenching tools, the men were to erect fortifications on Bunker Hull. The indefatigable Prescott was the key leader on the American side in the ensuing battle.

The area north of Boston was dominated topographically by Bunker Hill and the lower Breed's Hill in front of it. On June 16 the American militiamen occupied Bunker Hill, the highest ground and a favorable position as long as the adjacent land and narrow escape route could be held. In order to repel the expected British disembarkation, the militia also occupied Breed's Hill, which was closer to Charlestown and was lower and more vulnerable to a flanking attack.

In reaction to this colonial move, on the morning of June 17 the British sixth-rate ships *Glasgow* (24 guns) and *Lively* (20 guns) and the sloop *Falcon* (14 guns) shelled the American positions, while the armed transport *Symmetry* (18 guns) and two gunboats raked Charlestown Neck. Meanwhile, British commander Lieutenant General Thomas Gage called a council of war. He and a majority rejected a plan put forth by Major General Henry Clinton for an immediate landing by 500 men south of Charlestown Neck and behind the American redoubts to trap the colonial forces in the peninsula. Gage and the others held that interposing a force between two hostile bodies was a violation of sound military practice.

The plan that was adopted called for landing a strong force below Moulton Point on the southeast corner of the peninsula followed by a march up the east side along the Mystic River. This would flank the American position and have the British out of range of musket shot. The British could then take the Americans from the rear. The British attack was delayed until high tide in the early afternoon, and in the interval the Americans extended their lines to cover such a possibility.

In preparation for the landing, the British third-rate ship of the line *Somerset* (68 guns), two floating batteries, and guns at Copp's Hill in Boston shelled the

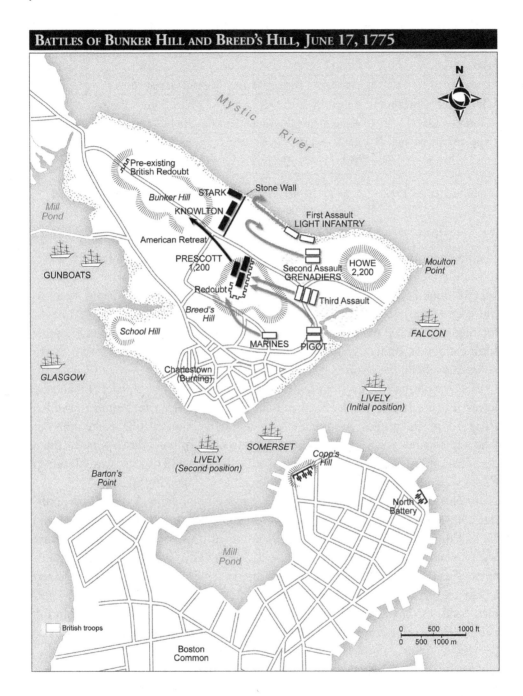

**BATTLES OF BUNKER HILL AND BREED'S HILL, JUNE 17, 1775**

American redoubt; the *Glasgow* and *Symmetry* and two gunboats shelled Charlestown Neck; and the guns of the *Falcon* and *Lively* swept the ground in front of Breed's Hill to clear it for the landing. While this was in progress, 28 British barges crossed to Charlestown Peninsula with some 1,500 troops under Major General William Howe. At about 1:00 p.m., they came ashore without opposition at Moulton Point and then formed up in three ranks on Moulton's Hill as Howe examined the American position.

Painting *Death of General Warren*, by John Trumbull, depicts the Battle of Bunker Hill of June 17, 1775. Trumbull was himself a participant in this sanguinary fight between American militiamen and British Army regulars that had profound effect on the Revolutionary War. (National Archives)

Howe could see that the situation had changed since the early morning, for the American breastworks now extended eastward. There was still an opportunity to flank the American position, but Howe was concerned about the presence of American troops on Bunker Hill. The men there were constructing a covering works, but Howe mistook them to be a reserve. He could also see colonial reinforcements marching to Breed's Hill; these were New Hampshire men under colonel John Stark (other colonial militia units had refused to cross into Charlestown Peninsula). In all, some 2,500–4,000 colonial militia and six small cannon now opposed the British regulars. Major General Israel Putnam had command.

Reluctant to impose his own force between the two bodies of colonial troops on Breed's Hill and Bunker Hill, Howe rested his men and called up reinforcements. These having arrived, he addressed the men and then ordered an attack on the American breastworks. Although the British ships continued to provide covering fire, Howe's own artillery was useless, for the guns' ammunition boxes were found to contain solid shot for 12-pounders rather than the 6-pounder guns on hand. He ordered the guns to fire grapeshot, but the distance was too great for it to be effective.

Howe still hoped to carry out a flanking attack by smashing the American left while appearing to carry out a frontal assault. This did not work out as planned, for the American left proved to be too strong. Twice the British were thrown back with heavy losses. It was 90 degrees, and the soldiers were carrying heavy packs, which did not come off until the third and final assault. The uphill climb also prevented the British from charging with bayonets during the American reload. The British troops also tended to fire high. On their side, the Americans demonstrated excellent fire discipline, with Putnam reportedly ordering "Don't fire until you see the whites of their eyes." He also ordered the men to fire low.

Having received some 400 reinforcements, sent to Howe after the failure of the first assault, and with the American militia out of powder, the British took Breed's Hill with bayonets. The militia withdrew to Bunker Hill and then across Charlestown Neck to the mainland, suffering most of their casualties in the retreat. They then began to fortify Winter Hill and Prospect Hill on the road to Cambridge. The British troops did not cross Charlestown Neck.

Although the British had won, it was at a very high cost. Of 2,400 men engaged, Howe's force suffered 1,054 casualties (including 82 officers), 226 of them dead. Probably some 1,500 Americans of perhaps 3,200 on the peninsula had actually taken part in the fighting; of these, some 140 were killed, 380 were wounded, and 39 were captured. In terms of percentage of casualties to forces engaged, Bunker Hill was one of the most sanguinary battles of the entire century. The battle shook Howe and may well have contributed to his subsequent failure as commander in chief to press home attacks against the Americans. Perhaps most important, the Battle of Bunker Hill demonstrated that relatively inexperienced colonial forces could stand against British regulars in pitched battle.

Spencer C. Tucker

### Further Reading

Brooks, Victor. *The Boston Campaign.* Conshohocken, PA: Combined Publishing, 1999.

Chidsey, Donald Barr. *The Siege of Boston.* Boston: Crown, 1966.

French, Allen. *The Siege of Boston.* Spartanburg, SC: Reprint Co., 1969.

Ketchum, Richard M. *Decisive Day: The Battle for Bunker Hill.* Garden City, NY: Doubleday, 1974.

Ward, Christopher. *The War of the Revolution,* Vol. 1. New York: Macmillan, 1952.

## Canada Campaign

| Date | August 1775–July 1776 | |
|---|---|---|
| Location | Canada | |
| Opponents (*winner) | *British | American Patriots |
| Commander | Major General Sir Guy Carleton | Brigadier General Richard Montgomery; Colonel Benedict Arnold |
| Approx. # Troops | 800 British regulars | 2,750 men (initial strength) |
| Importance | The British secure Canada. Had the American effort here succeeded, it might have added Canada to the United States. | |

On June 1, 1775, the Continental Congress decided to dispatch American expeditionary forces to Canada in an effort to capture both Montreal and Quebec. The

Americans hoped thereby to add Canada to the Revolutionary cause but also to seal the back door to America for the British up the St. Lawrence River.

The Montreal Expedition began first. On August 28, 1,200 men departed Fort Ticonderoga up Lake Champlain in an array of watercraft to capture St. Johns (present day St. Jean) on the Richelieu River. Major General Philip Schuyler had command. St. Johns was held by only 200 British regulars with several cannon, and Schuyler soon increased his strength to some 1,700 men, more than twice the number of British regulars in all of Canada. He also had five cannon and three mortars, but he was duped regarding British strength, and his initial assault went awry. Schuyler, who was ill, then handed over command to Brigadier General Richard Montgomery.

Reinforcements and the news that Indians loyal to the British had departed revived American morale. Montgomery now had 2,000 men, and while the British had strengthened St. Johns, its garrison still numbered only 500 men. Instituting a siege, Montgomery cut communications with Montreal. Meanwhile on September 25, Colonels Ethan Allen and John Brown with several hundred men attempted to take the weakly held Montreal, but Brown's force failed to get into the action, and Allen and most of his men were taken prisoner.

On October 18 Montgomery captured Chambly (near St. Johns), held by 89 British soldiers. There the Americans also secured 6 tons of powder, 3 mortars, 150 muskets, 6,500 cartridges, 500 hand grenades, 300 swivel shot, and 158 barrels of provisions. This action also severed the water route connecting St. Johns with Montreal.

On October 30 Montgomery turned back a British and Indian force of some 800 men under British governor of the province of Quebec Major General Sir Guy Carleton attempting to raise the siege, and on November 2 St. Johns surrendered. The Americans took 500 prisoners as well as 41 cannon. Montgomery could now proceed against Montreal, but the prolonged siege had forced him into a winter campaign.

On November 13 Montgomery secured the surrender of Montreal. Carleton and some 150 British regulars had loaded valuable stores aboard ships and sailed for Quebec, but American cannon at Sorel turned back the ships, and the Americans bluffed the British into surrendering the brigantine *Gaspee,* two other armed ships, eight smaller boats, and the stores. All British personnel were taken prisoner except for Carleton and several of his officers, who escaped shortly before the surrender.

On September 13, meanwhile, the second American expeditionary force, bound for Quebec, got under way when Colonel Benedict Arnold marched 1,051 men from Cambridge to Newburyport, Massachusetts. Five days later they sailed in a small flotilla for the Kennebec River, planning to proceed through the Maine wilderness to the St. Lawrence and then cross to Quebec.

Proceeding up the Kennebec, Arnold's men reached Gardinerstown on September 22, where 200 bateaux were waiting for them. Few of his men had any experience in these craft, which in any case were too heavy and too poorly built to operate all the way to the St. Lawrence. By September 24, Arnold had reached Fort Western (present-day Augusta).

Arnold expected the trip to the St. Lawrence to take 20 days, but in fact the expedition was in trouble as soon as it departed the last Maine outpost. Traversing the rapids proved difficult especially at Norridgewock Falls, reached on October 7. The bateaux scraped the rocks, opening seams, soaking gunpowder, and ruining supplies. Much of the passage was through boggy terrain, made more difficult by cold weather and heavy rains. Short of supplies, Arnold's men were soon starving. On October 25 Arnold lost nearly a third of his force when 300 men under Colonel Roger Enos voted to return home.

Finally, on November 9 following what was a remarkable trek of some 400 miles through the wilderness, Arnold reached Point Lévis opposite Quebec with 675 men. A shortage of boats and a winter storm, however, delayed his crossing until the night of November 13. The next day they were on the Plains of Abraham before Quebec. On November 15 Arnold unsuccessfully attempted to bluff Lieutenant Colonel Allan MacLean and his 1,200-man garrison into surrender.

Arnold believed that it would take 2,000 men and cannon to take Quebec. Learning that MacLean was planning a sortie against him, Arnold withdrew to Pointe-aux-Trembles to await the arrival of Montgomery from Montreal. Carleton, meanwhile, reached Quebec and assumed command there.

Montgomery arrived on December 2 along with 600 men, some artillery, the captured British supplies, and winter clothing. Together, he and Arnold had 1,250 men to face an equal number of Canadian defenders, who were in a fortified city with cannon. On December 5, Continental Army forces were again on the Plains of Abraham and initiated a loose siege of Quebec. Believing his militia to be unreliable, Carleton refused to engage the Americans outside the city.

Montgomery and Arnold lacked the means to maintain a complete siege, nor could they remain there indefinitely. They had limited supplies, and Arnold's enlistments were about to expire with no hope of renewal. Arnold and Montgomery therefore decided to stake all on an attack on December 31 with their approach masked by a blizzard.

It was a two-pronged American attack. Montgomery led 500 men in a southerly approach, arriving at Près de Ville by 4:00 a.m. Personally leading his men from the front against a fortified position, Montgomery and several dozen of his men were killed by fire from two British 3-pounder cannon. Montgomery's successor, Colonel Donald Campbell, then ordered a retreat.

Arnold, meanwhile, approached the city from the north. Arriving at Saint Roch with 700 men, he enjoyed more success but in the ensuing fighting was wounded in the knee and had to be evacuated. Major Daniel Morgan succeeded to the command and was able to penetrate the city. With Montgomery's southern force having withdrawn, however, Carleton was able to concentrate against the northern threat and prevent further advance. The Americans were surrounded, cut into small detachments, and by 9:00 a.m. were forced to surrender.

In the Battle of Quebec, the Americans lost 30 killed, 42 wounded, and 425 taken prisoner. British and Canadian militia forces suffered only 5 dead and 13 wounded.

Arnold collected the survivors and reestablished a loose siege of the city, retaining a tenuous hold on Quebec during the winter. On May 6, 1776, however, the British supply ship *Surprise* arrived, effectively ending the siege, and shortly thereafter Carleton drove off Arnold's force. On June 1, substantial Anglo-German reinforcements reached Quebec by sea via the St. Lawrence under British major general John Burgoyne and Brunswick major general Friedrich Adolf Riedesel Freiherr zu Eisenbach. Too late, the Americans reinforced in Canada with six regiments under Brigadier General John Sullivan, but smallpox ravaged his force.

Believing that it was held by only 300 men, on June 6, 1776, Sullivan sent Brigadier General William Thompson and 2,000 men against Trois Rivières, halfway between Quebec and Montreal. In the ensuing battle on June 8 the Americans were defeated, losing 40 dead, 30 wounded, and 236 captured. British losses were 8 dead and 9 wounded.

Carleton's caution allowed Sullivan's battered force to escape to Montreal. Sullivan hoped to hold Isle-aux-Noix, the last American post in Canada, but this proved impossible. Desperately short of supplies and with much of his army sick and now opposed by 8,000 British regulars and Hessian mercenaries, Sullivan returned to Crown Point at the end of July with what little remained of his force.

The Canadian Campaign was a complete failure. The error lay not in attempting it but in insufficiently supporting it. Had the campaign succeeded, it would no doubt have united Canada to the other British North American colonies and changed the entire course of the war.

Spencer C. Tucker

## Further Reading

Gabriel, Michael P. *Major General Richard Montgomery: The Making of an American Hero.* Madison, NJ: Fairleigh Dickinson University Press, 2002.

Lanctot, Gustave. *Canada and the American Revolution, 1774–1783.* Translated by Margaret M. Cameron. Cambridge, MA: Harvard University Press, 1967.

Morrissey, Brendan. *Quebec 1775: The American Invasion of Canada.* Translated by Adam Hook. Oxford, UK: Osprey, 2003.

Stanley, George. *Canada Invaded, 1775–1776.* Toronto: Hakkert, 1973.

## Battles of Lake Champlain/Valcour Island

| Date | October 11 and 13, 1776 | |
|---|---|---|
| Location | Near Valcour Island, Lake Champlain | |
| Opponents (*winner) | *Great Britain | United States |
| Commander | Royal Navy lieutenant Thomas Pringle | Brigadier General Benedict Arnold |
| Approx. # Ships and Troops | 25 small warships manned by some 700 men; 1,000 additional troops and perhaps 650 allied Indians | 15 small warships (2 schooners, 1 sloop, 4 galleys, and 8 gondolas manned by some 800 men) |
| Importance | Despite their loss, the Americans have forced the British to postpone their invasion of New York and rely on Lake Champlain as a supply route. | |

Control of Lake Champlain was vital for the Americans in supplying their efforts to conquer Canada during the American Revolutionary War. The lake was also crucial to British plans to separate New England from the other rebellious colonies. Both sides had used row galleys and other small craft on the lake in the winter of 1775–1776 during the Canada Campaign. Even after the American withdrawal from Canada, the Continental Congress ordered Major General Philip Schuyler to hold northern New York and authorized him to build "gallies and armed vessels" to secure both Lake Champlain and Lake George. Continental Army brigadier general Benedict Arnold had charge of construction, and neighboring colonies sent materials and shipwrights.

Arnold preferred row galleys and hoped to meet the British with eight, each armed with two heavy 24-pounders and two 18-pounders. Only four were completed in time to take part in the battle, however. Each was more than 72 feet in length with two masts and a lateen rig. Crew complement was 80 men. Most mounted two 12- or 18-pounders in the bow, two 12-pounders (along with possibly two 2-pounders) in the stern, and four 6-pounders in broadside. All carried smaller man-killing weapons known as swivels on their rails. As with all Lake Champlain squadron vessels, precise armament cannot be verified.

In 1935 one of Arnold's smaller ships, the gondola *Philadelphia,* was raised. Today it is displayed in the Smithsonian Institution, touted as the oldest U.S. Navy (actually army) warship in existence. The *Philadelphia* was an open boat 53′4″ in length. It had a single mast with a square course and topsail but was basically a rowing boat propelled by its crew of 45 men using long oars known as sweeps. The ship carried one 12-pounder on a slide mount at the bow, two 9-pounders on carriage mounts to fire over the rails, and eight swivels.

The British had both larger vessels and more guns on Lake Champlain. What they did not have was time. Winter would bring their operations to a halt because

The Battle of Valcour Island on Lake Champlain, New York (October 11 and 13, 1776) ended in an overwhelming British victory, but the existence of Brigadier General Benedict Arnold's small American flotilla had ensured that there would be no British invasion of New York from Canada that year. (Naval Historical Society)

their invasion route on the lake would freeze over. By early October, however, Major General Sir Guy Carleton's fleet was ready to move.

The resulting engagements between the British and Americans began at Valcour Island, about 50 miles north of Fort Ticonderoga, on October 11, 1776. Arnold's 800 men had 15 warships: 2 schooners, 1 sloop, 4 galleys, and 8 gondolas, with a combined throw weight of 703 pounds. He positioned his vessels at anchor in a crescent shape at the island so that the British would have to tack into position to engage them.

Commander of the British squadron Lieutenant Thomas Pringle had some 25 warships, many of them mounting heavier guns than those available to Arnold. Pringle's smaller vessels alone were nearly a match for all of those of the Americans. The British warships were served by 667 trained Royal Navy seamen and 1,000 British Army soldiers; their guns had a combined throw weight of 1,300 pounds.

On October 11 Pringle's vessels pounded the Americans for six hours. The Americans lost 1 schooner and 1 gondola, and 3 other vessels were badly damaged. The Americans also used up most of their ammunition. During the night, Arnold's remaining 13 vessels slipped past the British in an effort to reach Fort Ticonderoga. However, the wind changed from the south, and the Americans had to resort to their sweeps.

For a day the Americans kept ahead, but the British caught up, and a second engagement occurred on October 13 north of Crown Point. One galley struck, and Arnold beached and set afire another galley and four gondolas. Although they had lost

11 of their 15 vessels the Americans had only about 80 men killed and wounded, and perhaps 120 captured. Most got to Crown Point on foot, just ahead of Indians allied with the British. British losses were 40 killed or wounded and 3 small vessels sunk.

Although a tactical defeat for the Americans, the two small battles on Lake Champlain were also a strategic victory. They ended any possibility of a linkup in 1776 between Carleton's forces and those of Major General William Howe in New York. Carleton thought that it was too late in the year to begin a land campaign and withdrew. If the British had taken Ticonderoga and held it through the winter, mounting their 1777 campaign would have been easier and might have been a success. Instead, the 1777 British thrust southward ended in an American victory at Saratoga, the turning point of the war.

Spencer C. Tucker

### Further Reading

Allen, Gardner W. *A Naval History of the American Revolution,* Vol. 1. Cambridge, MA: Houghton Mifflin, 1913.

Chapelle, Howard I. *The History of the American Sailing Navy: The Ships and Their Development.* New York: Norton, 1949.

Nelson, James L. *Benedict Arnold's Navy: The Ragtag Fleet That Lost the Battle of Lake Champlain but Won the American Revolution.* New York: McGraw-Hill, 2006.

## Battles of Trenton and Princeton

| Date | December 26, 1776, and January 3, 1777 | |
|---|---|---|
| Location | Trenton and Princeton, New Jersey | |
| Opponents (*winner) | *United States | Great Britain |
| Commander | General George Washington | Colonel Johann Rall (Trenton); Colonel Charles Mawhood (Princeton) |
| Approx. # Troops | 2,400 men, 18 guns (Trenton); 5,000 men, 40 guns (Princeton) | 1,600 men, 6 guns (Trenton); 1,200 men, 9 guns (Princeton) |
| Importance | The battle restores confidence in the American cause, ends Patriot fear of Hessian mercenaries, and establishes George Washington's military reputation. | |

Continental Army commander General George Washington's first military campaign ended in near disaster. In July 1776, British commander in chief General William Howe and 32,000 British troops (the largest expeditionary force in British history until the 20th century) landed in New York and proceeded to drive Washington's troops from Long Island and Manhattan. Washington suffered one defeat after another; often his men simply broke and ran. Washington then left an isolated garrison at Fort Washington on the Manhattan side of the Hudson River, and in mid-November, supported by ships in the Hudson, British forces cut it off and captured it, taking 3,000 prisoners, 100 cannon, and a huge quantity of munitions. The same thing almost happened a few days later to the colonials at Fort Lee, across the Hudson in New Jersey.

Washington fled to the interior. Howe pursued in dilatory fashion, ignoring the Hudson to go after the Continental Army. Washington got away, his army safely behind the Delaware River. On December 13, 1776, British forces caught up with Major General Charles Lee, who had rejected Washington's orders to join him. The British captured Lee and some of his 4,000 men near Morristown, New Jersey.

The British then went into winter quarters, their forces covered by a line of outposts. The most important was located at Trenton, New Jersey, and was held by Colonel Johann Rall's Hessian mercenaries. What was left of Washington's force was deployed across the Delaware River from Trenton.

Washington's position was critical. Smallpox ravaged his force, and half of his 10,000 men were sick. To make matters worse, enlistments for most would expire in a few days, at the end of the year. Washington decided to risk everything and mount a surprise attack on Trenton. Everything depended on getting the men across the icy Delaware River at night to achieve surprise. Crossings by 5,500 men, horses, and artillery were to occur at three separate locations, with the forces converging on Trenton. If circumstances allowed, they could then advance on the British posts at Princeton and New Brunswick.

The attempt was planned for Christmas night, December 25. The crossing was to start at 5:00 p.m., with the attack at Trenton scheduled for 5:00 a.m. the next day. However, weather conditions were terrible, and the troops were slow to reach their assembly areas. As a consequence, the men began loading an hour later than planned. Shallow-draft wooden Durham boats, 40–60 feet long by 8 feet wide, transported the men across the river. Perfect craft for such an operation, the boats had a keel and a bow at each end. Four men, two to a side, used setting poles to push off the bottom and move the boats, which each also had a mast and two sails. Horses and artillery went across in Delaware River ferries.

All did not go smoothly, as a storm swept through. Of the three crossings, only the major one at McKonkey's Ferry under Washington with 2,400 men occurred in time for the planned attack. That force was divided into two corps, under Major Generals John Sullivan and Nathanael Greene. Colonel Henry Knox commanded the 18 pieces of artillery. Conditions were horrible. The men had to contend not only with the dark but also with wind, rain, sleet, snow, and chunks of ice in the Delaware. The password for the operation, "Liberty or Death," reflected its desperate nature.

Washington had planned for the crossing to be complete by midnight, but the last man was not across until after 3:00 a.m., and it was nearly 4:00 a.m. before the army formed and began to move. Washington's men were poorly clad for such an operation; some actually had no shoes and wrapped their feet in rags. The army having been formed, the men thus marched the nine miles to Trenton.

Washington was determined that the attack would succeed. When Sullivan informed him that the storm had wet the muskets, making them unfit for service, Washington replied, "Tell General Sullivan to use the bayonet. I am resolved to take Trenton." Washington's will, more than anything, kept the men going. On nearing Trenton, Washington split his force into the two corps to follow two different roads for a converging attack on the British outpost.

The attack began at 8:00 a.m., with the two columns opening fire within 8 minutes of one another. The battle lasted some 90 minutes. The Hessian garrison consisted of three regiments, 50 Hessian jaegers, and 20 light dragoons, about 1,600 men in all, along with six 3-pounder guns. Continental Army forces soon drove the Hessians back. Artillery played a major role, and here Washington enjoyed a six to one advantage, with his guns deployed to fire down the streets of the town. The battle itself was a confused melee of men fighting singly or in small groups. Rall rallied his men, intending a bayonet charge down Queen Street, but he was soon mortally wounded, and the Hessians were cut down by individual Americans with muskets and rifles and by artillery fire.

The Hessians lost 22 killed and 92 wounded. A total of 948 were captured. The remaining Hessians would also have been taken had the other columns gotten into position in time. The Continentals also secured a considerable quantity of arms and booty. The Americans lost only 2 men, both frozen to death, and 5 wounded. With little food or rest for 36 hours, Washington's men needed relief, and he was thus forced to suspend operations. On December 27 the Continentals were back across the Delaware.

Washington followed up Trenton with another foray across the Delaware. With the addition of other Continental Army troops and Pennsylvania militiamen, Washington now had some 5,200 men (3,600 of them, however, were unreliable militia) and 40 guns. On the evening of January 2, 1777, British major general Charles, Lord Cornwallis, came up with some 5,000 men, but Cornwallis believed that he had Washington trapped against the Delaware and delayed the attack until morning. That night, however, Washington and his men were able to escape. Leaving 500 men with picks and shovels to give the British the impression that he was reinforcing, Washington and his men, instead of recrossing the Delaware, took back roads to Princeton, New Jersey, where he routed 1,300 crack British troops under Lieutenant Colonel Charles Mawhood. The Americans suffered 35 killed or wounded. The British sustained 28 killed, 58 wounded, and 187 captured or missing. Washington then recrossed the Delaware.

These two small Continental victories changed the entire campaign. Washington called Trenton "A glorious day for our country," while British minister for the colonies Lord George Germain exclaimed in London that "All our hopes were blasted by the unhappy affair at Trenton." Trenton helped end the Continentals' fear of the

Hessian troops. More importantly, the two battles at Trenton and Princeton added immensely to Washington's prestige, which was at a low point a month before, and established his reputation as a general and a leader of men. The battles also restored Continental morale, which had been at its lowest point since the start of the war. In two weeks Washington had snatched victory out of the jaws of death and fanned the dying embers of American independence into flame again.

Spencer C. Tucker

**Further Reading**

Fischer, David Hackett. *Washington's Crossing.* New York: Oxford University Press, 2004.

Ketchum, Richard M. *The Winter Soldiers: The Battles for Trenton and Princeton.* New York: Anchor Books, 1975.

McPhillips, Martin. *The Battle of Trenton.* Parsippany, NJ: Silver Burdett, 1984.

Ward, Christopher. *The War of the Revolution,* Vol. 1. New York: Macmillan, 1952.

## Battles of Saratoga

| Date | September 19 and October 7, 1777 | |
|---|---|---|
| Location | Saratoga County, New York | |
| Opponents (*winner) | *United States | Great Britain |
| Commander | Major General Horatio Gates | Lieutenant General John Burgoyne |
| Approx. # Troops | 9,000 men (First Saratoga); 11,500 men (Second Saratoga) | 7,200 men (First Saratoga); 6,617 men (Second Saratoga) |
| Importance | An entire British army surrenders. Buoyed by this news, the French Crown decides to enter the war openly against the British. | |

British major general John Burgoyne returned to England early in 1777 and presented to King George III and Secretary of State for the Colonies Lord George Germain a plan to split off New England, the font of the rebellion, from the remainder of the colonies and thus snuff out the revolt. Burgoyne envisioned a three-pronged campaign. The major thrust would drive from Canada down the Lake Champlain–Hudson Valley corridor, while a secondary effort pushed eastward from Lake Erie up the Mohawk Valley. The two forces were to meet at Albany and join the third prong, a British drive up the Hudson River from New York City.

There were two principal problems with Burgoyne's plan. First, it took little account of logistics, and second, it depended heavily on simultaneous execution. The plan was further hampered by the fact that while being in approval of Burgoyne's plan, Germain also approved an entirely different plan submitted by British commander in North America Major General William Howe. Howe proposed to move

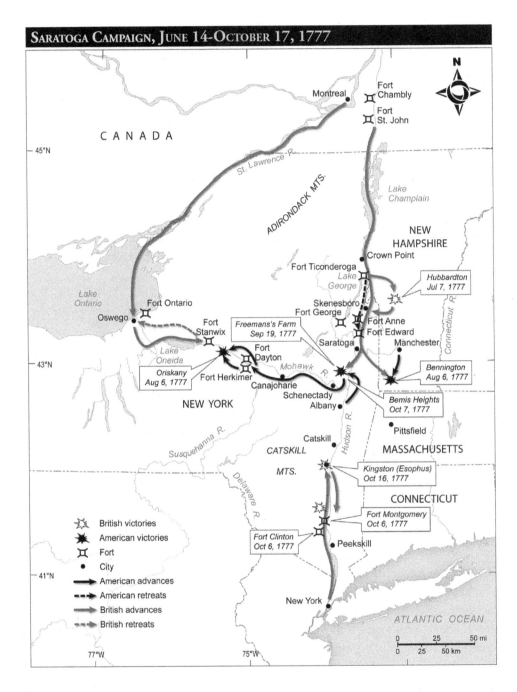

## SARATOGA CAMPAIGN, JUNE 14–OCTOBER 17, 1777

south from New York against Philadelphia. He believed that Continental Army commander General George Washington would commit the bulk of his army to defend the capital and that the rebel army might thus be destroyed.

Germain made no effort to reconcile these two plans, nor did he order the two commanders to cooperate. Neither Howe nor Burgoyne made any effort to coordinate with the other, although Howe did inform British commander in Canada

John Trumbull's painting depicting the surrender of British Lieutenant General John Burgoyne to Continental Army Major General Horatio Gates at Saratoga, New York, on October 17, 1777. The American victory here marked a major turning point in the Revolutionary War as it led France to enter the war openly on the American side. (National Archives)

Major General Sir Guy Carleton by letter of his intentions. Howe promised to position a corps in the lower Hudson River area to maintain communications through the Highlands, which he said might then "act in favor of the northern army," but he gave no assurances that it would move north; nor did Howe leave any instructions to this effect with the officer he left in command in New York, Major General Henry Clinton. Later, Clinton did send a force up the Hudson to a point above Hyde Park, but this was in the manner of a diversion, and he made no effort to join Burgoyne. Burgoyne saw Howe's letter to Carleton but did not change his plans.

Burgoyne, now a lieutenant general, and the main British force assembled at St. Jean, south of Montreal. Brigadier General Barry St. Leger led the secondary effort at Lachine. St. Leger had only 875 British, Loyalist, and Hessian troops, assisted by 1,000 Iroquois Indians under Joseph Brant. This force struck from Oswego into the Mohawk Valley, but the Indian massacre of civilians produced a widespread mobilization of militia, supported by units of the Continental Army under Major General Benedict Arnold. Although St. Leger's force campaigned in the Mohawk

Valley during July 25–August 25, much of this time was spent in a fruitless siege of Fort Stanwix (Fort Schuyler, present-day Rome, New York), and the force never joined Burgoyne.

Howe, meanwhile, left about one-third of his army under Major General Sir Henry Clinton to garrison New York and put to sea with some 16,000 men, sailing to the head of the Chesapeake Bay to approach Philadelphia from the south. Washington shifted his army to central New Jersey so he could act in either direction. As Burgoyne moved deeper into upper New York from Canada, however, Washington detached some of his best troops and most capable commanders to reinforce that front. The opportunity to cut off and destroy a British army away from Royal Navy support was simply too tempting. Once Howe's intent was clear, Washington had ample time to move south and protect Philadelphia.

The Continental Army met defeat in the Battle of Brandywine Creek on September 11, 1777, but managed to withdraw in good order. By the end of September, Howe had seized Philadelphia, but it was a hollow victory, devoid of military significance.

Burgoyne now faced a difficult decision. After capturing Fort Ticonderoga in early July, he had advanced slowly. By early August, he knew that Howe would not be reinforcing him and that St. Leger had been blocked. Burgoyne also knew that winter would freeze over his Lake Champlain supply line, and communications to Canada were threatened by colonial actions against Fort Ticonderoga. Then on August 16, Burgoyne suffered a disaster. He had detached a sizable force of Hessian mercenaries to secure provisions, and the American militia cut off and surrounded them at Bennington (in present-day Vermont). The British lost 207 killed and 696 captured; American casualties were only 30 killed or wounded. The Americans also secured supplies and weapons.

Burgoyne had only 30 days of provisions for his 7,000 men in addition to some 2,000 women and a number of children who accompanied the troops. Local supplies were practically nonexistent due to the work of Major General Philip Schuyler, commander of the Northern Department and the unsung hero of the campaign. Burgoyne's long supply lines and Schuyler's skillfully planned retreat (after he had destroyed the countryside) were the keys to the campaign. Schuyler's continued withdrawals and aloof manner made him unpopular with his men, however. With Major General Horatio Gates also intriguing against him, Congress relieved Schuyler of command on August 19 and replaced him with Gates, who subsequently quarreled with Arnold.

The Indians in Burgoyne's service also helped to create hostility against the British. The Indians scalped a white woman, ironically the fiancée of a British officer. Gates played this up with great success. Burgoyne inflamed the situation by threatening Indian reprisals against resisting Americans, which served to bring out militia in large numbers. Later the Indians, anticipating disaster, melted away, a serious loss for the British in gathering intelligence on American dispositions.

Burgoyne's advance, impeded at every turn by the Americans and slowed by the need to construct dozens of bridges and causeways across swamps and creeks, now was only a mile a day. On September 13–14 the British crossed to the west side of the Hudson River on a bridge of rafts. The troops at last reached Saratoga, only a few miles from their goal of Albany, but found their way blocked in a series of battles for control of the main Albany road. Collectively known as the Battles of Saratoga, these were the Battle of Freeman's Farm (First Battle of Saratoga) and the Battle of Bemis Heights (Second Battle of Saratoga).

The Battle of Freeman's Farm occurred on the afternoon of September 19. Some 6,000 Americans, their right flank anchored on the Hudson River, had established a fortified position of redoubts and breastworks on Bemis Heights, south of a 15-acre clearing known as Freeman's Farm. Burgoyne opened the battle when he ordered three regiments to attack across the clearing and dislodge the Americans from Bemis Heights. The British attack went poorly. Brigadier General Daniel Morgan and Arnold halted the advance, with Morgan's riflemen inflicting heavy casualties on the British, especially officers. Fortunately for Burgoyne, Gates refused to leave his entrenchments to support Arnold and Morgan. Hessian forces turned the American right flank, and that night the British encamped in the field. But they had failed to dislodge the Americans on Bemis Heights, the object of their attack. The British had also sustained some 600 casualties to only 300 casualties for the Americans.

The Americans were now reinforced, and by the time of the second battle, Gates had some 11,500 men to only 6,617 for Burgoyne. At a council of war on October 5, Burgoyne's officers pressed him to retreat while there was still an opportunity, but Burgoyne steadfastly refused and ordered a full-scale attack to turn the American flank. This prompted the second battle on October 7. Gates committed Morgan's riflemen on the British right flank. Brigadier General Ebenezer Learned's brigade was in the center, and Brigadier General Enoch Poor's brigade was on the left. Gates's refusal to commit his entire force mitigated the British defeat, but Arnold, who had quarreled with Gates and been removed from command, disregarded orders and charged onto the field to lead a general American assault that took two British redoubts. In the battle, the Americans sustained only about 130 casualties to 600 casualties for the British.

On October 8 Burgoyne ordered a general retreat, only to find that the Americans had blocked that possibility. On October 17, aware that Clinton would be unable to relieve him, Burgoyne formally surrendered his army of 5,895 officers and men. Gates granted the British paroles on condition that they not serve again in America, an action that Congress subsequently disallowed. Burgoyne was eventually cleared of any misconduct, but it was the end of his military career.

The British lost not only Saratoga but also Ticonderoga and the Highlands as well. All they had to show for the year's campaigning was the occupation of Philadelphia. The war now became a major issue in British politics. More important, the

Battles of Saratoga caused France, which had been providing extensive secret aid, to enter the war openly on the American side. On December 4 Benjamin Franklin, in Paris as an ambassador for the colonists, received the news of Burgoyne's surrender. Two days later King Louis XVI approved an alliance with the United States. A treaty was signed on February 6, 1778, and on March 11 Great Britain and France were at war.

For two years, France had been actively assisting the rebels with substantial quantities of military supplies, but the actual entry of France into the war was a threat to every part of the British Empire. The war then became largely a problem of sea power, accentuated when Spain declared war on England in 1779, followed by Holland in 1780. Participation of French Army regiments in concert with the French Navy made possible the defeat of the British Army in America.

Spencer C. Tucker

**Further Reading**

Black, Jeremy. *War for America: The Fight for Independence, 1775–1783.* Stroud, Gloucestershire, UK: Alan Sutton, 1991.

Ketchum, Richard M. *Saratoga: Turning Point of America's Revolutionary War.* New York: Henry Holt, 1997.

Lunt, James. *John Burgoyne of Saratoga.* New York: Harcourt, Brace, Jovanovich, 1975.

Ward, Christopher. *The War of the Revolution,* Vol. 2. New York: Macmillan, 1952.

## Battles of Kaskaskia and Vincennes

| Date | July 4, 1778, and February 23–25, 1779 | |
|---|---|---|
| Location | Illinois Country (present-day Illinois and Indiana ) | |
| Opponents (*winner) | *United States and allied Native Americans | *Great Britain, French Canadian militia, and allied Native Americans |
| Commander | Virginia Militia lieutenant colonel George Rogers Clark | British lieutenant governor Henry Hamilton |
| Approx. # Troops | Some 175 men and some allied Native Americans | Some 170 men and 60 allied Native Americans |
| Importance | Allows the Americans to lay claim to and to secure the entire region from the Alleghenies to the Mississippi River (nearly doubling the size of the United States) in the Treaty of Paris, which ends the war. | |

By 1776, the few white settlers in present-day Kentucky found themselves under attack by Native Americans from north of the Ohio River who had been encouraged by British lieutenant governor Henry Hamilton at Detroit. In the summer of 1776 one of these settlers, 24-year-old George Rogers Clark, who had declared for the Patriot cause, traveled to Williamsburg, Virginia, where he petitioned Governor Patrick Henry for assistance in defending Kentucky. In response, the Virginia government created Kentucky County in December and gave Clark 500 pounds of gunpowder. Following his return home in March 1777, Clark was appointed major of militia, with orders to defend Kentucky.

Fending off Native American attacks during the summer and autumn, Clark became convinced that Americans should attempt to wrest the Northwest Territory from British control. In October he again returned to Virginia and persuaded Henry to accept his idea. Success would relieve the pressure on Kentucky and loosen the British hold on all the territory north of the Ohio. Clark was aware that most of the white settlers in the region were of French extraction, and he saw them as potential allies.

The plan was approved by the Virginia General Assembly, which, however, was not informed of its true aims. Publicly Clark was to raise troops to defend Kentucky, but his secret instructions called on him to take Kaskaskia and, if feasible, Detroit. Commissioned a lieutenant colonel in the Virginia Militia, Clark in the spring of 1778 organized his men near Louisville.

On June 24 Clark set out with 175 men from Corn Island at the Falls of the Ohio across the Illinois Country toward Kaskaskia, at the confluence of the Illinois and Kaskaskia Rivers, arriving there on the evening of July 4. His men had not eaten in two days and were determined to take the place or die in the attempt. Surprising the garrison in the middle of the night, the men captured Kaskaskia without a shot being fired. Clark then informed the French-speaking inhabitants of the treaty of alliance between France and the United States and secured oaths of loyalty from them. Indeed, Catholic priest Father Pierre Gibault agreed to assist Clark upon the latter's assurance that the Catholic Church would be protected under the laws of Virginia.

Clark then extended his authority over other French settlements in the vicinity. Thanks to Gibault, who carried letters to the French settlers at Vincennes, that British outpost (there were no British regulars present at Fort Sackville) pledged its loyalty to the United States on July 20, and shortly thereafter Clark sent Captain Henry Helm and a small force to occupy the fort in August.

Hamilton, learning of Clark's occupation of the Illinois Country, marched on October 7 with a force of 175 white troops, mostly French Canadian militiamen, and 60 Indians to retake the lost posts. The French militiamen at Fork Sackvlle refused to fight, and Helm had no choice but to surrender it on December 17. Hamilton then suspended operations for the winter, planning to attack Kaskaskia the next spring and drive out the Americans there under Clark.

On January 29, 1779, Clark learned of Hamilton's recapture of Vincennes and decided to attempt to retake it immediately. He set out from Kaskaskia on February 5 with some 170 men, many of them French, and after a march of some 180 miles across freezing marshy plains of what is now the state of Illinois, he arrived at

Vincennes on February 23. Clark warned the inhabitants of his approach. The French were asked to remain in their homes, while British sympathizers were advised to seek refuge in Fort Sackville. Clark's men then nearly encircled the fort. Clark marched men back and forth with flags to create the impression of a far larger force. Hamilton at first refused Clark's demands for surrender, but in the ensuing skirmishing, American rifle fire killed 6 British defenders. Hamilton surrendered Fort Sackville and its 79-man garrison on February 25. Helm then took another British force of 40 men sent up the Wabash to secure supplies. Clark was now in full control of the Illinois Country.

The best-known action of the western theater in the American Revolutionary War, Clark's Illinois Campaign was a small operation but had vast strategic importance. Although Clark was unable to secure sufficient resources to move against Detroit or to completely halt Native American raids, his accomplishment helped the United States secure in the peace settlement following the war the entire region from the Alleghenies to the Mississippi River, nearly doubling the size of the United States.

Spencer C. Tucker

**Further Reading**

Harrison, Lowell H. *George Rogers Clark and the War in the West.* Lexington: University of Kentucky Press, 2001.

Palmer, Frederick. *Clark of the Ohio: A Life of George Rogers Clark.* Whitefish, MT: Kessinger, 2004.

Ward, Christopher. *The War of the Revolution.* 2 vols. New York: Macmillan, 1952.

## Battle of Kings Mountain

| Date | October 7, 1780 | |
|------|------------------|---|
| Location | Kings Mountain, South Carolina | |
| Opponents (*winner) | *United States | Great Britain |
| Commander | Colonels Isaac Shelby and William Campbell | British Army major Patrick Ferguson |
| Approx. # Troops | 900 Patriot militiamen | 1,000 Loyalist militiamen |
| Importance | Boosts Patriot morale and halts British efforts to secure North Carolina. | |

At the end of 1778, British commander in North America Lieutenant General Sir Henry Clinton had shifted the principal theater in the American Revolutionary War to the South, where there was strong Tory (Loyalist) sentiment. The campaign opened to great success, with the British capturing both Savannah, Georgia, and Charles Town (Charleston), South Carolina (the greatest Patriot defeat of the war). The British envisioned conquering a given area and then turning it over to a local Tory militia to hold, but the war in the South soon degenerated into a savage contest of Tory (Loyalist) versus Patriot, with both sides committing widespread atrocities.

After the capture of Charles Town, Clinton returned to New York, leaving in charge in the South able Lieutenant General Charles, Earl Cornwallis. In June, Cornwallis had detached forces under Major Patrick Ferguson of the 71st Regiment of Foot of American Volunteers to cover the area between the Catawba and Saluda Rivers. Ferguson was a capable 36-year-old officer who had designed a remarkable breech-loading rifle that could be fired five to six times a minute. He had received permission to raise his own regiment of riflemen from among American Tories. Known as the American Volunteers, it numbered some 1,300 men.

An implacable foe of the rebels, Ferguson had become widely known for his plundering of settlements in the Carolinas. He had also issued a challenge to the inhabitants of the Watauga settlements beyond the Appalachian Mountains to the west in what is now Tennessee that if they did not end their opposition to the Crown, he would cross the mountains, hang their leaders, and lay waste to their settlements.

The frontiersmen of the Watauga settlements decided that if there was to be fighting, it should not be on their own territory. Colonel Isaac Shelby and John Sevier issued a call for men. They called on Colonel William Campbell of Virginia, and he in turn summoned Colonel Benjamin Cleveland of North Carolina. By September 25, an all-militia force of some 900 men had assembled at Sycamore Flats on the Watauga River. Most of the men were mounted but, armed with the long rifle, would fight on foot.

Ferguson was moving south toward the British outpost of Ninety-Six when he learned that the backwoodsmen, as Ferguson called them, were converging against him. The Patriot militia force had now grown to 1,400 men, but its leaders decided that 900 of the best mounted men should press ahead in pursuit of Ferguson, with the remainder to follow as soon as they could.

Ferguson took up position at Kings Mountain in rural York County, just across the border in South Carolina and some 30 miles west of Charlotte. A seemingly strong position, Kings Mountain rose some 60 feet above the surrounding countryside and was some 500 yards long and 70–80 yards wide. Ferguson, expecting British reinforcements that never arrived, had detached some 200 men on a foraging expedition on the morning of October 7 when the Patriot militia arrived and surrounded his position.

This was a battle of American against American, with Ferguson being the only British officer present. The Patriots formed into groups and, taking advantage of cover and concealment on its wooded slopes, began working their way up Kings Mountain. The defenders, although well trained, were shooting downhill and tended to fire high. The Patriots were for the most part excellent marksmen.

The battle lasted little more than an hour. None of the Tories who took part escaped. A total of 157 were killed, 163 were wounded so badly that they were left on the field, and 698 were taken prisoner. Ferguson was among the dead. He had refused calls to surrender and had been killed in a volley of shots while he and some of his men were trying to break free. Patriot losses were only 28 killed and 62 wounded.

The Battle of Kings Mountain was one of the most important battles of the entire war. The battle was an immense boost to Patriot morale and temporarily halted efforts by Cornwallis to secure North Carolina. Upon learning of events, on October 14 he withdrew to Winnsboro, South Carolina, for the winter. The battle did have several negatives for the Continental Army in the South in that it seemed to end the immediate need to strengthen Patriot forces there and reinforced the mistaken belief held by some that militia alone could produce victory.

Spencer C. Tucker

## Further Reading

Allen, Thomas B. *Tories: Fighting for the King in America's First Civil War.* New York: HarperCollins, 2010.

Buchanan, John. *The Road to Guilford Court House: The American Revolution in the Carolinas.* New York: Wiley, 1997.

Dameron, J. David. *Kings Mountain: The Defeat of the Loyalists, October 7, 1780.* Cambridge, MA: Da Capo, 2003.

Ward, Christopher. *The War of the Revolution.* 2 vols. New York: Macmillan, 1952.

## Battle of Cowpens

| Date | January 17, 1781 | |
|---|---|---|
| Location | South of the Broad River, South Carolina, on the border with North Carolina | |
| Opponents (*winner) | *United States | Great Britain |
| Commander | Brigadier General Daniel Morgan | Lieutenant Colonel Banastre Tarleton |
| Approx. # Troops | Some 2,000 Continental Army and militia troops | 1,100 British regulars |
| Importance | Buoys Patriot morale and is an important step in the reconquest of South Carolina from the British. | |

On August 16, 1780, British forces had destroyed an American army under Major General Horatio Gates in the Battle of Camden in South Carolina. Continental Army commander General George Washington then chose Major General Nathanael Greene as the new commander of the Southern Department. While working to reconstitute American forces, Greene was obliged by circumstances to divide his forces. British Army commander in the South Lieutenant General Charles, Earl Cornwallis, sought to take advantage of this. In early January 1781 he dispatched Lieutenant Colonel Banastre Tarleton, his crack British Legion, and

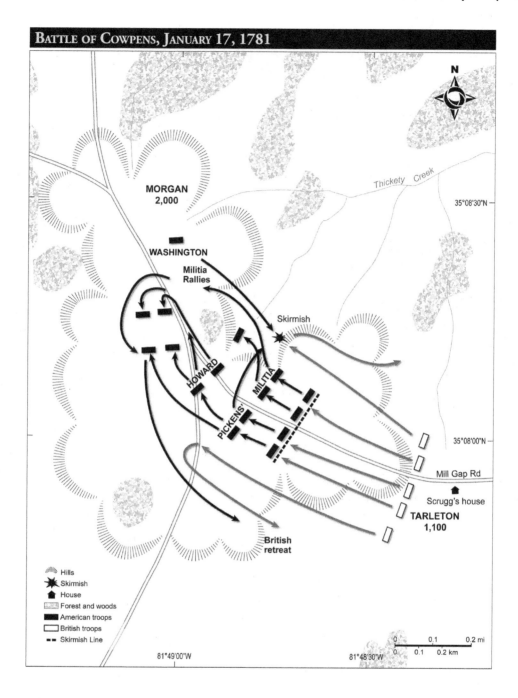

## BATTLE OF COWPENS, JANUARY 17, 1781

MORGAN
2,000

WASHINGTON

Militia
Rallies

Thickety Creek

35°08'30"N —

Skirmish

HOWARD

MILITIA

PICKENS'

35°08'00"N —

Mill Gap Rd

Scrugg's house

TARLETON
1,100

British
retreat

Hills
Skirmish
House
Forest and woods
American troops
British troops
Skirmish Line

N

0        0.1        0.2 mi
0    0.1    0.2 km

81°49'00"W

81°48'30"W

other units, totaling some 1,100 men, to seek out and destroy the smaller body of Greene's force under Continental Army brigadier general Daniel Morgan.

Tarleton and his men crossed the Pacolet River at night and advanced on Morgan's camp early on January 16, 1781. The Americans hastily withdrew, leaving their breakfast to the British. Morgan's men fell back on an area known as Hannah's Cowpens. Morgan was reluctant to attempt a crossing of the nearby Broad River to

In the Battle of Cowpens on January 17, 1781, British Army lieutenant colonel Banastre Tarleton was pursuing American forces under Brigadier General Daniel Morgan when he suffered a shattering defeat, thanks to Tarleton's failure to reconnoiter and Morgan's masterful deployment of his resources. (National Archives)

the north with Tarleton's force upon him and so elected to fight here. In making his dispositions, Morgan factored in Tarleton's known aggressive nature.

Counting militia, Morgan may have had about 2,000 men. Morgan selected a hill as the center of his position and arranged his forces in three lines: riflemen in the first line, militia in the second line, and the reliable Maryland and Delaware regiments in the third line, known as the Continental Line. He placed Lieutenant Colonel William Washington's cavalry out of sight behind the hill. Morgan instructed the Georgia riflemen in the first line to fire two rounds at the advancing British and then fall back; the second line, of North Carolina and South Carolina militiamen under Brigadier General Andrew Pickens, were also to fire two rounds before withdrawing. The regiments of the third line were at the top of the hill and were ordered to stand fast. Morgan's plan was fraught with risk, as retreat was now impossible thanks to the Broad River to the American rear, but the American commander gambled on Tarleton's impetuosity.

On January 17 Tarleton and his British Legion came upon the Americans. As Morgan had hoped, the overly confident Tarleton failed to reconnoiter and immediately attacked. After firing two rounds each as planned, Morgan's first two lines withdrew. Tarleton, not understanding that this was by design and believing that victory was now his, rushed forward to encounter the final American position of the Continental Line at the top of the hill, at which point the riflemen, militia, and Lieutenant Colonel Washington's cavalry came around both flanks and double-enveloped the attacking British. In the battle, which is sometimes called the American Cannae, Tarleton lost 90 percent of his force.

Tarleton himself escaped along with some of his cavalry, but he left behind on the field 100 dead, 229 wounded, and 600 unwounded prisoners. Morgan reported losses of only 12 killed and 60 wounded, but these were apparently only Continental Army soldiers, and recent scholarship puts Patriot losses at some 25 dead and 124 wounded. Morgan also secured some 800 muskets, 2 cannon, 100 horses, and all the British supplies and ammunition.

Morgan had in fact taken a considerable gamble, and his decision to fight was probably mistaken, although fortunately it had a happy outcome for the Patriot cause. Patriot morale now soared. This brilliant American victory completely transformed the situation in the South and the psychology of the war, so close to disaster just weeks following Camden. It was a turning point in the reconquest of South Carolina from the British and led Cornwallis into a chain of events that saw him end up at Yorktown, Virginia.

Spencer C. Tucker

### Further Reading

Babits, Lawrence E. *A Devil of a Whipping: The Battle of Cowpens.* Chapel Hill: University of North Carolina Press, 1998.

Davis, Burke. *The Cowpens-Guilford Courthouse Campaign.* Philadelphia: University of Pennsylvania Press, 2002.

Roberts, Kenneth. *The Battle of Cowpens: The Great Morale-Builder.* Garden City, NY: Doubleday, 1958.

Tucker, Spencer C. *Rise and Fight Again: The Life of General Nathanael Greene.* Wilmington, DE: ISI Books, 2009.

## Battle of Guilford Courthouse

| Date | March 15, 1781 | |
|---|---|---|
| Location | Just west of Guilford Courthouse, North Carolina (present-day Greensboro, North Carolina) | |
| Opponents (*winner) | *Great Britain | United States |
| Commander | Lieutenant General Charles, Lord Cornwallis | Major General Nathanael Greene |
| Approx. # Troops | 1,900 British regulars | 4,404 men: 4,243 infantry and 161 cavalry (1,490 Continental Army, remainder militia) |
| Importance | Regarded as a defeat by many British leaders because of its heavy casualties, the battle leads Cornwallis to move the bulk of North Carolina forces to Virginia. | |

In March 1781, Continental Army commander in the South Major General Nathanael Greene, having reunited his army's two main bodies, sought out British forces under Lieutenant General Sir Charles, Earl Cornwallis. On paper, Greene had the superior force: 4,404 men, including 4,243 infantry and 161 cavalry. This advantage was deceptive, for only one-third of his men (1,490) were Continental Army troops, and only about 500 of these were trained veterans. Cornwallis had only 1,900 men, but all were regulars, and almost all were disciplined veterans, steady under fire.

Greene chose as a battlefield position sparsely settled country just west of Guilford Courthouse, a North Carolina backcountry hamlet that he had previously reconnoitered. He broke camp at Speedwell Iron Works on Troublesome Creek on the morning of March 14 and arrived at Guilford Courthouse that afternoon. Cornwallis was some 10 miles to the southwest.

Greene expected a British attack the next day, moving up New Garden Road. He planned to defend a stretch of gradually rising terrain astride that road, forcing the British to attack him uphill and employing the same tactic that had worked so well in the Battle of Cowpens of positioning forces in three lines, with the militia in front. Forested terrain made it impossible for Greene to see the first two lines from his command position at the third line, however.

About a half mile west of Guilford Courthouse, Little Horseshoe Creek flowed in a more or less north-south direction. East of it lay open fields, and behind these were a rail fence and woods. Behind the fence line, Greene placed some 1,000 North Carolina militia, his least trained men, instructing them to fire off two rounds at the advancing British before falling back. Virginia militia formed the second line, about 300–400 yards farther back and in the woods. To stiffen their resolve, Greene mixed among them some Virginia Continentals.

The final line was about 400 yards beyond, at the top of a rise just before Guilford Courthouse. This line consisted of the 1,400-man Continental Line: two regiments from Maryland and two regiments from Virginia. Finally, Greene placed covering forces in the woods to each side of his lines.

There was no reserve. Greene had no intention of placing his army in jeopardy. If prudence required, he planned to withdraw north up Reedy Fork Road to Salisbury.

March 15 dawned bright and clear. Before first light, a courier informed Greene that Cornwallis was indeed moving against him. The British arrived shortly after noon, and Cornwallis immediately formed a line with a brigade on each side of the road and no reserve, a move demonstrating contempt for his opponent.

The battle opened almost immediately with American artillery fire, and the British replied. Following a 20-minute cannonade with little damage to either side, Cornwallis ordered his infantry forward. Too soon, with the British still about 150 yards or so from their fence line, the North Carolina militiamen opened a ragged fire. Although dozens of British soldiers fell, the vast majority continued on.

At about 50 yards, the British halted and delivered a volley of their own before charging with the bayonet. The North Carolina militiamen promptly fled into the woods, with many simply throwing down their weapons as they attempted to escape. Unfortunately for Greene, most of the militiamen did not join the Virginians but instead simply decamped altogether.

As Greene anticipated, the woods broke up the British formations, and the battle became fragmented, with small groups engaging one another. The Virginia militiamen fought well, but after about a half hour of fierce combat and several bayonet attacks, the British finally broke through the second American line and emerged from the woods, only to encounter an open fenced field and the third American line.

A well-aimed volley and an American counterattack with the bayonet drove the British back and into the woods again. This was the critical point in the battle. Greene might have ordered the Continental Line forward, but this chance at total victory would carry with it the risk of the destruction of his entire force, something he was not prepared to hazard. Greene ordered the Continentals to hold their positions, and the British left was thus able to regroup. Greene, meanwhile, rode up and down the American line, encouraging his men and in the process exposing himself to British fire.

It appeared that the Americans might carry the day, but on the British right/ American left, things were going differently. Here the British managed to break through the 5th Maryland Regiment, a unit experiencing its first battle, and turned the American left. Many of the Marylanders fled without firing a shot, and disaster was averted only when Lieutenant Colonel John Eager Howard's 1st Maryland Regiment wheeled and hit the advancing British in the flank and Lieutenant Colonel William Washington rode forward with his cavalry to strike the British from the rear.

To halt the American advance and stave off disaster, Cornwallis, whose horse had been shot from under him and who had only narrowly escaped capture, ordered his artillery to fire grapeshot into the melee. This action killed as many British troops as it did Americans but had the intended effect of breaking up the American counterattack. The outcome was still in doubt, but Greene refused to hazard his army. The gap in his line convinced him that he should order a retreat and preserve the bulk of his force. With most of the teams killed before the retreat began, the Americans were forced to abandon their guns and two ammunition wagons. The men then moved north up Reedy Creek Road, with Howard's Marylanders providing rear-guard protection. Although the British initially pursued the Americans, they soon gave it up. The next day under a flag of truce, both sides cared for their wounded and buried the dead.

In the battle, the Americans had sustained 264 casualties: 79 killed and 185 wounded, more than half of them militia. Another 294 militia were listed as missing. They had simply deserted and returned home. British casualties were much higher: 93 killed and 439 wounded, a number of them mortally. This amounted to a quarter of the force engaged.

Cornwallis reported a victory in glowing terms, but when it was announced it to Parliament, Opposition leader Charles James Fox responded by paraphrasing ancient King Pyrrhus of Epirus: "Another such victory would ruin the British army." Horace Walpole gave an even gloomier assessment, saying that the battle showed that the war was lost.

Despite his report, Cornwallis was frustrated by Greene's brand of war, writing that he was "quite tired of marching about the country in quest of adventures." Cornwallis now decided to withdraw to the coast, refit, and then move the bulk of his force north into Virginia. He hoped that there he could cut Greene's supply line. This decision, however, set up the Battle of Yorktown, which turned out to be the climactic engagement of the war. Meanwhile, Greene's forces came to control virtually all of interior North Carolina, South Carolina, and Georgia.

Spencer C. Tucker

## Further Reading

Babits, Lawrence E., and Joshua B. Howard. *Long, Obstinate, and Bloody: The Battle of Guilford Courthouse.* Chapel Hill: University of North Carolina Press, 2009.

Davis, Burke. *The Cowpens-Guilford Courthouse Campaign.* Philadelphia: University of Pennsylvania Press, 2002.

Tucker, Spencer C. *Rise and Fight Again: The Life of General Nathanael Greene.* Wilmington, DE: ISI Books, 2009.

Ward, Christopher. *War of the Revolution.* 2 vols. New York: Macmillan, 1952.

## Battle of the Chesapeake

| Date | September 5, 1781 | |
|------|-------------------|---|
| Location | Off the Virginia Capes, Atlantic Ocean | |
| Opponents (*winner) | *France | Great Britain |
| Commander | Admiral François Joseph Paul, Comte de Grasse | Rear Admiral Thomas Graves |
| # of Ships | 24 ships of the line | 19 ships of the line |
| Importance | Ends with the French Navy in control of the Chesapeake, enabling Continental Army and French forces to win the Battle of Yorktown. | |

French admiral François Joseph Comte de Grasse, with a powerful fleet of 28 ships of the line, had been campaigning in the West Indies. Indeed, after France's entrance into the American Revolutionary War in 1778, both Britain and France had deployed major fleet units there to try to secure the lucrative sugar trade of the

The naval Battle of the Chesapeake of September 5, 1781, between the British and French, while it was itself indecisive, had immense ramifications, for it made possible the subsequent land victory by the Americans and French over the British in the Battle of Yorktown. (DeAgostini/Getty Images)

other. De Grasse, however, planned to bring his fleet north during hurricane season and would then be free to act to support Continental Army and French Army land operations in North America. Washington hoped to retake New York, but de Grasse decided to sail instead to Chesapeake Bay. Washington immediately saw the possibilities of bagging the sizable British force under the command of Lieutenant General Charles, Earl Cornwallis, at the port of Yorktown on the Chesapeake Bay.

On August 27 British rear admiral Samuel Hood, with 14 ships of the line, stood into Chesapeake Bay on his way north from the West Indies. With no sign of the French, Hood sailed on to New York, where he joined the more senior Rear Admiral Thomas Graves with his 5 ships of the line. Graves also had heard nothing of de Grasse but informed Hood that French commodore Louis-Jacques Comte de Barras de Saint-Laurent, with 8 ships of the line, 4 frigates, and 18 transports, had sailed from Rhode Island the day before. The British assumed, correctly, that Barras was sailing south, probably for the Chesapeake. Graves and Hood, with their combined 19 ships of the line, set out to intercept Barras on August 31.

The day before, August 30, de Grasse had arrived in the Chesapeake with 28 ships of the line, 4 frigates, and 3,000 land troops under Major General Claude-Ann, Marquis de Saint-Simon. Disembarking the troops, de Grasse then ordered the transports and boats up the bay to ferry Washington's forces south.

Graves arrived in the Chesapeake on September 5, ahead of Barras. A French frigate signaled the British approach. Instead of swooping down on the unprepared French ships, Graves, hampered by an inadequate signaling system and unwilling to risk a general action against a superior enemy (28 ships of the line to 19), formed his ships into line ahead and waited for de Grasse to come out.

De Grasse, shorthanded with 90 of his officers and 1,500 sailors on ferrying duties up the bay but aware of his poor position, immediately set out with 24 ships of the line to meet the English. Hood and his officers had not had time to assimilate Graves's signals, and two signals were simultaneously flown: close action and line ahead at half a cable. Thus, while the British van bore down on the French, the British center and rear followed the van instead of closing. The vans engaged at 3:45 p.m., but the rest of both fleets remained out of action.

At 4:27 p.m. the line ahead signal was hauled down, yet it was not until 5:20 p.m. that Hood attempted to close with the French. But the French avoided close engagement.

The battle ended at sunset. The British sustained 336 casualties, and the French sustained 221 casualties. No ships were lost on either side although a number were damaged, and on September 11 Graves was forced to order the badly damaged *Terrible* (74 guns) scuttled.

On the morning of September 6 there was only a slight wind, and Graves chose to attempt repairs to his ships' masts and rigging. Inconclusive maneuvering followed over the next several days. On September 8 and 9, the French briefly gained the wind and threatened to reengage. On September 9, French frigates spotted the arrival of Barras's ships, and de Grasse turned back to the Chesapeake that night. Notified on September 13 that de Grasse was back in the Chesapeake but not yet aware of Barras's arrival there, Graves held a council of war with his captains, bringing the decision to return to New York, make repairs, gather additional ships, and then return. He arrived off Sandy Hook on September 20. On October 19, Graves and Hood sailed again from New York, this time with 25 ships of the line, but it was too late.

The Battle of the Chesapeake doomed Cornwallis. Cut off from reinforcement, he surrendered his army, representing one-third of British Army strength in North America, on October 19. This defeat brought down the British government and led London to seek peace. Thus, a tactically inconclusive naval battle ranks as one of the most significant strategic victories in world history.

Spencer C. Tucker

### Further Reading

Larrabee, Harold A. *Decision at the Chesapeake.* London: William Kimber, 1965.

Syrett, David. *The Royal Navy in American Waters, 1775–1783.* Aldershot, UK: Scolar, 1989.

Tilley, John A. *The British Navy and the American Revolution.* Columbia: University of South Carolina Press, 1987.

## Siege of Yorktown

| Date | September 28–October 19, 1781 | |
|---|---|---|
| Location | Yorktown, Virginia | |
| Opponents (*winner) | *United States, France | Great Britain |
| Commander | General George Washington; Lieutenant General Jean Baptiste Donatien de Vimeur, Comte de Rochambeau | Lieutenant General Charles, Lord Cornwallis |
| Approx. # Troops | 9,000 American troops (3,000 of them militia), 7,500 French | 9,000 (including Hessian troops) |
| Importance | The surrender of a third of the British troops in North America brings a new government to power in Britain, which institutes a policy of cutting British losses in America. | |

By 1781, the American Revolutionary War was in stalemate. After sustaining heavy casualties in the Battle of Guilford Courthouse (March 15, 1781) in North Carolina, however, British commander in the South, Lieutenant General Charles, Earl Cornwallis, decided to march the majority of his forces north into Virginia in an effort to destroy the Continental Army's supply lines southward into North Carolina.

Continental Army commander General George Washington hoped for a combined American and French assault on British-occupied New York, and toward that end he had positioned his main forces at White Plains. These numbered four infantry regiments, a battalion of artillery, and the Duc de Lauzun's 4,000-man French Legion under French lieutenant general Jean Baptiste Donatien de Vimeur, Comte de Rochambeau.

In May 1781 French admiral Jacques Comte de Barras arrived with a small squadron at Newport, Rhode Island, bringing news that Admiral François Joseph, Comte de Grasse, was on his way to the West Indies from France with a powerful fleet. Washington learned, however, that de Grasse would bring the fleet north during hurricane season.

In the meantime, Washington sent 1,200 men under Continental Army major general Marie-Joseph Paul Yves Roch Gilbert du Motier, Marquis de Lafayette, to trap British forces under the turncoat Brigadier General Benedict Arnold that had been operating along the James River in Virginia. Cornwallis arrived in Virginia just at this time and commanded about 7,000 men, approximately a quarter of British armed strength in North America. Cornwallis tried but failed to take Lafayette's much smaller force and then withdrew to the small tobacco port of Yorktown on the York River just off Chesapeake Bay. Lafayette followed.

On August 14 Washington learned that de Grasse would not be coming to New York but instead would sail to the Chesapeake Bay, arriving there later the same month and remaining until the end of October. Washington immediately saw the possibilities. If de Grasse could hold the bay while Washington came down from the land side, they might bag Cornwallis at Yorktown.

Washington ordered Lafayette to contain Cornwallis and on August 21 sent 2,000 American and 4,000 French soldiers south, leaving only 2,000 men under Major General William Heath to watch British forces at New York under British commander in chief in North America Lieutenant General Sir Henry Clinton. Not until early September did Clinton realize what had happened. Although promising Cornwallis a diversion, Clinton did little to help his subordinate.

On August 30 de Grasse arrived in the Chesapeake with 28 ships of the line and 3,000 land troops. He immediately disembarked the troops under the command of Major General Claude-Anne de Rouvroy, Marquis de Saint-Simon, and sent his transports and boats up the bay. During September 14–26, Washington and Rochambeau's troops were transported down Chesapeake Bay from Head of Elk (present-day Elkton), Baltimore, and Annapolis, Maryland, to land near Williamsburg, where they concentrated.

Barras, meanwhile, had sailed south from Newport with 8 ships of the line convoying 18 transports that were also carrying siege guns. British rear admiral Thomas Graves with 19 ships of the line set out on August 31 to intercept Barras and on September 5 arrived ahead of Barras at Chesapeake Bay. De Grasse stood out with 24 ships of the line to engage the British. The inconclusive Battle of the Chesapeake (also known as the Battle of the Capes) followed, ending in a tactical draw with damage and casualties but no ships lost on either side. Strategically, however, it was one of the most important naval battles in world history, for it left the French still in control of the bay. During the battle, Barras's ships arrived. Now facing even longer odds, Graves returned to New York to gather more ships, leaving Cornwallis, for the time being at least, to his own fate.

Marching from Williamsburg, Washington's combined American and French army arrived at Yorktown on September 28. Washington had some 9,000 American troops (3,000 were militia who played no role in the battle) and 7,500 French troops. He also had French field and siege artillery and the services of French engineers, who now directed a siege of Yorktown with European-style zigzag trenches and parallels dug toward the British defenses.

On October 9 the Americans and French began a bombardment. Two days later the allies began construction of a second siege line, this one only 400 yards from the British line. On the night of October 14, the allies stormed two key British redoubts. The French took No. 9 and the Americans seized No. 10, completing the second siege line. The allies were thus able to establish new firing positions that compromised the British defensive line. On October 15 the allies repulsed a desperate British counterattack. Too late, on the night of October 16, Cornwallis attempted to escape across the York River to Gloucester Point, which Washington had largely neglected. The plan was thwarted by a severe storm.

Now running low on food, on the morning of October 17 Cornwallis asked for terms, seeking parole for his men. Washington insisted that they surrender as prisoners of war, and Cornwallis agreed. On October 19 the formal surrender occurred: 8,077 British surrendered (840 seamen, 80 camp followers, and 7,157 soldiers). During the siege, the British lost 156 killed and 326 wounded; the allies lost 75 killed and 199 wounded (two-thirds of them French). Clinton arrived with a powerful fleet and 7,000 land troops a week later. De Grasse had already departed for the West Indies.

The battle was in fact an amazing bit of luck. The British had lost control of the American seaboard for one brief period, and as a result they lost the war. The consequences of the British defeat at Yorktown were momentous. A terrific shock in England, the defeat brought down the British government of Lord North, a hardliner, and ushered in a British policy of cutting its losses immediately, to the point of granting concessions to America, including independence, to separate it from its French ally.

Spencer C. Tucker

**Further Reading**

Davis, Burke. *The Campaign That Won America: The Story of Yorktown.* New York: Dial, 1970.

Lumpkin, Henry. *From Savannah to Yorktown: The American Revolution in the South.* Columbia: University of South Carolina Press, 1981.

Morrissey, Brenden. *Yorktown, 1781: The World Turned Upside Down.* London: Osprey, 1997.

## St. Clair's Defeat

| Date | November 4, 1791 | |
|------|------------------|---|
| **Location** | Near present-day Fort Recovery, Ohio | |
| **Opponents (*winner)** | *Native American Western Confederacy | United States |
| **Commander** | Little Turtle; Blue Jacket | Major General Arthur St. Clair |
| **Approx. # Troops** | Some 1,000 warriors | 902 troops |
| **Importance** | The greatest defeat suffered by the American military at the hands of Native Americans, it leads to the creation of the Legion of the United States. | |

In the late 1780s there was a significant increase in tensions in the Old Northwest Territory between white settlers and Native Americans from squatters settling on lands belonging to the Miami and Shawnee tribes. This vast territory included all of the land of the United States west of Pennsylvania and northwest of the Ohio

River and covered all of present-day Ohio, Indiana, Illinois, Michigan, Wisconsin, and the northeastern part of Minnesota.

Encouraged by the British, the Native Americans demanded that the whites fall back to the Ohio River. In June 1790 governor of the Northwest Territory Arthur St. Clair and commander of the Army of the United States Brigadier General Josiah Harmar decided on force to intimidate the Native Americans. President George Washington authorized the calling up of the Kentucky and Pennsylvania Militias, and on September 30, 1790, Harmar assembled 320 men of the 1st Infantry Regiment and 1,133 militiamen at Fort Washington (Cincinnati, Ohio). This understrength and inadequately trained and equipped force invaded Shawnee and Miami territory in October.

This first major military expedition for the standing Army of the United States ended in disaster, with Harmar foolishly dividing his force twice. During October 19–23 in a series of clashes not far from present-day Fort Wayne, Indiana, Harmar's men attacked Miami villages along the Maumee River and were defeated by Native Americans led by Miami chief Little Turtle in what is known as Harmar's Defeat. Harmar arrived back at Fort Washington on November 3, having suffered 129 killed and 95 wounded. Although exonerated in a court-martial, Harmar resigned his commission.

In March 1791 Congress voted to create a second army regiment. Congress also commissioned Governor St. Clair a major general and appointed him to replace Harmar. St. Clair, a former Continental Army general, was charged with leading a new foray into Indian country.

President George Washington insisted that St. Clair proceed in the summer, but logistics and supply problems slowed his preparations at Fort Washington. Ill with gout, St. Clair did little to prepare his men, who for the most part were poorly trained and disciplined. The expedition finally set out in October 1791.

St. Clair initially commanded about 2,000 men, the largest American military force since the American Revolutionary War. The force included some 600 regulars of the 1st and 2nd Infantry Regiments, 800 six-month conscripts, and 600 militia. Its objective was Kekionga, capital of the Miami tribe near present-day Fort Wayne, Indiana. St. Clair planned to erect a fort there to counteract British influence.

Desertion soon reduced St. Clair's force to fewer than 1,500 men. Some 200–250 camp followers (wives, children, laundresses, and prostitutes) accompanied them. St. Clair had problems maintaining order, especially among the militiamen and the new soldiers. Also, from their entry into Indian country, the force was under constant observation by warriors, and occasionally there were skirmishes.

By the beginning of November, desertion and illnesses had reduced St. Clair's force to some 1,120 men, including the camp followers. Only 52 officers and 868 enlisted and militia personnel were present for duty on November 3, when the force made camp on an elevated meadow, known as Fort Recovery, near the headwaters of the Wabash River. Even though Indians had been seen in the vicinity, St. Clair did not order construction of any defensive works.

The men had stacked arms and were preparing breakfast at dawn on November 4, 1791, when some 1,000 Native American warriors, led by Miami chief Little Turtle and Shawnee chief Blue Jacket, attacked. The Indians quickly overran the perimeter, and the militiamen simply broke and ran without their weapons. The regulars unstacked their arms and formed a line, firing into the attackers, who then fell back. Most of the Native Americans then mounted a flanking attack, while others shot down the artillerymen bringing up the guns, which were then spiked and abandoned.

When the troops were ordered to charge the Indians with the bayonet, the natives withdrew, but they then encircled the troops in the woods and defeated them. St. Clair had three horses shot from beneath him as he tried to rally the men. After several hours of fighting and facing total annihilation, St. Clair ordered the survivors to break free, abandoning both the wounded and camp supplies. The Indians pursued the troops for some three miles before breaking off to loot the camp.

St. Clair's force suffered 632 killed and 264 wounded of 920 engaged. This casualty rate of some 97 percent is the highest ever sustained by a U.S. Army unit. Nearly all of the estimated 200 camp followers were slain. Native American casualties are believed to have numbered 21 killed and 40 wounded. Known as St. Clair's Defeat, the Columbia Massacre, and the Battle of the Wabash, it was the greatest defeat sustained by the U.S. Army at the hands of Native Americans. St. Clair resigned, denied a court-martial by a furious President Washington.

This military disaster helped fuel passage of the Second Amendment to the Constitution (the right to bear arms) and the Militia Act of 1792. The defeat also led Congress to create the Legion of the United States. Thoroughly trained by its commander, Major General Anthony Wayne, the legion defeated the Indians in the Battle of Fallen Timbers on August 20, 1794.

Spencer C. Tucker

**Further Reading**

Guthman, William H. *March to Massacre: A History of the First Seven Years of the United States Army, 1784–1791.* New York: McGraw-Hill, 1970.

Lytle, Richard. *The Soldiers of America's First Army: 1791.* Lanham, MD: Scarecrow, 2004.

Sword, Wiley. *President Washington's Indian War: The Struggle for the Old Northwest, 1790–1795.* Norman: University of Oklahoma Press, 1985.

## Battle of Fallen Timbers

| Date | August 20, 1794 | |
|------|-----------------|---|
| Location | About 12 miles southwest of present-day Toledo, Ohio | |
| Opponents (*winner) | *United States | Native Americans |
| Commander | Major General Anthony Wayne | Blue Jacket |
| Approx. # Troops | Some 3,000 regulars, militiamen, and allied Native Americans | Some 1,500 Native Americans and 60 Canadian militiamen |
| Importance | This victory restores the prestige of the American military, breaks the power of the Native Americans in the Old Northwest Territory, and leads the British to evacuate their remaining garrisons below the Great Lakes. | |

Following the defeat by Native Americans of the U.S. Army expeditions into the Old Northwest Territory, the first led by Brigadier General Josiah Harmar in 1790 and the second led by Major General Arthur St. Clair in the autumn of 1791, Congress voted to establish the 5,000-man Legion of the United States, commanded by a major general and consisting of four sublegions led by brigadier generals. Washington appointed retired general Anthony ("Mad Anthony") Wayne to command the legion.

Wayne set up a training camp some 25 miles from Pittsburgh at a site he named Legionville and put the men through rigorous training. In May 1793 he moved the legion to Cincinnati and then a few miles north to a new camp, Hobson's Choice. In early October, Wayne moved north with 2,000 regulars to Fort Jefferson, the end of his defensive line. When Kentucky mounted militiamen arrived, Wayne moved a few miles farther north and set up a new camp, naming it Fort Greeneville (now Greenville, Ohio) in honor of his American Revolutionary War commander, Major General Nathanael Greene.

In December 1793 Wayne sent a detachment to the site of St. Clair's Defeat on the Wabash. On Christmas Day 1793 the Americans reoccupied the battlefield and constructed Fort Recovery on high ground overlooking the Wabash. Aided by friendly Native Americans, the soldiers recovered most of St. Clair's cannon, which the Native Americans had buried nearby. These were incorporated into Fort Recovery, which was manned by an infantry company and a detachment of artillerists.

Wayne's campaign timetable was delayed because of unreliable civilian contractors, Native American attacks on his supply trains, the removal of some of his men elsewhere, and a cease-fire that led him to believe that peace might be in the offing. But Miami chief Little Turtle, Shawnee war chief Blue Jacket, and other chiefs rejected peace negotiations, in part because of a speech by British governor-general in Canada Sir Guy Carleton, who predicted war between Britain and the United States and pledged British support for the Native Americans. In February 1794 Carleton ordered the construction of Fort Miamis on the Maumee River to mount cannon larger than those that Wayne might be able to bring against it, further delaying Wayne's advance.

On June 29, 1794, Little Turtle struck first, at Fort Recovery, Wayne's staging point for the invasion. A supply train had just arrived there and was bivouacked outside the walls when 2,000 warriors attacked. Although a number of soldiers were killed, the Native Americans were beaten back with heavy casualties, and two days later they withdrew. Never again were the Native Americans able to assemble that many warriors. The repulse also prompted some of the smaller tribes to quit the coalition and led to the eclipse of Little Turtle, who was replaced as principal war leader by the less effective Blue Jacket.

The Battle of Fallen Timbers on August 20, 1794. Major General Anthony Wayne's Legion of the United States defeated a Native American and Canadian militia force under Blue Jacket, restoring U.S. military prestige and breaking forever Native American power in the eastern region of the Northwest Territory. (Library of Congress)

Wayne now had 2,000 men. In mid-July, some 1,600 Kentucky militiamen under Brigadier General Charles Scott began to arrive. Wayne also could count on 100 Native Americans, mostly Choctaws and Chickasaws, from Tennessee. On July 28 Wayne departed Fort Greeneville for Fort Recovery. Washington warned that a third straight defeat "would be inexpressibly ruinous to the reputation of the government."

The Native Americans were concentrated at Miami Town, the objective of previous offensives, and the rapids of the Maumee River around Fort Miamis. In between was a 100-mile-long road along the Maumee River Valley. Wayne intended to build a fortification at midpoint on the road, allowing him to strike in either direction and forcing the Native Americans to defend both possible objectives. By August 3 he had established this position, Fort Adams, and had also built a second fortified position, Fort Defiance, at the confluence of the Auglaize and Maumee Rivers. Wayne then sent the chiefs a final peace offer. Little Turtle urged its acceptance, pointing out the strength of the force opposing them and expressing doubts about British support. Blue Jacket and British agents wanted war, which a majority of the chiefs approved.

Having learned of a Native American concentration near Fort Miamis, Wayne decided to move there first. After a difficult crossing of the Maumee River, on August 15 Wayne's men were still 10 miles from the British fort. Sensing an impending fight, Wayne detached unnecessary elements from his column to construct a possible fallback position, Fort Deposit, manned by Captain Zebulon Pike and 200 men.

On August 20 Wayne again put his column in motion, anticipating battle that day with either the Native Americans or the British. Indeed, some 1,500 braves and 60 Canadian militiamen were lying in wait for the Americans, hoping to ambush them from the natural defenses of what had been a forest before it had been uprooted by a tornado and transformed into a chaos of twisted branches and broken tree trunks.

Blue Jacket had expected Wayne to arrive on August 19 and was not anticipating the daylong delay. In preparation for battle, the Native Americans had begun a strict fast on August 18 and then continued it the next day. When the Americans did not arrive, many of the Native Americans, hungry and exhausted, departed for Fort Miamis.

Wayne marched his men so as to be ready to meet an attack from any quarter. His infantrymen were in two wings: Brigadier General James Wilkinson commanded the right, and Colonel John Hamtramck the left. A mounted brigade of Kentuckians protected the left flank, while legion horsemen covered the right flank. Additional Kentucky horsemen guarded the rear and served as a reserve. Well to the front, Major William Price led a battalion to trigger the Native American attack and allow Wayne time to deploy the main body.

When the Native Americans did open fire, Price's men fell back into Wilkinson's line. Wayne rallied his men and sent them to defeat the ambush with an infantry frontal attack driven home with the bayonet. At the same time, the horsemen closed on the flanks. The Native Americans were routed, fleeing the battle toward Fort Miamis. The killing went on to the very gates of the fort while the British looked on. Wayne's losses in the battle were 33 killed and 100 wounded (11 of them mortally wounded), while Native American losses were in the hundreds.

Although Wayne disregarded Fort Miamis, he destroyed Native American communities and British storehouses in its vicinity. The soldiers then marched to Miami Town. They occupied it without opposition on September 17 and razed it. They then built a fort on the site of Harmar's 1790 defeat, naming it Fort Wayne.

The Battle of Fallen Timbers broke forever the power of the Native Americans in the eastern region of the Old Northwest Territory. The battle also led the British to evacuate their garrisons below the Great Lakes and did much to restore U.S. military prestige. Wayne is justifiably known as the father of the U.S. Army.

On August 3, 1795, chiefs representing 12 tribes signed the Treaty of Greenville, Wayne having revealed to them that the British had agreed to withdraw their forts and recognize the boundary set in the 1783 Treaty of Paris. The Treaty of Greenville set a definite boundary in the Old Northwest Territory, forcing the Native Americans to give up once and for all the eastern and southern parts of the present-day state of Ohio and part of Indiana and Michigan. Increased settler movement into the Ohio Territory, ensuing Native American resentment, and a turn by Native Americans to the British, however, helped set the stage for the War of 1812 in the Old Northwest Territory.

Spencer C. Tucker

### Further Reading

Millett, Allan R. "Caesar and the Conquest of the Northwest Territory: The Wayne Campaign, 1792–95." *Timeline: A Publication of the Ohio Historical Society* 14 (1997): 2–21.

Palmer, Dave R. *1794: America, Its Army, and the Birth of the Nation.* Novato, CA: Presidio, 1994.

Tebbel, John W. *The Battle of Fallen Timbers, August 20, 1794.* New York: Franklin Watts, 1972.

## Battle of Tippecanoe

| Date | November 7, 1811 | |
| --- | --- | --- |
| **Location** | Near present-day Battle Ground, Indiana | |
| **Opponents (\*winner)** | \*United States | Native Americans |
| **Commander** | Indiana Territory governor William Henry Harrison | Tenskwatawa |
| **Approx. # Troops** | 970 U.S. Army troops and militia | 550–700 warriors |
| **Importance** | An important event leading to war with Britain, the battle causes many Americans to believe that the British have been arming Native Americans in the Old Northwest Territory. At the same time, the battle infuriates the Indians and causes many to rally to the British in the War of 1812. | |

Shawnee leader Tecumseh opposed any concessions to the white settlers who were expanding westward into Indian lands, but he realized that in order to mount effective resistance, he must form an alliance extending beyond the Shawnees. Tecumseh thus worked to create a Pan-Indian coalition that would be dedicated to the goal of protecting lands against white expansion.

Tecumseh and his half brother Tenskwatawa, known as the Prophet, had founded Prophetstown in May 1808 as the capital of their growing native confederacy. Located near present-day Lafayette, Prophetstown was not only the center for diplomatic activities among the tribes but was also a training ground for warriors. At its peak, more than 1,000 Indians were in residence there.

In November 1811 Tecumseh was absent from the village recruiting in the southern states for his confederation, and Tenskwatawa was in charge in his absence. At the same time, governor of the Indiana Territory William Henry Harrison

86°51'W

40°30'N

INDIANA

First Native
American attack

Burnet's Creek

BARTON

WELLS

Native
Americans

Native
Americans

SPENCER

retreat

DAVIESS

▲ U.S. camp
■ U.S. troops
Native Americans movement
→ U.S. troops movement

Common Road

0        250       500 ft
0    50    100 m

was determined to destroy Prophetstown. Harrison had aggressively pursued land cession treaties with the Native Americans. These treaties often included the payment of small sums of money for vast tracts of land. Tecumseh's growing confederation was a threat to this process and to whites in the Old Northwest Territory, and Prophetstown had become a symbol of British influence, although the Indian raids on American frontier settlements almost certainly did not originate with Tecumseh and Tenskwatawa.

Governors Ninian Edwards of the Illinois Territory and Benjamin Howard of the Missouri Territory both approved Harrison's proposed plan for a march up the Wabash River to the limits of the purchase of 1809. Harrison informed Secretary of War William Eustis of the plan, and Eustis responded that he favored approaching Tenskwatawa, asking him to disperse his followers, and, should he refuse, attacking him. Eustis also authorized Harrison to establish a new frontier post, but under no circumstances was he to antagonize the British.

The most important element of Harrison's expeditionary force, Colonel John Boyd's 4th U.S. Infantry, arrived at Vincennes, Indiana, from Philadelphia on September 19, 1811, having covered the 1,300 miles on foot and in boats. Six days later on September 25, Harrison gave the order to move out. A total of 970 men responded: 350 members of the 4th U.S. Infantry, 400 Indiana militia infantry, 84 mounted Indiana riflemen, 123 Kentucky dragoons, and 13 spies and guides. The march order consisted of a company of riflemen leading, followed 100 yards behind by a mounted troop and 50 yards behind it the infantry in column. Another mounted unit took up the rear 100 yards behind the infantry. Detached troops

The Battle of Tippecanoe, November 7, 1811. Fought near present-day Lafayette, Indiana, it was trumpeted as a victory over the Indians, but army and militia casualties had been heavy and the battle angered Native Americans and led many to side with the British in the War of 1812. Illustration by Kurz & Allison, circa 1889. (Library of Congress)

protected the flanks of the column 100 yards to either side. Each night the men prepared a fortified camp to protect against possible native attack.

As a consequence of these precautions, it took Harrison more than two weeks to cover the 65 miles from Vincennes to the bend in the Wabash River at present-day Terre Haute. There the men completed Fort Harrison on October 27 before moving to the mouth of the Vermillion River. Harrison now ordered the construction of a blockhouse, later called Fort Boyd, at the site.

Harrison had warned that whether he advanced farther would depend on Native American conduct, so when some warriors stole horses from the camp and someone fired into the camp on October 10, wounding a man, Harrison took these as justification to cross the Vermillion into Native American territory. More shots were fired into Harrison's advancing forces but without casualties. Harrison was now determined to destroy Prophetstown, and his officers urged that he attack without delay. However, on November 6 a native delegation requested talks, and against the advice of his subordinate commanders, Harrison accepted, with the parley scheduled for the next day.

The Indian delegation then suggested the campsite for Harrison's force. Harrison's enemies later claimed that the natives had selected an ideal ambush position, but in fact it was the best site in the area for defensive purposes. Located some two miles west of Prophetstown on an oak-covered knoll, it was a wedge-shaped area about 10 acres in area, bordered by wet prairie land and on the west side by Burnet's Creek.

Harrison ordered the men to bivouac fully clothed, with their weapons loaded and bayonets fixed. It was a cold night, and Harrison did not restrict fires so that the men could stay warm. In case of native attack, Harrison instructed that the men rise, advance a pace or two, and form a line of battle and return fire. Harrison was confident that he could hold during a night attack and then take the offensive when it was light. The horses were kept within the camp, and to warn of any attack, Harrison ordered the posting of a sizable night guard of 108 men. He did not, however, order the construction of breastworks, nor was he concerned about the possibility of fires illuminating the American positions.

Although Tecumseh had warned Tenskwatawa against an attack until the confederation was stronger and fully unified, Tenskwatawa ignored the advice. On the night of November 6, the natives discussed their options. Later Shabonee, a Potawatomi chief, testified that two Englishmen were present during the deliberations and had urged an attack. A captured African American wagon driver informed Tenskwatawa that Harrison had no artillery with him and that he planned to attack Prophetstown after his discussions with the natives the next day.

That night some 550 to 700 natives, largely Kickapoos, Potawatomis, and Winnebagos but also including Chippewas, Hurons, Mucos, Ottawas, Piankeshaws, Shawnees, and Wyanadots, worked themselves into a frenzy. Using fiery speeches, Tenskwatawa urged action. He claimed that the white man's bullets could not harm them because their powder had already turned to sand and their bullets to soft mud.

The warriors left Prophetstown during the night, and by 4:00 a.m. on November 7 they had surrounded Harrison's camp. One of the American sentinels, Stephen Mars, heard movement in the darkness and fired a shot or two before fleeing for the safety of the camp. He was killed before he could reach it, but his shot alerted Harrison's men. The Indians then let out war whoops and opened fire. The battle opened first on the northwest side of the camp. Unfortunately for Harrison's men, when they rose many were silhouetted against their own campfires, making them easy targets. Harrison himself mounted and rode to the sound of the firing. His own white horse had broken its tether during the night, and he rode a dark one. This probably saved his life, for the natives were looking for him on a white horse. His aide, Colonel Abraham Owen, who found Harrison's horse and rode it, was shot and killed.

Firing next erupted on the east side of the camp and then became general. During the battle, Tenskwatawa stationed himself on a high rock to the east and chanted war songs to encourage his followers. Informed early that some of his warriors had been slain, Tenskwatawa insisted that his followers fight on and promised an easy victory.

After two hours of fighting and when it was sufficiently light, Harrison sent out mounted men to attack the natives on their flanks. Soon afterward the disheartened natives were in retreat. In the battle, Harrison had lost 68 men killed and 126 wounded. The number of Native American dead is not known for certain. Thirty-seven bodies were found at the battle site, but this did not account for those who were carried off or died later from their wounds. Native American losses are estimated at no fewer than 50 killed and 70 or more wounded.

Worried by a false report that Tecumseh was nearby with a larger native force, Harrison ordered his men to fortify their position. A reconnaissance the next day revealed that Prophetstown had been abandoned, and Harrison then advanced on it. Among supplies abandoned there by the natives in their hasty withdrawal was some new British equipment. Harrison ordered the men to take what supplies they could and destroy the rest. Prophetstown and its supplies and food stocks were soon ablaze. Harrison's force then set out for Vincennes, 150 miles distant. The return march was agony for the wounded, who were tossed about in the carts and died at the rate of two or three per day.

The native warriors later came close to killing Tenskwatawa for his false predictions. Certainly the Battle of Tippecanoe also badly damaged Tecumseh's efforts to build a confederation to stave off white settlement. Tecumseh returned to Prophetstown several weeks later to find only ruins. He was never able to recover the momentum behind his confederation movement after the battle, although Prophetstown was rebuilt and reoccupied.

In the end, the battle only hardened positions on both sides. Frontiersmen were convinced that the British had been behind it all, while the encounter drove many Indians to ally with the British during the War of 1812. The British were also convinced of the need to aid the natives, if only in the defense of Canada. In effect, the Battle of Tippecanoe served to cement the British–Native American alliance. For all of these reasons, many have called the Battle of Tippecanoe the opening battle of the War of 1812.

Daniel W. Kuthy and Spencer C. Tucker

## Further Reading

Cave, Alfred. "The Shawnee Prophet, Tecumseh, and Tippecanoe." *Journal of the Early Republic* 22(4) (Winter 2002): 637–673.

Jortner, Adam J. *The Gods of Prophetstown: The Battle of Tippecanoe and the Holy War for the American Frontier.* New York: Oxford University Press, 2011.

Millett, Allan R. "Caesar and the Conquest of the Northwest Territory: The Wayne Campaign, 1792–95." *Timeline: A Publication of the Ohio Historical Society* 14 (1997): 2–21.

Tunnell, Harry D. *To Compel with Armed Force: A Staff Ride Handbook for the Battle of Tippecanoe.* Fort Leavenworth, KS: Combat Studies Institute, U.S. Command and General Staff College, 2000.

## Siege of Detroit

| Date | August 16, 1812 | |
|---|---|---|
| Location | Detroit, Michigan Territory | |
| Opponents (*winner) | *Great Britain | United States |
| Commander | Major General Isaac Brock | Brigadier General William Hull |
| Approx. # Troops | 730 British regulars and Canadian militiamen; 600 allied Native Americans | 582 U.S. Army regulars; 1,600 Ohio militiamen |
| Importance | Gives the British control of the Michigan Territory, assures the British of the loyalty of the settlers in Upper Canada, and causes many Native Americans to rally to the British. | |

After the U.S. declaration of war against Britain on June 18, 1812, on July 12 governor of the Michigan Territory and U.S. Army brigadier general William Hull crossed the Detroit River and invaded Upper Canada at the head of 600 regulars and 2,000 militiamen. This was part of a two-pronged U.S. invasion of Upper Canada but unfortunately for the United States was not simultaneous. Hull's forces quickly occupied Sandwich (present-day western Windsor, Ontario), but the general failed to move quickly against Fort Malden (present-day Amherstburg, Ontario) when he might easily have taken it. Hull's lack of initiative allowed British major general Isaac Brock, governor of Upper Canada, to both reinforce Fort Malden and then take the offensive himself.

On July 17 the British mounted a surprise attack on and captured the important U.S. outpost of Fort Mackinac on Michilimackinac Island in the strait between Lakes Huron and Michigan. Hull also suffered the loss of a militia force sent to secure supplies at the Raisin River when it was scattered by Shawnee leader Tecumseh's warriors in the Battle of Brownstown on August 5.

On August 8 Hull, concerned about these reversals and the threat to his supply lines posed by the large number of Native Americans who by reason of the British success had aligned against the United States and having received word of the approach of Brock with a relief column from Niagara, abandoned a belated plan to move against Fort Malden and withdrew back to Fort Detroit.

Hull then ordered Lieutenant Colonel James Miller and some 600 men of the 4th U.S. Infantry to the Raisin River. Near the Indian village of Maguaga, Miller encountered some 150 British troops and Canadian militiamen and an unknown number of Indians. The Americans repelled the British attack and routed their opponents, but the next day Hull ordered Miller to return to Detroit.

Hull's army was now effectively shut up in Detroit, and the general's disgusted subordinates began circulating petitions demanding his recall. Meanwhile, on August 13 Brock arrived at Fort Malden with reinforcements.

Hull ordered Captain Nathan Heald, commander of Fort Dearborn (present-day Chicago, Illinois), to evacuate that post. On August 15 the evacuees—54 U.S. regulars, 12 militiamen, and 27 dependents—were ambushed by some 500 Indians led by Chief Blackbird. The natives killed 42 and captured 51 in what the Americans came to call the Fort Dearborn Massacre.

On that same day, August 15, Brock arrived at Fort Detroit with 730 British and Canadians and 600 Native Americans under Tecumseh. They were supported offshore by the corvette *Queen Charlotte* (17 guns) and the brig *General Hunter* (10 guns). Brock called on a shaken Hull to surrender. Playing on Hull's fears, Brock also allowed to fall into Hull's hands a false document purporting to show that a large number of Indians were advancing on the fort.

On August 16 Brock and his men crossed the Detroit River and surrounded the fort. Brock paraded his men to give the impression of greater numbers and informed Hull that he would be unable to control the allied Native Americans if fighting began. Hull was deeply depressed by the possibility that women and children at Detroit might thereby be slain. Convinced that he was outnumbered and concerned over the Indian massacre of Americans but without consulting with any of his subordinates, the unnerved Hull sent his son out under a flag of truce to surrender that same day. Hull's subordinates reported that the American troops deeply resented this action.

Brock paroled the 1,600 Ohio militiamen but marched the 582 American regulars off to captivity. He also secured 33 cannon, 2,500 muskets, and the brig *Adams* (14 guns), which was taken into British service as the *Detroit*. Brock then quickly marched back to meet the American threat on the Niagara front.

Although the Americans recaptured Detroit a year later, the damage had been done. The loss of Detroit shocked the American public; gave the British control of the Michigan Territory; helped secure the loyalty of the citizens of Upper Canada, many of whom were recent American immigrants who had been expected to rally to the United States with the war; and caused even more Indians to rally to the British.

Released from captivity, Hull was court-martialed in the spring of 1814. Cleared of charges of treason and cowardice, he was found guilty of neglect of duty and sentenced to death, but President James Madison remitted this punishment in consequence of Hull's American Revolutionary War service. Hull spent the remainder of his life trying to clear his name. He claimed that his lines of communication could have been cut at any time either by land or water, that he was critically short of supplies, that the militiamen were unreliable, and that he had been promised a diversion in the East to distract the British. Not only had the diversion not been made, but Major General Henry Dearborn had concluded an armistice with the British.

Spencer C. Tucker

**Further Reading**

Bender, Mark L. "The Failure of General William Hull at Detroit in 1812 and Its Effects on the State of Ohio." Unpublished master's thesis, Kent State University, 1971.

Carter-Edwards, Dennis. "The War of 1812 along the Detroit Frontier: A Canadian Perspective." *Michigan Historical Review* 13(2) (Fall 1987): 25–49.

Dunnigan, Brian L. "'The Prettiest Settlement in America': A Select Bibliography of Early Detroit through the War of 1812." *Michigan History* 27(1) (March 2001): 1–20.

Gilpin, Alec R. *The War of 1812 in the Old Northwest.* East Lansing: Michigan State University Press, 1958.

Scott, Leonard. "The Surrender of Detroit." *American History Illustrated* 12(3) (March 1977): 28–36.

## Battle of Lake Erie

| Date | September 10, 1813 | |
|---|---|---|
| Location | Lake Erie | |
| Opponents (*winner) | *United States | Great Britain |
| Commander | Commodore Oliver H. Perry | Commander Robert H. Barclay |
| Approx. # Ships | 9 warships with a total of 54 guns (broadside weight of 936 pounds); 450 men | 6 warships with a total of 64 guns (broadside weight of 496 pounds); 565 men |
| Importance | Gives the Americans control of Lake Erie and makes possible the subsequent American recovery of Detroit and the land victory in the Battle of the Thames. | |

The Battle of Lake Erie was the U.S. Navy's first squadron-to-squadron victory and a critical naval engagement on the Great Lakes during the War of 1812. After the American surrender of Detroit on August 16, 1812, the U.S. Navy Department ordered the construction at Erie, Pennsylvania, of a squadron to counter British naval dominance of Lake Erie. Under Master Commandant Oliver Hazard Perry's direction, the Americans built two brigs and four gunboats at Erie and added three armed merchant vessels, while at the same time the British could build only one large brig at Amherstburg, Upper Canada (present-day Ontario).

On Lake Erie, British commander Robert H. Barclay commanded six Royal Navy ships with a total of 64 guns that had a broadside firepower of 496 pounds and a total weight of metal of 905 pounds. The nine American vessels mounted 54 guns with a broadside capability of 936 pounds of shot and a total weight of metal of 1,536 pounds. The two identical American brigs—the *Lawrence* and *Niagara* of 20 guns each—were armed with short-range carronades. The other ships in Perry's squadron were the brig *Caledonia* (3 guns), the schooner *Somers* (2 guns), the sloop *Trippe* (1 gun), and four gunboats: the *Tigress, Porcupine, Scorpion,* and *Ariel* (each mounting 1 to 4 guns). The two largest Royal Navy brigs—the *Detroit* (21 guns) and *Queen Charlotte* (17 guns)—were differently armed. The *Detroit,* Barclay's flagship, mounted long guns, while the *Queen Charlotte* was fitted with

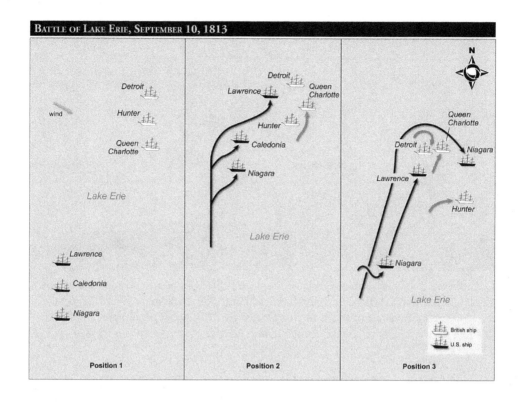

**BATTLE OF LAKE ERIE, SEPTEMBER 10, 1813**

Position 1 | Position 2 | Position 3

carronades. This decidedly mixed armament seriously complicated Barclay's tactical options. The other ships in the British squadron were the schooner *Lady Prevost* (13 guns), the brig *General Hunter* (10 guns), the sloop *Little Belt* (3 guns), and the schooner *Chippawa* (2 guns).

The resulting battle was a test of experience versus firepower. The British officers had more combat experience than their American counterparts, none of whom had ever been in a squadron battle, and the British probably shipped more men. The Americans had more experienced sailors and more gunnery practice. Both sides augmented their crews with soldiers. Perry ordered his novice captains to engage their designated foe and to maintain their place in the line of battle.

On the morning of September 10, 1813, the Americans at Put-in-Bay on Ohio's South Bass Island sighted Barclay's squadron emerging from the Detroit River. Barclay kept his line close together, while Perry approached with his squadron strung out over a span of two miles. Instead of waiting for the trailing vessels to close up, Perry impetuously headed straight for the *Detroit*.

Instead of closing with the *Queen Charlotte,* however, Perry's second-in-command, Master Commandant Jesse Duncan Elliott, kept the *Niagara* behind the *Caledonia* and did not engage the *Queen Charlotte.* That ship's commander brought his brig forward to assist the *Detroit* in the attack on Perry's *Lawrence.* In two hours of heavy fighting, the *Lawrence* sustained 80 percent casualties and

Commodore Oliver Hazard Perry's hard-fought victory over the British squadron led by Commodore Robert H. Barclay in the Battle of Lake Erie (September 10, 1813) gave the United States control of that lake and allowed the U.S. Army to go on the offensive and recapture Amherstburg and Detroit. (James, Barnes, *Naval Actions of the War of 1812*, 1896)

struck before Perry transferred his flag to the *Niagara,* ordered Elliott to bring up the trailing gunboats, and brought the *Niagara* through the British line, forcing all the ships in the British squadron to surrender one after another.

In the battle the Americans lost 27 killed and 96 wounded, the majority of them on the *Lawrence,* which had taken a terrible pounding. British personnel losses were 41 killed and 94 wounded, with Barclay among the latter.

The Battle of Lake Erie marked a rare time in history when an entire British squadron surrendered. Perry's ships then transported U.S. ground forces across Lake Erie, kept them supplied, and made possible the defeat of the British and their allied Indian forces there. The subsequent Battle of the Thames of October 5, 1813, broke British power west of Niagara.

The Battle of Lake Erie left a lasting legacy in Americans' memory of the War of 1812. First there is Perry's after-action message "We have met the enemy and they are ours," and second is Perry's battle flag emblazoned with "Don't Give Up the Ship," the alleged words of Captain James Lawrence that have been enshrined at the U.S. Naval Academy. The controversy over why Elliott did not bring the *Niagara* forward earlier also engendered considerable debate among the naval officer corps that lasted until Elliott's death in 1845.

David C. Skaggs

## Further Reading

Palmer, Michael A. "A Failure of Command, Control, and Communications: Oliver Hazard Perry and the Battle of Lake Erie." *Journal of Erie Studies* 17 (Fall 1988): 7–26.

Skaggs, David Curtis. *Oliver Hazard Perry: Honor, Courage and Patriotism in the Early U.S. Navy.* Annapolis, MD: Naval Institute Press, 2006.

Symonds, Craig. *Decision at Sea: Five Naval Battles That Shaped American History.* New York: Oxford University Press, 2005.

## Battle of the Thames

| Date | October 5, 1813 | |
|---|---|---|
| Location | Thames River, Upper Canada | |
| Opponents (*winner) | *United States | Great Britain |
| Commander | Major General William Henry Harrison | Major General Henry Procter; Shawnee chief Tecumseh |
| Approx. # Troops | 3,440 U.S. Army regulars and militia; some 160 allied Native Americans | 880 British troops; some 500 Native Americans |
| Importance | The climactic battle of the war in the Old Northwest and a rare land victory for the Americans to this point, it helps renew support for the war, especially in Kentucky. | |

Throughout 1813 the British and their Indian allies, commanded by Major General Henry Procter and Shawnee leader Tecumseh, had frustrated efforts by Major General William Henry Harrison to regain U.S. control over the Great Lakes region. When U.S. Navy master commandant Oliver Hazard Perry defeated the British in the Battle of Lake Erie on September 10, 1813, the Americans regained control of that key body of water, enabling Harrison to undertake an offensive to recapture Detroit and invade western Upper Canada.

Procter, his logistical support now all but cut off, hoped to withdraw from Detroit by moving through Upper Canada along the Thames River. Tecumseh strongly opposed Procter's decision, seeing it as evidence of abandonment by the British, who had promised the Indians their own lands. Eventually the allies reached a compromise to retreat but to make a stand somewhere along the route.

The British march from Sandwich began on September 24 with about 880 troops and perhaps 500 Native American warriors and their families. The withdrawal was not well organized and proceeded slowly, encumbered with considerable personal baggage. Soon the men were on half rations. Morale was low, and the officers were reportedly dissatisfied with Procter's leadership, although Lieutenant Colonel Augustus Warburton, second-in-command, resisted calls that he intervene to remove Procter.

On September 27 Harrison's army landed in Canada. He had almost 5,000 U.S. regulars and Kentucky militiamen. Harrison left Sandwich on October 2, the speed of his advance greatly enhanced by mounted Kentucky riflemen led by Colonel Richard M. Johnson. On October 4 the American column reached the third and

BATTLE OF THE THAMES, OCTOBER 5, 1813

unfordable branch of the Thames. Shawnee leader Tecumseh and his warriors had dismantled the bridge there and were then on the opposite side. Harrison ordered up two 6-pounders and used these to drive away the Indians and then ordered his men to set about repairing the bridge. In just two hours Harrison was again on the move. Johnson's Kentuckians then intercepted Procter a few miles from Moraviantown along the Thames River, the British having already set fire to watercraft they were using to transport their baggage and supplies on the river.

By the morning of October 5, it was clear to Procter that a final stand was inevitable. The ensuing engagement occurred near present-day Chatham, Ontario, along the Thames River and is known as the Battle of the Thames or the Battle of Moraviantown. Procter deployed his regulars in a wedge-shaped clearing in a beech forest. The left flank rested on the river, beside which ran the road to Moraviantown some three and a half miles to the east. The line ran some 250 yards to the north, ending at a small swamp. It then extended from the small swamp another 250 yards, where it ended at a large swamp. The left portion of the British line was held by 540 men of the 41st Regiment of Foot and 290 men of the Royal Newfoundland Regiment. Procter also positioned a 6-pounder artillery piece in the road to provide some support. The portion to the right of the small swamp was held by Tecumseh's 500 warriors. The British, however, had not erected any sort of earthworks or abatis by felling trees.

The Americans arrived before the British position at about 8:00 a.m. The American force numbered 140 regulars, 1,000 Kentuckians in Johnson's regiment, and about 2,300 Kentucky volunteers. There were also perhaps 160 allied Indians.

As Harrison was making his dispositions prior to an attack, Johnson learned that the British left was only thinly held by men standing about three feet apart. The situation seemed tailor-made for Johnson's mounted men, and he asked permission from Harrison to make an immediate charge. Harrison agreed. With many of the attackers screaming "Remember the Raisin!"—a reference to the Raisin River Massacre—the Kentuckians quickly drove through the British line. The British artillery piece having failed to fire, the Kentuckians then dismounted and used their rifles to attack the British from the rear. Attacked from both front and rear, the British line crumbled, and most of the men surrendered. Only the grenadier company of the 41st Regiment managed to escape intact.

The Indians, protected somewhat by the swamp, held their ground and halted Johnson's horsemen with musket fire, killing or wounding 15 of them. Johnson himself was wounded several times. Tecumseh, who had a premonition of his own death, was slain in combat. His body was never recovered (the natives said that it had been lifted up to heaven), but Johnson claimed to have killed him and was generally so credited. With the sizable American force converging on their position, the remaining Indians fled the battlefield.

The Battle of the Thames lasted less than an hour, with the British suffering 12 killed, 22 wounded, and some 600 captured. As many as 33 Native Americans were also slain. American casualties were 7 killed and 22 wounded. Procter, who escaped, was widely blamed for the defeat. He blamed his men, who he said had not carried out his orders. Procter demanded a court of inquiry, and when this was denied he appealed directly to British commander Frederick, Duke of York. This led to a court-martial and a finding that Procter had been guilty of failing to properly prepare for the retreat and of exercising poor tactical judgment. The court recommended that he be reprimanded and suspended from duty for six months. In the end he was only reprimanded, in July 1815.

Although a relatively minor action, the Battle of the Thames proved decisive and provided a rare victory for the United States. Even though the American side had enjoyed the advantage of greatly superior numbers, the Americans had defeated British regulars. The victory was received with great enthusiasm in Kentucky and helped renew public support for the war. Thereafter the battle was used to considerable political advantage by any on the American side who could claim to have participated in it. The climactic engagement of the war in the Old Northwest Territory, the Battle of the Thames destroyed the British position west of the head of Lake Erie (they retained only Fort Mackinac, kept by them until the end of the war) and broke forever Native American power in the territory. This opened that territory for white settlement west to the Mississippi River. After their victory, the American troops burned Moraviantown, a peaceful Indian settlement. Then, lacking naval support, which was needed elsewhere, and faced with the mass expiration of enlistments, they departed Canada for Detroit.

Steven J. Rauch and Spencer C. Tucker

### Further Reading

Antal, Sandor. *A Wampum Denied: Procter's War of 1812.* Ottawa: Carlton University Press, 1997.

Skaggs, David. "River Raisin Redeemed: William Henry Harrison, Oliver Hazard Perry, and the Midwestern Campaign, 1813." *Northwest Ohio History* 77 (Spring 2010): 67–84.

Sudgen, John. *Tecumseh's Last Stand.* Norman: University of Oklahoma Press, 1985.

## Battle of Horseshoe Bend

| Date | March 27, 1814 | |
|---|---|---|
| Location | Horseshoe Bend of the Tallapoosa River (some 12 miles east of Alexander City in present-day central Alabama) | |
| Opponents (*winner) | *United States | Red Stick Creeks |
| Commander | Tennessee Militia major general Andrew Jackson | Chief Menawa |
| Approx. # Troops | Some 3,000 militiamen, U.S. Army regulars, and allied Indians | 1,200 Red Stick Creek warriors, plus families |
| Importance | The battle brings major combat in the Creek War to an end and leads to the punitive Treaty of Fort Jackson, whereby the Creeks are forced to cede half of Alabama and part of Georgia to the United States. | |

A number of Creek Native Americans, who occupied most of present-day Alabama, resisted American encroachment upon their homeland. These militant Creeks, known as the Red Sticks, considered an attack by militiamen on a Creek party returning from a trip to Spanish Florida to purchase ammunition—the Battle of Burnt Corn (July 27, 1813)—as a declaration of war. Led by Peter McQueen and William Weatherford, the Red Sticks went on the warpath. They enjoyed some initial military success, capturing Fort Mims in southern Alabama on August 30, where they massacred upwards of 500 men, women, and children.

Soon the tables were reversed. In the autumn of 1813, militiamen from Georgia and the Mississippi Territory launched expeditions against the Red Sticks. Major General Andrew Jackson successfully led 2,500 Tennessee militiamen against the Creek settlements of Tallushatchee on November 3 and Talladega six days later. Meanwhile, Brigadier General James White successfully led other Tennessee militiamen against Hillibee on November 18.

In January 1814 Jackson returned to the offensive with a force of 1,000 militiamen. He was nearly defeated by the Creeks at Emuckfaw Creek on January 22 and at Enitachopco Creek two days later, sustaining about 100 casualties while

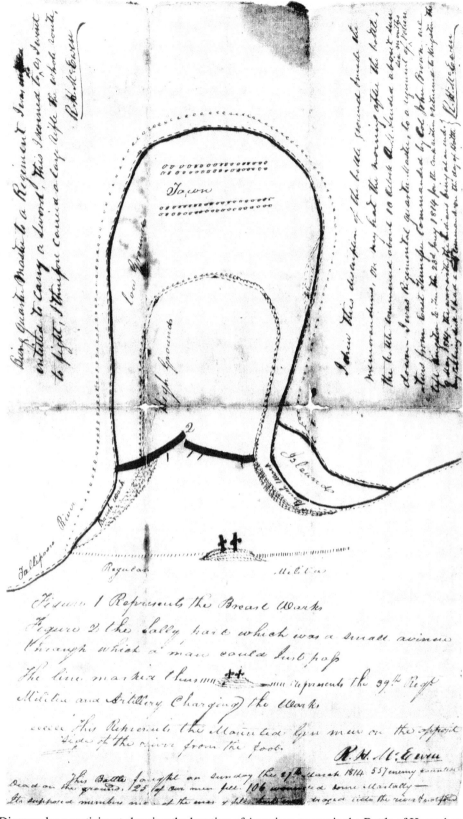

Diagram by a participant showing the location of American troops in the Battle of Horseshoe Bend. Fought along the Tallapoosa River in Alabama on March 27, 1814, this defeat of the Red Stick Creeks ended major combat during the Creek War. (Hulton Archive/Getty Images)

inflicting twice that number on the Native Americans. Jackson then retired to refit and gather up supplies for a final effort.

By February 1814, Jackson's force had grown to some 4,000 men. They were mostly militia but included the newly recruited 600-man 39th U.S. Infantry. The Creeks, some 1,200 strong, had previously fortified their encampment of about 100 acres at Horseshoe Bend, a bend formed by the Tallapoosa River. They constructed a log breastwork across the neck of the peninsula and collected canoes to flee across the river should that prove necessary. Jackson, who was aware of the Creek plans, nonetheless remained determined to attack the encampment.

Jackson arrived at Horseshoe Bend on the morning of March 27, 1814. He had with him some 3,000 men, including allied Cherokee and Creek warriors. Sensing the weakness of the Creeks' defensive position, he sent Tennessee Militia brigadier general John Coffee with mounted infantry and the friendly Native Americans to take position behind the bend and block the Indians from escape. Some of the allied Cherokees swam across the river and seized the canoes.

At about 10:00 a.m., Jackson ordered his two small cannon to bombard the hostile Creek fortifications. Coffee then employed the captured canoes to get some of his men across the Tallapoosa and assault the Creeks from behind. Flaming arrows fired by the Indian allies set much of the Creek settlement on fire. Despite these maneuvers, the defenders kept up a steady fire against their antagonists.

At about 12:30 p.m., Jackson ordered the 39th Infantry forward to carry out a frontal assault on the Creek breastworks. Although the Creeks fought desperately, they were soon overwhelmed and driven from the works. Fighting in small bands, the survivors were soon pinned against the river.

The battle now turned into a massacre. Many of the Creeks refused to surrender, and others were shot while swimming across the river in an attempt to escape. Jackson, a hardened soldier, described the carnage as "dreadful." Perhaps 800 hostile Indians were killed, and another 350, mostly women and children, were captured. The casualty tally among the militia and U.S. regulars was 26 killed and 106 wounded, while friendly Cherokees and Creeks suffered 23 killed and 47 wounded.

The Battle of Horseshoe Bend brought major combat in the Creek War to an end. Weatherford fled with a few survivors into Spanish territory but soon after surrendered. On August 9, 1814, Jackson compelled the Creeks, friend and foe alike, to sign the punitive Treaty of Fort Jackson, by which the Creeks ceded half of Alabama and part of Georgia to the United States. Jackson, now a national hero, also gained promotion to major general in the U.S. Army.

Paul David Nelson

## Further Reading

Burstein, Andrew. *The Passions of Andrew Jackson.* New York: Knopf, 2003.

Heidler, David S., and Jeanne T. Heidler. *Old Hickory's War: Andrew Jackson and the Quest for Empire.* Mechanicsburg, PA: Stackpole, 1996.

Kanon, Tom. "'A Slow, Laborious Slaughter': The Battle of Horsehoe Bend." *Tennessee Historical Quarterly* 58(1) (March 1999): 2–15.

Marquis, Christopher G. "Reckoning at Horseshoe Bend." *Military Heritage* 12(1) (August 2010): 42–49.

Paul, R. Kay. "Death at the Horseshoe—Birth of a Legend: Andrew Jackson's Campaign against the Creek Indians." Unpublished master's thesis, California State University, Dominquez Hills, 2007.

Turner, Jonathan S. "Horseshoe Bend: Epic Battle on the Southern Frontier." Unpublished master's thesis, Georgia Southern University, 1996.

## Battle of Chippawa

| Date | July 5, 1814 | |
|---|---|---|
| Location | Chippawa, Upper Canada (Ontario) | |
| Opponents (*winner) | *United States | Great Britain |
| Commander | Major General Jacob Brown; Brigadier General Winfield Scott | Major General Phineas Riall |
| Approx. # Troops | 4,000 regulars | 2,200 regulars, militia, and allied Indians |
| Importance | A tremendous boost to American morale, the battle also shows that the U.S. Army has come of age and that when properly trained it can hold its own against hardened British regulars. | |

The principal American land objective in the War of 1812 was the seizure of Canada. In preparing for the 1814 campaign, U.S. Army major general Jacob Brown, commanding the Left Division of the Army of the North, planned to clear British forces from the Niagara Peninsula, then cooperate with the American squadron on Lake Ontario to seize both York (present-day Toronto) and Kingston on the north shore of the lake. In preparation for the campaign, Brown sent Brigadier General Winfield Scott and his brigade to Buffalo, New York, on the Niagara frontier, to train. Scott's task was not easy. American forces were understrength, inadequately clothed, and led by officers of mixed capabilities. Unlike the British forces, very few of the officers and soldiers in Scott's brigade were professionals and had experienced more defeats than victories. Scott nonetheless implemented a rigorous training regimen based on the French drill manual, and when the time for the invasion arrived, his men were well trained and confident of victory.

Brown's Left Division also included two other brigades of infantry. Brigadier General Eleazar Wheelock Ripley arrived on the Niagara in mid-May and commanded the second brigade. The brigade also consisted of regular army soldiers,

Engraving based on an Alonzo Chappel painting depicting the American victory in the Battle of Chippawa, Ontario, Canada, July 5, 1814. (Bettmann/Corbis)

most of whom had received at least a partial benefit from Scott's training program. New York Militia brigadier general Peter P. Porter commanded the third brigade. Unlike the other two brigades, Porter's brigade consisted of militia volunteers and native warriors. The Iroquois of New York had initially tried to maintain their neutrality, but by 1814 they were persuaded that their interests lay with the American cause, and Red Jacket had brought 600 of his warriors into the American camp. A battalion of Pennsylvania volunteers joined the Left Division in mid-June, but they had little training. A battalion of artillery and a company of regular dragoons rounded out Brown's force.

British major general Phineas Riall commanded the British Right Division, charged with the defense of the Niagara Peninsula and the town of York. Lieutenant General Gordon Drummond, commander of all forces in Upper Canada, instructed Riall to aggressively defend his territory and retain Fort Niagara on the American side, which the British had captured the previous winter. Riall was also to hold Forts Erie and George on the Canadian shore and to throw back any American invasion. Based on past experience, both Drummond and Riall had a low opinion of American units and believed that a small British force would have few problems contending with a much larger American force.

In the early hours of July 3, 1814, Scott's brigade crossed in boats from Buffalo, on the New York shore, to beaches near Fort Erie in Upper Canada. Within hours, the Americans had surrounded the fort. Its commander, Major Thomas Buck, believing that defense in the face of heavier American artillery was futile, surrendered with his 137 men. Meanwhile, the remainder of Ripley's troops crossed the Niagara and entered Canadian territory.

The next day, Scott's brigade led the Left Division north along the left bank of the Niagara River. British lieutenant colonel Thomas Pearson, who commanded a small body of regulars, militia, and native warriors allied to the British, responded immediately to the American invasion. Pearson defended each stream across the American line of advance, forcing Scott to deploy and maneuver the British out of each position. By the end of the day on July 4, Scott had reached the Chippawa, an unfordable river flowing eastward and emptying into the Niagara. Behind the Chippawa, Pearson and Riall were gathering their forces to resist any American attempt to cross the river.

The land south of the Chippawa, where the battle would be fought, was flat and bounded on the east by the Niagara River and on the south by Street's Creek. Closest to the Niagara was a meadow covered in waist-high grasses. About three-quarters of a mile west of the Niagara, the meadow was bounded by a dense forest cluttered with fallen trees. A tongue of the forest in the north extended eastward so that the Americans south of Street's Creek could not see the bridge crossing the Chippawa River near where it emptied into the Niagara.

During the day on July 5, Brown waited for Porter's brigade to join the rest of his forces in camp south of Street's Creek. Brown intended to attack the British position north of the Chippawa on July 6. However, Riall was determined to cross the Chippawa and attack the American camp. He sent a body of militia and natives into the forest to fire on the Americans in camp while he gathered his regulars for the attack. The sporadic British fire was more irritating than deadly, but it did distract the defenders as planned.

Early in the afternoon, Brown met with Porter and his brigade about three miles south of the American camp and ordered Porter to clear the enemy from the forest. Accordingly, Porter formed about 850 Iroquois and Pennsylvanians into a long thin line perpendicular to the Niagara. At about 4:00 p.m., he and Red Jacket led the line northward through the forest, heading directly to the Chippawa River. Almost immediately, they encountered small bands of natives and Canadian militiamen and pushed them relentlessly back toward the British camp. The fight in the forest was brutal, particularly when warrior fought warrior. As the attackers drove forward, the integrity of their line dissolved into small packets of Iroquois and Pennsylvania volunteers. Meanwhile, as yet undetected by Porter, Riall dispatched three battalions of experienced infantry and two companies of artillery across the Chippawa straight for the American camp. Several light companies also deployed into the woods, where they ambushed and routed Porter's force with little difficulty.

Meanwhile, the main British force moved through the defile formed by the tongue of forest and out onto the plain. Riall pushed two battalions forward and kept a third in reserve. As soon as Brown saw dust thrown up by the British movement, he ordered Scott to take his brigade across Street's Creek and give battle. As Scott's battalions crossed the bridge over the creek, they immediately came under fire by the British artillery. Compared to previous engagements, the American advance was steadfast. Scott formed two battalions into line to face the British and sent a third into the forest to cover the withdrawal of Porter's men, who had fled precipitously upon encountering Pearson's troops.

As the British line approached that of the Americans, both sides opened a fierce musketry supported by artillery fire. During the exchange, Scott also maneuvered his battalions to overlap those of the British. Marching and firing smartly, the Americans brought the British advance to a halt. Soon Scott's third battalion, having dealt with Pearson's outnumbered force in the forest, exited the woods and approached the British flank. Under intense American fire, the British infantry wavered and slowly withdrew, the men ignoring the admonitions of their officers to stand and fight. Riall skillfully covered the withdrawal of his battered brigade north, back across the Chippawa River. As the British withdrew, they pulled the planking from the bridge. Brown wisely decided not to press the attack.

The British suffered more heavily than the Americans. Riall lost approximately 500 killed, wounded, or missing out of a force of 2,200 regulars, militia, and Native Americans. Brown reported 325 total casualties from his assigned divisional strength of 4,036, not all of whom were present. The American casualties fell heaviest on Scott's brigade, which endured a loss of 19 percent. The soldiers who fought at Chippawa would meet again 20 days later at Lundy's Lane, another bloody battle in which the Americans performed equally well.

The Battle of Chippawa established the American soldiers' faith in themselves and their officers. After a string of defeats, the Americans had engaged well-trained British regulars on an open plain and defeated them, a prospect seemingly unimaginable just months earlier. The battle served notice that the U.S. Army had come of age and had achieved tactical parity with the British. The Battle of Chippawa also propelled the military careers of Brown and Scott, whose brigade had borne the brunt of the fighting.

Richard V. Barbuto

## Further Reading

Barbuto, Richard V. *Niagara, 1814: America Invades Canada.* Lawrence: University Press of Kansas, 2000.

Daniels, James B. "The Battle of Chippewa." *American History* 42(4) (October 2007): 46–53.

Graves, Donald E. *Red Coats & Grey Jackets: The Battle of Chippawa, 5 July 1814.* Toronto: Dundurn, 1994.
Latimer, Jon. *Niagara, 1814: Final Invasion.* Oxford, UK: Osprey, 2010.

## Battle of Bladensburg

| Date | August 24, 1814 | |
|---|---|---|
| Location | Bladensburg, Maryland | |
| Opponents (*winner) | *Great Britain | United States |
| Commander | Major General Robert Ross | Brigadier General William Winder |
| Approx. # Troops | 4,500 regulars | 500 regulars and 5,500 militiamen |
| Importance | This fiasco allows British forces to take Washington and burn its government buildings and facilities. | |

In 1814 the British took the offensive in America on several fronts, including a Mid-Atlantic amphibious campaign. Toward that end, substantial land reinforcements arrived from Bermuda, including 2,500 battle-hardened regulars detached from British forces in France and commanded by Major General Robert Ross. Preceded by naval units under Vice Admiral Alexander Cochrane, this force arrived in the Chesapeake Bay on August 15. Counting the forces of Rear Admiral Sir George Cockburn already on hand, Cochrane had at his disposal 20 warships, including 4 ships of the line, and a large number of transports and storeships. With a battalion of 700 marines detached to operate ashore with the soldiers, total British ground strength was more than 4,500 men.

In order to mislead the Americans as to his real intent, Cochrane detached two squadrons of frigates—sending one up the Potomac River and the other up the bay to a point above Baltimore. At noon on August 19, 14 British ships started ascending the Patuxent River. Cochrane was able to mask the descent on Washington by making it appear that his target was Captain Joshua Barney's flotilla, which had sought refuge in the Patuxent.

The British troops came ashore at Benedict, 25 miles from the mouth of the river, and on August 20 began the march along the west bank of the Patuxent, flanked by light British vessels in the river. On August 22 the land forces reached Upper Marlborough, 40 miles from the mouth of the Patuxent. The American flotilla was cornered on the river at Pig Point, abreast Upper Marlborough. Following some fighting, Barney recognized the inevitable and abandoned his boats on August 21, scuttling them a day later as the British approached.

Cockburn argued strongly for a descent on Washington, and finally Ross agreed. They ignored a letter from Admiral Cochrane calling on them to return to Benedict,

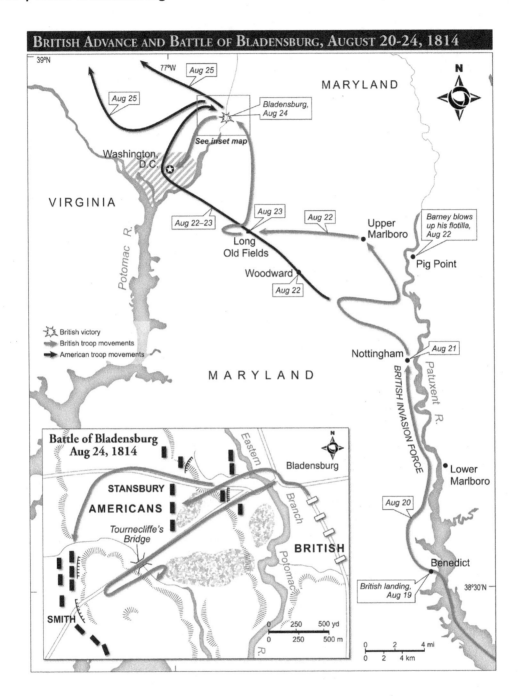

BRITISH ADVANCE AND BATTLE OF BLADENSBURG, AUGUST 20-24, 1814

with Cockburn arguing that they were past the point of return. One approach to the capital was along the eastern branch of the Potomac to a point where two bridges spanned the river. This was the most direct route, and the men of Barney's flotilla were soon defending the bridge that led to the navy yard. The second route, eight miles longer, was for the British to continue northwest to Bladensburg. Ross and Cockburn opted for the latter as less risky and more likely to afford surprise. During

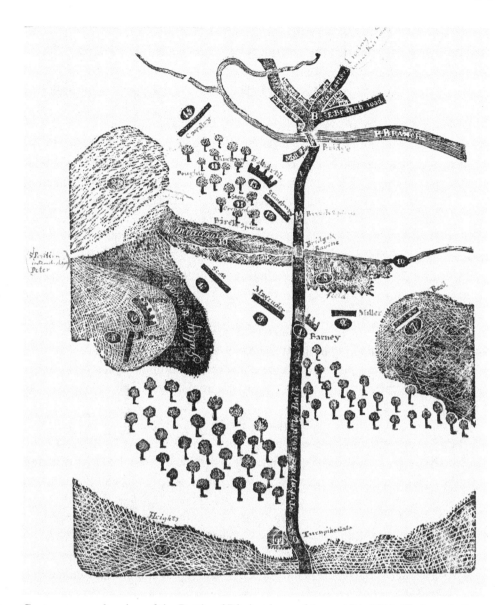

Contemporary drawing of the Battle of Bladensburg of August 24, 1814. Their rout of a far larger American force allowed the British to take Washington, D.C., and burn its public buildings. (Library of Congress)

the night of August 23–24, British troops reached Bladensburg. The British marines remained at Upper Marlborough in case the expedition met with failure and needed to retire.

The resultant defense of the national capital, commanded by Brigadier General William H. Winder, was one of the most embarrassing defeats ever sustained by American arms. Although Winder was severely handicapped in having to rely on what was essentially a militia force, virtually nothing had been done to prepare against a British attack on Washington. Even the last-minute felling of trees and the destruction of roads and bridges might have prevented the British descent on the capital.

As early as July 1, President James Madison had warned a cabinet meeting that he expected an attack on Washington. Madison selected Winder to command a newly created Tenth Military District covering Maryland, northern Virginia, and the District of Columbia. Winder was chosen in part because his uncle, Levin Winder, was governor of Maryland and a critic of the war. Brigadier General Winder had only some 500 regulars available, and the bulk of these were manning forts. As a result, on July 4 the federal government informed nearby states of a massive call-up of 93,500 militia, although Winder was prohibited from ordering any of them into active service until there was imminent danger. That danger now appeared, but few of the militiamen responded.

On August 24 Winder had some 6,000 men mustered at Bladensburg and arrayed in three lines within 30 miles of Washington to oppose the advance of perhaps 4,500 British soldiers. That very morning, Barney received permission to march his 400 seamen and marines to Bladensburg and immediately did so. They did not reach the field until after the battle had begun at 1:00 p.m. but were positioned to prevent a British advance down the Washington Pike. Some of the men served a battery of five naval guns; the remainder of the men acted as infantry.

The sailors and marines were virtually the only Americans to gain credit that day. Many of the militiamen simply broke and ran after a few volleys, terrified by the British Congreve rockets. Winder himself contributed to the defeat by ordering the militiamen to retire when many were still fighting well. Insufficiently trained to retire in good order, the militia prematurely stampeded, causing the battle to be known derisively as the Bladensburg Races. Only the sailors and marines held firm, but the British were able to work around them. The battle was over by 4:00 p.m. British casualties were 64 killed and 185 wounded; American losses were 10–12 killed, 40 wounded, and about 100 taken prisoner. Barney was among those wounded and taken prisoner.

The rout at Bladensburg allowed the British to take Washington that night and burn its public buildings. The British departed the next day and reembarked at Benedict on August 30 without interference. They then proceeded to Baltimore, Maryland, where they met rebuff.

Spencer C. Tucker

**Further Reading**

Lord, Walter. *The Dawn's Early Light.* New York: Norton, 1972.

Pitch, Anthony. *The Burning of Washington: The British Invasion of 1814.* Annapolis, MD: Naval Institute Press, 1998.

Taylor, Blaine. "Shaky Stand at Bladensburg." *Military Heritage* 6 (5) (April 2005): 66–71, 83.

# Battle of Plattsburgh

| Date | September 11, 1814 | |
|---|---|---|
| Location | Plattsburgh, New York | |
| Opponents (*winner) | *United States | Great Britain |
| Commander | Brigadier General Alexander Macomb; Master Commandant Thomas Macdonough | Lieutenant General Sir George Prévost; Captain George Downie |
| Approx. # Troops and Ships | 3,000 troops; 4 ships and 10 gunboats (86 guns); 3,000 troops | 10,000 troops; 4 ships and 12 galleys (94 total guns); as many as 10,500 troops |
| Importance | Having suffered rebuff in his land assault and defeat in the naval engagement, Prévost withdraws his army back into Canada. | |

Following the defeat of Napoleon in April 1814, Britain was able to send additional land and naval forces to North America. With these assets in place, the British planned to invade the United States successively from three points—Niagara, Lake Champlain, and New Orleans—as well as to raid simultaneously into the Chesapeake Bay. On the Niagara front, however, the Americans went on the offensive before the British forces could mount their attack. In July, U.S. troops captured Fort Erie and won important land victories at Chippawa and Lundy's Lane.

By mid-August, governor-general of Canada Lieutenant General Sir George Prévost assembled some 11,000 British regulars near Montreal to invade the United States by the classic route of Lake Champlain and the Hudson River. His immediate objective was the town of Plattsburgh, New York, and the U.S. naval base on Lake Champlain. Prospects appeared bleak for the United States, particularly as Secretary of War John Armstrong had mistakenly ordered the commander of U.S. forces in the Lake Champlain area, Major General George Izard, to move most of his men from Plattsburgh to the Niagara frontier.

The British land force then began to move down the western shore of Lake Champlain. Following skirmishes along Beekmantown Road, the British reached Plattsburgh on September 6, 1814. Despite its importance, the town was defended by only a single brigade of regulars under Brigadier General Alexander Macomb along with about 800 New York and Vermont militiamen, at most 3,000 men.

Prévost proved to be an inept commander. He failed to secure a ford across the Saranac River to his front and then, much to the consternation of his senior officers, suspended land operations pending the arrival of the supporting British naval squadron on Lake Champlain, commanded by Captain George Downie. Prévost was resolved to gain control of the lake before continuing his advance. Downie, however, had taken command of the squadron only on September 2 and was determined not to hazard it until his most powerful ship, the *Confiance,* was fully prepared and all its guns were mounted.

Prévost's land force remained inactive for nearly five days awaiting Downie's arrival, and Macomb used the delay to strengthen his defensive position, which consisted of three wooden forts and two blockhouses along the south bank of the Saranac River where it entered Lake Champlain. Although his forces were outnumbered almost 4 to 1, on the night of September 9 Macomb mounted a spoiling attack across the Saranac, with 50 men attacking a British rocket battery. The raid was successful, and the American force returned to its lines intact. Prévost nevertheless remained quiescent until the morning of September 11, when the British flotilla at last sailed into Plattsburgh Bay.

Immediately on Downie's arrival, Prévost ordered two brigades to begin the land attack. As the British flotilla engaged the U.S. Navy squadron under Master Commandant Thomas Macdonough, Major General Thomas Brisbane's brigade of 3,500 men attacked American troops in front of Plattsburgh to fix the defenders in place, while a second British brigade of 3,500 men under Major General Frederick Robinson searched for a ford on the Saranac in order to turn the American left flank. Prévost held a third brigade under Major General Manly Powers in reserve, ready to exploit any opportunity.

Unfortunately for the British, Robinson was late beginning his movement and lost additional time by marching down the wrong road. Brisbane also had difficulty in the face of determined resistance. Just as the British troops were registering progress against the outnumbered Americans, however, at 10:30 a.m. they received orders from Prévost to cease operations and withdraw immediately. Prévost took this decision in view of what had happened on the lake.

Downie's squadron of 4 ships—the frigate *Confiance* (39 guns), the brig *Linnet* (16 guns), the sloop *Chubb* (11 guns), and the sloop *Finch* (11 guns)—and 12 galleys mounting a total of 17 guns had rounded Cumberland Head and stood in to engage the American flotilla. The Americans had 4 ships—the frigate *Saratoga* (26 guns), the brig *Eagle* (20 guns), the schooner *Ticonderoga* (17 guns), and the sloop *Preble* (7 guns)—and 10 gunboats mounting a total of 16 guns. The two sides were closely matched in firepower as well. Macdonough had a great advantage in that his ships were carefully positioned. During the week in which he had time to prepare, he had placed his ships in line, setting out anchors so that they might easily be swung in either direction to utilize their guns to maximum advantage as the situation dictated. Because the American vessels were anchored, their crews could concentrate on working the guns. The British crews, on the other hand, were forced to work the sails and guns of their ships at the same time.

The naval battle involving a total of about 1,800 men lasted 2 hours and 20 minutes. The two largest ships, the American *Saratoga* and the British *Confiance,* inflicted significant damage on each other. Downie was killed, and with heavy personnel losses the *Confiance* struck to the Americans. Three other British vessels also surrendered. Three British galleys were sunk, and the remainder withdrew. But with all of his own galleys in sinking shape, Macdonough was unable to pursue. He had nonetheless won a classic victory. American casualties were 47 dead and 58 wounded; British casualties totaled 57 dead and at least 100 wounded.

The casualties in the fighting on land and in the water were relatively insignificant—British losses in the land battle totaled perhaps 250 men, while American losses were only about 150 men—but the battles had immense consequences. Deprived of his naval support and well aware of what had happened to a British invading army in 1777 in this same region under Lieutenant General John Burgoyne during the American Revolutionary War, Prévost ordered a general withdrawal. This ended all danger of a British invasion from the north during the remainder of the war. Macomb's troops were astonished at the British departure. For his stand, Macomb received a gold medal and promotion to major general. Prévost was subsequently recalled to England to face an official inquiry.

News of the victory also influenced the Ghent Peace Conference. Coupled with the American victories on the Niagara front and at Baltimore, Maryland, the Battle of Plattsburgh contributed greatly to the British decision to end the war on the basis of status quo ante bellum, without territorial concessions.

Spencer C. Tucker

**Further Reading**

Everest, Allan S. *The War of 1812 in the Champlain Valley.* Syracuse, NY: Syracuse University Press, 1981.

Fitz-Enz, David G. *Plattsburg, the Final Invasion: The Decisive Battle of the War of 1812.* New York: Cooper Square, 2001.

Skaggs, David Curtis. *Thomas Macdonough: Master of Command in the Early U.S. Navy.* Annapolis, MD: Naval Institute Press, 2003.

Stanley, George F. G. *War of 1812: Land Operations.* Ottawa: National Museums of Canada and Macmillan, 1983.

## Battle of New Orleans

| Date | January 8, 1815 | |
|---|---|---|
| Location | Some 5 miles south of New Orleans, Louisiana | |
| Opponents (*winner) | *United States | Great Britain |
| Commander | Major General Andrew Jackson | Lieutenant General Edward Pakenham |
| Approx. # Troops | 4,700 regulars and militiamen; 13 guns | 5,300 regulars |
| Importance | The last major battle of the war, it actually occurred after the Treaty of Ghent was signed and thus had no effect on the war's outcome. It did, however, propel Jackson into the presidency and helped perpetuate the militia myth, much to the detriment of the regular army. | |

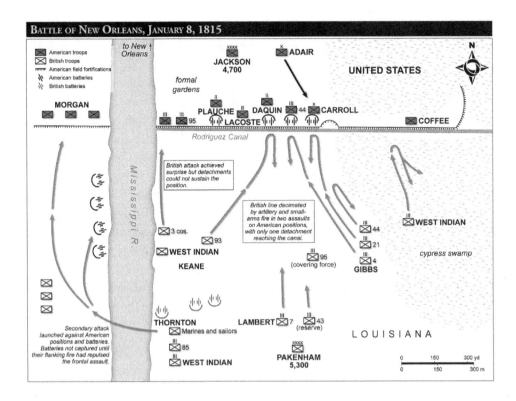

BATTLE OF NEW ORLEANS, JANUARY 8, 1815

British planning for an invasion of the Gulf Coast of the United States had been ongoing since early 1814, when the defeat of Napoleon enabled them to shift substantial military and naval resources to North America. The British planned a three-pronged assault to end the war. One army would invade the United States south from Canada, while another force operated in the Chesapeake region with the possibility of capturing Washington, D.C. A third assault, mounted from Jamaica, was to attack the Gulf Coast region by taking Mobile, Alabama, then moving overland to capture New Orleans. From there British forces would work their way north, up the Mississippi River. As part of this latter strategy, the British enlisted the aid of Creek Indians to disrupt American forces in the southern interior. Commander of the North American Station Vice Admiral Sir Alexander Cochrane was the overall architect of the campaign.

Throughout much of 1814 while the British were relocating forces for the Gulf Coast assault, American forces were busy fighting the Red Stick Creeks, who were allied with the British. Major General Andrew Jackson decisively defeated the Creeks in the Battle of Horseshoe Bend on March 27, 1814. His forces also successfully defended Mobile from a British naval attack on September 15, and he captured Pensacola from the British during November 7–9. In May 1814 Jackson had been promoted to major general in the regular army and given command of the Seventh Military District. He then gathered a force of regulars, militia, and volunteers and marched quickly toward New Orleans.

Major General Andrew Jackson at the Battle of New Orleans, January 8, 1815. This depiction of the battle shows Jackson (with drawn sword) as the heroic leader of U.S. forces. Jackson's thorough preparation for the battle was a major factor in the American victory in what was the most romanticized battle of the War of 1812. (Library of Congress)

Jackson was well aware of British intentions, for in early September 1814 Royal Navy captain Nicholas Lockyer of the brig sloop *Sophia* had established contact with pirate chieftain Jean Lafitte at Grande Terre on Lake Barataria, south of New Orleans, about cooperating with the British in their attack on the city. Lafitte feigned acceptance but then informed American authorities of the British overture, this despite the fact that his brother was jailed in New Orleans and the Americans were then making preparations to attack his pirate stronghold.

On November 27, 1814, the British sailed from Jamaica with a large task force of some 50 ships (including 7 ships of the line along with 7 frigates and numerous sloops and brigs) commanded by Admiral Cochrane and carrying some 6,500 British Army regulars, 1,000 West Indian blacks, and 1,000 troops of the Royal Marines.

On December 1 Jackson arrived in New Orleans with his forces to bolster the 1,000 men already there and began preparing defenses. Jackson also ordered works prepared at Baton Rouge should it be necessary to fall back there.

Jackson had to decide which of the six available invasion routes the British would likely take. This was resolved on December 13, 1814, when the British fleet anchored at the entrance to Lake Borgne, 40 miles east of New Orleans, signaling that as their likely approach route. Indeed, they planned to move against New Orleans not from the south but instead from the east through Bayou Bienvenue, which drains the area east of the city and reaches from Lake Borgne within 1 mile of the Mississippi. Jackson now summoned to New Orleans 4,800 Tennessee infantrymen stationed throughout Louisiana; few actually arrived, however.

On December 14 Captain Lockyer led an attack by some 42 British launches and other craft to engage and capture five American gunboats defending Lake Borgne. Because of the shallowness of the lake, it took Major General Sir Edward Pakenham more than a week to land all his troops below New Orleans. In a surprise move, however, on December 23 Pakenham sent an advance force of 1,600 men under Major General Sir John Keane down Bayou Bienvenue and Bayou Mazant to near Villeré Plantation, only seven miles below the city where there were no defenses. The British swiftly captured American pickets there; they then paused for six hours. Keane hoped to push on to the city, but he was ordered to wait for reinforcements. This was a fatal mistake in retrospect, as the way to New Orleans lay open.

Informed of events, Jackson moved with typical resolve to counter this threat, and with some 2,000 men supported by the schooner *Carolina* (14 guns), on the night of December 23–24 he launched a raid on the British position. Keane's peninsula veterans, while surprised, fought well but failed to pursue. Rebuffed, Jackson then withdrew to a point about five miles south of the city. Taking advantage of the dry, shallow Canal Rodriguez, Jackson set up a line of breastworks. On Christmas Day, Pakenham arrived to assume personal command of the British forces.

On January 1, 1815, Pakenham sent out a reconnaissance in force resulting in an inconclusive artillery duel between the two sides, with the Americans getting the better of it. Pakenham then called up reinforcements, and these arrived on January 6. Unfortunately for the British, in that week's delay Jackson also received reinforcements in the form of 2,000 Kentucky militiamen (although only 700 were armed) under Brigadier General John Adair. The Americans also used the time to improve their fortifications and position 16 artillery pieces.

Pakenham now prepared for a full infantry assault. Shortly before 7:00 a.m. on January 8, 1815, he launched a frontal assault on the American line with 5,300 men. Jackson had some 4,000 men deployed across his front and 1,000 in reserve. In what was the largest battle of the War of 1812, the British troops proved to be easy targets for American artillery fire and steady rifle and musket fire delivered by a three-deep line of defending infantry.

In order to scale the American ramparts, the British troops were to bring along ladders and fascines; however, the 44th Regiment neglected these tools and sent men back to retrieve them, causing the attack to be delayed and the surprise of a dawn assault to be lost. Pakenham ordered the attack across 650 yards of open terrain in close-order formation. At 500 yards American artillery opened fire, with shell and shot ripping into the closely packed British formations. After Jackson ordered the artillery to cease-fire, American infantrymen opened fire as the British were a mere 300 yards from their lines. American artillery from the left continued to fire. Through this fusillade of fire the British troops kept advancing, reaching the base of Canal Rodriguez, where they stopped, allowing the American defenders to pour fire down upon the hapless troops. The 93rd Highlanders attempted to come to the aid of their comrades, but they too were raked by withering American fire.

Pakenham rode forward to rally his men and was mortally wounded. The only British success came on the west bank of the Mississippi River, where a brigade of the 85th Regiment supported by Royal Navy and Royal Marine detachments overwhelmed the American militiamen guarding the line.

Following the deaths of both Pakenham and his second-in-command, Major General Samuel Gibbs, Major General John Lambert took command of the British forces and ordered a withdrawal. In the battle of only some 75 minutes, the British sustained nearly 40 percent casualties: 291 dead, 1,262 wounded, and 484 taken prisoner. The strength of the Americans' position can be seen in their losses of only 13 dead, 39 wounded, and 19 missing. Jackson, cognizant of British strength, allowed them to withdraw unmolested.

On January 9, ships of Cochrane's task force approached American Fort St. Philip on the Mississippi River some 45 miles south of New Orleans. The bomb vessels *Aetna* and *Meteor,* supported by three sloops and a schooner, commenced a bombardment. The American garrison of 306 men, commanded by Major Walter H. Overton, held out for nine days of British shelling, with 2 men killed for some 1,000 shot and shells fired before the British withdrew on January 18.

On January 25 the British troops returned to their ships and departed. British casualties for the entire New Orleans campaign were 2,459; the Americans suffered but 333 casualties. In an effort to mitigate the effects of the New Orleans disaster, the British then moved against Fort Bowyer, Alabama.

The Battle of New Orleans was the last significant battle of the War of 1812. The battle actually occurred a week after the signing of the Treaty of Ghent on December 24, 1814, that ended the war and was thus meaningless as far as terms ending the war were concerned. However, the battle nonetheless proved to be a great boost for American nationalism and helped propel Jackson into the presidency. The lopsided nature of the victory also helped perpetuate the cherished American militia myth, much to the detriment of the regular army, during the next decades.

Rick Dyson and Spencer C. Tucker

### Further Reading

Aitchison, Robert. *A British Eyewitness at the Battle of New Orleans: The Memoir of Royal Navy Admiral Robert Aitchison, 1808–1827.* Edited by Gene A. Smith. New Orleans: Historic New Orleans Collection, 2004.

Cummings, Edward B. "E Pluribus Unum: The American Battle Line at New Orleans, 8 January 1815." *On Point: Journal of Army History* 14(3) (December 2008): 6–12.

Reilly, Robin. *The British at the Gates: The New Orleans Campaign and the War of 1812.* New York: Putnam, 1974.

Remini, Robert V. *The Battle of New Orleans.* New York: Penguin, 1999.

## Battle of the Alamo

| Date | February 23–March 6, 1836 | |
|---|---|---|
| Location | San Antonio, Texas | |
| Opponents (*winner) | *Mexico | Republic of Texas |
| Commander | Mexican president and general Antonio López de Santa Anna | Jim Bowie; William B. Travis |
| Approx. # Troops | 3,000–4,000 men | 187 men |
| Importance | Served as a rallying cry for Texans, renewing their determination to continue the war. The battle also led to widespread support for the Texan cause throughout the United States. | |

In November 1835 a Texas provisional government was established to organize resistance to Mexican rule, and Sam Houston was named the commander of the Texan Army. Believing San Antonio to be too isolated to defend successfully, Houston sent Jim Bowie to withdraw the garrison stationed there. Bowie, however, became enamored of an abandoned 18th-century Spanish mission there, San Antonio de Valero, better known as the Alamo, which for several decades had served as a barracks for Mexican troops.

With some captured Mexican artillery and hard work, the garrison had already begun shoring up the crumbling mission. Bowie sent word to Houston that he would stay and defend the Alamo. Almost immediately, Bowie clashed with Colonel William B. Travis, the garrison's permanent commander, but the two decided to share command and make a stand at the Alamo. Only 150 men, including legendary frontiersman Davy Crockett, were in the Alamo when Mexican president General Antonio López de Santa Anna arrived with some 1,500 troops on February 23, 1836.

Santa Anna quickly ordered his troops, reinforced to 3,000–4,000 men on March 2, to surround the Alamo. He then commenced a round-the-clock bombardment to which the defenders were barely able to respond. Although they had cannon, gunpowder was in painfully short supply. The encirclement was not secure, and Travis (who assumed command when Bowie became ill) sent three riders out to summon aid. In answer to his appeals, 32 men rode in from Gonzales and forced their way at night through the incomplete Mexican investment. The final defense numbered only about 187 men, although the exact count remains in dispute. In any case, it was an impossibly small force to defend a perimeter encompassing the church and two sets of barracks around a very large open courtyard. The adobe walls were originally built to keep out the Comanches but were not sufficiently stout to withstand prolonged artillery fire.

On the night of March 5, the bombardment ceased. In the darkness, the Mexican troops quietly positioned themselves for a dawn attack. Only an overly eager

Painting depicting fighting between Texan defenders of the Alamo and Mexican soldiers within the walls of the fortress on March 6, 1836. Davy Crockett (shown here with his rifle above his head) was among those slain. (MPI/Getty Images)

soldier's cry alerted the garrison to the imminent danger before the attackers were upon them. The morning darkness, coupled with the inexperience of many of the Mexican troops, combined to make the assault unsuccessful, but the Mexicans re-formed and on their second attempt breached the walls. Once inside, they had such an overwhelming numerical advantage that the Texans had little chance of survival. Travis reportedly died early in the battle, and Bowie, according at least to legend, fought from his sickbed for a short time. The men inside the church building held out the longest but did not have the firepower to survive for very long. Mexican sources state that many of the defenders, possibly as many as half, fled the makeshift fortress to the southeast but were ridden down by Mexican cavalry men, who anticipated such a move.

By 8:00 a.m., the battle was over. All 187 Texan defenders, including Bowie and Crockett, were killed. The victorious Mexicans spared some 20 women, children, and African American slaves who had taken refuge in the Alamo. Mexican army casualties have been estimated at anywhere from 400 to 1,600.

In the 1970s, a diary allegedly kept by Enrique de la Peña, one of Santa Anna's staff officers, came to light. Although its veracity has been challenged, the journal describes the final moments of the battle in a way that brought traditional accounts into question. Since 1836, the generally accepted view was that all the defenders died in battle, but de la Peña's diary states that a handful, including Crockett, were taken prisoner. Although most of the officers recommended mercy, Santa Anna's reputation for ruthless suppression of rebellion showed itself again when he ordered the prisoners executed as traitors.

Although the siege at the Alamo slowed the Mexican campaign in Texas only by some two weeks, it provided the spark that motivated many to join General Houston's motley force. The Battle of the Alamo quickly became enshrined in the U.S. public's mind as one of the most heroic moments in American history. The cry "Remember the Alamo!" became a potent slogan for the Texas Revolution. On March 2 during the siege, Texas declared its independence.

Tim Watts

### Further Reading

Hansen, Todd, ed. *The Alamo Reader: A Study in History.* Mechanicsburg, PA: Stackpole, 2003.

Hardin, Stephen L. *Texian Iliad: A Military History of the Texas Revolution.* Austin: University of Texas Press, 1994.

Matovina, Timothy M. *The Alamo Remembered: Tejano Accounts and Perspectives.* Austin: University of Texas Press, 1995.

Winders, Richard Bruce. *Sacrificed at the Alamo: Tragedy and Triumph in the Texas Revolution.* Abilene, TX: State House Press, 2003.

## Battle of San Jacinto

| Date | April 21, 1836 | |
|---|---|---|
| Location | Near present-day La Porte, Texas | |
| Opponents (*winner) | *Republic of Texas | Mexico |
| Commander | General Sam Houston | President and General Antonio López de Santa Anna |
| Approx. # Troops | 910 men; 2 guns | 1,360 men; 1 gun |
| Importance | Secures the independence of Texas from Mexico. | |

On March 2, 1836, during the siege of the Alamo in San Antonio, Texas had declared its independence. Nonetheless, Mexican forces under Mexican president General Antonio López de Santa Anna won apparently decisive military victories at the Alamo on March 6 and at Coleto Creek on March 20. Santa Anna hoped to end the campaign by capturing Texas government officials at Harrisburg. On April 14, separating some 700 men from his main force, the Mexican Army of Operations in Texas, Santa Anna set out for Harrisburg. His advance units arrived there near midnight on April 15, only to learn that the Texas government had fled. Three days later Santa Anna ordered Harrisburg put to the torch, and he then moved to New Washington on the Gulf Coast. There he discovered that the Texas officials he sought had fled to Galveston Island.

Mexican general Antonio López de Santa Anna surrenders to generalissimo of Texan forces Sam Houston following the Battle of San Jacinto on April 21, 1836. (Library of Congress)

Commander of Texas forces General Sam Houston, meanwhile, learned from captured dispatches of Santa Anna's location and that his strike force was detached from the main body. Houston, who had been retreating steadily before the superior Mexican forces since departing Gonzales on March 13, moved swiftly to exploit the situation. On April 20 his force of 910 men was positioned near Lynch's Ferry on the Lynchburg-Harrisburg Road in the vicinity of present-day Houston, Texas, near the confluence of Buffalo Bayou and the San Jacinto River, to block Santa Anna from joining his main force. That afternoon, minor artillery exchanges and cavalry skirmishes occurred between the two sides. Meanwhile, Santa Anna got word of his situation to General of Brigade Martín Perfecto de Cos, who joined him on the morning of April 21 with 600 men.

With Cos's men, Santa Anna now commanded some 1,360 troops. Believing that he had the advantage, Santa Anna chose to rest his army and attack the next day. Meanwhile, shortly before noon on April 21, Houston held a council of war. Despite a majority opinion in favor of remaining on the defensive, Houston decided that he must attack before additional Mexican reinforcements could arrive.

At about 4:30 p.m., Houston led his men in a charge against the Mexicans, with the Texans shouting "Remember the Alamo!" and "Remember Goliad!" Santa Anna's failure to post sentries around his camp during the traditional Mexican afternoon siesta and his decision to set up camp with a swamp to the rear proved fatal.

Houston's assault turned into fierce hand-to-hand combat lasting less than 20 minutes. The bloodshed continued for several hours more, however, with the Texans killing hundreds of panicked Mexican soldiers, mired in the swamp surrounding Peggy Lake, in retribution for the slaying of prisoners at the Alamo and Goliad. At the end of the battle, 630 Mexicans were dead and 730 were captured, including 208 wounded. Surprisingly, the Texans suffered only 9 killed and 30 wounded, Houston among the latter. Santa Anna fled but was captured the next day.

San Jacinto was the decisive battle of the Texas Revolution. On May 14, 1836, Santa Anna signed the Treaty of Velasco, agreeing to withdraw Mexican forces beyond the Rio Grande in exchange for his safe return to Mexico. His return was contingent upon him lobbying for political recognition of the Texas Republic. Despite signing a treaty pledging recognition of an independent Texas, Santa Anna was held as a prisoner until November 20 before he returned in disgrace to Mexico in 1837. Mexico did not officially recognize Texan independence until the 1848 Treaty of Guadalupe Hidalgo, which ended the Mexican-American War. Yet for all intents and purposes, the Battle of San Jacinto freed Texas from Mexican control.

Charles F. Howlett and Spencer C. Tucker

### Further Reading

Hardin, Stephen L. *Texian Iliad: A Military History of the Texas Revolution.* Austin: University of Texas Press, 1994.

Moore, Stephen L. *Eighteen Minutes: The Battle of San Jacinto and the Texas Independence Campaign.* Plano: Republic of Texas Press, 2004.

Pohl, James W. *The Battle of San Jacinto.* Austin: Texas State Historical Association, 1989.

Williams, Amelia W., and Eugene C. Barker, eds. *The Writings of Sam Houston, 1813–1863.* 8 vols. Austin: University of Texas Press, 1938–1943.

## Battle of Buena Vista

| Date | February 22–23, 1847 | |
|---|---|---|
| Location | Puerto de la Angostura, Coahuila, Mexico | |
| Opponents (*winner) | *United States | Mexico |
| Commander | Major General Zachary Taylor | General Antonio López de Santa Anna |
| Approx. # Troops | Some 4,800 men | 16,000 men |
| Importance | Although a tactical draw, the battle is a strategic victory for the United States in that it ends the threat to the U.S. position in northern Mexico. | |

During September 21–24, 1846, the U.S. Army of the North, commanded by Major General Zachary Taylor, fought and defeated Mexican forces in the Battle of

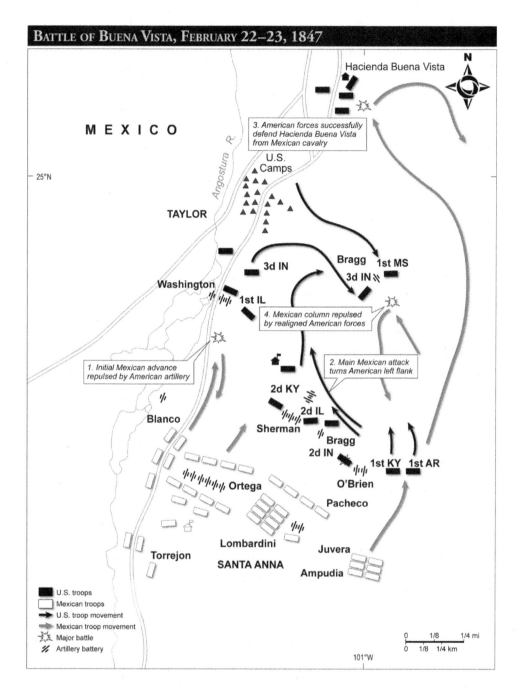

**BATTLE OF BUENA VISTA, FEBRUARY 22–23, 1847**

Hacienda Buena Vista

N

MEXICO

3. American forces successfully defend Hacienda Buena Vista from Mexican cavalry

U.S. Camps

25°N

TAYLOR

Bragg     1st MS

3d IN

3d IN

Washington

1st IL

4. Mexican column repulsed by realigned American forces

1. Initial Mexican advance repulsed by American artillery

2. Main Mexican attack turns American left flank

2d KY

2d IL

Blanco

Sherman

Bragg

2d IN

1st KY   1st AR

Ortega

O'Brien

Pacheco

Lombardini

Juvera

Torrejon

SANTA ANNA

Ampudia

■ U.S. troops
□ Mexican troops
➤ U.S. troop movement
➤ Mexican troop movement
✴ Major battle
∥ Artillery battery

0   1/8   1/4 mi
0   1/8   1/4 km

101°W

Monterrey. Following the capture of this important northern Mexican city and much to Taylor's displeasure, U.S. president James K. Polk approved shifting most of Taylor's forces to Major General Winfield Scott for a landing at the port of Veracruz and a march overland from that point to Mexico City. Beginning in January 1847, U.S. forces in northern Mexico were gradually siphoned off. Taylor then concentrated most of his remaining forces around the city of Saltillo.

Following the killing of a U.S. courier and the recovery of his dispatches, Mexican general Antonio López de Santa Anna, located at San Luis Potosí some 250 miles to the south, learned of the approximate size of Taylor's force and Scott's intention to attack the Mexican capital via Veracruz. Santa Anna quickly gathered an army to march north with the plan to defeat Taylor's reduced army and force the Americans out of northern Mexico, then return south to meet Scott.

Santa Anna set out with some 20,000 men, but only about 15,000 of these were able to make the difficult march north. At first unwilling to believe that Santa Anna was moving against him, Taylor learned for certain on February 21, 1847, that the Mexican army was nearby. Taylor then decided to abandon Saltillo as Santa Anna's army approached. The Americans first advanced seven miles to Agua Nueva but then backtracked to the more easily defended Angostura Mountain pass, halfway between Agua Nueva and Saltillo. Americans know the resulting battle for the nearby Hacienda Buena Vista, while Mexicans remember it by the name of the pass. Taylor had some 4,700 men to face Santa Anna, who had 15,000 men.

Taylor ordered his second-in-command, Brigadier General John Wool, to set up a defensive position. The Americans chose the difficult high ground in large part to offset the Mexican advantage in cavalry. As the Americans prepared to meet the Mexican attack, Santa Anna arrived at Agua Nueva with his exhausted troops. Taylor returned from Saltillo on the morning of February 22 and saw the Mexicans deploying. Perceiving Taylor's withdrawal as weakness, Santa Anna demanded that the Americans surrender, which Taylor promptly rejected.

The battle began on the afternoon of February 22. Mexican light infantry under General Pedro de Ampudia, who had previously faced Taylor while in command of Mexican forces at Monterrey, tried to scale the mountain on the American left but was rebuffed. By evening, skirmishing between the two sides had ceased.

A light rain fell that night as both sides repositioned their forces for the main battle expected the next day. Early on February 23, Santa Anna ordered the main assault. Advancing up the Saltillo Road, the Mexicans were halted by fire from an American artillery battery in the pass commanded by Captain John M. Washington. Meanwhile, the Mexicans were having success on the American left. There two Mexican divisions drove back the vastly outnumbered American 2nd Indiana Regiment and three artillery pieces. American reinforcements were rushed forward to slow the Mexican advance, while Wool, who exercised tactical control of the battle, ordered the center to slowly retire, supported as it did so by artillery fire. Taylor arrived to help rally the men.

At the same time, Mexican cavalry moved around the American left to attack Hacienda Buena Vista in the American rear. There wagon train guards and some of the troops who had retreated earlier met and repulsed the cavalry. Wool was able to form a new battle line and halt the Mexican breakthrough. That afternoon the Mexicans turned back a U.S. counterattack. The Mexicans then launched their own attack in turn and took two American artillery pieces. American artillery, which played perhaps the key role in the battle, halted any further Mexican advance, however.

That afternoon Santa Anna withdrew, and the battle was over. During the night the Mexicans began retracing their steps south so that Santa Anna might defend against Scott's invasion force. Taylor had expected a renewal of the Mexican attack the next day and was surprised to learn of the Mexican departure. He did not pursue.

The Battle of Buena Vista claimed U.S. casualties of 267 dead, 456 wounded, and 23 missing. Mexican losses were far higher, on the order of 600 killed, 1,000 wounded, and 1,800 missing. The battle brought Taylor additional laurels and assisted him in his successful bid for the presidency in 1848. The battle also marked the end of major combat in northern Mexico. Although Santa Anna had suffered significant losses at Buena Vista, he was nonetheless able to reconstitute his forces to face Scott's forces moving west from Veracruz to Mexico City.

Paul J. Springer and Spencer C. Tucker

**Further Reading**

Lavender, David. *Climax at Buena Vista: The American Campaigns in Northeastern Mexico, 1846–47*. Philadelphia: Lippincott, 1966.

Nichols, Edward J. *Zach Taylor's Little Army*. Garden City, NY: Doubleday, 1963.

Winders, Richard Bruce. *Mr. Polk's Army: The American Military Experience in the Mexican War*. College Station: Texas A&M University Press, 1997.

## Siege of Veracruz

| Date | March 9–29, 1847 | |
|---|---|---|
| Location | Veracruz, Mexico | |
| Opponents (*winner) | *United States | Mexico |
| Commander | Major General Winfield Scott | General of Division Juan Morales |
| Approx. # Troops | 10,000 men | 4,000 men |
| Importance | Following the largest amphibious landing to this point in American history, the U.S. capture of the port of Veracruz provides the Americans a secure supply base for the overland campaign to Mexico City. | |

Veracruz, the largest port in Mexico and the principal entrepôt for the Mexican capital, was a key strategic objective in the campaign to capture Mexico City during the Mexican-American War (1846–1848). When Major General Zachary Taylor's invasion of northern Mexico proved insufficient to force the Mexican government to agree to a peace treaty acceptable to the James K. Polk administration, Major General Winfield Scott conceived of a plan to withdraw much of Taylor's force and use these troops himself for a descent on Veracruz and then a march inland to take the capital of Mexico City.

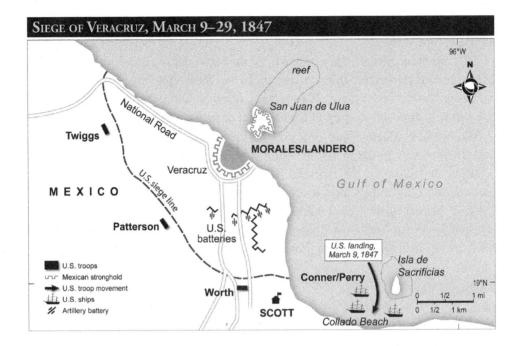

SIEGE OF VERACRUZ, MARCH 9–29, 1847

At the onset of war in 1846, Secretary of the Navy George Bancroft, acting under the direction of President Polk, ordered a blockade of the Mexican Gulf Coast ports. In order to secure a base to support blockade operations, Commodore David E. Conner seized Antón Lizardo on the Mexican coast 12 miles south of Veracruz. American blockaders could not safely approach the port at Veracruz, however, as it was protected by cannon in the fortress of San Juan de Ulúa, a massive island reef fortification approximately a half mile offshore.

Mexican president and army commander General Antonio López de Santa Anna learned of the American plans from dispatches taken from a slain U.S. courier. Santa Anna decided to march his army north to defeat the weakened Taylor, drive U.S. forces from northern Mexico, and then return south to defeat the American invasion at Veracruz.

Meanwhile, preparations for the U.S. invasion proceeded. Conner advocated a landing near Antón Lizardo, where naval gunfire could protect troop transports and destroy any opposition on the beaches. This would avoid the guns at San Juan de Ulúa. Scott, on the other hand, held that landing troops near the small town rather than closer to Veracruz would actually hamper operations by lengthening his supply lines. He also urged that any landing occur no later than February 1, 1847, as any significant delay could trap American forces in the Mexican coastal lowlands during the annual yellow fever outbreak.

Unfortunately for Scott's plans, the landings at Veracruz were delayed by politics in Washington. Although Scott was the most experienced U.S. general and the logical person to take command, Polk did not want to name him to that position. Polk, a Democrat, feared that the glory resulting from a successful invasion would assist Scott, a Whig, should he decide to seek the presidency in 1848. Polk

Depiction of the surrender of Veracruz, Mexico, on March 29, 1847, following a 21-day siege by U.S. troops during the Mexican-American War. (N.C. Brooks, *A Complete History of the Mexican War*, 1849)

much preferred Senator Thomas Hart Benton, a loyal Democrat, as commander. The Senate, however, blocked Polk and awarded command of the undertaking to Scott, but the delays prevented Scott from maintaining his desired timetable. The invasion was further delayed by the lack of available landing craft capable of bringing troops directly to the shore in sufficient numbers to overwhelm any local defenses.

For the invasion, Scott gathered 15,000 men at Tampico. Most of the U.S. regulars engaged at Veracruz had been requisitioned directly from Taylor's army at Monterrey, which made an enemy of Taylor. Scott selected Isla de Sacrificios, a small island near Veracruz, as the staging point for the invasion. The joint army-navy task force set out on March 3, 1847.

Despite earlier interservice arguments, the army and navy cooperated well in the actual landings, with the navy efficiently transporting troops to and from the staging area. The landing was scheduled for March 8, but signs of an approaching norther forced a one-day postponement. The operation occurred at Collado Beach on March 9, 1847. Specially designed surfboats that were carried aboard the transports worked very well.

Mexican general of division Juan Morales commanded the Veracruz defenses. He had under his immediate control 3,000 troops in Veracruz and 1,000 troops garrisoning San Juan de Ulúa. Morales also disposed of some 100 artillery pieces in the two locations. However, he decided not to contest the landings but instead to await a siege from behind his powerful fortifications. As a result, by midnight on March 9 in what was the largest U.S. amphibious landing until World War II, more than 10,000 American troops had reached the shore without a single casualty.

After observing the Veracruz defenses, Scott refused to commit his troops to an attempt to storm the walls. Instead, he opted to surround the city and rely on naval gunfire to reduce the defenses. In addition to shipboard artillery fire, the navy off-loaded a number of heavy guns and provided crews to man them in order to supplement army firepower ashore. The navy guns included two 8-inch cannon firing 64-pound explosive shell. They proved highly effective in the siege operations.

On March 22 after almost two weeks of preparations, Scott ordered the bombardment of Veracruz. When Morales requested a truce, Scott demanded the surrender of the city as a condition of any negotiations. Morales then resigned his post and was succeeded by General of Brigade José Juan Landero Bauza, who requested surrender terms from Scott on March 25. Scott demanded the unconditional surrender of the city, which Landero finally offered on March 28. The siege was officially lifted on March 29.

Landero's capitulation included the surrender of San Juan de Ulúa, allowing American transport vessels to enter the harbor directly without fear of attack. Scott's conquest of Veracruz opened the interior of Mexico to invasion, and the siege allowed Scott's army to reach the safety of elevated mountain passes before the onset of yellow fever season. From Veracruz, Scott began his highly successful Mexico City Campaign, arriving on the outskirts of the Mexican capital in August 1847.

Paul J. Springer

## Further Reading

Bauer, K. Jack. *The Mexican War, 1846–1848.* New York: Macmillan, 1974.

Bauer, K. Jack. *Surfboats and Horse Marines: U.S. Naval Operations in the Mexican War, 1846–48.* Annapolis, MD: U.S. Naval Institute, 1969.

Eisenhower, John S. D. *So Far from God: The U.S. War with Mexico, 1846–1848.* New York: Random House, 1989.

Johnson, Timothy D. *A Gallant Little Army: The Mexico City Campaign.* Lawrence: University Press of Kansas, 2007.

Winders, Richard Bruce. *Mr. Polk's Army: The American Military Experience in the Mexican War.* College Station: Texas A&M University Press, 1997.

# Battle of Cerro Gordo

| Date | April 17–18, 1847 | |
|---|---|---|
| Location | Near Xalapa, Veracruz State, Mexico | |
| Opponents (*winner) | *United States | Mexico |
| Commander | Major General Winfield Scott | General Antonio López de Santa Anna |
| Approx. # Troops | 8,500 men | 12,000 men |
| Importance | Scott is able to move his expeditionary force out of the yellow fever belt and into the Valley of Mexico for the advance on Mexico City. | |

After securing their base at Veracruz, Mexico, U.S. forces under Major General Winfield Scott moved west along the National Road toward their objective of Mexico City. Near Xalapa in Veracruz state, a large hill officially named El Telégrafo but known by the local residents as Cerro Gordo dominated the area. Just west of Plan del Río, the National Road entered a defile. There Mexican president General Antonio López de Santa Anna, with 12,000 men and 43 guns, established a defensive position in the hopes of trapping Scott's forces. Not only did Santa Anna seek a decisive victory on the battlefield, but he also hoped to delay Scott's march from the coast, thereby keeping American forces in the lowlands for the upcoming yellow fever season. To avoid this, Scott, with 8,500 men, was forced to offer battle in terrain that greatly favored the Mexican defenders.

Learning of Santa Anna's position, Scott sent Brigadier General David Twiggs ahead with some 2,600 men and artillery. Twiggs arrived in Plan del Río on April 11 and sent his engineer, Lieutenant P. G. T. Beauregard, to scout the Mexican positions. Beauregard reported that the Mexicans could be flanked if the Americans secured the hill of La Atalaya, just before El Telégrafo. Twiggs, however, made preparations for a frontal assault on the Mexican positions and informed Scott of this. Twiggs estimated Mexican strength at 4,000 men, whereas Santa Anna in fact commanded some 14,000 men.

Major General Robert Patterson's division of volunteers arrived on April 12. Patterson's brigade commanders, Brigadier Generals Gideon Pillow and James Shields, talked Twiggs out of an assault that day. On April 14 Patterson, previously bedridden with fever, postponed any attack until Scott's arrival. When Scott arrived at Plan del Río, he refused to commit his army to a hastily planned assault on unknown forces and instead ordered a thorough reconnaissance of the Mexican positions. Captain Robert E. Lee reported that Santa Anna had sent few men to defend the Mexican left flank, convinced that the rough terrain in that sector would prevent any American attack from that direction. Lee also noted that the left flank of the Mexican line was indeed passable and that U.S. forces might thereby bypass Mexican defenses unobserved and envelop the entire Mexican line. In effect, if sufficient troops could move down the path without being detected, they could seize the Jalapa Road behind El Telégrafo at the village of Cerro Gordo. American forces would then be in position to trap Santa Anna's entire force.

Scott ordered the trail that Lee had discovered to be widened, with an attack to occur on the morning of April 18. Lee would lead Twiggs's division, supported by Shields's brigade, around the Mexican line. On April 17 Twiggs and Shields began their flanking maneuver. A brief skirmish with Mexican pickets soon expanded into a full-blown battle, however, alerting Mexican forces on La Atalaya to the American presence. Colonel William S. Harney led an attack on that hill, routing the defenders and chasing them to Cerro Gordo. Because of Twiggs's attack on La Atalaya, Santa Anna believed that Scott's objective was the capture of El

Telégrafo, not the Jalapa Road, despite information provided by a U.S. deserter that Scott intended to capture the National Road beyond the Mexican positions.

On the morning of April 18, Harney led an assault on El Telégrafo. Despite reinforcements dispatched by Santa Anna, the defenders could not prevent the Americans from taking its summit. At the same time, Shields's brigade, supported by a brigade under Colonel Bennett Riley, moved around the hill. Outflanking the Mexican defenders, the brigade struck the Mexican camp at Cerro Gordo. The surprise appearance of American troops in the rear of their positions panicked the now-disorganized Mexican forces, turning a tactical defeat into a rout.

American casualties after two days of hard fighting totaled 63 killed and 353 wounded. The Mexican army lost approximately 1,000 killed and wounded, with an additional 3,000 captured and paroled under oath not to participate in further fighting. The Americans also secured 43 guns and virtually the entire Mexican baggage train, including personal effects belonging to Santa Anna and his staff. Although the majority of Santa Anna's men managed to escape up the National Road to Jalapa, Scott was able to move his army out of the yellow fever belt and reorganize it for the movement into the Valley of Mexico.

Paul J. Springer and Spencer C. Tucker

**Further Reading**

Bauer, K. Jack. *The Mexican War, 1846–1848.* New York: Macmillan, 1974.

Clary, David A. *Eagles and Empire: The United States, Mexico, and the Struggle for a Continent.* New York: Bantam, 2009.

Eisenhower, John S. D. *So Far from God: The U.S. War with Mexico, 1846–1848.* New York: Random House, 1989.

Johnson, Timothy D. *A Gallant Little Army: The Mexico City Campaign.* Lawrence: University Press of Kansas, 2007.

## Battle for Mexico City

| Date | September 8–14, 1847 | |
|---|---|---|
| Location | Mexico City and vicinity, Mexico | |
| Opponents (*winner) | *United States | Mexico |
| Commander | Major General Winfield Scott | General Antonio López de Santa Anna |
| Approx. # Troops | 7,200 men | 16,000 men |
| Importance | Gives the Americans control of the Mexican capital, bringing peace negotiations and an end to the war. | |

In March 1847, U.S. Army major general Winfield Scott commenced a brilliant campaign to capture Mexico City as a means to end the war. After the successful Siege of Veracruz (March 9–29, 1847), Scott moved his forces inland on the

National Road toward the capital city. On August 20 at Churubusco and Contreras, following other battles en route, Scott fought a pair of battles that left the American army only three miles south of Mexico City and opened the route for a final assault on the capital. However, Mexican forces under Mexican president and army commander General Antonio López de Santa Anna still outnumbered the Americans more than 2 to 1 (some 16,000 men to 7,200).

Scott decided to feign an attack on the southern road leading into Mexico City while concentrating his forces to the west and southwest. On September 8, 1847, Major General William J. Worth's division launched an ill-prepared assault on El Molino del Rey, a series of low stone buildings only two miles southwest of the capital. Worth's attack eventually succeeded through sheer force of numbers, but the poorly planned advance cost him 118 killed, 665 wounded, and 18 missing, nearly a quarter of his division. Mexican losses were 269 killed, 500 wounded, and 852 captured. Worth's troops also discovered that earlier intelligence reports claiming that El Molino del Rey contained a cannon foundry were false. Thus, the battle produced no tangible gains for the U.S. forces.

As the American forces moved through El Molino del Rey, they could see Chapultepec Castle, the final major Mexican defensive position outside of the city. The castle appeared to be a strong position, incorporating earthworks, ditches, stone walls, and an elevated position. However, Santa Anna provided only 800 troops to defend Chapultepec, an insufficient number for its extensive size.

On September 13, two American divisions, commanded by Major General John A. Quitman and Major General Gideon J. Pillow, attacked Chapultepec from two directions after a two-hour preparatory artillery barrage. The Americans employed scaling ladders to assail the parapets, forcing the castle's commander, Major General Nicolás Bravo, to surrender the fortification. Among the Mexican defenders were young cadets from the Mexican Military Academy immortalized as Los Niños Héroes (Boy Heroes).

The capture of Chapultepec did not end the battles to take Mexico City but did free American forces for a direct assault on the capital. Surging American forces soon assaulted the Belén Gate at the southwestern edge of the city and the San Cosmé Gate to the west. As darkness fell, Scott called off the attack to regroup his forces for the final assault, scheduled for the following day.

Scott ordered his troops forward on September 14, 1847, but to his surprise, Santa Anna had withdrawn his army from Mexico City to the town of Guadalupe Hidalgo, three miles north of the capital. Rather than pursue Santa Anna's retreating force, Scott continued to advance on Mexico City. Scott correctly perceived that the capture of the capital would lead to the collapse of the Mexican will to continue the struggle and would eventually compel Mexico to negotiate an end to the war.

Scott marched his troops into the central plaza on the morning of September 14. Within hours of the triumphant demonstration of the conquering army and the hoisting of the Stars and Stripes, the urban poor began to attack the occupying U.S. soldiers with stones, bottles, and other loose objects. The riot finally ended on September 16 thanks to the intervention of members of the Mexico City town council, who worked feverishly to restore public order, fearing that the uprising might ignite a popular revolt that would cause even more damage to the city. Scott's forces then began a period of American occupation that lasted until the signing of the Treaty of Guadalupe Hidalgo on February 2, 1848.

Scott's casualties in the attack on Mexico City were remarkably light. He lost fewer than 1,000 soldiers in the fighting near Chapultepec and at the gates of the city while inflicting losses of more than 3,000 on the Mexican defenders, including the capture of some 800 prisoners. With the exception of the bloody assault at El Molino del Rey, Scott's entire campaign had been remarkably efficient, allowing him to move a small but effective army on hostile terrain against a numerically superior enemy fighting on its home territory. In a period of only six months, Scott had driven from the coast to the capital, fought in a series of victorious engagements, and moved into occupation of the enemy's capital.

Paul J. Springer

**Further Reading**

Bauer, K. Jack. *The Mexican War, 1846–1848*. New York: Macmillan, 1974.

Granados, Luis Fernando. *Sueñan las piedras: Alzamiento ocurrido en la ciudad de México, 14, 15, y 16 de septiembre de 1847*. Mexico City: Ediciones Era, 2003.

Johnson, Timothy D. *A Gallant Little Army: The Mexico City Campaign*. Lawrence: University Press of Kansas, 2007.

## Battle of Fort Sumter

| Date | April 12–14, 1861 | |
| --- | --- | --- |
| Location | Charleston harbor, Charleston, South Carolina | |
| Opponents (*winner) | *Confederacy | United States |
| Commander | Brigadier General P. G. T. Beauregard | Major Robert Anderson |
| Approx. # Troops | 500 men; 48 guns | 85 men; 43 guns |
| Importance | The Confederates begin the Civil War. | |

The election of Abraham Lincoln as president of the United States prompted the states of the Deep South to secede from the Union. South Carolina was the first, on December 20, 1860. Mississippi, Florida, Alabama, Georgia, Louisiana, and Texas followed suit. Meeting in Montgomery, Alabama, on February 8, 1861, representatives of the seven seceded states proclaimed the establishment of the Confederate States of America and the next day elected as president Jefferson Davis of Mississippi.

Of the major federal military installations in the Deep South in early April 1861, only Fort Sumter in Charleston Harbor, South Carolina, and Fort Pickens on Santa Rosa Island off Pensacola, Florida, remained in Union hands. After a month of seeking a way to resupply Sumter and hoping for a cooling of Southern passions, U.S. president Abraham Lincoln concluded that he had to send relief expeditions to these forts or surrender them to the South. This, however, ran the risk of causing Virginia and other border states to secede.

On April 10, a relief expedition sailed for Sumter. Commanded by Gustavus F. Fox, the expedition consisted of only the screw sloop *Pawnee* (8 guns) and the U.S. Revenue Service side-wheeler *Harriet Lane* (4 guns) escorting the supply ship *Baltic,* carrying 200 reinforcements and supplies. The side-wheel steam frigate *Powhatan* (16 guns) was to have been included, but Lincoln secretly diverted it to relieve Fort Pickens, although its absence probably did not affect the outcome at Sumter.

On April 6 Lincoln directed State Department clerk Robert S. Chew to proceed to Charleston and inform Governor Francis W. Pickens that the president had ordered the resupply of Major Robert Anderson's garrison at Sumter. Chew was instructed to inform Pickens that this would be "of provisions only" and that if no armed attempt was made to thwart this effort, no additional men, arms, or ammunition would be introduced without prior notification or a Confederate attack.

Pickens promptly informed President Davis in Montgomery, Alabama, and Davis ordered Brigadier General P. G. T. Beauregard at Charleston to demand the surrender of Fort Sumter. If refused, Beauregard was to reduce the fort. Beauregard made this demand on April 11. Following an unsatisfactory reply from Major Anderson, Beauregard ordered fire opened before the Union relief expedition could arrive.

The shelling of Fort Sumter commenced at 4:30 a.m. on April 12, 1861. Beauregard and some 500 men employed 30 heavy guns and 18 mortars. Anderson had only 85 men and 43 civilian engineers. Fort Sumter held 43 guns, but to conserve ammunition, Anderson ordered return fire restricted to six guns only. At about 7:00 a.m., Captain Abner Doubleday, Anderson's second-in-command, fired the first shot in defense of the fort. The firing continued all day, with the Federals firing slowly to preserve ammunition. That night Fort Sumter ceased fire, but the Confederates still lobbed an occasional shell at the fort. Although the Union relief expedition had arrived off Charleston Harbor, rough weather precluded any attempt to launch boats to resupply Sumter, and without the powerful *Powhatan,* Fox was reluctant to expose his ships to enemy fire.

Heavy Confederate shelling recommenced on April 13, while Union return fire was limited to one gun every 10 minutes. With the Confederate batteries holding the Union ships at bay, with Sumter nearly out of food, and with fires having broken out in the fort, after 34 hours of bombardment Anderson arranged a truce on the afternoon of April 13 and formally surrendered on April 14.

As part of the terms of capitulation, Sumter's garrison was permitted to run the American flag back up the flagpole and fire a 100-gun salute to it. Firing commenced at 2:00 p.m., but on the 50th shot, powder sparks ignited stacked shells, which exploded, killing one Union soldier (Private Daniel Hough) outright and wounding two others, one (Private Edward Galloway) mortally. They were the only casualties in the engagement that began the bloodiest war in U.S. history. Anderson and his garrison were subsequently evacuated by the Union ships off Charleston and returned to the North.

The shelling of Fort Sumter galvanized opinions on both sides and ended any sympathy in the North for the Confederate cause. With the South having fired on the U.S. flag, a patriotic fervor swept the North. Whether Lincoln had intended to maneuver the South into this is unclear, but on April 15 he declared the existence of an "insurrection" and called for 75,000 volunteers to serve for three months. America was now at war with itself.

Spencer C. Tucker

**Further Reading**

Detzer, David R. *Allegiance: Fort Sumter, Charleston and the Beginning of the Civil War.* New York: Harcourt, 2001.

Tucker, Spencer C. *Blue and Gray Navies: The Civil War Afloat.* Annapolis, MD: Naval Institute Press, 2006.

Wise, Stephen R. *Gate of Hell: Campaign for Charleston Harbor, 1863.* Columbia: University of South Carolina Press, 1994.

# First Battle of Bull Run

| Date | July 21, 1861 | |
|---|---|---|
| Location | Manassas Junction, Virginia, 22 miles west of Washington, D.C. | |
| Opponents (*winner) | *Confederacy | United States |
| Commander | Brigadier General Pierre G. T. Beauregard | Brigadier General Irvin McDowell |
| Approx. # Troops | 18,000 men | 18,000 men |
| Importance | A significant boost to Southern morale, this Confederate tactical victory prevents a Union descent on Richmond and nets the South a considerable quantity of weapons; the battle also signals that the war will be protracted. | |

With the Civil War already under way, the public and press in the North clamoring for action, and 90-day enlistments in some volunteer regiments about to expire, President Abraham Lincoln ordered a military offensive against the Confederate capital of Richmond. He took this step against the advice of his professional

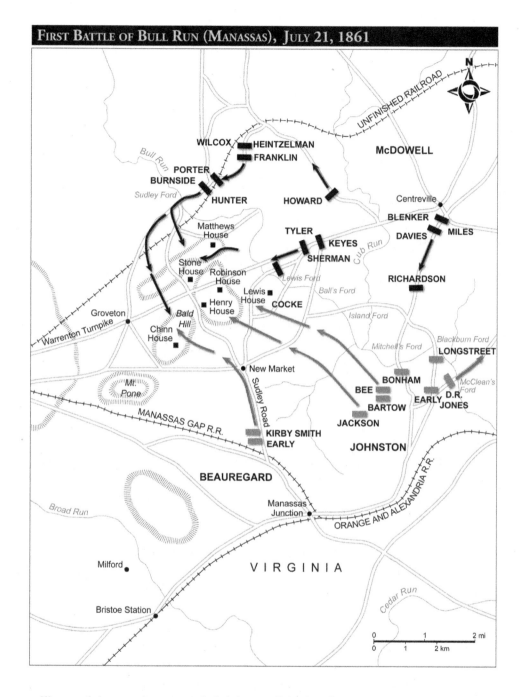

### FIRST BATTLE OF BULL RUN (MANASSAS), JULY 21, 1861

military advisers, who counseled delay until Union forces could be better trained and organized.

The Union offensive was to begin with the capture of the strategically important Confederate rail intersection of Manassas Junction, Virginia, located some 29 miles southwest of the federal capital and just west of Bull Run. Brigadier General Irvin McDowell, commanding the Department of Northeastern Virginia at Washington,

The First Battle of Bull Run, July 21, 1861. Inexperienced Union troops were unable to carry out Brigadier General Irvin McDowell's attack plan, and defending Confederate forces under P. G. T. Beauregard won a clear-cut victory in this first large land battle of the Civil War. (Library of Congress)

D.C., was to march to Manassas with 35,000 men and defeat some 22,000 members of the Confederate Army of the Potomac under Brigadier General P. G. T. Beauregard. As McDowell moved against the Confederates from the east, Major General Robert Patterson, commanding the Department of Pennsylvania with another 18,000 Union troops, had the important assignment of preventing Confederate troops in the Shenandoah Valley from reinforcing Beauregard from the west.

McDowell, a career staff officer with no command experience, departed Washington on July 16, but his advance was glacial. It took two days for his army to reach Centreville, northeast of the meandering stream of Bull Run. Here McDowell ordered a reconnaissance by Brigadier General Daniel Tyler's division. Tyler's troops clashed with two Confederate brigades at Blackburn's Ford, after which McDowell spent two more days organizing his forces and developing a battle plan.

McDowell's delay proved costly to the Union side, for it enabled Brigadier General Joseph Johnston and some 10,000 Confederates to elude Patterson and move by the Manassas Gap Railroad from the Shenandoah Valley to reinforce Beauregard in the first troop movement by rail in U.S. history. Patterson did not learn of the Confederate movement until July 20, and by then, all of Johnston's men except one brigade had joined Beauregard.

The First Battle of Bull Run (First Battle of Manassas) opened early on the morning on July 21, 1861. Each commander planned to carry out an envelopment of the eastern flank of the other: McDowell attempting to cut off Beauregard from reinforcement from the west, and Beauregard attempting to sever McDowell's line of communication to Washington. Both plans proved difficult for poorly trained troops to execute. In any case, inadequate orders delayed execution of the Confederate attack. By 2:00 a.m. on July 21, McDowell had some 12,000 men moving west on the Warrenton Pike to a ford on Bull Run at Sudley Springs. At 5:00 a.m., Union artillery beyond Bull Run opened up on the Confederate lines as Union infantry there feigned an attack south from Centreville against the eight-mile-long Confederate defensive line.

Already three hours behind schedule, the Union flanking attack began with apparent promise. However, Confederate scouts had detected the Union movement and reported it, allowing Beauregard to rush reinforcements from the Confederate right to the threatened northwest some miles distant. Battle was fully joined in midmorning, with Confederate troops under Colonel Nathan G. Evans bearing the brunt of the Union assault. Beauregard's reinforcements arrived on the battlefield piecemeal, but Confederate troops under Brigadier General Bernard E. Bee and Colonel Francis S. Bartow managed to hold against the disjoined Union attacks until noon. Union numbers then began to tell as the Confederates were driven back to Henry House Hill. A Union victory appeared in the offing, with only a Virginia brigade under Brigadier General Thomas J. Jackson and South Carolinians led by Colonel Wade Hampton holding formation. Exhorting his disoriented soldiers to stand firm, Bee saw Jackson's positions and shouted to his men, "Look, there's Jackson standing like a stone wall. Rally behind the Virginians." Shortly thereafter Bee was mortally wounded, but he had given Jackson his sobriquet of "Stonewall."

Halted by the steady stream of Confederate reinforcements, the Federals now regrouped. For two hours, the battle raged back and forth with charges and counter charges. Beauregard and Johnston both arrived on the scene to take personal charge of the Confederate defense, and Beauregard directed a counterattack across Henry House Hill, which captured Union batteries and by 4:00 p.m. had sent Union troops reeling back. At first the Union withdrawal was orderly, but then an artillery shell tore into a wagon on Cub Run Bridge, causing a bottleneck on the main route to Centreville. The retreat then became a confused, panicky stampede back to Washington. Adding to the confusion and congestion were the numerous carriages of the civilians who had come out of Washington to witness what they expected to be a major Union victory.

This significant tactical victory was a great boost to Southern morale and garnered the Confederates a sizable collection of discarded Union weapons and supplies. The victory hardly changed the strategic situation, however, for the Confederates were themselves little better organized than their opponents and in any case were incapable of a major offensive against Washington. Union casualties in the battle numbered 2,896: 460 killed, 1,124 wounded, and 1,312 missing or deserted. Confederate casualties were 1,982: 387 killed, 1,582 wounded, and 13 missing. The casualty totals were modest by the standards of the war's future engagements, but both sides now realized that more resources would be necessary to secure victory in the war.

Jeffrey D. Bass and Spencer C. Tucker

**Further Reading**

Beatie, Russel H. *Army of the Potomac: Birth of Command, November 1860–September 1861.* New York: Da Capo, 2002.

Detzer, David. *Donnybrook: The Battle of Bull Run, 1861.* New York: Harcourt Books, 2004.

McPherson, James. *Battle Cry of Freedom: The Civil War Era.* New York: Oxford University Press, 1988.

Robertson, James I., Jr. *Stonewall Jackson: The Man, the Soldier, the Legend.* New York: Macmillan, 1997.

## Battle of Hampton Roads

| Date | March 8–9, 1862 | |
|---|---|---|
| Location | Hampton Roads, Virginia | |
| Opponents (*winner) | *United States | Confederacy |
| Commander | Lieutenant John Worden | Flag Officer Franklin Buchanan; Lieutenant Catesby ap Roger Jones |
| # of Ships | Union squadron of 5 wooden warships and the ironclad *Monitor* (total 204 guns) | Confederate ironclad *Virginia* and 3 small wooden gunboats and 2 wooden tenders of the James River Squadron (total 35 guns) |
| Importance | Although the battle is a draw (both sides claim victory), it enables the Union Peninsula Campaign to go forward. | |

Following the Union defeat in the First Battle of Bull Run (July 21, 1861), Major General George B. McClellan assumed command of Union forces. McClellan thought that he had a better way to get to Richmond. He would take advantage of Union control of the sea to bring troops south by water and attack Richmond from the east up the peninsula formed by the York and James Rivers. Thus, the Peninsula Campaign (March–August 1862) set up a naval confrontation.

The Union transports at Hampton Roads, Virginia, however, were now threatened with destruction by the Confederate ironclad *Virginia.* This ship was the rebuilt U.S. Navy steam frigate *Merrimac,* scuttled by Union forces withdrawing from the Norfolk Navy Yard but raised and rebuilt by the Confederates as an ironclad ram. Flag Officer Franklin Buchanan, commander of the James River Squadron, took command. The *Virginia* mounted 10 guns: 6 9-inch Dahlgren smoothbores in broadsides plus 2 6.4-inch and 2 7-inch Brooke rifles at bow and stern.

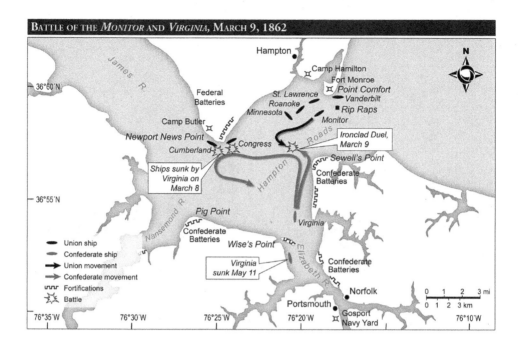

On March 8, 1862, the *Virginia* sortied from Norfolk on its maiden voyage. Most in the crew thought that it was a shakedown run, but Buchanan was determined to attack the Union warships protecting the transports. He ordered a course set for the Union warships and employed his ship's ram to sink the sailing sloop *Cumberland* (24 guns). He then attacked and burned the frigate *Congress* (50 guns). While maneuvering to escape, the frigate *Minnesota* (40 guns), the Union flagship, ran aground. With its pilots uncertain of the shoal water and with Buchanan having been wounded in an exchange of fire with Union troops ashore, the *Virginia* retired at dusk. Its crew was confident that they would complete their work of destruction the next day.

As the Confederates departed, the Union ironclad *Monitor* put into the roads. Commanded by Lieutenant John Worden, this revolutionary warship was far more maneuverable than the *Virginia* but only a fraction of its size. The *Monitor* mounted only two guns, both 11-inch Dahlgrens. Hastily completed, it had nearly sunk the day before while under tow south, and there were serious doubts that it would prove to be a worthy opponent for the *Virginia*.

The next morning, March 9, the *Virginia*, now commanded by Lieutenant Catesby ap Roger Jones in place of the wounded Buchanan, steamed out to attack the *Minnesota*. The *Monitor* then appeared in front of the grounded Union flagship. The battle occurred from about 8:00 a.m. until noon and was fought at very close range, with both warships constantly in motion. The *Virginia* rammed the more nimble *Monitor*, but since the Confederate ironclad had lost its ram in the *Cumberland* the day before, this did little damage. The *Monitor*'s gunners meanwhile tried to cripple their antagonist's vulnerable propeller and rudder.

Currier & Ives lithograph of the Battle of Hampton Roads on March 9, 1862, between the USS *Monitor* and the CSS *Virginia*. The battle marked the beginning of a new era in naval warfare. (Library of Congress)

The *Monitor*'s guns could fire only once every seven or eight minutes, but its rotating turret meant that the guns were a target only when they were about to fire. Almost all of the *Monitor*'s shots registered, and the *Virginia* sustained damage. Although the *Virginia* fired more shots, most went high and had little effect. Worden was temporarily blinded by the direct hit of a shell that struck the pilothouse, however. In the resultant confusion the *Monitor* drifted away from the battle, and when the ship's new commander, Lieutenant Samuel Greene, brought it back into position, he saw the *Virginia* departing. Jones interpreted the *Monitor*'s actions as meaning that the Confederates had won, and with his own ship having sustained damage, he returned to Norfolk for repairs.

Tactically the Battle of Hampton Roads was a draw, but the *Virginia* had been hit 50 times and was leaking. The *Monitor* had sustained only 21 hits and was virtually undamaged. The battle between the two ironclads was not renewed, but in merely surviving the *Monitor* ensured the safety of the Union transports and supply ships and thus McClellan's entire operation. The engagement also led to so-called Monitor Mania in the North. Of 56 ironclads laid down by the North during the war, 52 of these were of the *Monitor* or turreted type. In effect, the battle marked a new era in naval warfare. The battle also sparked a frantic effort by both sides to manufacture larger-caliber guns capable of penetrating the new iron armor.

Spencer C. Tucker

**Further Reading**

DeKay, James Tertius. *Monitor.* New York: Walker, 1997.

Holzer, Harold, and Tim Mulligan. *The Battle of Hampton Roads: New Perspectives on the* USS Monitor *and CSS* Virginia. New York: Fordham University Press, 2006.

Smith, Gene A. *Iron and Heavy Guns: Duel between the* Monitor *and* Merrimac. Abilene, TX: McWhiney Foundation Press, 1998.

## Jackson's Shenandoah Valley Campaign

| | | |
|---|---|---|
| **Date** | March 23–June 9, 1862 | |
| **Location** | Shenandoah Valley of Virginia | |
| **Opponents (*winner)** | *Confederacy | United States |
| **Commander** | Major General Thomas J. "Stonewall" Jackson | Major General Irvin McDowell; Major General Nathaniel P. Banks; Brigadier General James Shields; Major General John C. Frémont |
| **Approx. # Troops** | Never more than 18,000 men | 52,000 men |
| **Importance** | Jackson's successes cause President Abraham Lincoln to withhold McDowell's corps from joining the Army of the Potomac against Richmond. | |

In March 1862, Union forces led by Major General George McClellan launched a powerful effort to seize the Confederate capital of Richmond. Steamships transported more than 100,000 men of the Army of the Potomac to Fort Monroe, Virginia, after which on April 4 the Union troops began an advance up the peninsula formed by the York and James Rivers. Concerned that Confederate forces in the Shenandoah Valley under Major General Thomas J. "Stonewall" Jackson would take advantage of the absence of McClellan's army and drive on Washington, President Abraham Lincoln insisted on withholding Major General Irvin McDowell's powerful I Corps of some 40,000 men at Fredericksburg. Originally scheduled to proceed overland and join McClellan at Richmond, I Corps would be withheld until Union troops under Major General Nathaniel P. Banks could clear the valley. Banks would then cover Washington, permitting McDowell to link up with McClellan to take Richmond.

Well aware that General Joseph E. Johnston had only 60,000 men available to protect Richmond, General Robert E. Lee, military adviser to Confederate president Jefferson Davis, recommended that Jackson be reinforced and ordered to demonstrate in the Shenandoah Valley to draw the largest number of possible Union reinforcements from McClellan. Davis concurred.

In early 1862 Jackson's command numbered only about 4,000 men. Arrayed against them were some 15,000 Union troops under Major General John C. Frémont to the west, 10,000 soldiers under Banks to the north, and McDowell's 40,000 men to the east.

On February 27, 1862, McClellan ordered Banks to cross the Potomac at Harpers Ferry with his corps and move against Jackson, who evacuated Winchester on March 11 and withdrew to the vicinity of Mount Jackson. Lincoln insisted that Washington be covered, and upon McClellan's order, Banks left a division under Brigadier General James Shields to push south against Jackson while Banks moved east to Manassas with the remainder of his men to cover the approach to Washington and release McDowell.

Jackson marched 41 miles in only two days with some 4,500 men and attacked Shields, with 9,000 men, at Kernstown on March 23. Colonel Nathan Kamball of Shields's command fed more men into the battle and fought the Confederates to a draw. Brigadier General Richard B. Garnett's Stonewall Brigade ran out of ammunition and withdrew without orders, opening a gap in the Confederate line into which the Federals rushed, forcing Jackson to withdraw in confusion. In Jackson's only defeat of the campaign, the Confederates suffered 718 casualties compared to only 590 for the Union.

Shields, however, reported that Jackson must have been reinforced, and this led Lincoln to order Banks to return to the valley and to keep McDowell's corps near Fredericksburg. Thus Kernstown, a tactical defeat for Jackson, served the larger Confederate strategic purpose of denying McClellan the services of 40,000 men.

Concerned about Jackson's Shenandoah Valley activities, Lincoln inserted himself into northern Virginia operations and ordered the separate commands there to move against Jackson. There was, however, no one overall Union commander in the valley, a fatal flaw.

Banks was moving slowly south up the valley with some 15,000 men, while Frémont with another 20,000 men moved on Staunton from the west. Leaving 8,000 men under Brigadier General Richard S. Ewell to contain Banks, on April 30 Jackson marched rapidly westward with some 10,000 men to engage Frémont. On May 6 Jackson arrived at Staunton with his so-called foot cavalry, having covered 92 miles on foot and another 25 miles by train. Pushing west, late on the afternoon of May 7 Jackson's leading elements under Brigadier General Edward "Allegheny" Johnson encountered Brigadier General Robert H. Milroy's brigade at the front of Frémont's army. Milroy's men withdrew as Brigadier General Robert C. Schneck rushed to his support. Schneck, who was senior, assumed command and deployed his 6,000 troops around McDowell. The Confederates occupied the nearby key terrain feature of Stilington's Hill.

On May 8, Schneck attacked. In the four-hour Battle of McDowell (also known as the Battle of Stilington's Hill), 2,800 Confederates turned back all assaults by 2,300 Union troops. That night Schneck withdrew into the Alleghenies. In the battle, the Confederates lost 45 killed and 423 wounded; Union losses were 26 killed, 227 wounded, and 3 missing.

After a brief respite, Jackson moved down the valley to confront Banks. Moving north in the Luray Valley, Jackson used as a screen the 50-mile-long Massanutten Mountain that bisects the Shenandoah and Luray Valleys. Heading west through the mountain's single pass at New Market on May 21, he again turned north. On May 23, with his movements effectively screened by Colonel Turner Ashby's cavalry, Jackson attacked Union forces at Front Royal commanded by Colonel John R. Kenly.

In the Battle of Front Royal, the Confederates had about 3,000 men engaged; the Union had only 1,063 men. Forced back through the town, Kenly withdrew to Cedarville, where the Confederates broke through the Union lines and forced a surrender. In the fighting the Confederates suffered only some 50 casualties; Union losses were 904: 32 killed, 122 wounded, and 750 taken prisoner. Banks then withdrew the rest of his force rapidly toward Winchester, with Jackson in pursuit. Lincoln, alarmed by developments, again halted McDowell from moving south against Richmond.

As Banks attempted to reorganize his force in defensive positions to hold Winchester, Jackson and Ewell drove on Winchester, with Ewell coming in from the southeast. The First Battle of Winchester (May 25) pitted some 16,000 Confederates against 6,500 Union troops. Banks chose to fight here in order to give his supply train of 550 wagons a chance to reach Williamsport, but poor Union dispositions allowed the Confederates to flank the Union position. The Union troops panicked and fled through Winchester and across the Potomac River 35 miles to the north, abandoning thousands of weapons and considerable supplies. Jackson's men were too exhausted to pursue much beyond Winchester. During the three-day flight from Front Royal to Winchester, Confederate losses were 400 killed or wounded; Union losses totaled 3,500 men, half of the force, with 3,000 of these prisoners. The Confederates also secured 9,000 small arms, 2 cannon, and large quantities of supplies and much-needed medicines.

This First Battle of Winchester and Jackson's subsequent occupation of Harpers Ferry spread panic in Washington and fanned fears of a descent on the federal capital by Jackson. Lincoln again halted McDowell, who was about to move south to join McClellan, and ordered him to send 20,000 men (10,000 men under Shields trailed by an equal force under Major General Edward O. C. Ord) to Front Royal and ordered Frémont to move east to Harrisonburg. If these two forces met at Strasburg, they could cut off Jackson's escape route south.

Moving swiftly, Jackson avoided the Union trap, withdrawing his 15,000 men along with his prisoners and captured supplies. Clearing Winchester on May 31, he passed through Strasburg and reached Harrisonburg on June 5. Jackson left Ewell to hold Union troops under Frémont at Cross Keys, while Jackson and the rest of his command moved to Port Republic to meet the Union forces under Shields.

In the Battle of Cross Keys (June 8), Ewell's 5,000 men repulsed Frémont's attack, and that night most of Ewell's men marched to Port Republic. The remaining troops followed the next day.

On June 9 Jackson was at Port Republic, east of the South Fork of the Shenandoah River. Shields sent two brigades forward to probe the Confederate position and appealed to Frémont to join him as soon as possible. Jackson ordered an attack, which was repulsed with heavy casualties. He then sent Brigadier General

Richard Taylor's brigade through woods, turning the Union left and forcing a withdrawal. Jackson, with about 6,000 men, had defeated 3,500 Union troops. The Union side suffered 1,008 casualties, including 558 taken prisoner; Confederate losses were also heavy at 816. Ewell's men, meanwhile, burned the North River Bridge behind them, and Frémont, arriving too late to assist at Port Republic, was reduced to watching events across the rain-swollen river.

Port Republic was the final victory in Jackson's remarkable Shenandoah Valley Campaign. During a span of 48 days with never more than 18,000 men, Jackson's command marched 646 miles and defeated three Union armies totaling four times his own strength in four pitched battles, six large skirmishes, and numerous minor actions. Jackson had inflicted some 8,000 Union casualties to fewer than 2,500 losses of his own. He then slipped out of the valley to join Lee on the Virginia Peninsula for the critical battles to save Richmond.

Jackson's Shenandoah Valley Campaign is considered one of the most brilliant operations in military history and raised Jackson to hero status in the Confederacy. More important than his own victories, however, was the impact of his campaign on the far more important Peninsula Campaign to the west.

James Brian McNabb and Spencer C. Tucker

## Further Reading

Cozzens, Peter. *Shenandoah 1862: Stonewall Jackson's Valley Campaign.* Chapel Hill: University of North Carolina Press, 2008.

Gallagher, Gary W., ed. *The Shenandoah Valley Campaign of 1862.* Chapel Hill: University of North Carolina Press, 2003.

Krick, Robert K. *Conquering the Valley: Stonewall Jackson at Port Republic.* New York: William Morrow, 1996.

Robertson, James I., Jr. *Stonewall Jackson: The Man, the Soldier, the Legend.* New York: Macmillan, 1997.

## Battle of Shiloh

| Date | April 6–7, 1862 | |
|---|---|---|
| Location | Hardin County, Tennessee, on the Tennessee River | |
| Opponents (*winner) | *United States | Confederacy |
| Commander | Major General Ulysses S. Grant; Major General Don Carlos Buell | General Albert Sidney Johnston; General Pierre G. T. Beauregard |
| Approx. # Troops | Army of the Tennessee (39,000 men); Army of the Ohio (36,000 men) | Army of Mississippi (44,000 men) |
| Importance | The first great meat-grinder battle of the war, it opens the way for Union forces to advance into northern Mississippi, presaging the Confederate defeat in the western theater. | |

Fought on April 6–7, 1862, on the west bank of the Tennessee River just north of the Mississippi state line, the Battle of Shiloh was, up to that time, the bloodiest battle of American history. (Library of Congress)

By April 1862, Union forces had driven the Confederates from Kentucky and Tennessee; had opened the Tennessee River to Florence, Alabama; and were preparing a conquest of the Mississippi. Stung by defeats at Fort Henry (February 6, 1862) and Fort Donelson (February 13–16) and the loss of Nashville (February 25), commander of Confederate Department No. 2 General Albert Sidney Johnston was determined to engage and defeat the Federals. He called up reinforcements and ordered a concentration at Corinth, Mississippi.

The strategy promulgated by Major General Henry Halleck, commander of the Union Department of the Mississippi, was to send forces down the Mississippi but also sever Confederate railroad lines across the region and take the town of Corinth, a key railhead. Halleck ordered Major General Ulysses S. Grant and his Army of West Tennessee (soon to be renamed the Army of the Tennessee) to link up with Major General John Carlos Buell's Army of the Ohio, which was marching from Nashville. The two would then operate together in a joint offensive against Corinth. Seizing the town would cut two important Confederate railroads: the west-east Memphis & Charleston Railroad, connecting the Mississippi, Memphis, and Richmond, and the north-south Mobile & Ohio Railroad.

Grant's six divisions of nearly 39,000 men arrived at Pittsburg Landing on the banks of the Tennessee River, some 23 miles north of Corinth. Grant pushed his men two miles inland on the west bank of the river, where they set up camp and waited for Buell's 36,000 men, delayed by heavy rains. Grant's troops were loosely arrayed near a small Methodist church named Shiloh (Hebrew for "place of peace"), which gave name to the ensuing battle.

Grant, however, had neglected to send any reconnaissance parties to ascertain Confederate strength. More preoccupied with his own offensive plans, he largely ignored defensive arrangements. By early April, Grant's men were scattered throughout the area, with no attempt having been made to form any sort of battle line or even throw up rudimentary earthworks.

The Confederates were not quiescent, however. Johnston was well aware of both Grant's arrival at Pittsburg Landing and probable Union intentions and was determined to strike Grant and destroy his army before Buell could arrive. Johnston organized his army into four corps under Major Generals Leonidas Polk, Braxton Bragg, and William J. Hardee, and Brigadier General John C. Breckinridge. On April 3, Johnston set out with 44,000 men from Corinth for Pittsburg Landing; however, rains turned the roads into quagmires, making progress slow and difficult. On April 5 Johnston's men were a scant four miles southwest of Shiloh, although their arrival went unnoticed by Union forces.

On April 6 at about 5:00 a.m., Johnston's men clashed with Union pickets and then struck the awakening Union army in full force, nearly overwhelming the unprepared Federals. The Confederate troops first hit Brigadier General William Tecumseh Sherman's division. Ill-prepared, it fell back. The Confederates then attacked the divisions commanded by Brigadier General Benjamin M. Prentiss and Major General John A. McClernand. Their troops, plus those of Sherman's reformed division, then confronted the Confederates during the next three hours in costly fighting that slowed the Southern assault. Superior numbers finally told, however, and the Confederate overran the Union defenders.

The Confederates were hindered not only by the stubborn Union defense but by ill-trained troops who stopped to loot the abandoned Union camps. A faulty battle plan also contributed, with the four corps becoming hopelessly tangled. The offensive ground to a halt as units became disorganized. Afforded time to redeploy, Grant, who was not on the field when the attack came, rushed to the landing from nearby Savannah, Tennessee, and began to organize a defensive position around the landing. He slowly re-formed a solid defensive front centered on a sunken road held by Prentiss's men. Grant ordered it held at all costs. The Confederates described the bitter fighting there as the Hornets' Nest.

The Southerners, meanwhile, had lost their commander. At about 2:00 p.m. while directing an attack on the Union lines, Johnston was struck in the leg by a bullet that severed an artery. He bled to death on the field. General P. G. T. Beauregard then assumed command of the Southern forces. Fighting raged across the field. The Confederates massed 62 guns and finally blasted Prentiss into submission. He and some 2,000 defenders of the Hornets' Nest surrendered at around 5:30. By the evening of April 6, although Union forces had been driven from their camp, they had developed a strong defensive position around Pittsburg Landing, backed by well-placed artillery and protected on their flanks by ravines and by the heavy guns of two gunboats in the river to their rear. That evening in a controversial decision, Beauregard suspended the Confederate attack, expecting to complete the destruction of the Union army in the morning.

During the night, however, lead elements of Buell's army and Major General Lew Wallace's division arrived and were immediately hurried into the line. On April 7 to Beauregard's surprise, Grant struck first. At about 7:30 a.m., Federal forces began steadily pushing the Confederates back. The fighting that day was as bloody as the combat of the previous day. Late that afternoon, Beauregard pulled his battered and exhausted army back to Corinth. The Union army did not pursue.

The Battle of Shiloh was over. The first great meat-grinder battle of the war, it had cost the Union 13,038 casualties (1,745 killed, 8,408 wounded, and 2,885 captured). The Confederates lost 10,694 (1,723 killed, 8,012 wounded, and 959 missing or captured). The grisly total of 23,732 causalities from this single battle was more than the United States had suffered in all of its previous wars combined. The carnage shocked Americans, North and South.

The Union victory at Shiloh was of tremendous consequence in the war. Although criticized for his lack of preparation, Grant had survived and proven himself to be an aggressive commander. Although temporarily demoted by Halleck afterward, Grant withstood calls for his head and was sustained by President Abraham Lincoln, who famously stated that "I can't spare this man. He fights." The battle ultimately doomed the Confederate cause in the West. After a tortoise-like advance and siege directed by Halleck, the Confederates abandoned Corinth in June.

Rick Dyson

### Further Reading

Daniel, Larry J. *Shiloh: The Battle That Changed the Civil War.* New York: Simon and Schuster, 1997.

Roland, Charles Pierce. *Albert Sidney Johnston: Soldier of Three Republics.* Austin: University of Texas Press, 1964.

Smith, Timothy B. *The Untold Story of Shiloh: The Battle and the Battlefield.* Knoxville: University of Tennessee Press, 2006.

## Seven Days' Campaign

| Date | June 25–July 1, 1862 | |
|---|---|---|
| Location | West of Mechanicsville near Richmond, Virginia | |
| Opponents (*winner) | *Confederacy | United States |
| Commander | General Robert E. Lee | Major General George B. McClellan |
| Approx. # Troops | 97,000 men | 104,000 men |
| Casualties | 20,204 (3,494 killed, 15,758 wounded, and 952 missing/captured) | 15,855 (1,734 killed, 8,066 wounded, 6,055 missing/captured) |
| Importance | The battle reverses the momentum of the war, causing McClellan to break off the Peninsula Campaign and end the Union threat to Richmond. | |

In the early spring of 1862, Union general in chief Major General George B. McClellan had begun his campaign up the Virginia Peninsula formed by the York and James Rivers westward toward the Confederate capital of Richmond, where he was to be joined in the final assault by a Union corps under Major General Irwin McDowell, held back at the insistence of President Abraham Lincoln to protect Washington. McClellan's campaign suffered from constant delays, and he became known as the "Virginia Creeper" for his glacial advance. He was hoodwinked and delayed in a siege of Yorktown (April 5–May 3), and his advance was blunted at Williamsburg (May 5), but by mid-May the Union army seemed poised to close in on the Confederate capital.

Meanwhile, General Robert E. Lee, then military adviser to Confederate president Jefferson Davis, supervised construction of impressive field fortifications to protect Richmond's eastern flank. McClellan brought up heavy artillery and fortified his positions east of the city, hoping to shell Richmond and its defenders into submission. General Joseph E. Johnston, commanding Confederate forces outside of Richmond, chose to strike at one isolated section of the Union army and destroy it before reinforcements could arrive and McClellan's artillery could be put in place. The resulting engagement at Seven Pines (May 31–June 1) was a confused, poorly managed battle with no clear victor. Johnston was severely wounded during the battle.

The carnage seemed to unnerve McClellan, however, and reinforced his overly cautious nature. He also dithered, waiting for McDowell's corps to be released, but Lincoln held it back in light of Major General Thomas J. "Stonewall" Jackson's brilliant Shenandoah Valley Campaign. On June 1 Davis named Lee to assume command from the wounded Johnston, and Lee decided to strike with full force with the aim of not just driving the Union army away but also destroying it. Recalling Jackson from the Shenandoah Valley, Lee prepared to move with 97,000 men against McClellan, with 103,000 men.

On June 25 McClellan advanced with Major General Joseph Hooker's division of III Corps south of the Chickahominy River in an attempt to seize a position from which to bombard Richmond. In the ensuing Battle of Oak Grove, the Confederate division of Major General Benjamin Huger gave ground grudgingly, with McClellan gaining very little in the day's action. Lee meanwhile massed most of his army north of the river for an attack on Brigadier General Fitz John Porter's isolated V Corps.

Lee's first attack came on June 26 at Mechanicsville, or Beaver Dam Creek. The Union army was divided by the Chickahominy River and was vulnerable. This began a solid week of relentless combat, and neither army had experienced anything like it. Leaving only a small force to defend the direct routes to Richmond, Lee struck McClellan's army with overwhelming force. The Confederates took heavy casualties, attacking across swampy ground, but the Union defenders pulled back the next day.

The next day, June 27, an even bigger battle occurred at Gaines' Mill, where Union defenders took advantage of high ground overlooking Boatswain's Swamp. Again the Confederates attacked and endured heavy losses. They finally reached the hill's crest, broke through at sunset, and won a pyrrhic victory. That night V Corps withdrew across the Chickahominy to join the rest of McClellan's army.

This sudden and relentless onslaught by Lee further unnerved McClellan, and he shifted from an offensive stance to one that would simply save his army from destruction. McClellan decided to pull his scattered army back and move to the James, where the Union Navy could supply him and provide fire support from its warships.

The next battle was fought on June 29 at Savage's Station, as Lee's army now crossed to the south side of the Chickahominy. It was another day of Confederate attacks and Union retreat but ended inconclusively. McClellan continued his withdrawal. The best chance for Lee to defeat McClellan's army was at White Oak Swamp and Glendale, on June 30. In savage fighting, the Confederates came close to breaking the Union lines, but the defenders held on, bringing reinforcements into the fight that lasted into the night. The engagement ended with no clear victor.

The final battle of the campaign occurred on July 1 at Malvern Hill. There Union artillery occupied the high ground, supported by several corps of infantry. Again, poor coordination doomed the Confederates as they mounted several attacks over open ground and took frightening losses, giving McClellan's forces a victory.

Following that engagement, McClellan pulled back to prepared positions at Harrison's Landing on the James River. Total losses for the Seven Days' Campaign were 15,855 for the Union (1,734 killed, 8,066 wounded, and 6,055 missing or captured) and 20,204 for the Confederates (3,494 killed, 15,758 wounded, and 952 missing or captured).

The Seven Days' Campaign is frequently neglected in Civil War scholarship, but it was important for many reasons. The campaign reversed the momentum of the war, doomed McClellan's Peninsula Campaign, and saved Richmond from a Union occupation. Indeed, within a few months, Lee had taken the war into the North with an invasion of Maryland. Although the Confederate victory had come at a high cost, the campaign showcased Lee's considerable abilities and his penchant for aggressiveness and risk taking. The campaign also saw the emergence of the Army of Northern Virginia as a formidable offensive fighting force. McClellan, on the other hand, continued to cause controversy, blaming others—including the Lincoln administration—for his woes and repeatedly requesting more men. McClellan's performance in the Seven Days' Campaign contributed to Lincoln's decision to replace him.

Robert M. Dunkerly

## Further Reading

Burton, Brian. *Extraordinary Circumstances: The Seven Days Battles.* Bloomington: Indiana University Press, 2001.

Sears, Stephen W. *To the Gates of Richmond.* New York: Ticknor and Fields, 1992.

Wheeler, Richard. *Sword over Richmond.* New York: Harper and Row, 1986.

## Battle of Antietam

| | | |
|---|---|---|
| **Date** | September 17, 1862 | |
| **Location** | Near Sharpsburg, Maryland | |
| **Opponents (*winner)** | *United States | Confederacy |
| **Commander** | Major General George B. McClellan | General Robert E. Lee |
| **Approx. # Troops** | 87,000 men | 41,000 men |
| **Importance** | Lee's invasion of the North is halted, and the Union victory helps ensure that Republicans retain control in the U.S. House of Representatives. President Abraham Lincoln uses the Union victory to announce the Preliminary Emancipation Proclamation. | |

On September 4, General Robert E. Lee and his Army of Northern Virginia began an invasion of the North. Lee hoped to cut key rail lines west and isolate the federal capital of Washington, D.C., with Harrisburg, Pennsylvania, as his probable objective. Southern leaders believed that a significant land victory might bring British and French diplomatic recognition of the Confederacy.

Lee's army crossed the Potomac River and moved east of the Blue Ridge Mountains. Arriving at Frederick, Maryland, on September 7, Lee divided his army into five separate parts, three of which were to converge on and take the major Union arsenal at Harpers Ferry. Overestimating Lee's strength, Major General George B. McClellan, reinstated by President Abraham Lincoln as commander of the Union Army of the Potomac, proceeded with his customary caution; in reality, his forces outnumbered Lee's two to one.

McClellan also fumbled away an incredible intelligence advantage. Near Frederick, some of his soldiers discovered a copy of Lee's orders wrapped around three cigars; the orders were verified by a Union officer who identified the handwriting of Lee's adjutant. McClellan now knew the entire disposition of Lee's forces. Despite this, McClellan moved with the same glacial speed that had earned him the nickname "Virginia Creeper" during the Peninsula Campaign. He delayed a full 18 hours before putting his army in motion and pushing through the Blue Ridge passes. On September 14 in small but intense engagements in the Battles of South Mountain and Crampton's Gap, Confederate forces held off the Union advance.

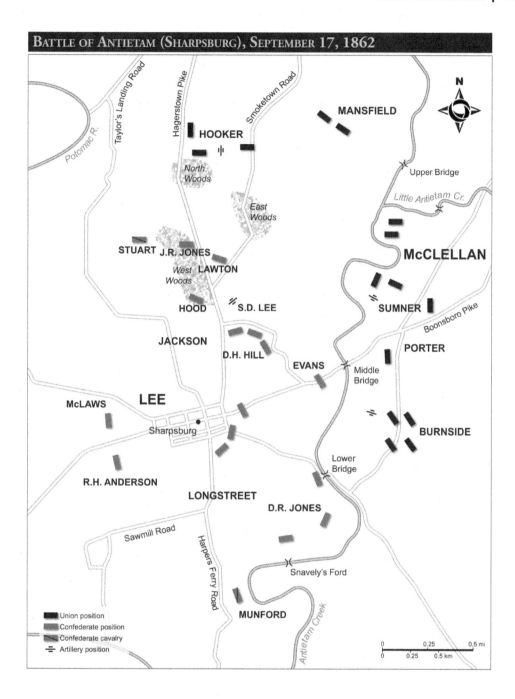

BATTLE OF ANTIETAM (SHARPSBURG), SEPTEMBER 17, 1862

Lee's army was then split in three main bodies spread out over 20 miles. Although initially inclined to retreat on learning of McClellan's moves, Lee decided to stand and fight. Lee ordered his remaining forces to join him as soon as possible and positioned his three available divisions along a low ridge extending about 4 miles north to south, just east of Sharpsburg and west of Antietam Creek. Hilly

Aftermath of the Battle of Antietem of September 17, 1862: Confederate dead along Hagerstown Road, Maryland. (Library of Congress)

terrain enabled Lee to mask his inferior resources. The resultant battle was fragmented, in large part because of the terrain.

On the afternoon of September 15, the major part of the Army of the Potomac was within easy striking distance of Lee, who had only 18,000 men available. Had McClellan attacked then, Lee would have been routed. But Lee predicted that his adversary would not move that day or the next. Indeed, McClellan wanted first to rest his troops and then spent the entire day of September 16 placing his artillery and infantry and inspecting the line.

While McClellan dallied, Confederate major general Thomas J. "Stonewall" Jackson's corps arrived from Harpers Ferry, giving Lee 30,000 men and leaving absent only three of his nine divisions. Even with Jackson's corps, though, Lee would be outnumbered 41,000 to 87,000. McClellan said after the battle that he thought that Lee had 120,000 men. This is hard to believe, for McClellan planned a double envelopment to hit Lee's flank and then smash the Confederate center.

Lee was in position to observe and command throughout the battle. McClellan remained more than a mile to the rear, unable to observe the battle in progress and with little idea of what was going on. McClellan also failed to take advantage of his superior numbers. He withheld an entire corps (20,000 men failed to see battle) and employed a piecemeal rather than simultaneous form of attack. Each Union corps was committed by successive oral orders from headquarters, without informing the other corps commanders and without instructions for mutual support. This process was compounded as corps commanders sent their own divisions to the attack in piecemeal fashion. In sharp contrast, Lee gave great latitude to his subordinate commanders. McClellan also failed to employ his cavalry to cut Confederate lines of communication and prevent Confederate reinforcements from moving to the battlefield from the south. Even a delay of an hour or two might have changed the battle, because Lee's remaining divisions arrived on the battlefield at the critical juncture, about 10:30 a.m. on September 17, with the Union attack already in progress.

The Battle of Antietam opened early on the morning of September 17 with an attack by Major General Joseph Hooker's 12,000-man I Corps against the Confederate left, held by Jackson's corps. Hooker's men drove the Confederates back into the West Woods. Lee called up Brigadier General John Bell Hood's Texas Brigade, which repulsed the Union attack.

Amid the smoke and ground fog, the battle lines were only 50 or even 30 yards apart. Units were destroyed as soon as they began to fight. The 1st Texas Regiment of Hood's Brigade lost more than 82 percent of its men killed or wounded in 20 minutes, the highest loss percentage North or South of any regiment in the war. Successive Union attacks on the Confederate left by Major General Joseph Mansfield's XII Corps and Brigadier General Edwin Sumner's II Corps also met rebuff.

At the Confederate center, meanwhile, a crisis developed as some 3,000 Confederates under Major General Daniel H. Hill fought to hold the Sunken Road, which came to be known as "Bloody Lane." Union major general William B. Franklin's VI Corps mounted three separate assaults there, all of which failed. Then two Union regiments were able to enfilade the Confederate position on the Sunken Road, forcing the Confederates to fall back and opening a gap between the Confederate center and left. Confederate troops under Hill managed to plug the hole in time. Lee then ordered Jackson to counterattack the Union right, a move that was not successful. McClellan failed to take advantage of the situation and commit his reserves, however.

On the Union left, Major General Ambrose Burnside's IX Corps spent the morning trying to carry a bridge over Antietam Creek. Union forces finally crossed the creek via fords, but the Confederates withdrew to higher ground. By the time Burnside was ready to renew the attack, the last division of Lee's army, commanded by Major General Ambrose P. Hill, had arrived. Despite being exhausted from their forced march, they defeated the Union assault. The battle was over.

Union casualties totaled 12,401: 2,108 dead, 9,540 wounded, and 753 missing (15 percent). Confederate losses were 10,316: 1,546 dead, 7,752 wounded, and 1,018 missing (26 percent). The Battle of Antietam (Sharpsburg) was the bloodiest single day of fighting during the entire Civil War.

Lee waited a day and then pulled back into Virginia. McClellan failed to pursue. Lincoln was furious and soon removed McClellan from command. McClellan might have destroyed Lee on the September 17 or the day after, but in the words of one historian of the battle, he was "so fearful of losing that he would not risk winning."

The inconclusive Battle of Antietam nevertheless had important results. Lee's defeat weakened Confederate hopes of securing recognition from Britain and France. Never again was the Confederacy as close to winning recognition abroad. The battle also helped ensure that the Democrats did not win control of the U.S. House of Representatives in the November elections. A 1 percent shift in the vote would have brought Democratic control and trouble for Lincoln. The Union victory also allowed Lincoln the opportunity on September 22 to issue the Preliminary Emancipation Proclamation, which freed as of January 1, 1863, all slaves in areas still in rebellion against the United States. This document transformed a war to preserve the Union into a struggle for human freedom.

Spencer C. Tucker

## Further Reading

Gallagher, Gary W., ed. *Antietam: Essays on the 1862 Maryland Campaign.* Chapel Hill: University of North Carolina Press, 1999.

McPherson, James M. *Crossroads of Freedom: Antietam.* New York: Oxford University Press, 2002.

Murfin, James V. *The Gleam of Bayonets: The Battle of Antietam and Robert E. Lee's Maryland Campaign, September 1862.* Baton Rouge: Louisiana State University Press, 2004.

Priest, John M. *Antietam: The Soldier's Battle.* New York: Oxford University Press, 1994.

Sears, Stephen W. *Landscape Turned Red: The Battle of Antietam.* New York: Ticknor and Fields, 1983.

## Battle of Chancellorsville

| Date | May 1–4, 1863 | |
|---|---|---|
| Location | Spotsylvania County, Virginia | |
| Opponents (*winner) | *Confederacy | United States |
| Commander | General Robert E. Lee | Major General Joseph E. Hooker |
| Approx. # Troops | 61,000 men | 134,000 men |
| Importance | In his most masterful battle of the war, Lee gambles boldly and defeats a Union army more than twice the size of his army, preventing yet another Union descent on Richmond. | |

On December 13, 1862, at Fredericksburg, Virginia, on the Rappahannock River, Confederate commander of the Army of Northern Virginia General Robert E. Lee won his most one-sided victory of the war when Union major general Ambrose Burnside's Army of the Potomac had attacked Lee's prepared positions on Marye's Heights. Burnside's 113,000 Union troops had been shattered by 75,000 Confederates. Union losses were nearly 11,000 men against Confederate casualties of only 4,600. With morale in the Army of the Potomac at a nadir, on January 25, 1863,

A Union artillery battalion before the Battle of Chancellorsville (May 2–4, 1863). The battle was Confederate general Robert E. Lee's greatest triumph but it brought the mortal wounding of Lieutenant General Thomas J. "Stonewall" Jackson. (Library of Congress)

U.S. president Abraham Lincoln replaced Burnside with one of his most outspoken critics, Major General Joseph Hooker. The aggressive and boastful Hooker, who had long sought the position, retrained the army and built its esprit de corps.

Lee meanwhile kept his forces in position below the Rappahannock. With Lincoln urging an advance on Richmond, Hooker planned to cross the Rappahannock River to the west of Fredericksburg, assaulting Lee's left and rear at Chancellorsville. Hooker had 134,000 men, while Lee had fewer than 61,000. Hooker sought to utilize his superior numbers in a double envelopment, with the eastern pincer under Major General John Sedgwick to demonstrate against Lee at Fredericksburg.

Hooker began his march westward on April 27, and two days later the army was across the Rappahannock. On April 30 Hooker's troops entered the Wilderness, an area of thick woods and underbrush 10 miles west of Fredericksburg. By that evening, 75,000 Union troops occupied areas to Lee's rear, while Sedgwick with 40,000 men threatened the Confederates at Fredericksburg.

Then in the midst of this offensive, Hooker suddenly halted his advance to consolidate and see what Lee would do, thereby forfeiting the initiative. Hooker also erred in sending 10,000 Union cavalry under Major General George Stoneman in a wide sweep south below Fredericksburg to destroy Confederate supply depots. This uncovered the Union right wing and denied Hooker vital intelligence regarding Lee's intentions.

Lee responded with a daring maneuver. Learning from his cavalry commander, Major General J. E. B. Stuart, that Hooker's right flank was "in the air," Lee planned a double envelopment of a double envelopment. It was a military masterpiece in which a small force attempted to surround a much larger one. Lee with about 17,000 men would demonstrate in front of the Union line to hold Hooker in place, while in a daring gamble Lieutenant General Thomas J. "Stonewall" Jackson with 28,000 men would march around the Union right flank. Success rested on Hooker's failure to exploit the Confederate separation or determine Jackson's intentions.

Jackson set off on May 2, with the march taking most of the day. His force was detected disengaging, but this was taken to mean that Lee was about to withdraw. Hooker ordered Union major general Daniel Sickles, commander of III Corps, to attack. His halfhearted advance further weakened the Union line, while Major General Oliver O. Howard, whose XI Corps occupied the far Union right flank, failed to make any defensive preparations, despite Hooker's instructions that he do so.

When Jackson's blow came at about 5:30 p.m., it was a complete surprise and enfiladed the Union line. Union troops reeled back in confusion. Darkness, increasing Union resistance, and the loss of Confederate unit cohesion in the woods all prevented a Union catastrophe, however. That evening Jackson was shot by his own men in front of his own lines while reconnoitering in the woods. On May 3 Stuart, replacing Jackson, resumed the Confederate attack, further constricting Hooker's lines.

Meanwhile, a second part to the battle, sometimes known as the Second Battle of Fredericksburg, was unfolding. On the night of May 2, Hooker ordered Sedgwick to attack. Sedgwick, despite having four times Major General Jubal A. Early's 10,000 men, believed that he was outnumbered and had not moved from the Fredericksburg heights. On May 3, however, Sedgwick advanced with 25,000 men from Fredericksburg, broke through Confederate positions, and advanced against Early at Salem Church.

Lee now feinted again. Leaving just a small force against Hooker, Lee turned east to deal with the new threat. Hooker's own force vastly outnumbered that of Lee but did not move. Sedgwick, surrounded on three sides and unaided, was forced to retire back across the Rappahannock during the night of May 4.

On May 5 Hooker withdrew his army back across the Rappahannock. The battle was over.

Although the Battle of Chancellorsville was Lee's military masterpiece, it also might have been the South's costliest victory. Union casualties were far higher than those for the Confederates: 17,197 to 13,303. However, the Union losses amounted to 13 percent of effectives, while the Confederate casualties amounted 21 percent of effectives and would be much more difficult for the Confederates to replace. Particularly grievous was the loss of Jackson. He died on May 10 of complications from his wound. The Army of Northern Virginia was never quite the same without him, and Lee sorely missed Jackson in the Battle of Gettysburg two months later.

Spencer C. Tucker

**Further Reading**

Furguson, Ernest B. *Chancellorsville, 1863: The Souls of the Brave*. New York: Knopf, 1992.

Sears, Stephen W. *Chancellorsville*. Boston: Houghton Mifflin, 1996.

Sutherland, Daniel E. *Fredericksburg & Chancellorsville: The Dare Mark Campaign*. Lincoln: University of Nebraska Press, 1998.

# Siege of Vicksburg

| Date | May 18–July 4, 1863 | |
|---|---|---|
| Location | Vicksburg, Mississippi | |
| Opponents (*winner) | *United States | Confederacy |
| Commander | Major General Ulysses S. Grant | Lieutenant General John C. Pemberton |
| Approx. # Troops | 77,000 men | 33,000 men |
| Importance | Effectively severs the Trans-Mississippi West theater from the remainder of the Confederacy and cements support in the Midwest for the Union cause. | |

The struggle for the city of Vicksburg on the Mississippi River was one of the most important battles of the American Civil War (1861–1865). Control of the Mississippi was vital for the Union. This would allow the North to cut off the Trans-Mississippi West from the rest of the Confederacy and bind the Midwest to the Union cause by securing the movement of its goods to the Gulf of Mexico. The Union assault against Confederate positions on the river began in early 1862. While Flag Officer Andrew Hull Foote's Western Flotilla moved down the Mississippi and tested its northern defenses, Flag Officer David G. Farragut's West Coast Gulf Blockading Squadron moved to take New Orleans and proceed upriver from there.

The northern Union flotilla worked in combination with Union Army forces ashore to capture a series of Confederate strongholds: Island No. 10 on April 8, Fort Pillow on June 4, and Memphis on June 6. On April 24 Farragut's ships ran past the Confederate forts at the river's mouth, and Union forces occupied New Orleans on May 1. The Union now controlled virtually the entire length of the Mississippi except for Vicksburg, Mississippi.

Vicksburg, located on a bend in the mighty river, was the key. Confederate lieutenant general John C. Pemberton commanded its defenses. Attempts at naval assault failed in May and June 1862, and in late summer and autumn the Confederates reinforced the city from the east and added a bastion downstream at Port Hudson, Louisiana, giving the South control of the intervening length of river.

In October 1862 Major General Ulysses S. Grant took command of the Army of the Tennessee. Operating from Memphis, he attempted but failed to take the city in

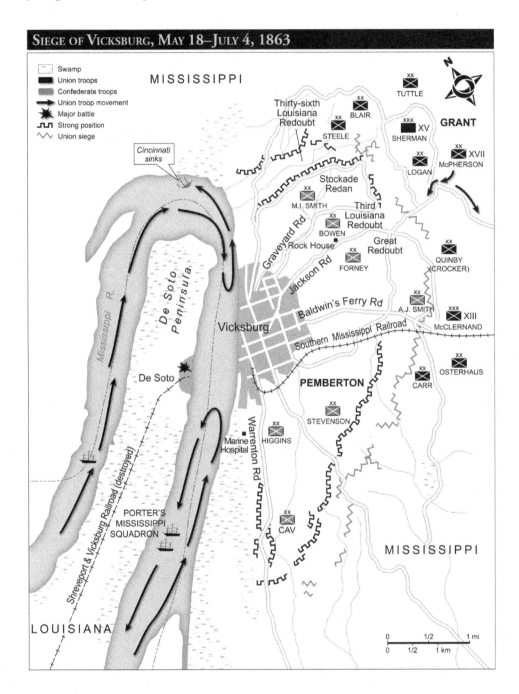

**SIEGE OF VICKSBURG, MAY 18–JULY 4, 1863**

the First Vicksburg Campaign (October 16–December 29, 1862). Vicksburg was strongly fortified and protected by the natural defenses of its high bluffs facing the river and swamps to the north. The city was most vulnerable from the south and east, but these were remote from Grant's supply base to the north at Memphis.

In January 1863 Grant encamped his Army of the Tennessee on the Louisiana side of the river, above Vicksburg, and began a series of unsuccessful efforts to get around the city, assisted by Rear Admiral David Dixon Porter's flotilla via various creeks and bayous.

Then on March 29, 1863, Grant cut loose from his base, crossed the Mississippi above Vicksburg, and marched down the Louisiana side of the river to a point south of the city where Porter's ships, which ran past the Vicksburg batteries on the night of April 16–17 during the Second Vicksburg Campaign (April 1–July 4, 1863), ferried him across the river on April 30. In effect, Grant planned to attack Vicksburg from the rear.

Defying instructions from Washington, Grant abandoned his base at Grand Gulf and marched northeast with 20,000 men, carrying supplies in wagons and partially living off the land. Grant believed that any delay would give the Confederates time to reinforce and fortify. He therefore employed a daring cavalry raid to keep Pemberton confused as to his movements. Grant quickly took Jackson, Mississippi, held by only 6,000 Confederates. The Union troops there destroyed everything of military value. Abandoned by Grant, the town was soon reinforced by the Confederates but was no longer available as a logistical center for Vicksburg to the west.

Confederate theater commander General Joseph E. Johnston ordered Pemberton to advance from Vicksburg and cut Grant's tenuous supply line. Grant learned of this plan through a spy and countered Pemberton's move. The two armies met at Champion's Hill on May 16. Grant commanded 32,000 men, and Pemberton commanded 25,000 men. Although the battle was hard fought, Grant was victorious. Union casualties amounted to some 2,500 men, while the Confederates sustained 4,000 losses. Pemberton was forced back into the Vicksburg perimeter. Johnston had warned Pemberton not to get shut up in Vicksburg and to abandon the city if necessary, but Pemberton thought that he knew better. On May 18, Union troops took up position facing the Confederate eastern defenses of Vicksburg.

Outnumbered at the outset of the campaign, Grant had marched 200 miles in less than three weeks, had won five battles, and had shut up the opposing army in a fortress. Grant then made two futile and poorly planned assaults against Vicksburg on May 19 and 22 before he settled down to a prolonged siege. Union siege guns as well as guns on the Union ships in the river kept the city and the Confederate lines under constant bombardment. At night, Union soldiers advanced their trenches ever closer to the Confederate lines. The strain on the inhabitants of Vicksburg was immense. Food was in short supply, and starvation soon set in, with people subsisting on whatever they could find. To escape the bombardment, they dug caves in the hard clay hillsides.

Two days' march to the east at Jackson, Johnston hovered with some 31,000 men raised specifically to lift the siege. Grant, reinforced, countered with a heavily manned line of eastward-facing defenses. Despite the urging of Confederate authorities, Johnston never attempted to test these or to relieve the garrison.

After six weeks, at 10:00 a.m. on July 4 Pemberton surrendered Vicksburg and 29,495 men. Union casualties of First and Second Vicksburg Campaigns amounted to around 9,000 men. Confederate casualties were 10,000, not counting prisoners.

Port Hudson, the remaining Confederate stronghold on the Mississippi, consequently surrendered on July 9. The entire Mississippi was under Union control, and the Confederacy was split north to south.

The capture of Vicksburg greatly benefitted the Union. Coming at the same time as the great Union victory at Gettysburg, the capture of Vicksburg lifted Northern morale and depressed morale in the South. The Trans-Mississippi West was cut off from the rest of the Confederacy. Midwestern farmers could now use the Mississippi for their goods, and this brought that region solidly behind the Union war effort.

Spencer C. Tucker

### Further Reading

Arnold, James R. *Grant Wins the War: Decision at Vicksburg.* New York: Wiley, 1997.

Ballard, Michael B. *Pemberton: A Biography.* Jackson: University Press of Mississippi, 1991.

Bearss, Edwin C. *The Vicksburg Campaign.* 3 vols. Dayton, OH: Morningside, 1995.

Winschel, Terrence J. *Vicksburg: Fall of the Confederate Gibraltar.* Abilene, TX: McWhiney Foundation Press, 1999.

Winschel, Terrence J., ed. *Triumph and Defeat: The Vicksburg Campaign.* Campbell, CA: Savas, 1998.

## Battle of Gettysburg

| Date | July 1–3, 1863 | |
|------|----------------|---|
| Location | Gettysburg, Pennsylvania | |
| Opponents (*winner) | *United States | Confederacy |
| Commander | Major General George Gordon Meade | General Robert E. Lee |
| Approx. # Troops | 94,000 men | 74,000 men |
| Importance | The battle represents the high-water mark for the Confederacy and tips the military and diplomatic scales decisively in the Union's favor. | |

Following his brilliant victory at Chancellorsville in May 1863, commander of the Confederate Army of Northern Virginia General Robert E. Lee fended off suggestions that part of his army be sent west to reinforce Vicksburg. Believing Vicksburg to be lost, Lee presented Confederate president Jefferson Davis with a plan to invade Pennsylvania. Far from an effort to take pressure off Vicksburg or to support a Southern peace offensive, it was instead a spoiling attack designed to delay an expected new offensive by Major General Joseph Hooker's Army of the Potomac and secure the rich resources of Pennsylvania. The Army of the Potomac had an edge in manpower of about 85,000–90,000 to 70,000 and in artillery pieces of 372 to 274, but these numbers were closer than they had been or would be again.

A wood engraving of a drawing by A. R. Waud in 1863 depicting Pickett's Charge against Union positions on Cemetery Ridge at Gettysburg, Pennsylvania, on July 3, 1863. The Battle of Gettysburg was a turning point in the Civil War. (Library of Congress)

On June 3, Lee's army began moving west from around Fredericksburg, Virginia. Hooker moved on a parallel route north of the Rappahannock River, keeping his own forces between Lee and Washington, D.C. Lee then headed north through the Shenandoah Valley, crossing the Potomac River through Maryland and into Pennsylvania. Lee planned to take Harrisburg and cut Union communications to the west. He would then be in position to threaten Baltimore and Washington and hoped thereby to force Hooker to attack him.

By the end of June, Lee's three corps, under Lieutenant Generals Richard Ewell, A. P. Hill, and James Longstreet, were widely scattered in southern Pennsylvania. Because there had been no word from his cavalry commander, Major General J. E. B. Stuart, who was to screen the Confederate right flank in the march north, Lee assumed that the Union army was not a threat. But Stuart had become separated from the main Confederate force and circled behind the Union troops moving north. On the evening of June 28 with his own forces dangerously dispersed, Lee learned that Hooker's army was massing near Frederick, Maryland. Union forces were closer to portions of Lee's army than these were to each other. If Lee did not concentrate at once, he ran the risk of having his army destroyed in detail.

The Confederates assembled at Gettysburg, a little town of 2,400 people but a major road hub. The Army of Northern Virginia came in from the northwest, and the Army of the Potomac came in from the south. As of June 28, the Union forces had a new commander, Major General George Gordon Meade. Hooker had hesitated at Chancellorsville in early May, allowing Lee, with half his own numbers, to win. Lincoln and his advisers doubted that Hooker could stand up to Lee. Meade, one of Hooker's corps commanders, was regarded as stolid and unflappable.

Preliminary contact between the two forces occurred near Gettysburg on June 29. Union cavalry under Brigadier General John Buford entered Gettysburg and sighted A. P. Hill's Confederate infantry west of the town. Buford sent word to Major General Joseph Reynolds, commander of the Union I Corps, and attempted to hold Gettysburg as both sides rushed resources forward.

The Battle of Gettysburg lasted three days. The first day, July 1, was a Confederate victory. Reynolds reached the town in midmorning and moved his infantry forward to replace Buford's cavalry but was killed while placing his units. In early afternoon Major General Oliver O. Howard's Union XI Corps reached the field, but in the fierce fighting that followed, the Confederates drove the Union troops back through Gettysburg into strong positions on Cemetery Hill and Culp's Hill.

The first day's battle had been costly for the Union; two-thirds of the 18,000 Federals engaged were casualties. Reynolds and Buford had purchased sufficient time, however, for the resultant Union defensive line, which came to be known from its shape as the Fishhook, was Meade's greatest single advantage in the battle. The Fishhook was anchored on the right by Culp's Hill and then ran westward to Cemetery Hill and south along Cemetery Ridge to Little Round Top and Big Round Top. Union cavalry screened the flanks. The Confederates, meanwhile, occupied Seminary Ridge, a long partially wooded rise to the west that paralleled Cemetery Ridge.

The second day of battle, July 2, revealed the advantage of the Fishhook, as Meade, operating from interior lines, could more easily shift troops and supplies than could Lee. Longstreet, commanding I Corps, urged Lee to secure the Round Tops at the south of the Union defensive line and then swing around behind the Union forces, threatening Baltimore and Washington to draw Meade from his defensive positions. Lee, however, decided on a two-pronged attack on the Union flanks.

These attacks were not simultaneous, though, enabling Meade to contain both. Longstreet's march to avoid Union observation posts took much of the afternoon. Nonetheless, his two-division attack against Major General Daniel Sickles's III Corps on the Union left was successful. Sickles had abandoned Cemetery Ridge and moved in advance of the rest of the Union line, forming a salient where he was completely unsupported. Locations here became famous from the fighting: the Peach Orchard, the Wheatfield, and Devil's Den. Meade shifted forces south, and although Sickles's men were driven back to Cemetery Ridge, they held there. The Confederates also failed to take Little Round Top, thanks to Colonel Joshua Chamberlain's badly outnumbered 20th Maine Regiment, which arrived there just in time. Had the Confederates been successful here, Longstreet could have enfiladed the entire Union line.

The fighting then shifted to the Union center. Although Hill attacked with insufficient numbers, one Confederate brigade briefly secured a foothold on Cemetery Ridge. To the north at twilight, two Confederate brigades were pushed back from

Cemetery Hill, and Ewell's attack on Culp's Hill was also rebuffed. The second day ended in a draw.

Although Longstreet expressed opposition, Lee now planned a massive attack from Seminary Ridge against the center of the Union line, held by Major General Winfield Scott Hancock's II Corps. At the same time, the Confederate cavalry under Stuart, which had arrived only the day before, would sweep around the Union line from the north.

At about 1:00 p.m. on July 3, the Confederates began a massive artillery barrage with some 160 guns from Seminary Ridge. More than 100 Union guns on Cemetery Ridge replied in a two-hour cannonade. Then the guns fell silent, and the Confederates began an attack over a mile of open ground in ranks a mile wide, with battle flags flying as if on parade. There were three divisions in the charge that day, with Major General George Pickett's in the center. The two other divisions faded away and streamed back toward the Confederate lines, leaving Pickett's division alone and exposed to enfilading Union fire. Only a few hundred Confederates reached the Union line, and they were halted there. Of 12,000–13,500 men, Pickett lost 8,000–10,000 that day. The Confederate cavalry, meanwhile, was defeated five miles east of the battlefield by Union cavalry.

Lee then shortened his line. He remained in place along Seminary Ridge the next day hoping that Meade would attack him, but the Union commander refused to take the bait. Finally, on the night of July 4 Lee decamped, taking advantage of darkness and heavy rain to mask his withdrawal. Lee proceeded down the Cumberland Valley and back into Virginia with captured booty and 6,000 Union prisoners.

In the battle itself, Meade lost 23,055 men: 3,155 killed, 14,531 wounded, and 5,369 captured or missing. Lee's losses are given as 23,231 (4,708 killed, 12,693 wounded, and 5,830 captured or missing) but might have been as high as 28,000 men. Although the South trumpeted a victory, cooler heads could see that the battle was a Confederate defeat. The Union victory at Gettysburg coupled with the simultaneous success at Vicksburg, Mississippi, decisively tipped the military-diplomatic balance in favor of the North.

Spencer C. Tucker

**Further Reading**

Coddington, Edwin B. *The Gettysburg Campaign: A Study in Command.* New York: Scribner, 1984.

Hess, Earl J. *Pickett's Charge: The Last Attack at Gettysburg.* Chapel Hill: University of North Carolina Press, 2001.

Pfanz, Harry W. *Gettysburg: Culp's Hill and Cemetery Hill.* Chapel Hill: University of North Carolina Press, 1993.

Pfanz, Harry W. *Gettysburg: The Second Day.* Chapel Hill: University of North Carolina Press, 1987.

Woodworth, Steven E. *Beneath a Northern Sky: A Short History of the Gettysburg Campaign.* Wilmington, DE: Scholarly Resources, 2003.

## Overland Campaign

| Date | May 4–June 12, 1864 | |
|------|---------------------|---|
| **Location** | Virginia | |
| **Opponents (*winner)** | *United States | Confederacy |
| **Commander** | Lieutenant General Ulysses S. Grant; Major General George Gordon Meade | General Robert E. Lee |
| **Approx. # Troops** | 120,000 men | 60,000 men |
| **Importance** | Although the Union Army of the Potomac absorbs heavy losses, the Confederate Army of Northern Virginia never quite recovers from the Union hammer blows. | |

New Union Army general in chief Lieutenant General Ulysses S. Grant planned his spring 1864 campaign to take advantage of superior Union numbers in a massive multipronged simultaneous effort to prevent the Confederates from shifting their dwindling resources to counter any one Union thrust. In the western theater, Major General William T. Sherman would move against the Confederate Army of Tennessee in northern Georgia and drive on the vital railroad and manufacturing center of Atlanta. Meanwhile, Major General Nathaniel P. Banks would advance on Mobile. In the eastern theater, Major General George Gordon Meade's Army of the Potomac, the major Union field force of some 120,000 men, would drive south from Culpepper, Virginia, against General Robert E. Lee's Army of Northern Virginia to capture Richmond in what became known as the Overland Campaign. Grant planned to accompany Meade's army in the field. At the same time, Major General Benjamin F. Butler's 39,000-man Army of the James was to proceed up the south bank of the James River and cut Lee off from the Lower South. Finally, Brigadier Generals George Crook and William W. Averell would proceed against the Shenandoah Valley from the west, while Major General Franz Sigel moved south to clear the Shenandoah Valley and seize the railheads of Staunton and Lynchburg. To meet Grant, Lee had 60,000 men supported by another 30,000 men under General P. G. T. Beauregard in the vicinity of Richmond and Petersburg.

The Overland Campaign began on May 4, 1864, when the Army of the Potomac crossed the Rapidan River in an effort to turn the right flank of the Army of Northern Virginia. The next day the two armies fought in the densely wooded area known as the Wilderness. Lee attacked Grant's left flank, using the woods and terrain to partially nullify the Union numerical advantage. The ensuing fighting was intense, and many wounded burned to death as brush fires engulfed parts of the battlefield. In the end, Lee outmaneuvered his opponent, inflicting 17,500 Union casualties for Confederate casualties estimated at some 7,500. Lee, however, had failed to stop Grant, for unlike previous rebuffs by Lee, this time the Army of the Potomac continued south, slipping around Lee's flank in an effort to get between the Army of Northern Virginia and Richmond.

Meanwhile, on May 5 during the Bermuda Hundred Campaign, Butler's Army of the James landed at Bermuda Hundred, a neck of land north of City Point at the confluence of the James and Appomattox Rivers and only 15 miles south of Richmond. The way to the capital appeared open. Richmond and Petersburg were virtually undefended, with their garrisons then being only about 5,000 men. The inept Butler fumbled away this golden opportunity, however. That same day Beauregard, commanding the Confederate Department of North Carolina and Southern Virginia with 18,000 men, assumed direction of Confederate defenses at Petersburg and ordered Major General George E. Pickett to contain Butler. Pickett rushed men to Bermuda Hundred, and with Butler slow to move, the Confederates bottled up the Union troops there.

Following the Battle of the Wilderness, the Army of the Potomac continued its southeastern movement toward Richmond. Grant again tried to outflank Lee's Army of Northern Virginia at the crossroads village of Spotsylvania Courthouse. Lee anticipated the move and got there first, with his men quickly throwing up entrenchments. Bloody trench warfare occurred during the next two weeks (May 7–21). On May 10, Grant hurled three corps against the Confederate lines. That evening on a very narrow front known as at the Mule Shoe, a salient in the center of the line, Colonel Emory Upton massed 12 regiments, and following an intense and concentrated artillery bombardment, they broke through at this point but were unable to exploit the situation.

Upton's limited success persuaded Grant to try the same tactic with an entire corps—Major General Winfield Scott Hancock's II Corps—at the tip of the salient. Grant's inactivity while preparing for the attack led Lee to believe that Grant was preparing to withdraw, and Lee shifted artillery from the area of the Mule Shoe, where Hancock struck with his 20,000-man corps in a predawn assault on May 12. The Union troops enjoyed initial success, taking 4,000 prisoners and shattering Major General Edward Johnson's division of Lieutenant General Richard S. Ewell's II Corps, with Johnson being among the prisoners. A furious counterattack by Major General John B. Gordon's division of Ewell's corps sealed the gap and staved off disaster. With no reserves readily available to exploit the situation, however, the Union attack ran out of steam. Subsequent Union attacks were not coordinated, and Lee was able to restore his line.

Meanwhile on May 11, Union major general Philip H. Sheridan's 10,000-man cavalry corps raided south. At Yellow Tavern, about six miles above Richmond, Sheridan encountered 4,500 Confederate cavalry led by Major General J. E. B. "Jeb" Stuart. Sheridan drove the Confederates from the field, and Stuart was mortally wounded, a major loss for the Confederacy. Union casualties totaled 625, while the Confederates lost about 1,000, including 300 prisoners.

At Spotsylvania Courthouse, Lee withdrew to a newly prepared line, which Grant assaulted six days later on May 18, only to be repulsed. On May 21 following additional heavy fighting, Grant decamped, again attempting to outflank Lee's right, cutting it off from Richmond. In the Spotsylvania fighting, Union casualties totaled 14,267 men, while Lee lost more than 10,000.

Again Lee anticipated Grant's move and established strong positions on the North Anna River on May 22, the day before Grant arrived. The ensuing Battle of the North Anna (May 23–26) was a series of small engagements, with Grant suffering 1,973 casualties and Lee suffering perhaps 2,017.

On May 27 Grant again put the Army of the Potomac in motion, moving eastward. A delay during Grant's crossing of the Pamunkey River provided Lee time to again place his Army of Northern Virginia between Richmond and the Union Army of the Potomac. On May 28, Union and Confederate cavalrymen again clashed in the Battle of Haw's Shop (also known as the Battle of Hawe's Shop and the Battle of Enon Church) in Hanover County, with each side suffering about 300 casualties. While the Union army crossed the Pamunkey River without incident, Lee once more moved faster than Grant expected, establishing a strong defensive position along Totopotomoy Creek. On May 29, Union forces dug in on the opposite bank of the Totopotomoy. Following cavalry engagements and minor infantry skirmishes during May 28–29, Grant ordered a general advance on May 30. Hancock's II Corps captured some entrenchments in the center of the Confederate lines but was unable to advance farther. Lee ordered Major General Jubal A. Early on the Confederate right to strike at Major General Gouverneur Warren's V corps probing the Confederate flank, but Major General Richard Anderson, ordered to assist Early, failed to arrive in time, and Early's attack was repulsed. The Battle of Totopotomoy Creek resulted in 731 Union casualties; the Confederates lost 1,159.

Once again Grant ordered another flanking maneuver south, this time toward the town of Cold Harbor. Grant now had some 108,000 men; Lee, having been reinforced by 14,000 men drawn from the Shenandoah Valley and operations along the James River, commanded 59,000 men. Lee was able to fortify and entrench at Cold Harbor, while Grant impatiently flung his army at the formidable Confederate position. The result was a stinging rebuff to Grant in one of the bloodiest battles of the war.

On June 3, Grant hurled three corps in a frontal assault against Lee. Within minutes the Federals sustained some 7,000 casualties. Grant admitted that this was a major mistake. Casualty estimates for the entire Battle of Cold Harbor (May 31–June 12, 1864) vary greatly but are probably on the order of some 13,000 Union troops to only 4,600 Confederates.

Now preparing to send the Army of the Potomac across the James River, Grant next ordered Sheridan and two divisions of his Cavalry Corps westward into Louisa County to cut the Virginia Central Railroad and join with Union forces in the

Shenandoah Valley, now commanded by Major General David Hunter, who had replaced Sigel. Grant planned for their combined forces to take the key Confederate rail center of Lynchburg and then join him at Richmond. Lee countered by sending his own cavalry commander, Major General Wade Hampton, and two cavalry divisions after Sheridan. Lee also dispatched Early's corps to Lynchburg to check Hunter.

During June 11–12, Sheridan and Hampton clashed in a confused battle at Trevilian Station. Sheridan enjoyed success on the first day, but the tables were turned on June 12 when the dismounted Confederate cavalrymen turned back several determined dismounted Union attacks. Sheridan withdrew after destroying about six miles of the Virginia Central Railroad. He never linked up with Hunter, who, although he outnumbered Early, withdrew from Lynchburg.

Now in a bold move that caught Lee by surprise, on the night of June 12–13 the Army of the Potomac secretly decamped from its trenches at Cold Harbor and, screened by cavalry, crossed the James River on a pontoon bridge more than 2,100 feet in length and moved against the lightly defended city of Petersburg, a vital transportation and supply center for Richmond. On June 15 Major General William F. Smith, commanding XVIII Corps of the Army of the James, failed to seize the initiative and let an incredible opportunity to take Petersburg slip away. Meanwhile, Beauregard's outnumbered forces bought Lee valuable time, repulsing a series of Union attacks on June 16 and 17. On June 18, Lee's army moved into prepared works at Petersburg, and Grant reluctantly opted for a siege. This long siege from June 13, 1864, to April 3, 1865, continued to sap Confederate strength.

The Overland Campaign was necessary in order for the Union to win the war. Despite reverses, most notably that of the Battle of Cold Harbor, the nearly six-week-long campaign was a Union strategic success, with Grant now besieging Petersburg. The campaign was, however, the bloodiest in American history. The Union side suffered some 55,000 casualties (7,600 killed), while Confederate losses totaled some 32,600 (4,200 killed). Grant had been attacking, however, and Lee's losses were in fact higher in terms of forces engaged (more than 50 percent) than those for Grant (some 45 percent). And while Grant could replace his losses, Lee simply could not. The Army of Northern Virginia never quite recovered from the hammering it had received.

Spencer C. Tucker

## Further Reading

Grimsley, Mark. *And Keep Moving On: The Virginia Campaign, May–June 1864.* Lincoln: University of Nebraska Press, 2005.

Hess, Earl J. *Trench Warfare under Grant and Lee: Field Fortifications in the Overland Campaign.* Chapel Hill: University of North Carolina Press, 2007.

## Atlanta Campaign

| Date | May 5–September 2, 1864 | |
|---|---|---|
| Location | Northern Georgia | |
| Opponents (*winner) | *United States | Confederacy |
| Commander | Major General William T. Sherman | General Joseph E. Johnston; General John B. Hood |
| Approx. # Troops | 98,500–112,000 men | 50,000–65,000 men |
| Importance | Union forces capture the key Confederate transportation hub of Atlanta. General Sherman is free to initiate his March to the Sea, and President Abraham Lincoln's chances of reelection are greatly enhanced. | |

Between May 5 and September 2, 1864, Major General William T. Sherman led more than 100,000 Union troops in an effort to capture the important Confederate manufacturing and rail center of Atlanta, Georgia. In March 1864 Ulysses S. Grant had been promoted to lieutenant general and given command of the Union Army. His strategic plan called for all Union forces to take the offensive on the same date, roughly May 5, 1864. Earlier in the war, the Confederates had been able to move their resources to different theaters depending on which Union army was active, thus partially neutralizing the North's numerical superiority. Grant's strategy, which had the strong support of President Abraham Lincoln, would prevent this. The two main thrusts would be aimed at the two major Confederate armies, the Army of Northern Virginia under General Robert E. Lee and the Army of Tennessee under General Joseph E. Johnston in northern Georgia.

While the Union Army of the Potomac and the Union Army of the James, under Grant's immediate direction, moved into Virginia in the Overland Campaign with the goals of destroying Lee's Army of Northern Virginia and taking Richmond, commander of the Division of the Mississippi Major General Sherman was to take the Armies of the Ohio, the Tennessee, and the Cumberland and defeat Johnston's army in Georgia, seizing Atlanta.

Johnston's 45,000-man Army of Tennessee was in a strong defensive position in the mountains of northern Georgia but had two major weaknesses: it was supplied by just a single railroad from Atlanta and faced a force more than twice its size.

On May 5, 1864, Sherman began the Atlanta Campaign. The forward-most Union position was 23 miles south of Chattanooga, about 120 miles from Atlanta, while Johnston's Confederate army was in and around Dalton, Georgia. Sherman's plan was simple. Major General James B. McPherson's Army of the Tennessee would move through the mountain passes to the west of Dalton, placing itself behind Johnston along the railroad. This move would either trap the Confederate army at Dalton or force it to retreat. While the flanking movement was under way, Major General George Thomas's Army of the Cumberland would press Johnston's front to distract the Confederates from McPherson's movements.

A Union artillery battery at a former Confederate fort near Atlanta during Major General William T. Sherman's 1864 Atlanta Campaign. (Library of Congress)

General Johnston, realizing that his position was untenable, soon abandoned Dalton and moved his army south some 18 miles to Resaca. Union soldiers were overjoyed at having driven the Confederates from such a well-fortified position, and many in the Confederate government in Richmond now doubted that Johnston would be able to defend Atlanta.

In Resaca, the Confederates dug in behind earthworks surrounding the city. Lieutenant General William Hardee commanded Johnston's right wing, Lieutenant General John Bell Hood held the center, and Lieutenant General Leonidas Polk commanded the left wing.

On May 14 Sherman ordered his forces to press Resaca on all fronts. The Battle of Resaca lasted two days. Johnston made a determined effort to hold Resaca, but Sherman again threatened his line of retreat, and in the end Johnston was forced to fall back closer to Atlanta. The Confederate army abandoned the town on the night of May 15, crossing the Oostenaula River on pontoon bridges. In the battle Johnston had sustained some 5,000 casualties, while Sherman suffered 6,000.

Johnston continued to move his army south, crossing the Etowah River and burning the bridge behind his army. The Confederates fortified Allatoona Pass in the Appalachian foothills, blocking any direct advance toward Atlanta. Sherman decided to repeat his flanking strategy that had proven successful against Dalton and Resaca. On May 23 Sherman sent his army west toward Marietta, Georgia. He believed that by threatening this important city, he could force Johnston to abandon Allatoona Pass.

Johnston detected the Union move toward Marietta and was able to place part of Hood's and Hardee's corps at New Hope Church directly in the Union path. On May 25 Major General Joseph Hooker's XX Corps of the Army of the Cumberland was surprised by this Confederate force behind earthworks. In the ensuing battle of May 25–27, Hooker lost some 1,600 killed or wounded; the Confederates lost far fewer troops.

Sherman now ordered New Hope bypassed, forcing Johnston to abandon that position. Standing between Sherman's position and Marietta were three mountains. The closest to the Union line was Kennesaw Mountain, some 1,200 feet high and the center of the Confederate line. Instead of his usual flanking movement, Sherman ordered a direct assault on the entrenched Confederates on Kennesaw Mountain on June 27. Major General George Thomas's Army of the Cumberland carried out the main assault. The battle was a one-sided Confederate victory. The Union army sustained more than 3,000 casualties, compared to perhaps 750 for the Confederates. Sherman has been criticized for the losses incurred in consequence of his impatience with the flanking strategy.

Following the battle, Sherman once again sent the Army of the Tennessee on a wide flanking movement, forcing Johnston to abandon Kennesaw Mountain and Allatoona Pass. By July 3, Johnston retreated across the Chattahoochee River. The Union army followed closely, bridged the river in two places, and began moving forces across. Johnston withdrew again, moving the majority of his army and guns into Atlanta.

Convinced that Johnston would not defend Atlanta, Confederate president Jefferson Davis replaced Johnston with his subordinate, John Bell Hood, on July 17. Much has been made of personal animosity between Davis and Johnston that made Davis quick to believe any negative report about his field commander, but all outward appearances indicated that Johnston would not fight for Atlanta, and Davis could not allow that.

Sherman and his senior officers expected bold action from the much more aggressive Hood. Despite having lost the use of his arm at Gettysburg and losing a leg at Chickamauga, Hood retained his belief in offensive tactics. On July 20 he ordered his men to attack the Union Army of the Cumberland north of the city. This engagement, known as the Battle of Peachtree Creek, held brief promise, only to end in failure for Hood. Two days later Hood unleashed his force on the Army of the Tennessee west of the city in the fierce Battle of Atlanta, in which General McPherson was killed. On July 28 east of Atlanta, Hood struck again in the Battle of Ezra Church but was soundly defeated. Despite the singular success of his cavalry in thwarting Union raids, Hood could do little to stop Sherman's envelopment of Atlanta.

Hood settled into the Atlanta defenses, while Sherman's men fortified outside the city and began shelling it. After nearly a month, on August 27 Sherman pulled much of his manpower out of line. Leaving a small force to man the trenches and guard the railroad bridge over the Chattahoochee River, Sherman sent the rest of his men to the west of Atlanta to again attempt to cut the Confederate supply line.

Thinking that the Union army was withdrawing, Hood was slow to respond. On August 30 the Army of the Tennessee, under its new commander, Major General Oliver Otis Howard, reached the city of Jonesboro, cutting the Macon & Western Railroad, Hood's only line of retreat and supply. Hood then ordered General Hardee and Lieutenant General Stephen Lee to Jonesboro to drive Howard out and reopen the rail line. In the Battle of Jonesboro (August 31–September 1), the Confederates sustained heavy casualties and were unable to retake the railroad. In the meantime, the Army of the Ohio cut the railroad between Jonesboro and Atlanta, rendering Atlanta untenable. On the night of September 1, Hood and the Confederates destroyed their supply stocks and munitions inside Atlanta and evacuated south to Lovejoy Station. The next day the Union forces entered the city.

The objective of the campaign—the destruction of the Confederate army—was not achieved, for Hood had escaped to Alabama with what remained of his army. However, Sherman had accomplished a great deal. Although Hood's army was still active in the field, Sherman possessed the resources to address Hood without abandoning the offensive in Georgia and was thus free to move largely unchallenged to Savannah. The news of the fall of Atlanta was received with joy in the North and gloom in the South. At a cost of only 20,000 casualties, as compared to at least 27,000 men for the much smaller Confederate army, Sherman was able to drive the Confederates some 140 miles into Georgia and take a city as important to the Southern cause as Richmond. The capture of Atlanta just three months before the 1864 presidential election has often been credited with ensuring President Abraham Lincoln's reelection and the continuation of the Civil War.

Wesley Moody

### Further Reading

Castel, Albert. *Decision in the West: The Atlanta Campaign of 1864.* Lawrence: University Press of Kansas, 1992.

Johnston, Joseph E. *Narrative of Military Operations, Directed, during the Late War between the States.* New York: D. Appleton, 1874.

Key, William. *The Battle of Atlanta and the Georgia Campaign.* Atlanta: Peachtree Publishers, 1981.

Sherman, William T. *Memoirs of General W. T. Sherman.* New York: Library of America, 1990.

## Siege of Petersburg

| Date | June 15, 1864–April 3, 1865 | |
|---|---|---|
| Location | Vicinity of Petersburg and Richmond, Virginia | |
| Opponents (*winner) | *United States | Confederacy |
| Commander | Lieutenant General Ulysses S. Grant; Major General George Gordon Meade | General Robert E. Lee |
| Approx. # Troops | 67,000 men, growing to 125,000 | Average of 52,000 men |
| Importance | General Lee's Army of Northern Virginia is gradually whittled away, eventually forcing him to attempt to break out to the west and south, culminating in his surrender at Appomattox a week later. | |

Union soldiers before battle during the Siege of Petersburg, Virginia. The Union siege lasted from June 15, 1864, to April 3, 1865. The longest such effort of the Civil War, it presaged the trench warfare of World War I. (National Archives)

In the Overland Campaign (May 4–June 12, 1864), Union Army general in chief Lieutenant General Ulysses S. Grant accompanied Major General George Gordon Meade's Army of the Potomac in a drive southward to take the Confederate capital of Richmond. Although the Army of the Potomac suffered heavy casualties and was unable to dislodge Lee in the Battle of Cold Harbor (May 31–June 12), Grant was determined to keep the offensive going and now decided to shift his forces south of the James to concentrate on Petersburg.

Located 20 miles south of Richmond, this city of 18,000 people was the key rail supply point for the Confederate capital. If Grant could take Petersburg, it would force the evacuation of Richmond. Meanwhile, on June 9 Union major general Benjamin Butler, aware that Lee had sent resources north to meet Grant at Cold Harbor and that Petersburg was only lightly held, tried but failed to take the city with his Army of the James. In what is known as the First Battle of Petersburg, some 2,500 Confederates under Brigadier General Henry A. Wise defeated 4,500 attacking Union troops along the so-called Dimmock Line east of the city.

On the night of June 12–13, the Army of the Potomac secretly decamped from its trenches at Cold Harbor and crossed the James on a hastily constructed 2,100-foot pontoon bridge. On June 15 Grant sent 15,000 men against Petersburg, then held by General P. G. T. Beauregard and only 5,400 Confederates. Grant committed Major General William F. Smith's XVIII Corps of the Army of the James and Major General Winfield S. Hancock's II Corps of the Army of the Potomac. Grant's two commanders cost him a chance to end the war in 1864. Smith failed to press the assault, while Hancock, without definite orders, did not lend Smith adequate support.

During the next three days Beauregard gambled boldly with significant effect, taking forces containing Butler at Bermuda Hundred to reinforce against Grant and turn back successive but poorly coordinated Union attacks. By the morning of June 16, some 14,000 Confederates faced 50,000 Federals. Lee, at first unaware of the magnitude of Grant's relocation, finally answered Beauregard's pleas for reinforcements. Both sides continued to reinforce, and by June 18 some 67,000 Union troops faced 20,000 Confederates.

Within a week there was stalemate, and both sides dug in. Temporary field fortifications ultimately became elaborate siege lines presaging those of World War I and extending some 30 miles from the eastern outskirts of Richmond and Petersburg around to the south and then southwest of Petersburg itself.

This was not actually a siege in the strict definition of the term in which supply lines were completely cut, nor was the campaign strictly limited to Petersburg, for the Union goal was the capture of Richmond, and there was thus considerable fighting over a wide area. The campaign might best be called the longest sustained operation of the war and also saw the largest concentration of African American troops during the conflict.

Soldiers on both sides endured periodic enemy shelling that included on the Union side fire from mammoth 13-inch siege mortars. Both sides labored to improve their defensive works while contending with alternating heat and cold, rain, thick mud, and choking dust. Desperate circumstances facing many families on the home front in addition to the difficult conditions in the trenches brought growing Confederate desertions, especially during the winter of 1864–1865.

Petersburg residents suffered along with the troops. Food was in short supply, and the city was within range of Union guns. During the fighting, more than 500 buildings were destroyed.

The key for the Confederates was continued control of the roads and railroads from the south and the west that supplied both Petersburg and Richmond. As early as June 21, Grant attempted to extend his position westward and secure control of the Confederate rail lines: the Richmond & Petersburg Railroad; the Southside Railroad, which ran west to Lynchburg; and the Weldon Railroad (Weldon & Petersburg Railroad), which ran north from Weldon, North Carolina.

In the Battle of Jerusalem Plank Road (June 21–23), Union forces fought an inconclusive battle for control of the Weldon Railroad. At the same time, Union cavalry divisions under Brigadier Generals James H. Wilson and August Kautz raided to the south and southwest. This raid of June 22–30 destroyed 60 miles of track, but the lines were soon back in operation, and the raid cost 1,445 Union casualties, about a quarter of the force involved.

In the First Battle of Deep Bottom (July 27–29), Grant ordered Hancock to fix the Confederates at Chaffin's Bluff, while Major General Philip H. Sheridan led two cavalry divisions across the James southeast of Richmond in an abortive effort to take the capital or at the least ride around the city from the east and north and cut the Virginia Central Railroad from the Shenandoah Valley.

On July 30 in the most dramatic action of the campaign, Union forces detonated a huge mine in a tunnel dug by Pennsylvania miner troops under a major Confederate fort. Inept Union planning for the following attack, a late change in plans, and poor Union leadership coupled with an effective Confederate reaction turned this Battle of the Crater into a Union fiasco, with nearly 3,800 casualties compared to only 1,500 Confederate losses.

In the Second Battle of Deep Bottom (August 13–20), Grant attempted another thrust against Richmond, this time led by Hancock. The attack was designed in part to prevent Lee from dispatching reinforcements to aid Lieutenant General Jubal A. Early's operations in the Shenandoah Valley, and in this at least the attack was successful.

Grant then sent Major General Gouverneur K. Warren's V Corps to attack the Weldon Railroad. The Federals ended up fighting on the defensive in the Battle of Globe Tavern (August 18–21) but did tear up considerable track along this key Confederate railroad. Grant then sent Hancock's II Corps against the Weldon Railroad. Although the Confederates won the Second Battle of Reams Station (August 29), they permanently lost an important portion of the Weldon line, forcing them to send supplies by wagon during part of the route. Most subsequent fighting occurred to the west as Grant endeavored to secure the Southside Railroad, connecting Petersburg to Lynchburg, and Boydton Plank Road.

In the Battle of Chaffin's Farm (September 29–30), also known as the Battle of New Market Heights, Butler's Army of the James crossed the James River to attack the Richmond defenses north of that river. Although the Federals enjoyed initial success, the Confederates contained the attack and then erected a new line of works.

Grant knew that to meet Butler's attack, Lee had been forced to weaken his line elsewhere. Grant sought to take advantage by attempting to extend his left flank to cut Confederate lines of communication southwest of Petersburg. He committed four infantry divisions and one cavalry division to the attack and, in the Battle of Peebles' Farm (September 30–October 2), extended his left flank.

Lee, concerned about the heightened Union threat to Richmond from the east, attacked the Union right flank on Darbytown Road on October 7. Although they routed the Union cavalry, the Confederates were halted on New Market Road. On October 13, Union forces assaulted the Confederates north of Darbytown Road but were repulsed. Butler again attacked during October 27–28 but was repulsed in the Battle of Fair Oaks and Darbytown Road.

Taking advantage of his superior numbers and Butler's attack, Grant sent more than 30,000 Union troops under Hancock to the west. The Federals suffered rebuff in the major Battle of Boydton Plank Road (October 27–28). The Confederates continued to control this key supply route throughout the winter.

In early February 1865, Union troops again attacked the Boydton Plank Road. In the Battle of Hatcher's Run (February 5–7), Lee sustained heavy casualties but again drove the Union troops back. The Federals, however, had extended their left flank to the Vaughan Road crossing of Hatcher's Run.

Lee was well aware of the growing disparity in manpower. Grant now had some 125,000 men, while Lee had only 50,000. Lee also knew that General Sheridan had rejoined Grant from the Shenandoah Valley with an additional 10,000 cavalry. To disrupt an anticipated major Union attack (actually planned for March 29), Lee planned a major attack against Union Fort Stedman on March 25.

Launched with half of Lee's infantry under Major General John B. Gordon, the attack on Fort Stedman enjoyed initial success, and the Confederates occupied the fort. However, the Federals counterattacked and restored the line. This was Lee's last attempt to breach the Union defenses.

On April 1 Sheridan, with four Union cavalry divisions and infantry of V Corps, crushed a Confederate force in the Battle of Five Forks, a major road intersection 10 miles west-southwest of Petersburg and about 5 miles west of where Lee's lines ended. The next day Grant flung his troops in a massive assault on the thinly held Confederate lines, which collapsed. Only a valiant stand at Fort Gregg saved the retreating Confederates from total defeat, but the Federals were in Petersburg by nightfall. The longest siege operation in American military history had ended.

Lee now evacuated Richmond and headed west, hoping to link up with General Joseph E. Johnston in North Carolina. Grant pursued, and Lee, cut off by Union cavalry, surrendered his remaining troops to Grant at Appomattox Courthouse on April 9, 1865. The Civil War was almost over.

Spencer C. Tucker

## Further Reading

Greene, A. Wilson. *The Final Battles of the Petersburg Campaign: Breaking the Backbone of the Rebellion.* Knoxville: University of Tennessee Press, 2008.

Horn, John. *The Petersburg Campaign, June 1864–April 1865.* Conshohocken, PA: Combined Books, 1993.

Sommers, Richard J. *Richmond Redeemed: The Siege at Petersburg.* Garden City, NY: Doubleday, 1981.

Trudeau, Noah Andre. *The Last Citadel: Petersburg, Virginia, June 1864–April 1865.* Baton Rouge: Louisiana State University Press, 1991.

## Battles of Franklin and Nashville

| Date | November 30 and December 15–16, 1864 | |
|------|-----------|------|
| Location | Tennessee | |
| Opponents (*winner) | United States | Confederacy |
| Commander | Major General John Schofield (Battle of Franklin); Major General George Thomas (Battle of Nashville) | General John Bell Hood |
| Approx. # Troops | 28,000 men (Franklin); 55,000 men (Nashville) | 20,000 men (Franklin); 30,000 men (Nashville) |
| Importance | Effectively breaks up the Confederate Army of Tennessee and marks the end of large-scale combat in the western theater. | |

After evacuating Atlanta, Georgia, on September 1, 1864, Confederate general John Bell Hood moved his forces northwest of the city to sever the rail lines supplying Major General William T. Sherman's Union army group. Failing to bring Hood to battle, Sherman returned to Atlanta and departed that city on November 15 to march across Georgia to Savannah. Sherman left about half of his force under Major Generals George Thomas and John Schofield to check Hood.

Reinforced by Major General Nathan Bedford Forrest's cavalry, Hood marched westward into Alabama and then turned northward into Tennessee in November. Hood planned to isolate and destroy Schofield's 30,000 troops before they could unite with the equal number of men under Thomas who were holding Nashville. On November 29 Forrest's cavalry and some of Hood's infantry reached Spring Hill, where they could block Schofield's line of march. However, Schofield cleared Confederate cavalry from the road after some skirmishing, while the Confederate infantry remained idle.

Infuriated at Schofield's escape, Hood pursued and caught up with the Union general on the afternoon of November 30. The Union troops entrenched at Franklin with the Harpeth River to their rear. Hood rejected Forrest's advice to outflank the Union army and decided on a frontal assault on Schofield's army in the hopes of destroying it, as the river would block a Union escape. Hood also chose not to wait for his artillery or Lieutenant General Stephen D. Lee's corps to arrive and ordered a frontal assault without artillery support.

Late in the afternoon, some 22,000 Confederate infantrymen charged the Union line, where Schofield had deployed about 28,000 defenders. Despite suffering heavy losses from Union artillery and rifle fire as they crossed the open ground, some Confederate units, including Major General Patrick Cleburne's division, reached and broke the Union line near its center. Fierce hand-to-hand combat ensued as Schofield ordered reserves forward to seal the breach. The Confederate infantrymen were eventually driven back, and supporting attacks on the Union flanks by Confederate cavalry were also repulsed. Sporadic fighting continued until about midnight.

The Battle of Franklin virtually destroyed Hood's army. Confederate casualties totaled approximately 1,750 killed, including 6 generals, and 5,500 wounded or captured. Union losses were given as 189 dead (although this number was surely higher), 1,033 wounded, and 1,104 missing or captured (undoubtedly a number of these were dead).

Although Hood held the field the following day, he was unable to prevent the successful retreat of Schofield's command to Nashville. Believing that he could overtake Schofield's force, Hood chose to pursue. General Thomas was waiting in Nashville, however, with a large and well-disposed army, and while Hood wanted redemption for his losses at Franklin, Thomas envisioned a completely different result.

Hood arrived at Nashville on December 2 and began to fortify his position. Lieutenant General Ulysses S. Grant, Union Army general in chief, telegraphed Thomas from City Point, Virginia, urging him to attack Hood before he could reinforce and better prepare his positions. But Thomas overestimated Hood's numbers and feared that he himself lacked sufficient strength, particularly cavalry, to defeat Hood in such an assault. Thomas refused another suggestion to attack on December 9 and thereafter did not follow numerous orders to attack because temperatures had plummeted, and ice and snow covered the ground. During Thomas's delays, Hood strengthened his positions in the hills south of Nashville.

Grant was concerned about the delays in attacking Hood because he believed that Hood might get around Thomas and push for the Ohio River. Grant toyed with the idea of replacing Thomas with Schofield and even cut orders to be carried to Nashville by Major General John A. Logan, who was authorized to supersede Thomas upon his arrival if he had yet to act.

On December 15 Thomas, with major components of the Armies of the Cumberland, the Ohio, and the Tennessee (some 55,000 men in all), finally attacked Hood's Army of Tennessee, which had 30,000 men. Thomas flanked both sides of Hood's position and took Montgomery Hill in the process. Hood then repositioned his men and dug in overnight. The next morning the Federals charged up Overton Hill and what became known as Shy's Hill toward the waiting Confederates. By late afternoon on December 16, Thomas and his men had crushed the Confederates. Hood was routed, and Confederate soldiers were fleeing from the battlefield. It was as decisive a victory as either side had seen in a major battle to that point. The Confederates may have suffered as many as 1,300 killed or wounded. At least 4,500 were taken prisoner or missing. Federal losses totaled approximately 3,000.

A 10-day Union pursuit to the Tennessee River followed. Confederate major general Nathan Bedford Forrest's cavalry helped screen the withdrawal. Finally on December 27, the last of Forrest's men crossed the Tennessee River. On December 29 Hood's men marched to Tupelo, Mississippi, bringing an end to the Franklin and Nashville Campaign. Fewer than 20,000 men remained in the Army of Tennessee when it crossed into Mississippi, where that remnant was broken up, with some units sent to Mobile while others made the long journey to North Carolina to join General Joseph Johnston's forces. Hood was relieved of command at his own request later that January. The Battles of Franklin and Nashville were among the worst military disasters for the Confederacy in the war. The battles effectively destroyed the Army of Tennessee as a fighting force and marked the end of major combat in the western theater.

Jim Piecuch, A. W. R. Hawkins III, and David Coffey

**Further Reading**

Gallagher, Gary W., Stephen D. Engle, Robert K. Krick, and Joseph T. Glatthaar. *The American Civil War: This Mighty Scourge of War.* Oxford, UK: Osprey, 2003.

Horn, Stanley F. *The Decisive Battle of Nashville.* Baton Rouge: Louisiana State University Press, 1984.

Knight, James R. *The Battle of Franklin: When the Devil Had Full Possession of the Earth.* Charleston, SC: History Press, 2009.

Sword, Wiley. *The Confederacy's Last Hoorah: Spring Hill, Franklin, & Nashville.* New York: HarperCollins for the University of Kansas Press, 1992.

## Red Cloud's War

| Date | 1866–1868 | |
|---|---|---|
| Location | Wyoming and Montana Territories | |
| Opponents (*winner) | *Lakota and Cheyenne Native Americans | U.S. Army |
| Commander | Oglala Lakota chief Red Cloud | Colonel Henry B. Carrington |
| Approx. # Troops | 2,000–3,000 warriors | 700 U.S. Army soldiers and 300 civilians |
| Importance | The most successful Native American War against the United States, with Washington acceding to Red Cloud's demands, including recognition of Cheyenne and Lakota control of the Powder River region. | |

The discovery of gold in Idaho and Montana in 1862 and 1863 opened a new front in the ongoing conflict between white settlers and the Plains Indian tribes. Although the American Civil War was still in progress, thousands of adventurers and fortune seekers nevertheless flocked to the area, and pressure mounted to establish more direct lines of access to the Virginia City goldfields. To respond to these challenges, army officials finally adopted the route pioneered by John Bozeman that extended from Fort Laramie on the North Platte River and the Oregon Trail northwestward along the eastern base and around the northern shoulder of the Bighorn Mountains and on to Virginia City. Although the Bozeman Trail was nearly

Indian Peace Commission members meet with Sioux Nation leaders at Fort Laramie, Wyoming, in 1868. The resulting Fort Laramie Treaty ended Red Cloud's War. The treaty guaranteed the Lakota ownership of the Black Hills, but the U.S. government seized the land after gold was discovered there. (National Archives)

400 miles shorter than other routes to the region, it also cut through hunting grounds reserved for the Sioux, Northern Cheyennes, and Arapahos by the Harney-Sanborn Treaties of 1865.

In 1866 U.S. government representatives, under considerable public pressure and also lured by the gold in the region that might relieve the financial stress of the Civil War, engaged the tribes in new negotiations in an effort to gain passage through their lands. Although a few chiefs signed new treaties at Fort Laramie, others led by Oglala Sioux chief Red Cloud quit the discussions when Colonel Henry B. Carrington marched in with a battalion from the 18th Infantry on his way to establish posts along the Bozeman Trail. This occurred well before agreements with all the tribes had been reached.

On June 17, 1866, Carrington's battalion of about 700 men, plus several cavalry units and hundreds of mule teams hauling large quantities of equipment and supplies, departed Fort Laramie and headed toward the Bighorn Mountains. At Fort Reno, located on the Powder River many miles from the nearest telegraph station, Carrington relieved two companies of the U.S. 5th Volunteers, consisting of former Confederate prisoners who had aligned with the Union and agreed to frontier service in exchange for their freedom. Farther to the northwest some 225 miles from Fort Laramie, Carrington constructed his headquarters on the Piney tributary of the

Powder River, which he named Fort Phil Kearny. Five companies stayed at Fort Phil Kearny, while the remaining two marched another 90 miles to establish Fort C. F. Smith on a bluff some 500 yards from the Bighorn River.

Fort Phil Kearny almost immediately came under Native American attack and, during its brief existence, remained in an almost continual state of siege. On December 21, 1866, Red Cloud's warriors attacked a wagon train six miles from the fort. Captain William Fetterman, who had boasted that he could ride through the whole Sioux Nation with just 80 men, asked to lead a relief column. Native decoys lured Fetterman from the fort, and against Carrington's orders, Fetterman crossed the ridge toward hundreds of waiting warriors. In a carefully executed ambush, the Sioux annihilated Fetterman's entire force, including 2 civilians who had accompanied the soldiers to test their new Henry repeating rifles.

The army was more successful in two other notable actions on the Bozeman Trail. In August 1867 Cheyenne and Sioux warriors launched separate but seemingly coordinated attacks known as the Hayfield Fight (August 1, 1867) and the Wagon Box Fight (August 2, 1867). In the Hayfield Fight, 19 soldiers and 6 civilians from Fort C. F. Smith under Lieutenant Sigismund Sternberg, equipped with converted breech-loading Springfields and several repeating rifles, held off a superior force with the loss of 3 killed and 3 wounded. In the Wagon Box Fight near Fort Phil Kearny, Captain James Powell and 31 men positioned themselves behind wagons that had their running gear removed. There they managed to hold at bay a force of several hundred warriors for four hours, with only 3 killed and 2 wounded.

Despite these small victories, the days of the Bozeman Trail were numbered. After eight months of negotiations, the majority of the tribal leaders finally agreed to the terms of a new treaty, but it was not until November 6, 1868, that Red Cloud signed the document at Fort Laramie that officially ended Red Cloud's War. The 1868 treaty met almost all of the Sioux demands, including the abandonment of Fort Reno, Fort Phil Kearny, and Fort C. F. Smith and the closing of the Bozeman Trail. The treaty also recognized Native American dominion over the Powder River Country and vast hunting grounds in Wyoming and Montana and set aside most of the Dakota Territory west of the Missouri River as the Great Sioux Reservation. For the first time in its history, the U.S. government had negotiated a peace that had conceded everything demanded by the opposing party and extracted nothing in return.

Bret F. Wood

## Further Reading

Bell, William G. "Winning the West: The Army in the Indian Wars, 1865–1890." In *American Military History,* edited by Maurice Matloff, 300–318. Washington, DC: Office of the Chief of Military History, 1973.

Cohen, Felix S. *Handbook of Federal Indian Law.* Washington, DC: U.S. Department of the Interior, Office of the Solicitor, 1945.

Mattes, Merrill J. *Fort Laramie Park History, 1834–1977*. Washington, DC: U.S. Department of the Interior, 1980.

Schuetz, Janice E. *Episodes in the Rhetoric of Government-Indian Relations*. Westport, CT: Greenwood, 2002.

## Battle of Palo Duro Canyon

| Date | September 28, 1874 | |
|---|---|---|
| Location | Palo Duro Canyon, south of Amarillo in the Texas Panhandle | |
| Opponents (*winner) | *U.S. Army | Cheyenne, Comanche, and Kiowa Native Americans |
| Commander | Colonel Ranald S. Mackernzie | Chiefs Iron Jacket, Poor Buffalo, and Lone Wolf |
| Approx. # Troops | 450 men of the 4th Cavalry and Native American scouts | Unknown |
| Importance | Ends the Red River War. | |

Violence on the southern Plains escalated between Native Americans and settlers, culminating in what became known as the Red River War. On June 27, 1874, a fierce battle occurred between buffalo hunters and a large force of Native American warriors at Adobe Walls, and unrest was increasing on the reservations of Indian Territory (Oklahoma), which also served as safe havens for marauding Cheyenne, Comanche, and Kiowa bands. Responding to events, Lieutenant General Philip H. Sheridan, commander of the massive Military Division of the Missouri, ordered a five-pronged campaign to converge on previously impregnable Native American sanctuaries on the Llano Estacado (Staked Plain) in the Texas Panhandle.

One of the largest of the five columns, led by Colonel Ranald S. Mackenzie, pressed northwest from Fort Concho, Texas, with eight companies of the 4th Cavalry, arguably the most potent frontier regiment, and five companies of infantry. After establishing a forward supply base and leaving three companies of infantry to protect it, Mackenzie pushed onward. By late September, his force approached Palo Duro Canyon near the site of an inconsequential engagement on August 30 between Colonel Nelson Miles's command pushing south from Kansas and a formidable array of Cheyenne, Comanche, and Kiowa warriors. Supply problems had curtailed Miles's effort, however, leaving the field to Mackenzie. On September 26 a Comanche party failed to stampede the well-picketed army horses and was easily driven off by the soldiers. Meanwhile, scouts reported the location of a large encampment, miles in length, containing hundreds of lodges within the canyon.

In the predawn darkness of September 28, 1874, Mackenzie's cavalry descended into the canyon single file on a precarious trail that was completely exposed. At daybreak as each company reached the bottom, the troops charged through the villages, scrambling surprised Cheyennes, Comanches, and Kiowas who attempted in vain to defend their homes. Typical of a Mackenzie fight, casualties were amazingly low, with only three Indians killed and one soldier badly wounded. However, so complete was the surprise that the Indians could only escape with what they could carry, leaving behind almost all food, shelter, and other supplies, which they had painstakingly stockpiled for winter. Almost all of the supplies went up in smoke when Mackenzie ordered the villages torched.

More significant and even more devastating for the warriors was the loss of some 1,500 ponies, captured by the quick-thinking and hard-riding troops of Captain Eugene Beaumont's company. A final heartbreaking blow came when Mackenzie deprived the Native Americans of any hope of recapturing the herd. As a longtime practitioner of total war, Mackenzie understood the value of the ponies. After culling out some 350 horses for his men and his scouts, he ordered the remainder—more than 1,000—shot.

The Battle of Palo Duro Canyon cemented Mackenzie's reputation as one of America's most successful Indian fighters. The battle also revealed the vulnerability of the Indian refuge on the Staked Plain and signaled the end to a cherished way of life for the tribes of the southern Plains. The battle was the decisive engagement of the Red River War that led to the final subjugation of the Comanches and Kiowas. Although campaigning continued into 1875, the Indians' ability to sustain themselves in the field had been destroyed. Within a year, the last of the holdouts trickled into the reservation at Fort Sill in Indian Territory.

David Coffey

**Further Reading**

Haley, James L. *The Buffalo War: The History of the Red River Indian Uprising of 1874*. Norman: University of Oklahoma Press, 1985.

Pierce, Michael D. *The Most Promising Young Officer: A Life of Ranald Slidell Mackenzie*. Norman: University of Oklahoma Press, 1993.

Utley, Robert M. *Frontier Regulars: The United States and the American Indian, 1866–1891*. New York: Macmillan, 1973.

## Battle of the Little Bighorn

| Date | June 25–26, 1876 | |
|------|------------------|---|
| Location | Near the Little Bighorn River, Big Horn County, Montana | |
| Opponents (*winner) | *Oglala Sioux, Cheyennes, and Arapahos | U.S. Army |
| Commander | Chief Crazy Horse | Lieutenant Colonel George A. Custer |
| Approx. # Troops | 1,800 warriors | 647 soldiers |
| Importance | The best known of all U.S. Army–Native American military engagements, its outcome shocks the American public and leads to the dispatch of significant reinforcement and the hunting down of the so-called hostiles. | |

*Custer's Last Fight,* a painting depicting the defeat of members of the 7th Cavalry
Regiment under Lieutenant Colonel George A. Custer in the Battle of Little Big
Horn, June 25–26, 1876. (Corel)

The discovery of gold in the Black Hills in 1874 and the failure of efforts by the
U.S. Army to prevent incursions into Sioux lands by growing numbers of miners
searching for gold led to the Great Sioux War of 1876–1877 (also known as the
Black Hills War and the Sioux and Northern Cheyenne War). Additionally, the Native Americans were resentful of wagon trains and U.S. proposals to run the Northern Pacific Railroad across their buffalo hunting grounds.

Commander of the Division of the Missouri Lieutenant General Philip H.
Sheridan was called to Washington in November 1865, and plans were drawn up
for military action against the bands of Sioux and Northern Cheyennes who refused to come to the Indian agencies or had simply left reservations. Concerned at
being seen as launching an unprovoked war, the Ulysses S. Grant administration
instructed Indian agents to insist that the Indians return to the reservations by
January 31, 1876, or face military action. A number of the Sioux not on the reservations, including Hunkpapa Lakota Sioux medicine man Sitting Bull, insisted that
they must first hunt buffalo and that they would return to the reservations in the
spring, but government leaders refused any extension of the deadline to placate
either the Sioux or Indian agents, who pointed out that weather conditions would
not allow the Lakotas to meet it.

With hundreds of Sioux under Sitting Bull and Oglala Lakota chief Crazy Horse
having failed to report to the reservations, on February 8 Sheridan issued orders for
the subjection of the recalcitrant Sioux and their return to the reservations by force.
The ensuing Great Sioux War would be the toughest Native American challenge
for the army since before the War of 1812.

Sheridan's plan for a winter campaign was stymied by delays but involved three
converging columns. Brigadier General Alfred H. Terry, in charge of the Department

of the Dakota, had overall command. With 1,000 men, he was to move from the east along the Yellowstone River. At the same time, Brigadier General George Crook would proceed north from Fort Fetterman, Wyoming, with 1,000 soldiers and some 260 allied Shoshone and Crow Indians, while Colonel John Gibbon with another 450 men would march from Fort Ellis and the west. The three columns were to converge on the Yellowstone River. With nearly 3,000 men committed, army leaders were confident of victory.

Crook's column was the first to make contact with the hostiles. On June 17, 1876, while proceeding up the south bank of the Rosebud River in present-day Big Horn County, Montana, Crook fought an unusual sustained six-hour battle with at least 1,500 and as many as 4,000–6,000 Lakota Sioux and Cheyennes led by Crazy Horse. The battle was inconclusive, and the Indians, aware of the forces converging against them, withdrew. Although Crook claimed victory, he was forced to retire and regroup, while his adversaries in the battle were able to take part in the subsequent major battle.

Unaware of Crook's rebuff, Terry pressed on. He and Gibbon united their columns and, learning that the Sioux were camped along the Little Bighorn River, proceeded there. Leading the advance were Lieutenant Colonel George A. Custer and his 7th Cavalry Regiment. A general in the Civil War and a veteran of the Plains fighting, Custer was also an inveterate glory seeker frustrated that he had not yet regained his former rank. He also denigrated Native American fighting abilities.

Custer was unaware that he was approaching probably the largest assemblage of Indian power ever: some 10,000–15,000 people, at least 4,000 of them warriors. Ordered to scout the Rosebud and Bighorn River Valleys, Custer and his 647 men, including 35 scouts, came upon the Indian camp on June 25. Ignoring orders not to attack until the command could be concentrated, Custer proceeded alone. He divided his 12 companies into three columns with the plan to attack the camp from different directions. Major Marcus Reno and Captain Frederick Benteen each assumed command of three companies, but the largest body of six companies of 212 troops proceeded under Custer's direct command.

In the ensuing Battle of the Little Bighorn, none of Custer's columns got very far. Reno's smaller column was soon halted by the Indians. It was subsequently joined by the other column under Benteen, the arrival of which probably saved Reno's men from annihilation. Reno and Benteen then constructed a defensive position on bluffs (known today as Reno Hill). Digging rifle pits, they were able to hold out here until rescued by Terry two days later.

Custer, meanwhile, was surrounded by more than 1,000 warriors led by Crazy Horse. Many of the warriors had repeating Winchester rifles and were thus better armed than Custer's men, who had the slower-firing Trapdoor Springfield. Within two hours, Custer's force was wiped out; all 212 men were killed. More than 100 were killed or wounded in the other two columns. In all, 268 were killed, and

55 were wounded. These figures represent nearly 40 percent of the regiment's pre-battle strength. The Custer family lost four of its members in addition to George: two brothers, Captain Tom Custer and Boston Custer; a nephew, Armstrong Reed; and a brother-in-law, Lieutenant James Calhoun. There is no consensus on Indian casualties, which were probably 50–200 or more.

Terry and Gibbon reached the field two days later on June 27 and buried the dead. Lacking the logistical capability to sustain a larger force in the field for long, the Native Americans had moved off, separating into smaller bands. Had they remained together, they might have defeated Terry and Gibbon as well.

The Battle of the Little Bighorn, also known as Custer's Last Stand and, by the Indians involved, as the Battle of the Greasy Grass, shocked the American people. Washington immediately dispatched reinforcements to the region and directed the army to hunt down the "hostiles." Although it took time to locate the elusive bands, the Native Americans soon were rounded up. Many were starving and came in voluntarily to army posts. General recognition of the mistreatment of Native Americans in the settlement of the West and the role of the army in this has led to the battle being viewed as a tragic encounter forced by the relentless westward U.S. expansionist movement and the efforts of Native Americans to defend their traditional way of life.

Spencer C. Tucker

### Further Reading

Connell, Evan S. *Son of the Morning Star: Custer and the Little Bighorn.* New York: North Point, 1984.

Miller, David H. *Custer's Fall: The Native American Side of the Story.* Norman: University of Nebraska Press, 1985.

Sarf, Wayne Michael. *The Little Bighorn Campaign, March–September 1876.* Conshohocken, PA: Combined Books, 1993.

Sklenar, Larry. *To Hell with Honor: Custer and the Little Big Horn.* Norman: University of Oklahoma Press, 2000.

## Battle of Wounded Knee

| Date | December 29, 1890 | |
|---|---|---|
| Location | Wounded Knee Creek, South Dakota | |
| Opponents (*winner) | *United States | Miniconjou Sioux |
| Commander | Colonel James W. Forsyth | Chief Big Foot (Spotted Elk) |
| Approx. # Troops | 500 men; 4 artillery pieces | At least 146 killed (350 men, women, and children) |
| Importance | This tragic encounter, still viewed by many as a massacre, brings finis to the Indian Wars. | |

By 1890, most of the western Native American tribes had been relegated to reservations, their lands and culture systematically eliminated. In the early 1870s Wovoka, an influential Northern Paiute medicine man, began preaching a popular peace tenet known as the Ghost Dance that dictated a life of moral behavior combined with traditional Native American customs and that above all denounced violence. Many of the beleaguered western tribes embraced this religion. The Sioux, however, distorted this creed into a more militant doctrine against white oppression.

Many of the Lakota Sioux (Teton Sioux), long fed up with the inept Indian agents of the Pine Ridge Agency, took up the Ghost Dance and moved off their reservations. U.S. Army commanders on the northern Plains grew apprehensive and worried that other Sioux bands would join the Pine Ridge contingent. Major General Nelson A. Miles, commanding the Military Division of the Missouri, soon ordered the arrest of Sitting Bull and Big Foot (also known as Spotted Elk), two prominent Sioux leaders who it was feared might bring about this alliance.

On December 15, 1890, Sitting Bull was killed in a scuffle when Indian police tried to arrest him. The respected Big Foot, whose Miniconjou band resided at the Cheyenne River Agency, agreed to go to Pine Ridge at the invitation of the chiefs there. His mission was to mitigate dissension among the Oglalas and Brulés and not to promote violence. Big Foot and his people managed to evade troops posted to block his path but were intercepted at Wounded Knee Creek.

Colonel James W. Forsyth's 7th Cavalry was ordered out to disarm Big Foot's village, and on the morning of December 29 some 500 troopers surrounded the Indian encampment near Wounded Knee Creek on the Lakota Pine Ridge Reservation in South Dakota. The Sioux warriors were lined up and ordered to hand over all weapons. Despite being outnumbered and with four Hotchkiss cannon aimed at the encampment, the Native Americans refused to surrender their Winchester repeating rifles. Tension grew as troops began to ransack the lodges and a medicine man known as Yellow Bird began to dance and incite the Sioux to action.

A scuffle occurred, and a shot rang out. Both sides then fired on the other. The resulting melee was a brief, brutal hand-to-hand combat involving clubs, knives, and rifles. Once the fight was over, the artillery shelled the village. At least 146 Native Americans were killed (84 men, 44 women, and 18 children); some estimates put the number of dead much higher. Big Foot was among those killed. Some 150 Native Americans managed to escape, a number of whom later froze to death. Army casualties in the fight were 25 dead and 39 wounded.

A related skirmish occurred the following day at Drexel Mission Church, four miles north of Wounded Knee, where a group of Sioux who had escaped the earlier battle burned four sheds. They also ambushed a squadron of the 7th Cavalry, killing one trooper and wounding six others. Native casualties in the engagement are not known. The patrol was rescued by members of the 9th Cavalry Regiment, who had been trailing the Sioux from the White River. This ended the wider Battle of Wounded Knee.

General Miles, hoping to prevent further violence, surrounded the disgruntled Native Americans at a distance with more than 3,000 soldiers. He then employed a combination of diplomacy and threat of force to secure the surrender of the last of the Sioux on January 15, 1891. A grand review of the soldiers was staged on January 21 before hundreds of Sioux.

Colonel Forsyth, meanwhile, was relieved of command. A court of inquiry concluded that the soldiers did indeed try to avoid killing women and children but that their proximity to the village made these deaths unavoidable. It was never established which side fired first. Forsyth was exonerated. Miles charged him with dereliction of duty, but Forsyth was later restored to command. Clearly, Forsyth had not understood the danger. Miles had cautioned him against placing the troops in close proximity to the Native Americans, but with his overwhelming manpower, Forsyth had not anticipated or prepared for confrontation.

The last major battle between the U.S. Army and Native Americans, the Battle of Wounded Knee, also known as the Wounded Knee Massacre, was not premeditated; rather, it was a major military blunder that could have been avoided. More than 120 years later, it remains for Native Americans a powerful symbol of their subjugation by whites.

William Whyte

**Further Reading**

Brown, Dee. *Bury My Heart at Wounded Knee.* New York: Holt, Rinehart and Winston, 1970.

Utley, Robert M. *Frontier Regulars: The United States and the American Indian, 1866–1891.* New York: Macmillan, 1973.

Wooster, Robert. *The Military and United States Indian Policy, 1865–1903.* New Haven, CT: Yale University Press, 1988.

# Battle of Manila Bay

| Date | May 1, 1898 | |
|---|---|---|
| Location | Manila Bay, Philippine Islands | |
| Opponents (*winner) | *United States | Spain |
| Commander | Commodore George Dewey | Rear Admiral Patricio Montojo y Pasarón |
| # of Ships | 4 protected cruisers, 2 gunboats | 2 protected cruisers, 5 light cruisers |
| Importance | Makes it possible for the United States to land troops and take the city of Manila and ultimately the Philippine Islands from Spain. | |

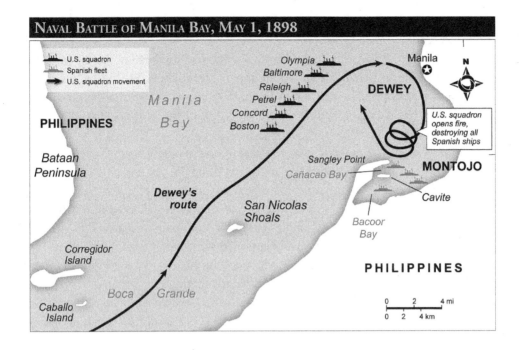

NAVAL BATTLE OF MANILA BAY, MAY 1, 1898

Commodore George Dewey's U.S. Asiatic Squadron was at Hong Kong when on April 23, 1898, Dewey was informed by British acting governor Major General Wilsone Black that war had been declared between the United States and Spain. Black then issued a proclamation of British neutrality and ordered Dewey's ships to leave Hong Kong's territorial waters by noon the next day.

Dewey repaired to Mirs Bay, an anchorage in Chinese waters, and there received a cablegram from Washington ordering him to the Philippines. The cablegram instructed him to "commence operations at once, particularly against the Spanish fleet. You must capture vessels or destroy. Use utmost endeavors."

Dewey's squadron consisted of the protected cruisers *Olympia* (flagship), *Baltimore, Boston,* and *Raleigh;* the gunboats *Concord* and *Petrel;* and the *McCulloch,* a revenue cutter that was pressed into service. Dewey left behind the old paddle wheeler *Monocacy,* but two colliers also accompanied the squadron. He was concerned about his ammunition supply, for when the squadron departed for the Philippines, the ship magazines were only about 60 percent of capacity. Before sailing, he conferred with the former U.S. consul to the Philippines, Oscar Williams, who had left Manila under threat of his life on April 23. Williams briefed Dewey and his commanders on board the *Olympia* only an hour before their departure on April 27, confirming that the American squadron was superior to that of the Spanish, which would most likely be found in Subic Bay, 30 miles from Manila.

That same afternoon, the American ships departed Chinese waters. They made landfall at Cape Bolineau, Luzon, at daybreak on April 30. Dewey detached the *Boston* and *Concord,* later reinforced by the *Baltimore,* to make a quick

Illustration of the Battle of Manila Bay on May 1, 1898. The U.S. Navy's destruction of the Spanish squadron off Manila made possible the U.S. conquest of the Philippines. (Library of Congress)

reconnaissance of Subic Bay, and they soon determined that the Spanish squadron was not present. Reportedly, Dewey was pleased at the news and remarked that "Now we have them."

Dewey then ordered his ships to steam to Manila Bay, which the squadron entered on the night of April 30. He chose to ignore the threat of mines and the fortifications guarding the entrance to the bay. Dewey selected the Boca Grande channel, and the ships steamed in single file with as few lights as possible. Not until the squadron had passed the islet El Fraile did the Spaniards discover the American presence. Both sides then exchanged a few shots but without damage. The American ships were now into the bay. Detaching his two supply ships and the *McCulloch*, Dewey proceeded ahead, although he did not intend to engage the Spaniards until dawn.

The Spaniards had some 40 naval vessels in and around Manila, but most were small gunboats. Spanish rear admiral Patricio Montojo y Pasarón's squadron consisted of seven ships: the two large cruisers *Reina Cristina* and *Castilla* (of about 3,000 tons each and the latter of wood) and the five small cruisers *Don Juan de Austria, Don Antonio de Ulloa, Isle de Cuba, Marqués del Duro,* and *Isle de Luzon,* each of less than 1,200 tons and none with more than four 4.7-inch guns in the main battery. Other ships were undergoing repairs. The Spanish warships were greatly inferior in armament to the American squadron, the crews of which were also better trained.

Montojo originally had his ships at Subic Bay during April 26–29, but its promised shore batteries were not yet in place, and the harbor entrance had not been mined. The water there was also 40 feet deep. Pessimistic about his chances and reportedly deciding that if his ships were to be sunk he would prefer it to occur in shallower water, Montojo had returned them to Manila Bay. His captains concurred with the decision.

To help offset his weakness in firepower, Montojo anchored his ships in Cañacao Bay just south of Manila off the fortified naval yard of Cavite so that they might be supported by land batteries. There the water was only 25 feet deep, and if the ships were sunk or had to be scuttled, the Spanish crews would stand a better chance of escape. Not believing that there was any immediate threat from the Americans, Montojo went ashore for the night, only to be alerted to their presence by the sounds of the exchange of gunfire on Dewey's ships entering the bay.

Early on the morning of May 1 only a week after the declaration of war, Dewey's ships steamed toward Manila, with the *Olympia* leading followed by the *Baltimore, Raleigh, Petrel, Concord,* and *Boston.* Off Manila a little after 5:00 a.m., the Spanish shore batteries opened up with wildly inaccurate fire that inflicted no damage. The *Boston* and *Concord* returned fire. Dewey then turned his ships toward the Spanish squadron. As the American ships advanced in single line, two Spanish mines exploded at some distance away from the *Olympia* and without effect. At 5:40 a.m. about 5,000 yards from the Spanish line, Dewey turned to his flag captain Charles Gridley of the *Olympia* and said, "You may fire when you are ready, Gridley."

The ships of the American squadron then closed to about 3,000 yards and turned to the west, running parallel back and forth along the Spanish line and pounding it with their guns. The 8-inch guns of the U.S. cruisers, hurling 150-pound shells, exacted the most damage. The Spanish ships and shore batteries responded but failed to inflict significant damage. Dewey then called a halt to assess damage and the status of ammunition stocks, and at the same time he ordered breakfast served to the crews.

At 11:16 a.m., the U.S. ships stood in again to complete their work. Within little more than an hour, they had sunk the remaining Spanish vessels firing at them and had secured the surrender of the naval station at Cavite. Dewey then sent a message to the Spanish commander at Manila that if the shore batteries did not cease fire, he would shell and destroy the city. Shortly thereafter, the city's guns fell silent.

In the ships and at Cavite, the Spaniards suffered 167 dead and 214 wounded, all but 10 aboard the ships. Three of the Spanish ships were later salvaged and pressed into service by the Americans. The Americans had no men killed and only 8 wounded. Rarely was a victory more cheaply obtained.

Dewey then took Cavite and blockaded the city of Manila while awaiting army troops to take it. On June 30 Major General Wesley Merritt and 10,000 men arrived. On August 13 the soldiers, assisted by naval gunfire from Dewey's squadron and Filipino guerrillas under Emilio Aguinaldo y Famy, attacked Manila. After a short, nominal defense, the city surrendered.

The Battle of Manila Bay was the decisive naval engagement of the war. In only 10 weeks' time, the United States had secured an empire from Spain, and it was control of the ocean that had enabled the United States to do so. The Philippine Islands were taken to provide a bargaining chip to persuade Spain to conclude peace, but in the final peace agreement the United States decided to keep the islands. This led to a war with Filipino nationalists who wanted independence and set up the future confrontation between the United States and Japan.

Spencer C. Tucker

**Further Reading**

Conroy, Robert. *The Battle of Manila Bay: The Spanish-American War in the Philippines.* New York: Macmillan, 1968.

Dewey, George. *The Autobiography of George Dewey.* 1913; reprint, Annapolis, MD: Naval Institute Press, 1987.

Spector, Ronald. *Admiral of the New Empire: The Life and Career of George Dewey.* Baton Rouge: Louisiana University Press, 1974.

Trask, David F. *The War with Spain in 1898.* Lincoln: University of Nebraska Press, 1996.

## Battle of Kettle Hill

| Date | July 1, 1898 | |
|---|---|---|
| Location | Near Santiago, Cuba | |
| Opponents (*winner) | *United States | Spain |
| Commander | Brigadier General Samuel S. Sumner | Lieutenant General Arsenio Linares y Pomba |
| Approx. # Troops | 5,000 men | 750 men |
| Importance | Helps secure San Juan Heights, the last natural barrier to Santiago, and makes Theodore Roosevelt a national hero, boosting his political career. | |

A major U.S. strategic objective in the Spanish-American War was the occupation of Cuba. U.S. Army V Corps troops, commanded by Major General William R. Shafter, had landed at Daiquirí, some 16 miles east of Santiago, on June 22, 1898. Shafter's objective was Santiago, and Kettle Hill, held by some 750 Spanish troops, was the first objective before San Juan Heights, the last major natural barrier to the port of Santiago.

While Brigadier General Henry W. Lawton's 2nd Infantry Division attacked Spanish troops at the nearby town of El Caney, Brigadier General Jacob F. Kent's 1st Infantry Division and Major General Joseph Wheeler's Dismounted Cavalry Division advanced toward San Juan Heights. With Wheeler ill, Brigadier General Samuel S. Sumner had charge of the Dismounted Cavalry Division. Shafter, situated at El Pozo two miles away, had envisioned Lawton's troops defeating the

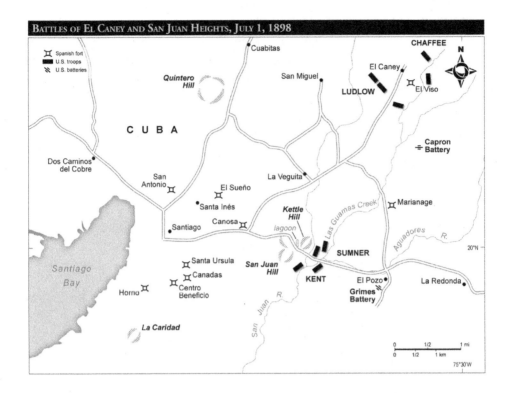

BATTLES OF EL CANEY AND SAN JUAN HEIGHTS, JULY 1, 1898

Spanish troops at El Caney in two hours and then moving south to join Kent's and Sumner's divisions for a combined assault on San Juan Heights.

The American attack on San Juan Heights, however, was delayed when Lawton's troops took longer than the anticipated two hours to quell Spanish resistance at El Caney. The men of the 2nd Infantry Division and the Dismounted Cavalry Division were meanwhile coming under fire from Spanish troops on the heights. After waiting for several hours and taking casualties from Spanish fire from the heights, many of the American officers grew impatient waiting for new orders from Shafter. At 1:00 p.m., three hours after the planned time for the assault and on his own responsibility, Sumner ordered an attack. On the left, Brigadier General Hamilton S. Hawkins's 1st Brigade of Kent's division moved up the western slope of San Juan Heights. Receiving important fire support from the Gatling Gun Detachment, they reached the summit.

At the same time that the infantry troops were securing San Juan Heights, Sumner's dismounted cavalrymen on the right flank were moving up Kettle Hill. The 9th U.S. Cavalry Regiment led the attack, closely followed by the 1st Volunteer Cavalry Regiment (the Rough Riders) and the 1st U.S. Cavalry. Meanwhile, the U.S. 3rd Infantry, 6th Infantry, and 10th Cavalry moved partway up the hill.

Lieutenant Colonel Theodore Roosevelt of the Rough Riders was among the first leaders at the top of the hill. He was one of the few officers to proceed on horseback, but a wire fence had forced him to dismount near the crest and make the last 40 yards on foot. There were no Spaniards there when the Americans reached the summit, as they had withdrawn ahead of the American advance. By 1:15 p.m., 15 minutes after the attack began, the Americans were in possession of Kettle Hill.

The Americans on Kettle Hill then opened an intense fire on San Juan Hill to the north. Securing permission from Sumner, Roosevelt led his men down the western slope, past a small lagoon, and up the northern extension of San Juan Hill to secure the part of San Juan Heights north of the El Pozo–Santiago Road. The Americans now controlled the eastern approaches to Santiago. That city surrendered on July 17, marking the effective end of the land campaign in Cuba.

The attack cost the Dismounted Cavalry Division 35 dead and 328 wounded and also made Roosevelt a national hero. He used reportage of his role in the battle to help win election as governor of New York in 1899 and nomination as the Republican vice presidential candidate in 1900. Roosevelt's role in the Battle of Kettle Hill was popularized by American journalists and illustrators. *New York Sun* journalist Richard Harding Davis, the best-known newspaper correspondent of the war, wrote eloquently of Roosevelt's charge up the hill. Frederic Remington's painting *The Charge of the Rough Riders* was even more laudatory of Roosevelt's heroism. Commissioned by Roosevelt himself, the painting depicts Roosevelt in the background on horseback, pistol drawn, leading the men forward. Although many of the Rough Riders wanted Roosevelt to receive the Medal of Honor, Secretary of War Russell Alger, upset that Roosevelt had written a report demanding the immediate return to the United States of troops suffering from disease, refused to endorse the recommendation. Nevertheless, on January 16, 2001, President William Jefferson Clinton posthumously awarded Roosevelt the Medal of Honor for his actions at Kettle Hill and San Juan Hill. Although the award came more than a century after the deed, Roosevelt was the first president of the United States to receive the highest U.S. award for valor.

Michael R. Hall and Spencer C. Tucker

## Further Reading

Azoy, A. C. M. *Charge! The Story of the Battle of San Juan Hill.* New York: Longmans, 1961.

Konstam, Angus. *San Juan Hill, 1898: America's Emergence as a World Power.* Westport, CT: Praeger, 2004.

Samuels, Peggy, and Harold Samuels. *Teddy Roosevelt at San Juan: The Making of a President.* College Station: Texas A&M University Press, 1997.

Walker, Dale L. *The Boys of '98: Theodore Roosevelt and the Rough Riders.* New York: Forge, 1999.

## Second Battle of the Marne

| Date | July 15–18, 1918 | |
|---|---|---|
| Location | Vicinity of the city of Rheims, France | |
| Opponents (*winner) | *France, United States, United Kingdom, and Italy | Germany |
| Commander | General de Division Ferdinand Foch | General der Infanterie Erich Ludendorff; Crown Prince Wilhelm |
| Approx. # Troops | 68 divisions (54 French, 8 U.S., 4 British, 2 Italian); 3,080 guns, 250 tanks | 48 German divisions; 6,353 guns |
| Importance | U.S. troops play a key role in halting the last German drive of the Ludendorff Offensive. The Allies now take the offensive themselves and hold it for the remainder of the war. | |

At dawn on July 15, German Army first quartermaster general and General der Infanterie Erich Ludendorff launched his fifth offensive, Operation MARNESCHUTZ-RHEIMS, known to history as the Second Battle of the Marne and the Champagne-Marne Offensive. This was the last German effort to try to win World War I in 1918 before arriving American Expeditionary Forces manpower could tip the scale decisively in favor of the Allies. Ludendorff's overly ambitious plan involved a double envelopment by General der Infanterie (U.S. equivalent lieutenant general) Crown Prince Wilhelm's Army Group east and west of the city of Rheims, with the goal of taking both it and the vital railroad running from Paris to Nancy. General der Infanterie Hans von Boehn's Seventh Army was to move up the Marne, while Generaloberst (U.S. equivalent full general) Karl von Einem genannt von Rothmaler's Third Army struck south toward Châlons-sur-Marne. Ludendorff believed that his offensive would force French général de division Ferdinand Foch, the supreme Allied commander, to pull his remaining reserves from Flanders. Ludendorff also believed that within a few days of victory at Rheims, he would be able to launch his planned Operation HAGEN and finish off the British to the north.

However, there was no guarantee that the Germans would not continue up the Marne Valley to Paris, and the offensive brought fear reminiscent of the summer of 1914 to the French capital. The sound of the heavy guns in the battle could be heard clearly in the French capital, some 50 miles distant.

Général de Division Henri Joseph Eugène Gouraud's French Fourth Army defended east of Rheims, while the French Sixth Army under Général de Division Jean Marie Degoutte was west of that city, almost to Château-Thierry on the Marne. In all, 48 German divisions faced 36 French divisions. The advantage in artillery also lay with the Germans: 6,353 guns to only 3,080 for the Allies.

Ludendorff launched his offensive at dawn on July 15. The offensive was the farthest south and east of all the German drives of 1918. Deserters and prisoners

French troops drive back the Germans near the Marne River. This final German offensive during July 15–18, 1918, was a turning point in World War I. Americans played an important role in the defeat of this German offensive. Their failure here meant that the Germans had lost the war. (National Archives)

betrayed most of the German plan, however, including its timing. The German artillery preparation began at 1:10 a.m. on July 15, but at midnight the French artillery had initiated an enhanced program of harassing and interdicting fire, and at 1:20 a.m. the French commenced full counterpreparation artillery fire, the intensity of which caught the Germans by surprise with their infantry in its assembly areas, inflicting many casualties.

At 4:50 a.m., Germany infantrymen began their attack behind a creeping barrage that included gas. West of Rheims, the French counterpreparation artillery fire separated the Seventh Army's infantry from its creeping barrage and disrupted the German bridging operation across the Marne. By nightfall on July 15, the Germans had crossed some six divisions to the south bank of the Marne, but hardly any artillery had gotten across the river. The bridgehead was now about 12 miles wide and 3 miles deep. At this point French artillery, working in conjunction with aircraft, concentrated on the bridges in order to cut off the Germans on the south bank.

East of Rheims, the German First and Third Armies encountered far heavier French artillery fire than anticipated but little French infantry resistance. At about 7:30 a.m. the German creeping barrage reached its maximum range and lifted. The attackers then found themselves facing a fully manned zone defense that hardly had been touched by the German artillery preparation or the creeping barrage. The Germans had walked into a trap. Knowing the timing of the attack, the Fourth Army had abandoned its frontline positions except for light security forces. The massive German artillery preparation had mostly struck empty ground.

By nightfall on July 15, Ludendorff's Operation MARNESCHUTZ-RHEIMS was already a failure. The fighting dragged on, however. Ludendorff ordered the Third Army to halt its attack and the Seventh Army on the west flank to consolidate its gains. On July 17 the Germans began bringing up artillery from the Seventh Army to support the First Army's attack on Rheims.

The French then launched a surprise counterattack, for even as the battle for Rheims raged, Foch had carefully assembled a reserve of 20 divisions—2 American and 18 French—along with 350 tanks. Early on July 18, he launched a counteroffensive with Général de Division Charles Mangin's Tenth Army and Général de Division Jean Degoutte's Sixth Army to its right against the Blücher salient on both sides of Château-Thierry, precisely the same area that the Germans had stripped of reinforcing artillery the day before.

The U.S. 1st and 2nd Divisions spearheaded the Tenth Army's attack, which fell on the right side of the Rheims salient five miles south of German-held Soissons. Although casualties were heavy for the Allies (the 1st Division, commanded by Major General Charles P. Summerall, alone sustained 7,200 casualties that day, and the 2nd Division, commanded by Major General James G. Harbord, sustained nearly 5,000 casualties), the attack succeeded brilliantly. The 1st Division captured 3,800 prisoners and 70 guns from the 7 German divisions it encountered, while the 2nd Division took 3,000 prisoners and 75 guns. In all, the Allies took 12,000 prisoners and 250 guns from 11 German divisions. The Second Battle of the Marne ended the German threat to Paris, and from this point on the Allies held the initiative on the Western Front.

Spencer C. Tucker

## Further Reading

Essame, Hubert. *The Battle for Europe, 1918.* London: Batsford, 1972.

Holmes, Richard. *The Western Front.* New York: TV Books, 2000.

Paschall, Rod. *The Defeat of Imperial Germany, 1917–1918.* Chapel Hill, NC: Algonquin, 1989.

Pitt, Barrie. *1918: The Last Act.* New York: Ballantine, 1963.

Wynne, Graeme. *If Germany Attacks: The Battle in Depth in the West.* London: Faber and Faber, 1940.

Zabecki, David T. *The German 1918 Offensives: A Case Study in the Operational Art of War.* New York: Routledge, 2006.

Zabecki, David T. *Steel Wind: Colonel Georg Bruchmüller and the Birth of Modern Artillery.* Westport, CT: Praeger, 1994.

## Saint-Mihiel Offensive

| Date | September 12–16, 1918 | |
|---|---|---|
| Location | Saint-Mihiel salient south of Verdun in eastern France | |
| Opponents (*winner) | *United States and France | Germany |
| Commander | General John J. Pershing | General der Infanterie Georg von der Marwitz |
| Approx. # Troops | 18 divisions (14 U.S., 4 French); 3,000 guns, 400 tanks, 1,500 aircraft | 10+ divisions |
| Importance | The first independent offensive operation for a U.S. army in the war, it significantly improved the Allies' military position in France and established the fighting reputation of the American Expeditionary Forces. | |

Following the Aisne-Marne Campaign (July 18–August 6, 1918) and the end of the German threat to Paris, French marshal Ferdinand Foch, Allied commander on the Western Front, gave American Expeditionary Forces (AEF) commander General John J. Pershing permission for an independent U.S. Army action. For more than a year, Pershing had hoped for an attack to pinch out the Saint-Mihiel salient (named for the town at its tip) that intruded into Allied lines south of Verdun and threatened the Paris-Nancy railroad line. The salient was also the entrance to the important Briey Basin that supplied Germany with much of its iron ore. After sometimes acrimonious debate, Foch finally agreed to Pershing's proposed offensive in what would be the first major battle of the war planned and carried out by the AEF.

Pershing had wanted the offensive to be the beginning of a drive all the way to Metz, but with the Amiens Offensive (August 8–15) having gone well, Foch ordered Pershing to limit his assault to reaching the base of the salient and then to shift his forces west in order to attack north of the Marne in the Meuse-Argonne sector. Pershing was bitterly disappointed with this decision, and rejecting this plan was probably a mistake on the part of Foch. The Americans believed, with some justification, that Pershing's plan would have yielded greater gains than British field marshal Sir Douglas Haig's attack toward Cambrai, which was the basis of Foch's subsequent operations.

Fourteen American and four French divisions were assigned to First Army for the Saint-Mihiel operation. While the AEF had ample small arms, the priority given by the United States at British and French insistence to the shipment of infantrymen rather than supporting arms (such as artillery, engineers, and aviation units and their equipment) meant that First Army was lacking in these and other support units. The French made up this shortfall by loaning the Americans more than half the artillery as well as nearly half the tanks and aircraft required for the offensive.

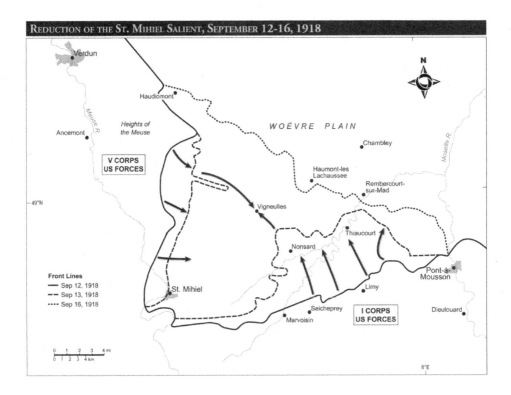

First Army would have more than 3,000 guns, 400 tanks, and 1,500 aircraft. The British and French provided the bulk of the artillery support. Lieutenant Colonel George S. Patton commanded the 304th Tank Brigade of 267 French light Renault tanks in what would be the first combat for U.S. tankers. U.S. Army colonel William Mitchell directed a heterogeneous air force of American, French, British, Italian, and Portuguese units in what would turn out to be the largest single air operation of the war. The American squadrons flew 609 of the airplanes, which were of French or British manufacture.

The offensive commenced before dawn on September 12 with a four-hour artillery bombardment and a threefold assault on the salient. The main attack was largely a pushing action mounted against the south face of the salient by two American corps. On the left, Major General Joseph T. Dickman's IV Corps (from left to right the 1st, 42nd, and 89th Divisions in line, with the 3rd Division in reserve) would operate on a front from Limey westward to Marvoisin. On the right, Major General Hunter Liggett's I Corps (from left to right in the line the 2nd, 5th, 90th, and 82nd Divisions, with the 78th Division in reserve) would operate along the line from Pont-à-Mousson on the Moselle westward to Limey.

Major General George H. Cameron's V Corps (from left to right, the 8th Brigade of the 4th Division, the French 15th Colonial Division, and the 26th Division, with the remainder of the 4th Division in reserve) would experience its first combat action. It was to mount a secondary thrust against the west face of the salient along the heights of the Meuse from Mouilly north to Haudimont. First Army's reserve consisted of three American divisions: the 35th, 80th, and 91st.

To fix the Germans in the salient, the French mounted an attack against the apex of the salient. The attack was carried out by the II Colonial Corps (from left to right, the 2nd Cavalry Division, the 26th Infantry Division, and the 39th Colonial Division). Altogether, Allied forces involved in the offensive totaled more than 650,000 men: some 550,000 American and 100,000 Allied (mostly French) troops.

German Army General der Artillerie (U.S. equivalent lieutenant general) Max von Gallwitz's Fifth Army had responsibility for this sector of the front. Gallwitz had at his disposal eight divisions and a brigade in the line and about two division equivalents in reserve. The Germans, then desperately short of manpower, recognized the threat and the need for a shorter line that could be held by fewer troops, and Gallwitz had begun withdrawing troops from the salient the day before the Allied offensive began.

The attack went much better than anticipated, especially in the southern part of the salient, where the Germans had already thinned out their forces. Although many of the tanks became bogged down in mud, they were hardly needed. Aware that the Germans were withdrawing, Pershing ordered the offensive speeded up and also ordered a nighttime pursuit. By the morning of September 13, the 1st Division, advancing from the east, had linked up at Vigneulles with the 26th Division from the west, and before evening all objectives in the salient had been captured. At this point, Pershing halted any further advances so that American units could be withdrawn for the coming offensive in the Meuse-Argonne sector. By September 16, the salient was entirely cleared.

This first major operation of an independent American army resulted in the capture of some 16,000 Germans and 257 guns at a cost of 7,000 American casualties. The operation also eliminated the threat of an attack on the rear of Allied fortifications at Nancy and Verdun, greatly improved Allied lateral rail communications, and opened the way for a possible future offensive to seize Metz and the Briey Basin in the unlikely event that Foch should change his mind.

Spencer C. Tucker

## Further Reading

Bonk, David. *St. Mihiel 1918: The American Expeditionary Forces' Trial by Fire*. London: Osprey, 2011.

Coffman, Edward M. *The War to End All Wars: The American Military Experience in World War I*. 1968; reprint, Lexington: University Press of Kentucky, 1998.

Hallas, James H. *Squandered Victory: The American First Army at St. Mihiel*. Westport, CT: Praeger, 1995.

Marshall, George C. *Memoirs of My Services in the World War, 1917–1918*. Boston: Houghton Mifflin, 1976.

Mauer, Mauer. *The U.S. Air Service in World War I*, Vol. 3, *The Battle of St. Mihiel*. Washington, DC: Office of Air Force History, 1979.

## Meuse-Argonne Offensive

| Date | September 26–November 11, 1918 | |
|---|---|---|
| Location | Meuse-Argonne region of northeastern France | |
| Opponents (*winner) | *United States | Germany |
| Commander | General John J. Pershing | General der Kavallerie Georg von der Marwitz |
| Approx. # Troops | More than 1.2 million men | More than 450,000 men |
| Importance | The largest military operation for the American Expeditionary Forces (AEF) in the war, it greatly assisted the Allied victory of November 1918. | |

Having seized the initiative after the failure of the German Ludendorff Offensive (March 21–July 18, 1918), French marshal Ferdinand Foch, Allied commander in chief, planned one great pushing action along the entire front from Ypres to Verdun. His goal was to expel the Germans from France by winter with the plan to win the war the next spring. The offensive was scheduled to begin in the last week of September, with Foch determined to prevent the Germans from carrying out a phased withdrawal in which they could destroy communications and materiel. The German high command's refusal to sacrifice the huge stores collected behind the front lines contributed to Allied success by delaying the withdrawal of its armies.

Foch's plan called for a pincer movement with the objective of capturing Aulnoye and Mézières, the two key junctions in the lateral rail system behind the German lines. The loss of either of these would seriously affect the German withdrawal. Foch assigned to the British Expeditionary Force the northern thrust against Aulnoye. The American Expeditionary Forces (AEF) received the task of driving on Mézières. At the same time, the Flanders Army Group of Belgian, French, and British forces would drive on Ghent, while the French armies in the Oise-Aisne region would push all along their front in order to lend support to the main pincer attack.

AEF commander General John J. Pershing decided to make his major effort between the Heights of the Meuse on the east and the western edge of the densely wooded Argonne Forest. The designated attack area of about 20 miles across was difficult terrain, broken by the central north-south ridge that dominates the Meuse and Aisne River Valleys. Montfaucon, Cunel, and Barricourt were heavily fortified. The Germans, now masters of defensive warfare, had also created an elaborate defense-in-depth of three separate strong belts, backed up by a fourth less well constructed line. These took full advantage of the wooded, difficult terrain of the Argonne Forest region. Pershing hoped to be able to push through the German defensive lines, break into the open territory beyond, strike at the German flanks, and, in a coordinated drive with the French Fourth Army to the American left, cut the vital Sedan-Mézières railroad line.

U.S. Army soldiers in French-built Renault tanks advancing at the start of the Meuse-Argonne Offensive (September 26–November 11, 1918) on the Western Front. (National Archives)

Pershing's plan was greatly complicated by the fact that several hundred thousand French troops had to be moved out of the assembly areas, and then the AEF had to be moved in. Thanks to brilliant staff work by First Army lieutenant Colonel George C. Marshall, assistant chief of staff, G-3 (Operations), more than 400,000 members of the AEF and 2,700 guns from the Saint-Mihiel Offensive (September 12–16, 1918) were repositioned across the rear of the attacking army in order to be ready for the commencement of the offensive on September 26. Still, this meant that many untested U.S. divisions would be in the forefront of the attack.

The Meuse-Argonne Offensive was the largest operation for the United States in the war, ultimately involving some 1.2 million AEF personnel. The offensive included the U.S. First Army, initially commanded by Pershing, of three corps (10 divisions) attacking abreast and Général de Division Henri Joseph Eugène Gouraud's French Fourth Army on its left. At first the defending German forces numbered only five divisions, but during the course of the offensive these increased to some 450,000 men of General der Kavallerie (U.S. equivalent lieutenant general) Georg von der Marwitz's Fifth Army of Army Group Gallwitz.

Pershing's dispositions called for each of his three corps to have three divisions in line and one in corps reserve. On the left was I Corps (from left to right the 77th, 28th, and 35th Divisions, with the 92nd Division in reserve), which was to advance paralleling the French Fourth Army to its left. The center was held by V Corps (from left to right the 91st, 37th, and 79th Divisions, with the 32nd Division in reserve). Pershing planned that V Corps would strike the decisive blow. Holding the AEF right was III Corps (from left to right the 4th, 80th, and 33rd Divisions, with the 3rd Division in reserve), which was to advance up the west side of the

Meuse River. Eastward across the Meuse, the American front extended in direct line some 60 miles; this part of the line was held by the French IV and II Colonial Corps and the American IV Corps in the Saint-Mihiel sector.

Supporting First Army were nearly 4,000 guns, two-thirds of which were manned by American artillerymen. Pershing had 190 light French Renault tanks, mostly with American personnel. He also had some 820 aircraft, 600 of them flown by Americans.

The first phase of the offensive occurred from September 26 to October 3. The attack began on September 26 at 5:30 a.m., with the AEF advancing seven miles in the first two days. Circumstances forced the Americans to undertake frontal assaults against the well-entrenched Germans, who on September 29 were reinforced by six new divisions. Although the Americans sustained heavy casualties, they managed to penetrate the first two German lines. Supply shortages, inexperience, and lack of tank support all stopped the American forces before the third German line, however.

In the second phase of the offensive, October 4–31, the attack was renewed, this time against 20 German divisions. Again, there was no room for maneuver. The inexperienced American divisions that had led the first phase were replaced by veteran units, which slowly ground their way forward despite heavy American casualties, especially from German air attacks of the frontline troops. First Army air units retaliated with bombing raids against German assembly areas for counterattacks.

Despite insufficient numbers of troop replacements, American penetrations forced the Germans to bring up reserves from other parts of the Western Front, aiding Allied advances elsewhere. Two notable incidents during this phase of the campaign were the fight of the so-called Lost Battalion of the 77th Division (October 2–7) and the feat of Corporal Alvin C. York. Meanwhile, French premier Georges Clemenceau, not understanding the difficulties facing the Americans and the necessity of costly and slow battering-ram tactics, tried without success to have Pershing relieved of command.

On October 16 the AEF's Second Army, commanded by Lieutenant General Robert Lee Bullard, commenced operations at Toul in the Saint-Mihiel sector. Pershing took command of the new army group of two armies, while Lieutenant General Hunter Liggett commanded First Army. Following American breakthroughs of the Siegfried (Hindenburg) Line, by the end of October the Argonne had been largely cleared of Germans. The American advance here facilitated that of the French Fourth Army on the American left to the Aisne River.

Before the third and final phase of the offensive during November 1–11, new American divisions replaced those that were worn out, new roads were constructed and existing ones were improved, and the supply system was also revamped. Most Allied units serving with the AEF were also withdrawn. Before resumption of the offensive, long-range 14-inch naval guns mounted on railway cars hurled 1,400-pound projectiles some 25 miles against the German positions. Also, 41 tons of gas shells drenched the Bois de Bourgogne and neutralized 9 of the 12 German artillery batteries there.

On November 1, First Army units began the assault of the now strengthened fourth German defensive line. Penetration of it was both rapid and spectacular. In the center of the front on the first day, V Corps advanced some six miles and captured Buzancy, forcing German units west of the Meuse to make a hasty withdrawal. During the night of November 3, the 2nd Division advanced five miles, clearing the Bourgogne Forest and enabling the installation of long-range artillery capable of shelling the railroad stations at Longuyon and Montmédy, through which the Germans were attempting to withdraw men and equipment. A juncture also occurred of the AEF with Gouraud's French Fourth Army on its left flank.

By the evening of November 6, elements of I Corps reached the Meuse opposite the southern part of the city of Sedan, 21 miles from their starting point a week earlier. This enabled the Allies to deny the Germans access to the Sedan-Mézières railroad, the chief goal of the campaign. Allied commander in chief Foch now shifted the First Army left boundary eastward so that the French Fourth Army might capture Sedan, erasing the stain to French honor that had occurred with the French surrender there in September 1870. American units were closing up along the Meuse and east of the river and were advancing toward Montmédy, Briny, and Metz when the armistice went into effect on November 11.

More than 1.2 million members of the AEF had taken part in the 47-day Meuse-Argonne Campaign, the largest battle in American history to that time. Not until the Battle of the Bulge (December 1944–January 1945) would these numbers be surpassed. In his report on the offensive, Pershing noted that 22 American and 4 French divisions had engaged and defeated 47 German divisions, representing 25 percent of Germany's divisional strength on the Western Front. Although the Germans had suffered some 100,000 casualties (including 26,000 taken prisoner) and lost 847 guns and some 3,000 machine guns, losses for the attackers had also been heavy. First Army sustained some 117,000 casualties (18,000 dead); this figure is close to half of all U.S. battlefield losses in the war.

Spencer C. Tucker

## Further Reading

Braim, Paul F. *The Test of Battle: The American Expeditionary Forces in the Meuse-Argonne Campaign.* Shippensburg, PA: White Mane, 1998.

Coffman, Edward M. *The War to End All Wars: The American Military Experience in World War I.* 1968; reprint, Lexington: University Press of Kentucky, 1998.

Marshall, George C. *Memoirs of My Services in the World War, 1917–1918.* Boston: Houghton Mifflin, 1976.

McHenry, Herbert L. *As a Private Saw It: My Memories of the First Division, World War I.* Indiana, PA: A. G. Halldin, 1988.

## Attack on Pearl Harbor

| Date | December 7, 1941 | |
|---|---|---|
| Location | Pearl Harbor, Hawaii | |
| Opponents (*winner) | *Japan | United States |
| Commander | Vice Admiral Nagumo Chūichi | Admiral Husband E. Kimmel; Lieutenant General Walter C. Short |
| # Ships | 6 aircraft carriers, 2 battleships, 2 heavy cruisers, 1 light cruiser, 9 destroyers, 3 submarines, 5 (prepositioned) midget submarines, and 8 tankers; 411 aircraft | 8 battleships, 8 cruisers, 30 destroyers, 4 submarines, and 49 other ships; 390 aircraft |
| Importance | With destruction of the U.S. Pacific Fleet's battleships, the Japanese can carry out their conquest of Southeast Asia without the threat of immediate U.S. naval interference. They have also purchased time to build up their planned defensive ring but have united Americans behind the effort to defeat them. | |

Japanese leaders, faced with U.S. economic sanctions that included an embargo on oil as a consequence of their invasion of China and takeover of French Indochina, decided on war with the United States. Supreme commander of the Japanese fleet Admiral Yamamoto Isoroku developed a plan designed to gain time for the Japanese to establish a defensive ring in the Southwest Pacific. The previous strategy was to carry out the southern conquests while the battle fleet waited in home waters for the arrival of the U.S. Pacific Fleet, which the Japanese expected would have been savaged by torpedo and air attacks on the long voyage to the Far East.

Yamamoto took advantage of the fact that in the summer of 1940, U.S. president Franklin Roosevelt had ordered the Pacific Fleet relocated from San Diego, California, to Pearl Harbor in the Hawaiian Islands. Yamamoto believed that the United States would need two to three years to recover from a blow at Pearl Harbor, giving the Japanese time to build up their defensive ring. He also hoped that the attack might cause the United States to lose heart and negotiate with Japan.

As the Japanese gathered intelligence through their Honolulu consulate, their fleet, already possessing the world's finest naval air arm, went through intensive training. The Japanese plan took advantage of the recently increased range of the Zero fighter. The British attack on the Italian fleet at Taranto on November 11, 1940, had shown that torpedo attacks by aircraft were possible in shallow waters. Japanese bombers also carried armor-piercing shells fitted with fins. When the shells were dropped vertically as bombs, no deck armor could withstand them.

The Japanese knew that Pacific Fleet commander Admiral Husband E. Kimmel brought the fleet back into Pearl Harbor on weekends, and the ships would not be

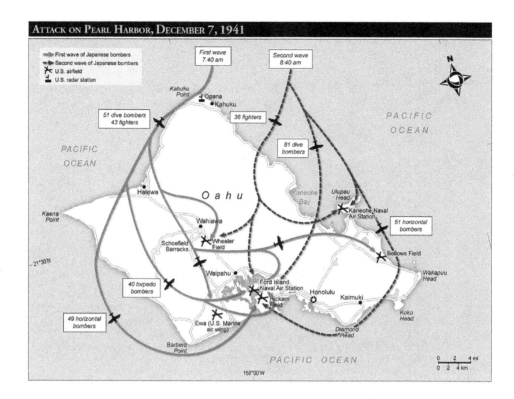

ATTACK ON PEARL HARBOR, DECEMBER 7, 1941

fully manned then. A Sunday was the natural choice for the attack, and after mid-December the weather was likely to be unfavorable for concurrent Japanese amphibious landings in Malaya and the Philippines. On the night of December 6–7 there would be no moonlight, aiding the surprise approach. The chief Japanese targets were the carriers and then the battleships, oil tanks, port facilities, and aircraft on the ground.

Vice Admiral Nagumo Chūichi commanded the Japanese task force. It was centered on six carriers with 411 aircraft, of which 360 were slated to be employed in two attack waves; 350 actually took part (183 in the first wave and 167 in the second wave). These numbered 129 high-level bombers, 103 dive-bombers, 40 torpedo-bombers, and 78 fighters. Escorting the strike force were two battleships, three cruisers, nine destroyers, three submarines, and eight tankers. The air strike was to coincide with an attack by midget submarines.

The submarines departed Japan on November 21, while the carrier strike force sortied on November 26. The Japanese arrived off the Hawaiian Islands undetected, and Nagumo ordered the aircraft launched some 275 miles north of Pearl Harbor between 6:00 and 7:16 a.m. (Hawaii time) on December 7. Two warnings should have made a difference. The Japanese submarines were detected, and U.S. destroyers sank one at 6:51 a.m. and another at 7:00 a.m. Also, radar warned of the approaching aircraft, but this was interpreted as B-17s coming from the mainland and therefore ignored.

Sailors in a motor launch rescue a seaman in the water from the U.S. Navy battleship *West Virginia,* sunk during the Japanese attack on the U.S. Pacific Fleet at Pearl Harbor on December 7, 1941. (Library of Congress)

Of eight U.S. battleships at Pearl Harbor, the Japanese sank four and severely damaged the others. Damage to the infrastructure of Pearl Harbor was superficial. In two strikes the Japanese sank three destroyers and four smaller vessels and damaged three light cruisers and a seaplane tender. Some 188 American aircraft were destroyed, and 63 were badly damaged; most had been packed together to protect against ground sabotage. The Japanese lost only five midget submarines, along with 29 planes destroyed and 70 damaged. U.S. casualties totaled 3,535 people killed or wounded; Japanese killed were fewer than 100.

Ultimately all U.S. battleships were refloated except the *Arizona,* and all of these except the *Oklahoma* saw subsequent service. The loss of U.S. life in the attack, while tragic, was not catastrophic for the subsequent U.S. war effort and certainly was far less than what it would have been had the fleet been caught at sea.

Thanks to the attack, though, the Japanese could carry out their operations in the Southwest Pacific without threat of U.S. naval interference. The Japanese also gained time to extend and build up their defensive ring. The main drawbacks were that the strike missed the chief target, the U.S. carriers, which were on ferrying duties. Had the Japanese mounted an additional strike and destroyed the oil tanks and facilities, the Pacific Fleet would have been forced to relocate to San Diego. Nagumo did not want to risk his own ships, however. He had achieved his objectives at virtually no cost and worried about the location of the U.S. carriers. The fleet would return home.

Although their attack had a historical parallel in their strike without declaration of war on the Russian fleet at Port Arthur in 1904, the Japanese had intended to keep within the bounds of legality. They planned to present a declaration of war to the U.S. government a half hour before the attack, but its extreme length and delays in decoding at the Japanese embassy in Washington meant that it was not ready for delivery until a half hour after the attack.

The failure of the carefully scripted Japanese scenario secured the moral high ground for Washington on what President Roosevelt referred to as "a day that will live in infamy." This was the primary negative for Japan. Coming without declaration of war, the attack aroused such anger in the United States as to sweep away any isolationist sentiment and mobilize the entire nation behind the war effort.

For Americans, the air strike on Pearl Harbor produced widespread criticism of the authorities and suspicion that factors beyond mere ineptitude were responsible for the disaster. These conspiracy theories have persisted, but there is no proof that Roosevelt knew about the Japanese plan or sought Pearl Harbor as a means of bringing the United States into the war.

Spencer C. Tucker

**Further Reading**

Morison, Samuel Eliot. *History of United States Naval Operations in World War II,* Vol. 1, *The Rising Sun in the Pacific, 1931–April 1942.* Boston: Little, Brown, 1948.

Prange, Gordon W., with Donald M. Goldstein and Katherine V. Dillon. *At Dawn We Slept: The Untold Story of Pearl Harbor.* New York: McGraw-Hill, 1981.

Prange, Gordon W., with Donald M. Goldstein and Katherine V. Dillon. *Pearl Harbor: The Verdict of History.* New York: McGraw-Hill, 1986.

Willmott, H. P., with Tohmatsu Haruo and W. Spencer Johnson. *Pearl Harbor.* London: Cassell, 2001.

## Battle of Bataan

| Date | December 8, 1941–April 9, 1942 | |
|---|---|---|
| Location | Bataan Peninsula, Luzon, Philippine Islands | |
| Opponents (*winner) | *Japan | United States |
| Commander | General Homma Masaharu | General Douglas MacArthur; Major General Jonathan M. Wainwright; Major General Edward P. King |
| Approx. # Troops | 75,000 men | 80,000 men (67,500 Filipinos and 12,500 Americans) |
| Importance | The Japanese secure possession of Luzon in the Philippines, but the great majority of Filipinos remain loyal to the United States. | |

The Bataan Peninsula on the Philippine island of Luzon is about 25 miles long and 20 miles wide and extends into Manila Bay. Bataan figured prominently in U.S. lieutenant general Douglas MacArthur's plans to defend the Philippines against possible Japanese attack, which called for U.S. and Philippine forces to withdraw onto that peninsula and hold there until the arrival of reinforcements from the United States.

Confident that he could defend Luzon at the beaches, though, MacArthur changed the plan. This included scrapping the prepositioning of supply depots on both Bataan and the island of Corregidor, at the tip of the peninsula, sufficient for 43,000 men on Bataan and 7,000 on Corregidor for 180 days. MacArthur had at his disposal 22,400 U.S. regulars (including 12,000 well-trained Philippine Scouts), 3,000 Philippine Constabulary troops, and 107,000 poorly trained and poorly equipped Philippine Army troops. He also planned to employ submarines and B-17 bombers against any Japanese invasion force. There were a large number of potential landing points, however, and a lot would depend on where the Japanese came ashore.

MacArthur kept most of his regulars back near Manila. The extensive Philippine coastline was covered only by the Philippine Army, which meant that the Japanese would encounter little resistance coming ashore. Moreover, much of Admiral Thomas C. Hart's already weak U.S. Asiatic Fleet was withdrawn, leaving only 4 destroyers, 28 submarines, and some torpedo boats. U.S. air assets in the islands were also woefully inadequate. MacArthur's air commander, Brigadier General Lewis Brereton, had 35 B-17s and 90 fighter aircraft, most of them modern P-40s, plus a dozen Philippine Army fighters.

News of the Japanese attack at Pearl Harbor reached Manila at 2:30 a.m. on December 8, 1941. Ground fog delayed an early morning Japanese strike by 500 Formosa-based aircraft against the Philippines, but this turned to Japan's advantage. On learning of the Pearl Harbor attack, Brereton sought MacArthur's approval for an immediate air strike on Japanese warships and shipping assembled at Takao Harbor, Formosa, for the invasion of the Philippines. MacArthur refused without explanation. He later held that his task was to defend the Philippines rather than initiate an attack.

U.S. bombers and fighters ordered into the air as a precaution therefore returned to base. Thus with few exceptions, all U.S. aircraft in the Philippines were on the ground when, without advance warning, late on the morning of December 8 Japanese aircraft arrived over Clark Field. Japanese planes also struck Iba Field. By the end of the day, 17 of the 35 B-17s had been destroyed, along with 55 of 72 P-40s and many of the older fighters. Only 7 Japanese planes were shot down. Although the army and navy commanders at Pearl Harbor had been sacked for their shortcomings, MacArthur not only escaped censure but on December 22 was promoted to full general.

On December 8 the first Japanese troops came ashore on Bataan. Two days later they landed unopposed at Aparri on the north end of the big island of Luzon. The Philippine Army infantry broke and ran on the first appearance of the invaders. U.S. major general Jonathan Wainwright, commander of the North Luzon Force, had assumed that the landings would take place in the Lingayen Gulf, on the eastern side of the island, and had the bulk of his forces there. The main body of 43,000 men of Lieutenant General Homma Masaharu's Fourteenth Army came ashore from 85 transports in the southern Lingayen Gulf only on December 22.

MacArthur now reverted to the original plan of withdrawing all his forces into the Bataan Peninsula. Aided by the fact that Japanese strength was half their own, the bulk of MacArthur's troops had withdrawn into the peninsula by the beginning of January 1942. Unfortunately for the defenders, many supply dumps, relocated when MacArthur altered his plans, were lost in the hasty retreat.

Japanese command of the air and the sea precluded resupply. The defenders immediately went on half-rations. MacArthur also had to feed some 67,500 Filipino troops and 12,500 U.S. troops, along with 26,000 civilians on Bataan and Corregidor, rather than the 43,000 of the original plan. Many of the defenders soon fell victim to malaria, malnutrition, and dysentery.

Despite the terrible conditions, MacArthur's forces put up a stout defense. Although the Japanese pierced the main defensive line in January, the Filipinos and Americans withdrew to a second defensive line about 15 miles from the tip of the peninsula and held there against strong Japanese assaults in late January and early February. Assisted by PT boat attacks and artillery fire from Corregidor, the defenders also defeated Japanese invasion attempts on the western coast of the peninsula behind the battle line. Homma then decided to await reinforcements from Japan.

Because the Pacific Fleet had been shattered in the Pearl Harbor attack, Washington deemed it impossible to attempt immediate relief of the islands. Rather than yield a tremendous propaganda advantage to the Japanese with the capture of the U.S. commander in the Far East, U.S. president Franklin D. Roosevelt ordered MacArthur out to Australia on February 22. MacArthur, who had been raised to full general on December 22 but was derisively referred to by many of the defenders as "Dugout Doug" for his failure to leave Malinta Tunnel on Corregidor (he visited Bataan but once), departed on March 11 and was later awarded the Medal of Honor.

Wainwright took up command of the Philippines, with Major General Edward P. King in charge of the defense of Bataan. Rations were now one-fourth of normal, which seriously affected the ability of the defenders to fight. Disease and sickness continued to extract a heavy toll. Reinforced, Homma attacked on April 3 and broke through. In two days the Japanese drove back the defenders some 10 miles, and on April 9 King had no option but to surrender. The Battle of Bataan claimed the lives of some 20,000 Americans and Filipinos. Roughly 2,000 escaped to Corregidor. The Japanese took 76,000 prisoners, some 64,000 Filipino soldiers and 12,000 Americans.

The Japanese forced the weakened survivors to march 55–60 miles to prisoner-of-war camps. Most of the prisoners were sick and hungry, and there was little food. While the Japanese were unprepared for the large influx of prisoners, they also ignored the norms of warfare, even denying the prisoners water. Up to 650 Americans and 5,000–10,000 Filipinos died in the infamous Bataan Death March to Camp O'Donnell. Another 1,600 Americans and 16,000 prisoners perished in the first six or seven weeks of imprisonment.

The fight then shifted to Corregidor, separated from Bataan by only two miles. This short distance enabled the Japanese to bombard the island by artillery. They also attacked from the air. On May 5, the Japanese mounted a successful amphibious assault in which they employed tanks. The next day, his resources exhausted and with less than three days of water remaining, Wainwright ordered U.S. forces throughout the Philippines to surrender. Formal resistance ended on June 9, although some soldiers escaped into the jungle to continue the fight through guerrilla warfare.

What is remarkable about the Philippine campaign is not its result, which was a foregone conclusion, but the skill and determination of the American and Filipino defenders, who waged a spirited defense for six months. Tokyo had expected the conquest to take only two months, and General Homma was called home to Japan in disgrace. Perhaps the greatest surprise was the loyalty of the Filipinos to the United States. The Japanese expected Filipino forces to rally to them, but that did not happen. During the campaign and the long Japanese occupation that followed, the vast majority of the Filipino people remained loyal to the United States.

Spencer C. Tucker

**Further Reading**

James, D. Clayton. *The Years of MacArthur,* Vol. 2, *1941–1945.* Boston: Houghton Mifflin, 1975.

Mallonée, Richard. *Battle for Bataan: An Eyewitness Account.* New York: I Books, 2003.

Morton, Louis. *United States Army in World War II: The War in the Pacific; Fall of the Philippines.* Washington, DC: Office of the Chief of Military History, United States Army, U.S. Government Printing Office, 1953.

Whitman, John W. *Bataan: Our Last Ditch; The Bataan Campaign, 1942.* New York: Hippocrene Books, 1990.

## Battle of the Coral Sea

| Date | May 7–8, 1942 | |
|---|---|---|
| Location | Coral Sea, Pacific Ocean | |
| Opponents (*winner) | *United States | Japan |
| Commander | Rear Admiral Frank Fletcher | Vice Admiral Innoye Shigeyoshi; Rear Admiral Goto Aritomo; Vice Admiral Hara Chūichi |
| # Ships | Fleet carriers *Lexington* and *Yorktown* (total of 141 aircraft), 5 heavy cruisers, 7 destroyers | Fleet carriers *Shōkaku* and *Zuikaku* (total of 124 aircraft), light carrier *Shōhō* (30 aircraft), 4 heavy cruisers, 6 destroyers |
| Importance | Causes the Japanese to abort their invasion of Port Moresby and removes two of their carriers from the subsequent Battle of Midway. It also inaugurates a new era in naval warfare in which fleets do battle without ever coming within sight of one another. | |

Following their string of early military successes, the Japanese were understandably reluctant to go over to a defensive posture. They were also spurred in this course by a series of U.S. carrier raids early in 1942. While inflicting little damage, these were a blow to Japanese pride and led Japanese military leaders to shift resources.

The Japanese therefore decided to mount a major strike against Midway Island and then cut off the sea-lanes to Australia. They planned first to seize Tulagi as a seaplane base and then take Port Moresby, on the southern coast of New Guinea, bringing Queensland, Australia, within bomber range. Once that had been accomplished, Admiral Yamamoto Isoroku's Combined Fleet would occupy Midway. Following destruction of the U.S. Pacific Fleet reacting to the Midway attack, the Japanese planned to resume their southeastern advance to interdict the sea routes from the United States to Australia.

Vice Admiral Innoye Shigeyoshi at Rabaul in New Britain Island had overall command of the operation. He planned to seize Tulagi on May 3, 1942, and Port Moresby a week later. To prevent any U.S. interference with the landings, Innoye deployed two covering forces: the Close Covering Group centered on the light carrier *Shōhō* (30 aircraft), four heavy cruisers, and a destroyer, all under Rear Admiral Goto Aritomo, and Vice Admiral Hara Chūichi's Carrier Division 5 of the fleet carriers *Zuikaku* and *Shōkaku* (124 aircraft total). They were escorted by Vice Admiral Takagi Takeo's two heavy cruisers and six destroyers. An additional 150 Japanese aircraft were available at Rabaul. The two naval covering forces sortied from Truk in the Carolines, 1,000 miles north of Rabaul, on April 30 and May 1, respectively.

U.S. code breaking uncovered the outline of the Japanese plan. To intercept the Japanese, Pacific Fleet commander Admiral Chester W. Nimitz sent from Pearl

Struck by Japanese torpedoes and bombs, the U.S. aircraft carrier *Lexington* had to be abandoned and was later scuttled. Although a tactical victory for the Japanese, who had sunk one American fleet carrier and damaged another, the 1942 Battle of the Coral Sea was a strategic victory for the United States as the Japanese abandoned their invasion of Port Moresby. The battle also had an important impact on the subsequent 1942 Battle of Midway. (Library of Congress)

Harbor a task force under Rear Admiral Frank Fletcher centered on the carriers *Yorktown* and *Lexington*, with 141 aircraft between them. Royal Navy rear admiral J. G. Crace's small force of U.S. and Australian cruisers and destroyers joined him. Nimitz also ordered the carriers *Enterprise* and *Hornet*, returning from their raid on Tokyo, to the Coral Sea, but they arrived too late to participate in the action.

The first Japanese move went well, with troops going ashore at Tulagi on May 3. Warned of their approach, the small Australian garrison on the island was hastily extracted. The *Shōhō* then steamed north to join the larger Japanese force at Rabaul, bound for Port Moresby.

On May 4, aircraft from the *Yorktown* struck Tulagi, sinking a Japanese destroyer. The *Yorktown* then joined other Allied ships in the central Coral Sea. Meanwhile, the Japanese carrier group passed east of the Solomon Islands, entering the Coral Sea from that direction to take the U.S. carriers from the rear as they moved to intercept the Port Moresby invasion force. The U.S. force was entering the Coral Sea from the Solomons to the north en route to the Louisiade Islands and thence to Port Moresby. On May 5–6 the two carrier groups searched for one another without success, although at one stage they were only about 70 miles apart.

On May 7, Japanese reconnaissance aircraft reported sighting a carrier and a cruiser, whereupon Japanese aircraft launched an all-out bombing attack. They sank both ships, which turned out to be a tanker and an escorting destroyer. Hara then gambled on a night strike by 27 aircraft, but the Japanese attackers encountered U.S.

F4F Wildcat fighters. Some of the Japanese pilots located the American carriers but in the dark assumed them to be friendly and tried to land on them. Only 6 Japanese planes returned to their carriers.

On May 7 Fletcher's aircraft were also led astray by a false report and expended their effort on the covering force for the Port Moresby invasion. The aircraft sank the light carrier *Shōhō,* which went down in only 10 minutes. This had unforeseen consequences. With the loss of his air cover, Admiral Innoye ordered the invasion force to turn back.

On the morning of May 8, the two carrier forces at last came to blows. They were evenly matched. The Japanese had 121 aircraft, and the Americans had 122. The Japanese had four heavy cruisers and six destroyers, and the United States had five heavy cruisers and seven destroyers. The U.S. ships were under a clear sky, however, while the Japanese ships had the advantage of cloud cover. As a result, the carrier *Zuikaku* escaped detection. U.S. aircraft located and badly damaged the *Shōkaku,* however.

Seventy Japanese aircraft attacked the American carriers; the *Lexington* was struck by two torpedoes and three bombs. Subsequent internal explosions forced its abandonment, and the U.S. destroyer *Phelps* later sank it with torpedoes. The *Yorktown* was damaged. Both sides then departed the Coral Sea, the Japanese in the mistaken belief that both U.S. carriers had been sunk.

The Americans lost 74 planes, and the Japanese lost more than 80. But the Americans lost a fleet carrier, and the Japanese lost only a light carrier. Even so, the Americans had prevented the Japanese from realizing their principal objective of capturing Port Moresby. The Americans were also able to sufficiently ready the *Yorktown* to allow it to fight in the next big battle, at Midway, whereas the *Shōkaku* could not be readied in time for that second and decisive fight. The *Zuikaku,* which could have participated, was not able to take part in that battle simply because of a lack of trained pilots. Thus, while the Battle of the Coral Sea may have been a tactical Japanese victory, strategically it went to the Americans.

The Battle of the Coral Sea also inaugurated a new era in naval warfare. It was the first battle in naval history between fleets that never came in sight of one another. A greater repetition of this soon followed at Midway.

Spencer C. Tucker

## Further Reading

Dull, Paul S. *A Battle History of the Imperial Japanese Navy, 1941–1945.* Annapolis, MD: Naval Institute Press, 1978.

Hoyt, Edwin P. *Blue Skies and Blood: The Battle of the Coral Sea.* New York: S. Eriksson, 1975.

Lundstrom, John. *The First Team: Pacific Naval Air Combat from Pearl Harbor to Midway.* Annapolis, MD: Naval Institute Press, 1990.

Millet, Bernard. *The Battle of the Coral Sea.* Annapolis, MD: Naval Institute Press, 1974.

Morison, Samuel Eliot. *History of United States Naval Operation in World War II,* Vol. 4, *Coral Sea, Midway and Submarine Actions, May 1942–August 1942.* Boston: Little, Brown, 1949.

## Battle of Midway

| Date | June 3–6, 1942 | |
|---|---|---|
| Location | West and north of Midway Island, Central Pacific | |
| Opponents (*winner) | *United States | Japan |
| Commander | Rear Admiral Frank Fletcher; Rear Admiral Raymond A. Spruance | Admiral Yamamoto Isoroku; Admiral Nagumo Chūichi |
| # Ships | 27 ships (3 carriers); 348 aircraft, including 115 land-based at Midway | 86 ships (5 carriers) and 325 planes |
| Importance | The Japanese invasion of Midway is thwarted, and their fine carrier arm is devastated. Midway marks the turning point in the war in the Pacific. | |

The Battle of Midway was the decisive World War II naval engagement between the United States and Japan. With their amazing run of successes in the first months of the Pacific War, the Japanese were understandably reluctant to go on the defensive. Admiral Yamamoto Isoroku and his Combined Fleet staff wanted to secure Midway Island, 1,100 miles west of Pearl Harbor. They hoped that this would draw out the U.S. Pacific Fleet so they could destroy it.

The half dozen U.S. carrier raids from February to May 1942, especially the April 18 raid on Tokyo, helped silence Yamamoto's critics and produce approval for his Midway plan. Under the revised plan, the Japanese would advance deeper into the Solomons and take Port Moresby, on the southern coast of New Guinea. Yamamoto's Combined Fleet would then occupy Midway Island, which Yamamoto saw as a stepping-stone toward a possible Japanese invasion of Hawaii. In any case, Midway could be used for surveillance purposes. After the Midway operation and the destruction of the U.S. fleet, the Japanese would resume their southeastern advance to cut off Australia.

In the Battle of the Coral Sea (May 7–8, 1942), U.S. carriers caused the Japanese to call off the invasion of Port Moresby. Planning for the Midway attack nevertheless went forward. Yamamoto's plan was both comprehensive and complex, involving an advanced submarine force to savage U.S. ships on their way to Midway; an invasion force under Vice Admiral Kondo Nobutake of 12 transports with 5,000 troops, supported by 4 heavy cruisers and a more distant covering force of 2 battleships, a light carrier, and 4 heavy cruisers; Vice Admiral Nagumo Chūichi's First Carrier Force of 4 fleet carriers (the *Hiryū, Sōryū, Kaga,* and *Akagi*), with 2 battleships, 2 heavy cruisers, and a destroyer screen; and the main battle fleet under Yamamoto of 3 battleships (including the giant *Yamato,* his flagship), a destroyer screen, and a light carrier. The total Japanese force in the operation involved some 200 ships stretched over 1,000 miles of the North Pacific: 8 carriers (600 aircraft, including floatplanes), 11 battleships, 22 cruisers, 65 destroyers, 21 submarines, and numerous auxiliaries.

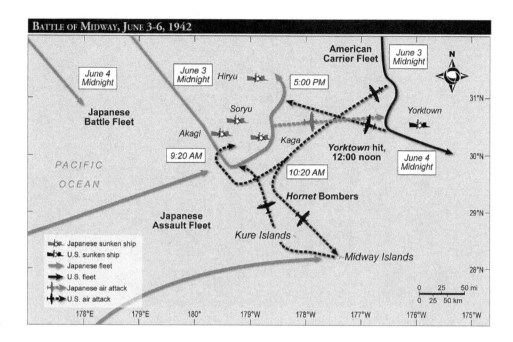

For the Aleutians, Yamamoto allotted an invasion force of 3 escorted transports carrying 2,400 troops, with a support group of 2 heavy cruisers, 2 light carriers, and a covering force of 4 older battleships. Apart from its tie-in with Midway, this force was to enable the Japanese to occupy Attu and Kiska, thus blocking a supposed U.S. invasion route to Japan.

The battle would begin in the Aleutians with air strikes on June 3, followed by landings on June 6. On June 4, Nagumo's carrier planes would attack the airfield at Midway. On June 6, cruisers would bombard Midway and troops would be landed, covered by the battleships. The Japanese expected that there would be no U.S. ships in the Midway area until after the landings, and their hope was that the U.S. Pacific Fleet would hurry north to the Aleutians, enabling the Japanese to trap it between their two carrier forces.

Commander of U.S. forces in the Pacific Admiral Chester W. Nimitz could only deploy 76 ships; he had no battleships and only 2 carriers fit for action. But by an astonishing effort, the *Yorktown,* heavily damaged in the Battle of the Coral Sea, was readied in 2 days instead of the estimated 90 days. Nimitz did have the advantage of an accurate picture of the Japanese order of battle, and thanks to code breaking, he was reasonably certain that Midway was the Japanese objective. By contrast, the Japanese had virtually no information on the Americans, but at this point in the war the Japanese tended to dismiss the Americans and exaggerate their own abilities.

Nimitz packed Midway with B-26 and B-17 bombers. He positioned the three U.S. carriers, with 233 planes, some 300 miles to the northeast. Nimitz hoped that the carriers would remain hidden from Japanese reconnaissance planes and counted

U.S. Navy Douglas SBD-5 Dauntless dive bombers prepare to attack the Japanese fleet on June 4, 1942, during the Battle of Midway. (National Archives)

on information about Japanese movements from Catalina aircraft based on Midway. He hoped to catch the Japanese by surprise, their carriers with planes on their decks.

Rear Admiral Raymond Spruance had tactical command of U.S. naval forces in the battle. The Japanese deployed 86 ships against 27 U.S. ships, and 325 planes against 348 (including 115 land-based aircraft) for the United States. Carrier strength was five for Japan and three for the United States.

On June 3, the day after the U.S. carriers were in position, American air reconnaissance detected the Japanese transports some 600 miles west of Midway. A gap in the search pattern flown by Japanese aircraft allowed the American carriers to remain undetected. In any case, the Japanese did not expect the U.S. Pacific Fleet to be at sea yet.

Early on June 4, Nagumo launched 108 aircraft against Midway, while a second wave of similar size was prepared to attack any warships sighted. The first wave did severe damage to Midway at little cost to itself, but the pilots reported the need for a second attack. Since his own carriers were being bombed by planes from Midway, Nagumo ordered the second wave of planes to change from torpedoes to bombs and to focus on the airfields.

Shortly thereafter, a group of American ships was spotted about 200 miles away, but the Japanese thought they were only cruisers and destroyers. Then at 8:20 a.m. came a report identifying a carrier. Most of the Japanese torpedo-bombers were now equipped with bombs, and most fighters were on patrol. Nagumo also had to recover the first wave of aircraft from the strike at Midway.

Nagumo accordingly ordered a change of course to the northeast. This helped him avoid the first wave of American dive-bombers. When three waves of U.S. torpedo-bombers attacked the Japanese carriers between 9:00 and 10:24 a.m., 47 of 51 were shot down by Japanese fighters or antiaircraft guns. The Japanese believed they had won the battle.

Two minutes later, however, 37 American dive-bombers from the *Enterprise* swept down to attack the Japanese carriers, while the Japanese fighters that had been dealing with the torpedo-bombers were close to sea level. With the torpedoes and fuel on their decks, soon the *Akagi* and *Kaga* were flaming wrecks. The *Sōryū* took three hits from *Yorktown's* dive-bombers that also arrived on the scene and soon was abandoned.

The *Hiryū*, the only Japanese fleet carrier still intact, then sent bombers against the *Yorktown*. A first strike sent three bombs into the carrier. Its crew worked to save the ship, but a second Japanese strike fatally damaged it and forced its abandonment. (A subsequent attempt to save the ship ran afoul of a Japanese submarine that penetrated the carrier's destroyer screen, hitting it with two torpedoes and also sinking the destroyer *Hammann*. The *Yorktown* finally sank on June 7.). Meanwhile, 24 American dive-bombers, including 10 from Yorktown, caught the *Hiryū*. It sank the next day. Yamamoto now suspended the attack on Midway, hoping to trap the Americans by drawing them westward. Spruance, however, refused to take the bait.

The Battle of Midway was a crushing defeat for Japan. The Americans lost the carrier *Yorktown* and about 150 aircraft, while the Imperial Navy lost four fleet carriers and some 330 aircraft, most of which went down with the carriers, and a heavy cruiser. The loss of the carriers and their well-trained aircrews and support personnel was particularly devastating. The subsequent Japanese defeat in the important Battle of Guadalcanal (August 7, 1942–February 7, 1943) was principally due to a lack of naval airpower.

The Battle of Midway also provided the Americans a respite until the end of 1942, when the new Essex-class fleet carriers began to come on line. In Nimitz's words, "Midway was the most crucial battle of the Pacific War, the engagement that made everything else possible."

Spencer C. Tucker

## Further Reading

Dull, Paul S. *A Battle History of the Imperial Japanese Navy, 1941–1945*. Annapolis, MD: Naval Institute Press, 1978.

Fuchida, Mitsuo, and Masatake Okumiya. *Midway, the Battle That Doomed Japan: The Japanese Navy's Story*. Annapolis, MD: Naval Institute Press, 1955.

Kernan, Alvin. *The Unknown Battle of Midway*. New Haven, CT: Yale University Press, 2005.

Parshall, Johnathan, and Anthony Tully. *Shattered Sword: The Untold Story of the Battle of Midway*. Washington, DC: Potomac Books, 2005.

Prange, Gordon W., with Donald M. Goldstein and Katherine V. Dillon. *Miracle at Midway.* New York: McGraw-Hill, 1982.

Smith, Peter C. *Midway, Dauntless Victory: Fresh Perspectives on America's Seminal Naval Victory of 1942.* Barnsley, UK: Pen and Sword Maritime, 2007.

## Battle of Guadalcanal

| Date | August 7, 1942–February 7, 1943 | |
|---|---|---|
| Location | Guadalcanal Island, Southwest Pacific | |
| Opponents (*winner) | *United States | Japan |
| Commander | U.S. Marine Corps major general Alexander A. Vandegrift; then U.S. Army major general Alexander Patch | Lieutenant General Hyakutake Haruyoshi |
| Approx. # Troops | 60,000 troops | 36,200 troops |
| Importance | The Japanese advance is halted, and U.S. forces take the offensive in the long road back to the Philippines and, ultimately, to the Japanese home islands. | |

Guadalcanal, an island in the Solomon chain northeast of Australia, lies on a northwest-southeast axis and is 90 miles long and on average 25 miles wide. Its southern shore is protected by coral reefs, and the only suitable landing beaches are on the north-central shore. Once inland, invading troops faced dense jungle and mountainous terrain, crisscrossed by numerous streams. The Guadalcanal campaign encompassed not only Guadalcanal but also Savo and Florida Island as well as the smaller islands of Tulagi, Tanambogo, and Gavutu.

During May–July 1942, the Japanese expanded their military presence in the central and lower Solomons. Units of Lieutenant General Imamura Hotishi's Eighth Army from Rabaul landed on Guadalcanal and on July 6 began construction of an airfield. U.S. military leaders were anxious to take the offensive following their June 1942 victory at Midway. News of the Japanese airfield prompted action, for this would place Japanese bombers within range of the advanced Allied base at Espiritu Santo. The United States sent a task force of some 70 ships. An amphibious force under Rear Admiral Richmond K. Turner lifted Major General Alexander A. Vandegrift's 19,000-man reinforced 1st Marine Division. Vice Admiral Frank J. Fletcher's three-carrier task force provided air support.

Neither side could allow the other to establish a major base on Guadalcanal, and the struggle was therefore a protracted, complex battle of attrition. The period August 1942–February 1943 saw some of the most bitter fighting of the entire war in any theater. There were some 50 separate actions involving warships or aircraft, including 7 major naval battles and 10 land engagements.

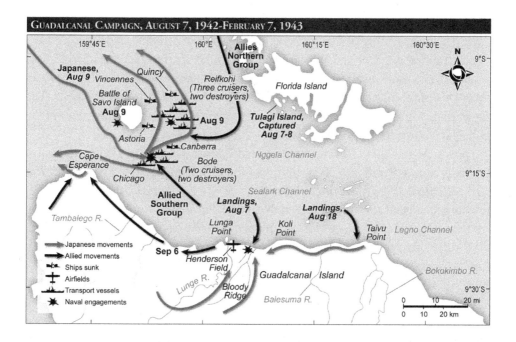

**GUADALCANAL CAMPAIGN, AUGUST 7, 1942–FEBRUARY 7, 1943**

On August 7, 1942, the marines went ashore at both Tulagi and Guadalcanal, surprising the small Japanese garrisons of 2,200 men on Guadalcanal and 1,500 on Tulagi. That same day the marines seized the airfield on Guadalcanal, which they renamed Henderson Field for a marine aviator killed in the Battle of Midway. Vandegrift immediately established a perimeter defense around the airfield.

The lack of a harbor made U.S. supply difficult, as did Japanese air and naval attacks. Coast watchers on islands did provide early warning of Japanese air and sea movements down the so-called Slot of the Solomon Islands. American land-based airpower controlled the Slot during the day, but the Japanese excelled at night fighting and initially controlled the Slot by night. The Japanese sent not their main fleet but instead small groups of ships.

Early on August 9 in the Battle of Savo Island, the Japanese administered the worst defeat ever suffered by the U.S. Navy, sinking four Allied cruisers (three U.S. and one Australian) and a destroyer for no ship losses of their own. However, the Japanese failed to attack the amphibious force. Fletcher had already withdrawn his carriers, and following the battle Turner withdrew his transports as well, despite the fact that many had not been unloaded. This left the marines without adequate supplies and forced them to rely on captured rations and Japanese construction equipment to complete the airfield.

On August 21, the day the Japanese mounted a major attack on the marine positions, the first U.S. aircraft landed at Henderson Field. From this point on the Japanese could not keep their ships in waters covered by the land-based U.S. aircraft, and they could not conduct an air campaign over the lower Solomons from as far away as Rabaul. U.S. air strength on Guadalcanal gradually increased to about 100 planes.

Both sides now reinforced. Peak Japanese strength would be some 36,000 men. At night the so-called Tokyo Express of Japanese destroyers and light cruisers steamed down the Slot and into the sound to shell marine positions and deliver supplies. The latter was an insufficient and haphazard effort that often took the form of drums filled with supplies pushed off the ships to drift to shore. The Japanese made a major mistake in failing to exploit the temporary departure of the U.S. Navy and not rushing substantial reinforcements to Guadalcanal.

During August 24–25 in the Battle of the Eastern Solomons, the Japanese lost the light carrier *Ryujo* and 90 aircraft, and the Americans suffered the carrier *Enterprise* damaged and lost three dozen aircraft. On August 31 a Japanese submarine torpedoed and severely damaged the carrier *Saratoga,* which was out of action for three months. The *Wasp,* the lone remaining U.S. carrier in the South Pacific, was badly damaged by torpedoes from a Japanese submarine on September 15, forcing its scuttling.

Actions ashore were marked by clashes between patrols. During September 12–14, the Japanese mounted strong attacks in an effort to seize U.S. positions on Lunga Ridge, overlooking Henderson Field from the south. Both sides continued building up their ground strength while naval and air battles raged over and off Guadalcanal.

During October 11–13, Japanese and U.S. covering forces collided in the Battle of Cape Esperance. The Japanese lost two ships, a cruiser, and a destroyer and had a cruiser heavily damaged. The United States lost a destroyer sunk and two cruisers damaged. The Americans upped their tally when U.S. aircraft from Henderson Field sank two more Japanese destroyers. Although not decisive, the Battle of Cape Esperance was the first U.S. night-action victory against the Japanese.

Vandegrift now had more than 23,000 men on the island, while Japanese lieutenant general Hyakutake Haruyoshi had about the same number. During October 23–25, the Japanese launched strong but widely dispersed and uncoordinated land attacks against Henderson Field, suffering 2,000 dead, while U.S. casualties were fewer than 300. Immediately after halting this Japanese offensive, Vandegrift began a six-week effort to expand the defensive perimeter to a point where the Japanese could not bring Henderson Field under artillery fire.

On October 26 in the Battle of the Santa Cruz Islands, U.S. aircraft badly damaged the light carrier *Zuiho* and the fleet carrier *Shokaku.* The U.S. carrier *Hornet* was sunk, and the *Enterprise* was badly damaged. The Japanese took such losses that they were unable to exploit the situation, however. The Japanese also lost 100 aircraft, about half as many as the Americans, who in 1942 produced more than five times as many aircraft than the Japanese and had a superior pilot replacement system.

During November 12–15, a series of intense sea fights took place off Guadalcanal. In the first fight, U.S. forces blocked Japanese efforts to land reinforcements. The Japanese also lost the battleship *Hiei* and two destroyers. The United States lost two cruisers and four destroyers. In the second fight, during November 13–14, the

Americans sank six Japanese transports and a heavy cruiser. During November 14–15 the Americans lost two destroyers, but the Japanese lost the battleship *Kirishima* and a destroyer. The Japanese also had six transports sunk and had to beach another four. U.S. forces now had round-the-clock control of the waters around the island. On November 30, U.S. and Japanese naval forces again clashed in the Battle of Tassafaronga. The Japanese lost one destroyer, while the Americans had a cruiser sunk.

On December 8 Vandegrift turned command of the island over to U.S. Army major general Alexander Patch, who organized his forces into XIV Corps, including the 2nd Marine Division (replacing the 1st Marine Division, which was withdrawn) and the army's 25th Infantry Division. At the beginning of January 1943 Patch commanded 58,000 men, while Japanese strength was fewer than 20,000 men. The Americans were now well fed and supplied, while the Japanese were losing men to sickness and starvation.

On January 10 Patch began an offensive to clear the island. In a two-week battle, the Americans drove the Japanese from a heavily fortified line west of Henderson Field. The Japanese were forced toward Cape Esperance, where a small U.S. force landed to prevent them from escaping by sea.

Tokyo had already decided to abandon Guadalcanal. In daring night operations during February 1–7, their destroyers brought off 10,630 men. The United States had committed 60,000 men to the fight for the island. Of these, the marines lost 1,207; army casualties came to 562. U.S. naval casualties were far greater than those on land. The U.S. Navy and U.S. Marine Corps lost 4,911, and the Japanese Navy and Army suffered some 31,000 dead. Counting land, sea, and air casualties, the struggle for Guadalcanal claimed 7,100 U.S. dead or permanently missing.

U.S. Navy ship losses included 2 aircraft carriers, 6 heavy cruisers, and 14 destroyers; the Japanese lost 2 carriers, 2 battleships, 3 heavy cruisers, 1 light cruiser, 11 destroyers, and 6 submarines. In the previous six months, Japan also lost 140 transports. Twenty-nine destroyers were damaged or in need of repair; their absence contributed to the later destruction of Japanese aircraft carriers. Particularly serious from the Japanese point of view was the loss of 2,076 aircraft (1,094 to combat) and so many trained pilots. The Japanese advance had now been halted, and General Douglas MacArthur could begin the long and bloody return to the Philippines.

Spencer C. Tucker

## Further Reading

Frank, Richard B. *Guadalcanal: The Definitive Account of the Landmark Battle.* New York: Random House, 1990.

Hammel, Eric. *Guadalcanal, Decision at Sea: The Naval Battle of Guadalcanal, November 13–15, 1942.* Pacifica, CA: Pacifica Press, 1988.

Takushiro Hatsutori. *Daitoa Senso Zenshi* [Complete History of the Greater East Asian War]. Tokyo: Hara Shobo, 1965.

Tregaskis, Richard. *Guadalcanal Diary.* New York: Random House, 1943.

## Operation TORCH

| Date | November 8, 1942 | |
|---|---|---|
| Location | Morocco and Algeria in North Africa | |
| Opponents (*winner) | *United States and Great Britain | Vichy France |
| Commander | Lieutenant General Dwight D. Eisenhower | Admiral Jean Darlan; General Charles Nguès |
| Approx. # Troops | 107,000 troops | 60,000 troops |
| Importance | U.S. forces gain valuable experience, and the Allies secure important bases for naval operations in the Mediterranean and air operations against Southern Europe as well as catch in a vice German and Italian forces being driven westward by the British Eighth Army. | |

Following the Japanese attack on Pearl Harbor, U.S. president Franklin D. Roosevelt and British prime minister Winston L. S. Churchill agreed that the Allies should first concentrate on Germany, the most powerful Axis opponent. Indeed, U.S. planners, especially U.S. Army chief of staff General George C. Marshall, sought the earliest possible invasion of France. However, the August 19, 1942, failure of Operation JUBILEE, the raid on Dieppe, France, forced the Americans to concede that an invasion across the English Channel lay many months if not years in the future. Churchill and British planners, meanwhile, attempted to interest the Americans in a more opportunistic approach that would include operations in the Mediterranean.

Roosevelt had promised Soviet leader Joseph Stalin that the Western Allies would undertake an invasion by the end of 1942 and was determined to honor that pledge. But if a cross-channel invasion was impossible, where might this take place? Churchill argued for attacks in the Mediterranean, against what he termed the "soft underbelly of Europe." Even before the Dieppe Raid (August 19, 1942), Roosevelt and Churchill had settled on an invasion of North Africa.

Gaining control of Vichy France–administered Morocco, Algeria, and Tunisia would provide bases for air operations to protect Allied Mediterranean shipping and from which to conduct strategic bombing raids against targets in Southern Europe. North Africa could also be used to mount invasions of the Mediterranean islands or even Italy or Greece. Not least, the invasion would provide badly needed combat experience for inexperienced U.S. troops against a military that was substantially inferior to the German Wehrmacht.

Roosevelt became the chief proponent of the operation and insisted on it over objections raised by many of his own service chiefs, including Marshall. Code-named TORCH, the invasion was to coincide with the planned breakout of British Empire forces at El Alamein in Egypt; the Allies hoped to crush Axis troops between their two forces. On October 23, British Eighth Army commander General

Some of the U.S. ships crossing the Atlantic to take part in Operation TORCH, the Allied invasion of French North Africa in November 1942, the largest amphibious operation to that point in history. (Corbis)

Bernard Montgomery initiated Operation LIGHTFOOT, the Battle of El Alamein. By November 2, the Eighth Army had broken through and began the pursuit of German generalfeldmarschall Erwin Rommel's Axis forces withdrawing westward.

The British favored landings in central North Africa, at Tunis and Bizerte in Tunisia, or at least in eastern Algeria, but the Americans were more cautious and won the point. The landings occurred at Casablanca in Morocco and at Oran and Algiers in Algeria. U.S. Army lieutenant general Dwight D. Eisenhower commanded the Allied Expeditionary Force. His deputy was another American, Major General Mark W. Clark. British Fleet admiral Andrew B. Cunningham directed the naval forces.

The landings in Morocco and Algeria constituted the largest amphibious operation in history to that time. The most westerly landing, that at Casablanca on the Atlantic, ensured the Allies a lodgment in North Africa even if the other two landings inside the Mediterranean went awry. Major General George S. Patton commanded the Western Task Force of 38,000 men, escorted by warships led by U.S. rear admiral Henry K. Hewitt. The force had departed from Norfolk, Virginia, in one of the longest expeditionary efforts in history.

The other two invasions were mounted from England and went ashore in Algeria. The Central Task Force under U.S. Army major general Lloyd Fredendall numbered nearly 41,000 men (37,100 Americans and 3,600 British), supported by British commodore Thomas H. Troubridge's covering warships. The 55,000-man Eastern Task Force headed for Algiers was largely British in composition (45,000 British troops and only 10,000 Americans), but to give the illusion that it was mostly American, U.S. major general Charles Ryder had command. Once Algiers was secured, British lieutenant general Kenneth A. N. Anderson would take charge. British vice admiral Sir Harold M. Burrough commanded its covering warships.

The Allies made every effort to emphasize the U.S. role and downplay British participation. Given the British attack against French ships at Mers-el-Kébir, Algeria, in July 1940 and British operations in Syria, Allied leaders rightly assumed that Americans would receive a far friendlier reception from French forces than would the British. Efforts were made to show the American flag wherever possible.

No one knew the extent to which French troops would resist the invasion. U.S. diplomat Robert Murphy made contact with Vichy French officials in North Africa, and on October 22 General Clark went ashore and met secretly near Algiers with French major general Charles Mast. However, this did not bring the desired agreement, and for the most part French troops resisted the landings.

Operation TORCH began early on the morning of November 8. Although taken by surprise, the French troops fought well. The unfinished French battleship *Jean Bart* at Casablanca, although incapable of movement, dueled with the U.S. battleship *Massachusetts.* Superior U.S. naval strength beat back a French naval sortie. In the battle, the French lost four destroyers and eight submarines either sunk or missing. The French at Casablanca surrendered on November 11.

The two Allied landings east and west of Oran encountered heavy French resistance. An attempt by two former U.S. Coast Guard cutters to run into the port failed, and a U.S. airborne battalion, flying all the way from Britain, was only partially successful in securing nearby airfields. At Algiers the frontal naval assault failed, but the city was soon ringed by Allied troops on the land side.

Within a matter of days, the Allies had secured their objectives. Overall Allied casualties were light; the total of 1,469 was well below that anticipated. Despite misgivings, Eisenhower negotiated with the commander of Vichy France's armed forces, former premier Admiral Jean Darlan, who was visiting in Algiers at the time of the landings. On November 11 Darlan agreed to order a cease-fire in return for heading the administration of French North Africa. (Darlan was soon assassinated, removing that embarrassment.)

Although the British were correct in that they could easily have landed farther east, German chancellor Adolf Hitler now decided to reinforce North Africa. Had these resources been sent to Rommel earlier, he might have secured the Suez Canal. Although Allied forces were unprepared for immediate overland operations, they were forced into conducting a land campaign by the prompt German reinforcement efforts, but Hitler's decision only delayed the inevitable and ensured that the ultimate Axis defeat in Tunisia would be more costly.

On November 9, meanwhile, Marshal Henri Philippe Pétain's Vichy French government responded to the invasion by severing diplomatic relations with the United States. Nonetheless, Hitler ordered German troops into "unoccupied" France. Their chief objective was to capture the French warships at Toulon. But on November 27, French crews frustrated this by scuttling 77 ships, including 3 battleships.

Operation TORCH had been successful. The subsequent Allied amphibious operations in Sicily, Italy, and Normandy benefitted immensely from the operation.

Spencer C. Tucker

**Further Reading**

Atkinson, Rick. *An Army at Dawn: The War in North Africa, 1942–1943.* New York: Henry Holt, 2002.

Breuer, William B. *Operation Torch: The Allied Gamble to Invade North Africa.* New York: St. Martin's, 1985.

Howe, George F. *The United States Army in World War II: Northwest Africa; Seizing the Initiative in the West.* Washington, DC: U.S. Government Printing Office, 1957.

Moorehead, Alan. *The March to Tunis: The North African War, 1940–1943.* New York: Harper and Row, 1967.

## Operation HUSKY

| Date | July 9–August 22, 1943 | |
|------|------------------------|---|
| **Location** | Island of Sicily in the Mediterranean | |
| **Opponents (*winner)** | *United States and Great Britain | Italy and Germany |
| **Commander** | General Dwight D. Eisenhower; General Sir Harold Alexander; General Bernard Montgomery; Lieutenant General George S. Patton Jr. | Generalfeldmarschall Albert Kesselring; General Alfredo Guzzoni; General der Panzertruppen Hans Hube |
| **Approx. # Troops** | 160,000 initial strength; peak strength 467,000 men | 300,000–365,000 men |
| **Importance** | The first Allied assault of Fortress Europe, it drives Italy from the war and provides an important base for future operations in the Mediterranean theater. | |

The Allied invasion of Sicily was to that point the largest amphibious landing in history. At the January 1943 Casablanca Conference, U.S. president Franklin D. Roosevelt and British prime minister Winston L. S. Churchill and their staffs discussed the next military objective to follow the final defeat of Axis forces in North Africa. The British favored a strike against the Axis southern flank that would avoid the strong German defenses in northern France, whereas U.S. Army chief of staff General George C. Marshall and the Americans sought an invasion of France across the English Channel as the shorter road to victory. Ultimately Roosevelt agreed with the British view that a southern advance would secure Allied Mediterranean shipping lanes, provide bombers bases from which to strike Axis Southern Europe, and perhaps drive Italy from the war. Thus, the next big offensive of the Western Allies was the invasion of Sicily, code-named HUSKY.

An American munitions ship blows up after being hit by a German bomb off Gela on July 11, 1943, during the Allied invasion of Sicily. (Getty Images)

U.S. general Dwight D. Eisenhower had overall command of Allied forces in the Mediterranean. His ground commander for HUSKY was British general Sir Harold Alexander, commander of Fifteenth Army Group. British admiral Andrew B. Cunningham commanded the naval forces, and Air Chief Marshal Sir Arthur Tedder commanded the supporting Allied air forces. British and American forces would participate in HUSKY in almost equal numbers. The Eastern Task Force would put ashore General Bernard Montgomery's British Eighth Army in southeastern Sicily from just south of Syracuse to the end of the southeastern peninsula. Eighth Army was then to advance along the coast, its final objective the port of Messina on the northeastern tip of the island. The Western Task Force would land Lieutenant General George S. Patton's U.S. Seventh Army in southeastern Sicily between Licata and Scoglitti. On securing the beachhead, Patton was to move inland to conduct supporting attacks and protect Montgomery's left flank. The newly formed Seventh Army had the supporting role, because Alexander believed that Montgomery's veteran troops were better suited for the chief offensive role. The Allies enjoyed air superiority with some 3,700 aircraft, as opposed to 1,600 for the Axis forces.

Sicily was defended by Italian general Alfredo Guzzoni's Sixth Army (consisting of seven static coastal divisions and four maneuver divisions) and German General der Panzertruppe (U.S. equivalent lieutenant general) Hans Hube's XIV Panzer Corps of the 15th Panzergrenadier Division and the Hermann Göring

Division. On July 10 the Germans reinforced with the 1st Parachute Division and the 29th Panzergrenadier Division. Axis strength totaled between 300,000 and 365,000 men.

The Allied invasion was preceded by an elaborate British deception, Operation MINCEMEAT, designed to convince the Germans that the Allies planned to invade Sardinia and islands in the eastern Mediterranean. The deception worked, causing German chancellor Adolf Hitler to shift some resources to those locations.

The invasion of Sicily, preceded by naval and air bombardment, began with airborne landings on July 9, 1943, the first large use by the Allies of such troops in the war. Few of the 144 gliders landed on their targets, and many crashed into the sea. The paratroopers were also widely dispersed. Worse, the invasion fleet fired on the second wave of transport aircraft in the mistaken belief that they were German aircraft and shot down 23 of the Douglas C-47 transport aircraft. Nonetheless, the widely dispersed airborne soldiers created confusion among the Axis defenders, disrupted communications, and, despite their light weapons, prevented some German armor units from reaching the invasion beaches.

The seaborne invasion began early on July 10 in bad weather. The second-largest landing undertaken by the Allies in the European theater of the war after the Normandy invasion (Operation OVERLORD), it involved two large task forces and 2,590 vessels. Operation HUSKY was the first Allied invasion of the war in which specially designed landing craft, including the DUKW truck, were employed.

Resistance from the Italian coastal defenses was weak, and by nightfall the Allies had secured the beachheads. At Gela, the Hermann Göring Division attacked the U.S. 1st Infantry Division but was driven off by naval gunfire. Inland, the rugged terrain and Axis resistance slowed the Allied advance, although Patton's forces reached the capital of Palermo on July 22 and several days later cut the island in two. The British occupied Syracuse with little resistance.

British and American forces were soon in competition to see which would be first to Messina, and a major controversy erupted when Montgomery expropriated an inland road that had been assigned to the Americans. This shift delayed the advance for two days and prolonged the campaign. Meanwhile, on July 25 Benito Mussolini fell from power in Italy as that government moved toward leaving the war.

In Sicily, Axis forces continued a tenacious defense. Allied forces pressed forward, aided by a series of small, skillfully executed amphibious operations on the northern coast east of San Stefano. On August 11, German Generalfeldmarschall (field marshal) Albert Kesselring ordered the evacuation of Axis forces, the Italians having already begun their exodus across the narrow Straits of Messina to Italy. The Italians brought out 62,000 personnel and 227 vehicles; the Germans evacuated 39,569 troops and 9,605 vehicles. It was thus something of a hollow victory when on August 17 Patton's forces reached Messina just hours after the last Germans had evacuated to Italy. Later that day, elements of the British Eighth Army also entered the city.

The conquest of Sicily claimed 11,843 British and 8,781 Americans killed, wounded, missing, or captured. The Germans suffered some 29,000 casualties, including 4,325 killed, 6,663 captured, and an estimated 18,000 wounded. Italian losses are estimated at 2,000 killed and 137,000 captured. The Axis side also lost up to 1,850 aircraft against only 375 for the Allies.

The invasion of Sicily was one of the most important Anglo-American campaigns of the war. It was the first assault by the Western Allies on Fortress Europe and another important experience in coalition planning. As such, the operation set important precedents. The invasion also achieved its goal of driving Italy from the war. On September 3 a new Italian government signed a secret armistice with the Allied powers.

The invasion of Sicily also had a major impact on U.S. military leadership in the European theater of operations. The operation brought the relief of Patton when the press reported that he had slapped two American soldiers suffering from battle fatigue; this was also probably the key in Roosevelt's selection of Eisenhower to command the Normandy invasion.

Anthony L. Franklin and Spencer C. Tucker

**Further Reading**

D'Este, Carlo. *Bitter Victory: The Battle for Sicily, 1943.* New York: E. P. Dutton, 1988.

Morison, Samuel Eliot. *History of United States Naval Operations in World War II,* Vol. 9, *Sicily-Salerno-Anzio, January 1943–June 1944.* Boston: Little, Brown, 1954.

Smyth, Howard McGraw, and Albert N. Garland. *Sicily and the Surrender of Italy.* Washington, DC: U.S. Government Printing Office, 1965.

# Schweinfurt-Regensburg Raids

| Date | August 17 and October 14, 1943 | |
|---|---|---|
| Location | Schweinfurt and Regensburg, Germany | |
| Opponents (*winner) | *Germany | United States |
| Commander | Luftwaffe Generalmajor Adolf Galland | Major General Ira Eaker |
| # Aircraft | Some 400 fighters | 376 B-17 bombers; 268 P-47 and 191 Spitfire fighter sorties (August 17); 291 B-17s (October 14) |
| Importance | The Americans learn a hard lesson about the strategic bombing of Germany. The raids force U.S. commanders to address a wide range of problems and speed up efforts to develop a long-range fighter capable of accompanying the bombers on their missions over Germany. | |

The Schweinfurt-Regensburg Raids of August 17 and October 14, 1943, were part of the Combined Chiefs of Staff bomber offensive initiated in June 1943. U.S. Army Air Forces (USAAF) leaders were determined, despite concerns about their effectiveness, to prove the efficacy of largely unescorted daylight precision bombing raids and the ability of strategic bombing to win the war.

The raids were designed to destroy five ball-bearing factories at Schweinfurt and the Messerschmitt aircraft complex at Regensburg. The mission was assigned to Major General Ira Eaker's Eighth Army Air Force in England. Both targets were far beyond the normal range of the USAAF's Boeing B-17 Flying Fortress strategic bomber. Regensburg, to be attacked by the 3rd Bombardment Group, was more than 500 miles from the English coast, while Schweinfurt, to be struck by the 1st Bombardment Group, was nearly 400 miles distant. German fighters would thus have ample opportunity to attack the bomber streams both coming and going. Once the Regensburg bombers had dropped their bombs, they were to fly on to North Africa. Eighteen squadrons of USAAF Republic P-47 Thunderbolts and 16 squadrons of Royal Air Force Supermarine Spitfires could provide protection only about 40 percent of the way.

Early morning fog on August 17 disrupted the plan for simultaneous attacks. Of the 3rd Bombardment Group's 146 B-17s, 122 reached their target; they dropped 250 tons of bombs on Regensburg. Four hours later, 184 of the 1st Bombardment Group's original 230 bombers dropped 380 tons of bombs on Schweinfurt. Of the 376 B-17s that took off, following aborts 361 crossed the Dutch coastline. Sixty (36 over Regensburg and 24 over Schweinfurt) were shot down, but 11 of the 301 bombers that made it to base were damaged beyond repair, and another 162 received some damage. The overall loss rate, including aircraft that had to be written off, was 19 percent. The Eighth Air Force lost 408 aircrew, 100 of them killed. U.S. gunners claimed to have downed 228 German fighters; actual losses were 27.

The raid did have some success. Nearly half of the machine tools in the Regensburg assembly plant were destroyed. Although the plant was back in production in less than four weeks, fighter production losses were on the order of 800 to 1,000 planes. Unknown at the time, the raid also destroyed the jigs for the fuselage of the Messerschmitt Me-262 jet fighter. German managers later speculated that this loss delayed the production of this aircraft by four critical months. At Schweinfurt, ball-bearing production suffered a temporary 50 percent drop-off. Double shifts, however, soon made up for this deficiency.

A belated attempt to renew the assault on Schweinfurt on October 14, the so-called Black Thursday Raid, cost the Americans 60 of 291 aircraft and more than 600 aircrew. Again, the raid had only limited success. This raid left 133 planes so badly damaged that it took four months to bring the Eighth Air Force back to anything approaching full strength. The Germans lost perhaps 35 fighters.

German minister of armaments and munitions Albert Speer believed that the Allies could have won the war in 1944 had they continued raids against the ball-bearing industry. Speer held in his memoirs that raids such as that at Schweinfurt could well have proven fatal if continued at a high level. The USAAF could not sustain such raids, however; they were simply too costly. The Eighth Air Force was losing some 30 percent of its strength each month, ensuring that few crews made it to the 25 missions necessary for rotation back to the United States. The loss rates for the bombers were totally unsustainable, and the attacks proved to Allied leaders that deep raids were impossible without long-range fighter escort.

The Schweinfurt-Regensburg Raids did force the USAAF to address a host of long-standing problems, including navigation and bombing procedures. The raids also sparked a crash program for mass production of a long-range fighter, hitherto inexplicably low on the list of military priorities. That aircraft appeared in the North American Aviation P-51 Mustang, probably the best all-around piston-engine fighter of the war. Mounting six .50-caliber machine guns and capable of a speed of 440 miles per hour (mph), it outclassed the Bf-109 in maneuverability and in speed by at least 50 mph. The P-51 Mustang could also carry 2,000 pounds of bombs. The British and Americans had been slow to utilize drop tanks. An obvious range extender for fighter aircraft, drop tanks had been utilized by the Japanese early on in operations against the Philippines. The P-51's range was 810 miles, but with two 75-gallon drop tanks, it had a round-trip range of 1,200 miles. A further 85-gallon internal tank extended this to 1,474 miles, and even with two drop tanks it could reach 400 mph and more. The Allies now had an aircraft with the range of a bomber and the speed and maneuverability of a fighter. The North American P-51 and the Republic P-47 Thunderbolt, another fine fighter and rugged ground-support aircraft, now also equipped with drop tanks, could protect the bombers to and from their targets.

The air war thus turned dramatically. In February 1944 the Allies carried out a series of massive raids against German aircraft factories and strikes against Berlin, forcing German fighters aloft so they could be destroyed.

Spencer C. Tucker

## Further Reading

Middlebrook, Martin. *The Schweinfurt-Regensburg Mission.* New York: Scribner, 1983.

Neillands, Robin. *The Bomber War: The Allied Air Offensive against Nazi Germany.* New York: Overlook, 2001.

Verrier, Anthony. *The Bomber Offensive.* New York: Macmillan, 1969.

## Battle of Tarawa

| Date | November 20–24, 1943 | |
|---|---|---|
| Location | Betio atoll, Tarawa, in the Gilbert Islands | |
| Opponents (*winner) | *United States | Japan |
| Commander | Major General Julian C. Smith | Rear Admiral Shibasaki Keiji |
| Approx. # Troops | 12,000 men of the 2nd Marine Division | 4,836 Japanese troops and Japanese and Korean laborers |
| Importance | The Americans learn important lessons in the conduct of amphibious operations and the need for certain specialized weapons and equipment. The battle becomes a symbol of U.S. Marine Corps gallantry. | |

The November 1943 capture of Tarawa in the Gilbert Islands was the first amphibious landing against a heavily defended coast since the Gallipoli Campaign during World War I (1914–1918). In terms of percentage of casualties, Tarawa was one of the bloodiest battles in U.S. military history but provided valuable lessons for subsequent amphibious operations.

Following the American victory on Guadalcanal in February 1943, Admiral Chester W. Nimitz, commander of U.S. forces in the Central Pacific, readied the Fifth Fleet for a strike in the Central Pacific. Commanded by Vice Admiral Raymond A. Spruance, the Fifth Fleet included 8 carriers, 7 battleships, 10 cruisers, and 34 destroyers. Rear Admiral Richmond K. Turner's Fifth Amphibious Force lifted U.S. Marine Corps major general Holland M. "Howling Mad" Smith's V Amphibious Corps. In addition to carrier-based naval aircraft, the Seventh Army Air Force provided support.

The 16 Gilbert atolls, ringed with coral reefs and at the time Japan's farthest eastern outpost, straddled the equator. The Japanese defense centered on Tarawa and Makin, some 100 miles apart. Betio, Tarawa's biggest island, contained a small airfield from which Japanese planes could threaten Allied shipping lanes between the United States and Australia. The invasion planners allocated 18,000 marines to Tarawa.

Beginning in mid-November 1943, U.S. Navy warships converged on the islands. U.S. Army Air Forces bombers attacked, followed by naval gunfire from battleships and cruisers and strikes by navy aircraft. Army forces landed on Makin on February 20 and secured it in four days.

The capture of Tarawa was not so easy. The citadel of its defense was Betio Island, only two miles long and several hundred yards across. The Japanese had built some 400 concrete pillboxes, bunkers, and strong points covered with logs and sand that were impervious to all but a direct hit. They also had 8-inch guns and had placed mines in gaps in the coral reefs and ringed the island with barbed wire.

Bodies of American dead on the beach at Tarawa in the Gilbert Islands. Of 5,000 marines in the initial assault, 1,500 were killed or wounded on November 20, 1943. (National Archives)

On the morning of November 20, the U.S. Marine Corps 2nd Division went ashore. As the marines came ashore, the 4,700 Japanese defenders, commanded by Rear Admiral Shibasaki Keiji, opened fire. Inadequate reconnaissance had failed to disclose inner coral reefs just below the surface of the water. Although the amtracs (amphibious tractors) carrying the first wave of assaulting troops could cross the reefs and most reached the beach, landing craft with the remainder of the men hung up on the reefs. The marines were thus forced to wade hundreds of yards through waist-deep water while under heavy Japanese fire.

Of 5,000 marines landed the first day, 1,500 were killed or wounded. The next day the divisional reserve landed. With no possibility of maneuver in such a small area, advance was slow and by frontal assault. Gradually the marines drove the defenders into the eastern part of the island. Most of them were killed in a suicidal November 22–23 night attack shattered by marine artillery and naval gunfire. The Japanese lost 4,690 men on Tarawa; the marines took only 17 Japanese prisoners, although 129 Korean laborers were also captured. The marines suffered 985 killed and 2,193 wounded. The casualties shocked Americans at home, and there were even calls for a congressional investigation.

The Americans learned important lessons from the operation. These included the need for better reconnaissance, more effective naval gunfire support (especially plunging fire to destroy fortifications), and additional flamethrowers, demolition charges, amtracs, and infantry firepower. The Battle for Tarawa became a symbol of U.S. Marine Corps gallantry.

Spencer C. Tucker

## Further Reading

Alexander, Joseph H. *Utmost Savagery: The Three Days of Tarawa.* Annapolis, MD: Naval Institute Press, 1995.

Graham, Michael B. *Mantle of Heroism: Tarawa and the Struggle for the Gilberts, November, 1943.* Novato, CA: Presidio, 1993.

Gregg, Charles T. *Tarawa.* New York: Stein and Day, 1984.

Wright, Derrick. *A Hell of a Way to Die: Tarawa Atoll, 20–23 November 1943.* London: Windrow and Greene, 1997.

## Invasion of Normandy

| Date | June 6, 1944 | |
| --- | --- | --- |
| **Location** | Normandy, France | |
| **Opponents (*winner)** | *United States, United Kingdom, Canada, Free France, Poland, Norway, Australia, and New Zealand | Germany |
| **Commander** | General Dwight D. Eisenhower | Generalfeldmarshall Gerd von Rundstedt; Generalfeldmarshall Erwin Rommel |
| **Approx. # Troops** | 2,700 ships manned by 195,000 men, transporting 130,000 troops, 2,000 tanks, 12,000 other vehicles, and 10,000 tons of supplies | 10,000 men |
| **Importance** | In the largest amphibious operation in history, the Allies carry out their long-promised invasion of western Europe. | |

At the Tehran Conference in November 1943, British prime minister Winston Churchill, U.S. president Franklin D. Roosevelt, and Soviet premier Joseph Stalin agreed to a major invasion of Europe via the English Channel as well as a landing in southern France and a major offensive by the Soviets on the Eastern Front. The Germans were well aware that the Western Allies would attempt a cross-channel invasion. Festung Europa (Fortress Europe) and its coasts of Holland, Belgium, and France bristled with German fortifications and booby traps. In mid-1942 the German Todt Organization began erecting Atlantic coast defenses and during the next two years expended some 17.3 million cubic yards of concrete and 1.2 million tons of steel on thousands of fortifications. The Germans also strongly fortified the channel ports, which German chancellor Adolf Hitler ordered turned into fortresses.

The Allies knew that they would likely not be able to count on the immediate use of any French ports, and in one of history's greatest military engineering achievements, thousands of laborers worked in Britain over many months to build two large artificial harbors. Known as Mulberries, these were to be hauled across

U.S. soldiers landing on the Normandy coast of France under heavy German machine gun fire, D-Day, June 6, 1944. (National Archives)

the channel from Britain and sunk in place; they were to ease resupply and allow the invaders to temporarily bypass the German-held ports. The Mulberries were of immense importance to the Allied cause.

In a close and near-seamless cooperation, British and French staff officers worked out precise and elaborate plans for a mammoth invasion of the Cotentin Peninsula in Normandy. U.S. general Dwight D. Eisenhower had overall responsibility, while British admiral Bertram H. Ramsay commanded the naval operation, code-named NEPTUNE, and British general Bernard Montgomery exerted overall command of the land forces. The planning document, first drawn up in the summer of 1943, described the object of the operation as being "to secure a lodgement on the continent, from which further offensive operations can be developed." In the weeks leading up to the landing, Allied air forces carried out a massive bombing campaign to isolate Normandy.

The landing was to be preceded by a night drop of three divisions of paratroops: the British 6th Division and the U.S. 82nd and 101st Divisions. The lightly armed paratroopers, operating in conjunction with the French Resistance, had the vital assignment of securing the flanks of the lodgement and destroying key transportation choke points to prevent the Germans from reinforcing the beaches. The German 21st Panzer and 12th SS Panzer Divisions were positioned just outside Caen. If they could reach the beaches, they would be able to strike the amphibious forces from the flank and roll them up.

The amphibious assault would occur early the next morning after the airborne assault. Five infantry divisions were to come ashore along a 50-mile stretch of

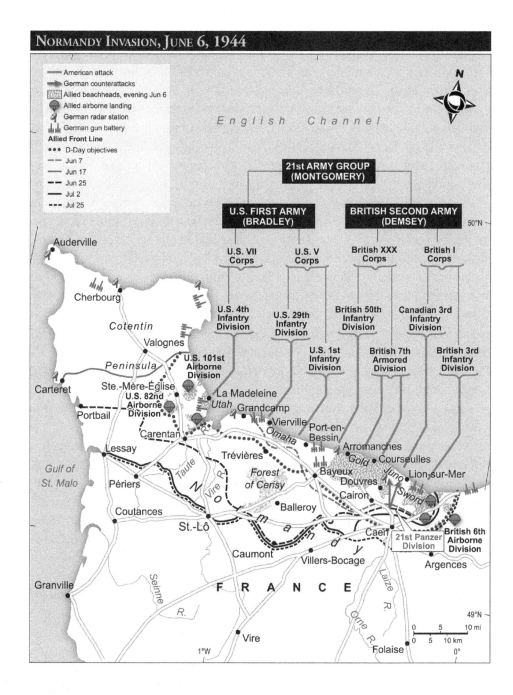

**NORMANDY INVASION, JUNE 6, 1944**

Legend:
- American attack
- German counterattacks
- Allied beachheads, evening Jun 6
- Allied airborne landing
- German radar station
- German gun battery
- **Allied Front Line**
- ••• D-Day objectives
- –– Jun 7
- — Jun 17
- –– Jun 25
- — Jul 2
- --- Jul 25

**21st ARMY GROUP (MONTGOMERY)**

**U.S. FIRST ARMY (BRADLEY)** — **BRITISH SECOND ARMY (DEMSEY)**

U.S. VII Corps — U.S. V Corps — British XXX Corps — British I Corps

U.S. 4th Infantry Division — U.S. 29th Infantry Division — British 50th Infantry Division — Canadian 3rd Infantry Division

U.S. 1st Infantry Division — British 7th Armored Division — British 3rd Infantry Division

U.S. 101st Airborne Division — U.S. 82nd Airborne Division — British 6th Airborne Division

21st Panzer Division

coast, divided into five sectors. The designated units and their beaches were, from west to east, the U.S. 4th Infantry Division, Utah; the U.S. 1st Infantry, Omaha; the British 50th Infantry, Gold; the Canadian 3rd Infantry, Juno; and the British 3rd Infantry, Sword.

The Normandy invasion was a vast undertaking. The airborne forces alone required 1,340 C-47 transports and 2,500 gliders. Ten thousand aircraft secured the skies, while naval support for the invasion numbered 138 bombarding warships, 221 destroyers and other convoy escorts, 287 minesweepers, 495 light craft, and 441 auxiliaries. In addition, some 4,000 landing ships and other craft of various sizes participated.

General Eisenhower faced a difficult decision, given terrible weather in the days leading up to the landing. Informed by his chief meteorologist that a break in the weather should occur, Eisenhower decided to proceed. The bad weather actually worked to the Allies' advantage, for the Germans did not expect a landing in such poor conditions.

The French Resistance was informed by radio code of the imminent attack, and the airborne forces took off. The drops occurred on schedule on the night of June 5–6, but thick cloud banks over Normandy that caused pilots to veer off course to avoid midair collisions in addition to German antiaircraft fire, jumpy flight crews, and Pathfinders that were immediately engaged in firefights on the ground and unable to set up beacons all led to premature drops and to paratroopers being scattered all over the peninsula. Some even fell into the English Channel, where they were dragged down and drowned by their heavy equipment. Gliders crashed into obstacles, and both gliders and paratroopers came down in fields that had been deliberately flooded by the defenders. Much equipment was thus lost. Nonetheless, the wide scattering of forces caused confusion among the Germans as to the precise Allied objectives. Airborne officers collected as many men as they could, and these improvised units were soon moving on the objectives, most of which were secured.

Success was likely if the Allies could establish a bridgehead large enough to build up their strength and overcome the German defenders. Once they broke out, the Allies would have the whole of France for maneuver. Their armies were fully mechanized, and the bulk of the defending German forces was not. German Generalfeldmarschall Erwin Rommel, who had charge of the coastal defenses, understood that the German defense was doomed unless it could destroy the invaders on the beaches. He told Hitler that "If we don't manage to throw them back at once, the invasion will succeed in spite of the Atlantic Wall."

Hitler failed to understand this and indeed welcomed the invasion as a chance to get at and destroy the British and U.S. forces. In Britain, they could not be touched; in France, they could be destroyed. "Let them come," he said. "They will get the thrashing of their lives."

The only real possibility for German success was the rapid introduction of Panzer reserves, but this was fatally delayed by two factors. The first was Allied air superiority of 30 to 1 over Normandy, including large numbers of ground-support aircraft, especially the Republic P-47 Thunderbolt and the North American P-51 Mustang. The second was Hitler's failure to immediately commit available resources. He was convinced that the invasion at Normandy was merely a feint and that the main thrust would come in the Pas de Calais sector.

Allied deceptions played a key role in deluding the Germans. The British actually controlled the entire German spy network in the United Kingdom and used it to feed disinformation to the Germans. In Operation FORTITUDE in particular, the British orchestrated two deceptions of immense importance to the success of the invasion. FORTITUDE NORTH suggested an invasion of Norway by a bogus British Fourth Army headquartered at Edinburgh, Scotland. To convince the Germans, the British employed radio nets and also created large numbers of decoy barges of canvas, wood, and wire; dummy gliders; and inflatable rubber tanks and trucks. Some German reconnaissance aircraft were then permitted to fly over these. This deception and perceived threat to his northern flank caused Hitler to shift some 400,000 men to Norway.

FORTITUDE SOUTH, on the other hand, was designed to convince Hitler that the landing at Normandy (Operation OVERLORD) was only a diversion and that the major invasion would indeed occur later in the closest English Channel crossing point, the Pas de Calais. The Allies created the First U.S. Army Group under General George Patton, still without command following an incident in which he had slapped soldiers suffering from combat fatigue in Sicily. The Germans expected Patton to command any Allied invasion of Europe. The U.S. First Army Group, a formation of 18 divisions and 4 corps headquarters, contributed nothing to the initial invasion, however.

Both deceptions involved feeding small bits of information to the Germans, some of it through the Double-Cross System and then letting the Germans draw the proper conclusions. The British plan worked to perfection. Not until late July did Hitler authorize the movement of the Fifteenth Panzer Army from the Pas de Calais to Normandy. The deception effectively immobilized 19 German divisions east of the Seine. Although units of the Fifteenth Army were moved west to Normandy before that date, they arrived piecemeal and thus were much easier to defeat.

The Normandy invasion began with some 2,700 vessels, manned by 195,000 naval officers and sailors, that transported 130,000 troops to France, along with 2,000 tanks, 12,000 other vehicles, and 10,000 tons of supplies. At about 5:30 a.m. on June 6, 1944, the bombardment ships opened up against the invasion beaches, engaging the German shore batteries. The first U.S. assault troops landed 30 to 40 minutes later, while the British landing craft were ashore 2 hours later.

The landing was in jeopardy only on Omaha Beach, where because of rough seas only 5 of 32 amphibious DD (duplex drive) tanks reached the shore. Support artillery was also lost when DUKW amphibious trucks were swamped by the waves. Some landing craft were hit and destroyed, and those troops of the 1st Infantry Division who gained the beach were soon pinned down by withering German fire. U.S. First Army commander Lieutenant General Omar N. Bradley even considered withdrawal.

At 9:50 a.m. the gunfire support ships opened up against the German shore batteries, and Allied destroyers repeatedly risked running aground to provide close-in gunnery support to the troops ashore; several destroyers actually scraped bottom. It was nearly noon before the German defenders began to give way. The 1st

Infantry Division overcame German opposition with sheer determination, reinforced by the knowledge that there was no place to retreat.

The landings on the other beaches were much easier, and the Allies suffered surprisingly light casualties overall for the first day: 10,000–12,000 men. A recent study suggests that a night landing would have produced fewer casualties. The Allies had employed these with great success in the Mediterranean, but Montgomery believed that overwhelming Allied air and naval power would make a daytime landing preferable.

One million men came ashore within a month. Unfortunately for the Allies, during June 19–20 a Force 6–7 storm severely damaged Mulberry A in the American sector. The storm also sank well over 100 small craft and drove many more ashore, bringing to a halt the discharge of supplies. Vital ammunition stocks had to be flown in. Mulberry A was abandoned, but a strengthened Mulberry B provided supplies to both armies until the end of the war.

The Allied ground offensive meanwhile proceeded slower than expected. By ordering his armies to fight for every inch of ground rather than withdraw along phased lines as his generals wanted, Hitler at first delayed the Allied timetable. Not until Operation COBRA (July 25–31) were the Allies able to break out, but Hitler's decision greatly speeded up the Allied advance at the end. Patton arrived in France on July 6. His Third Army soon parlayed the local breakthrough of COBRA into a theater-wide breakout and in a single month had liberated most of France north of the Loire.

Spencer C. Tucker

## Further Reading

Blair, Clay. *Ridgway's Paratroopers: The American Airborne in World War II.* Garden City, NY: Dial, 1985.

Hartcup, Guy. *Code Name Mulberry: The Planning, Building and Operation of the Normandy Harbours.* London: David and Charles, 1977.

Hesketh, Roger. *Fortitude: The D-Day Deception Campaign.* New York: Overlook, 2000.

Keegan, John. *Six Armies in Normandy: From D-Day to the Liberation of Paris, June 6th–August 25th, 1944.* New York: Viking, 1982.

Lewis, Adrian R. *Omaha Beach: A Flawed Victory.* Chapel Hill: University of North Carolina Press, 2001.

Masterman, J. C. *The Double-Cross System in the War of 1939–1945.* New Haven, CT: Yale University Press, 1972.

## Battle of Philippine Sea

| Date | June 19–21, 1944 | |
|---|---|---|
| Location | Philippine Sea | |
| Opponents (*winner) | *United States | Japan |
| Commander | Vice Admiral Marc A. Mitscher | Vice Admiral Ozawa Jisaburo |

| # Ships | 112 ships (7 fleet and 8 light carriers, 7 battleships, 8 heavy and 13 light cruisers, 69 destroyers, and 28 submarines); 956 aircraft | 55 ships (5 fleet and 4 light carriers, 5 battleships, 11 heavy and 2 light cruisers, and 28 destroyers); 476 carrier aircraft and some 300 land-based aircraft |
|---|---|---|
| Importance | Eliminates the Japanese naval air arm as an effective fighting force. | |

In June 1944 in Operation FORAGER, U.S. Pacific forces moved against the Japanese-held Mariana Islands in the central Pacific. Securing the Marianas would provide bases from which long-range Boeing B-29 Superfortress strategic bombers could strike Japan.

Steaming from Eniwetok 1,000 miles to the east, the U.S. V Amphibious Corps of 530 warships and auxiliaries, lifting more than 127,000 troops, proceeded to Saipan. Admiral Raymond Spruance had overall command. His Fifth Fleet and its chief strike force, Vice Admiral Marc A. Mitscher's Task Force (TF) 58, provided protection for the landing and V Amphibious Corps' ships. TF-58 included 15 carriers (7 fleet and 8 light), 7 battleships, 8 heavy cruisers, 12 light cruisers, 69 destroyers, and 956 aircraft.

The Japanese anticipated the U.S. move, and commander of the Combined Fleet Admiral Toyoda Soemu ordered Vice Admiral Ozawa Jisaburo to prepare a plan to lure U.S. warships, once they moved against the Marianas, into a decisive battle in the Philippine Sea. The Japanese designed this operation, code-named A-GO, to offset somewhat their inferiority in the air by employing land-based aircraft. For the engagement, the Japanese deployed some 90 percent of their surface naval strength: 9 aircraft carriers (5 fleet and 4 light), 5 battleships, 11 heavy cruisers, 2 light cruisers, 28 destroyers, and 473 aircraft.

Ozawa's forces were inferior to those of the Americans in every category except heavy cruisers. However, the Japanese planned to supplement their naval air arm with some 500 land-based aircraft on Yap, Guam, Tinian, and the Palaus. Nearly 100 bombers were ready to fly from Yokosuka if needed. Ozawa hoped to employ his longer-range aircraft to attack the U.S. carriers on their approach. When his own carriers were within range, he would launch a second strike and then land and rearm these aircraft on Guam to attack the American ships in a third strike before the Japanese planes returned to their carriers.

On June 15, the 2nd and 4th Marine Divisions went ashore on Saipan. Upon learning of this, Vice Admiral Ozawa immediately moved his ships into the Philippine Sea. Spruance, warned of their arrival by the U.S. submarine *Flying Fish,* on the afternoon of June 16 decided to postpone the invasion of Guam and detach 5 heavy and 3 light cruisers and 21 destroyers from the fire-support groups at Saipan to augment TF-58. This left 7 battleships, 3 cruisers, and 5 destroyers to protect the Saipan beachhead. On June 18 he concentrated the Fifth Fleet under Mitscher's tactical command some 180 miles due west of Tinian to search for the Japanese ships.

The resulting Battle of the Philippine Sea was the first fleet battle between the United States and Japan in two years and turned out to be pivotal. The Japanese employed 55 ships, the Americans 112. The battle was history's largest engagement between aircraft carriers.

Events went badly for the Japanese early on. Ozawa's ship dispositions were faulty and exposed his carriers to submarine attack. The U.S. submarine *Albacore* sank the *Taiho,* Japan's newest and largest carrier (and Ozawa's flagship), and the submarine *Cavalla* sank the fleet carrier *Shokaku.* Misled about the damage to Japanese land aircraft and unaware that most of them had been destroyed in strikes by planes from Mitscher's carriers, Ozawa believed that he could still count on heavy assistance from Guam.

On the morning of June 19, Ozawa launched four different attack waves against the American ships. Mitscher's fighters and antiaircraft fire downed most of them in what the Americans later referred to as the "Great Marianas Turkey Shoot." The Japanese carriers launched 324 planes but recovered only 56. Other Japanese planes were shot down over Guam or crash-landed there. The Americans lost only 30 aircraft. No U.S. ships were sunk, and only a few sustained damage. Meanwhile, Mitscher's planes attacked Guam and Rota to neutralize the Japanese airfields there. By 6:45 p.m., the battle was effectively over.

Spruance was not aware of Ozawa's exact location and therefore refused Mitscher's suggestion that he move west, as Spruance was concerned that the Japanese might be able to get between his ships and the Saipan landing sites. Mitscher sent out search missions during the morning and early afternoon of June 20, but not until 4:00 p.m. did the Americans definitively locate the Japanese ships at the extreme range of U.S. attack aircraft. Mitscher realized that an attack this late in the day would mean recovering the planes at night and that a number of them might run out of fuel and have to ditch, but he sent 216 aircraft against Ozawa's ships nonetheless.

The U.S. planes arrived at the Japanese ships just before dark and sank the carrier *Hiryu* and two tankers and damaged other vessels. The attack cost the United States 20 planes, but the Japanese lost 21. The homeward-bound U.S. aircraft were forced to find their carriers in the dark. Mitscher ignored the possibility of Japanese submarine attack, however, and lit his carriers. Still, 80 aircraft ran out of gas and either ditched or crash-landed. Destroyers later picked up most of the aircrews, leaving U.S. personnel losses for the day at 16 pilots and 33 crewmen. Spruance pursued the Japanese ships until the early evening of June 21, but he was slowed by the need of his destroyers to take on fuel. Ozawa meanwhile had accelerated his own withdrawal.

The Battle of the Philippine Sea remains controversial for its command decisions. Some historians have criticized Spruance for failing to push westward against the Japanese on the night of June 18–19, which might have yielded a more favorable launch position for Mitscher's aircraft. Mitscher also has been criticized for his failure to send out night searches on June 19–20 that might have located the Japanese ships sooner and allowed an early strike on June 20.

Nonetheless, the Battle of the Philippine Sea was a major defeat for Japan. Air combat and operational losses cost the Japanese approximately 450 aviators. Unable to replace either the carriers or the trained pilots, the vaunted Japanese naval air arm ceased to be a factor in the war. In the Battle of Leyte Gulf (October 23–26, 1944), the remaining Japanese carriers, bereft of aircraft, served as decoys.

Saipan was declared secured on July 9. This event so shocked Japanese leaders that the cabinet resigned on July 18. Guam was taken during July 21–August 10, and Tinian was taken during July 25–August 2, both after heavy Japanese resistance. Even while the fighting was in progress, U.S. Navy Construction Battalions (CBs, known as Seabees) were at work building runways and preparing facilities for the B-29s that would strike Japan.

Spencer C. Tucker

**Further Reading**

Dull, Paul S. *A Battle History of the Imperial Japanese Navy, 1941–1945.* Annapolis, MD: Naval Institute Press, 1978.

Morison, Samuel Eliot. *History of United States Naval Operations in World War II,* Vol. 8, *New Guinea and the Marianas, March 1944–August 1944.* Boston: Little, Brown, 1953.

Spector, Ronald H. *Eagle against the Sun: The American War with Japan.* New York: Free Press, 1985.

Y'Blood, William T. *Red Sun Setting: The Battle of the Philippine Sea.* Annapolis, MD: Naval Institute Press, 1980.

## Operation COBRA

| Date | July 25–31, 1944 | |
| --- | --- | --- |
| Location | Normandy, France | |
| Opponents (*winner) | *United States | Germany |
| Commander | Lieutenant General Omar N. Bradley; Major General J. Lawton Collins | General der Artillerie Erich Marcks |
| Approx. # Troops | 6 divisions and 100,000 men | 1 corps of understrength divisions |
| Importance | U.S. forces break through the German lines, enabling Lieutenant General George S. Patton's Third Army to carry out a brilliant exploitation deep into France. | |

Satisfaction with the success of the Normandy Invasion of June 6, 1944, dissipated to frustration when the tenacious German defense of the Cotentin Peninsula stifled Allied efforts to expand control beyond the initial beachheads. Supreme commander of the Allied Expeditionary Forces General Dwight D. Eisenhower had grown impatient with the disrupted timetable as British general Sir Bernard L. Montgomery failed to take Caen and Lieutenant General Omar N. Bradley's U.S. First Army remained stalled in the bocage, or hedgerow, country. To break the deadlock, two offensive plans were developed. Operation GOODWOOD, led by British lieutenant general Miles C. Dempsey, would fix the German attention on British forces seeking to capture Caen. Meanwhile, Bradley would launch Operation COBRA, a mobile ground attack to break out of the Cotentin Peninsula, drive west into Brittany, and culminate in a wide sweep to the southeast to stretch German defenses to the breaking point.

Tactical command for COBRA fell to aggressive VII Corps commander Major General J. Lawton Collins. Collins was allotted six divisions and almost 100,000 men for the attack. The plan hinged on a concentrated strike by heavy bombers to destroy a significant portion of the German lines. After the bombardment, an overwhelming ground attack by the U.S. 9th, 4th, and 30th Infantry Divisions would penetrate the disrupted German defenses and hold open a corridor for the exploiting mobile divisions.

Opposing Collins was German General der Artillerie (U.S. equivalent of lieutenant general) Erich Marcks's LXXXIV Corps. It had experienced heavy fighting and contained many understrength units, such as the Panzer Lehr Division, which could muster only 3,200 troops along a three-mile front.

A key element in the COBRA plan was to locate a point of penetration where there were sufficient parallel roads in the direction of the attack to allow follow-on forces into the breach. The most controversial aspect of the operation was carpet bombing by heavy bombers. Bradley designated a rectangular target box 2,500 yards wide and more than 7,000 yards long, and his IX Tactical Air commander, Major General Elwood "Pete" Quesada, met with Air Chief Marshal Sir Trafford Leigh-Mallory to coordinate the air attack. However, the competing needs for dropping maximum bomb tonnage, maintaining tactical positions for the infantry, and placing 1,500 bombers in the mile-wide corridor in a single hour could not be entirely reconciled.

Operation COBRA was scheduled for July 24, but overcast skies led Leigh-Mallory to call off the carpet bombing. Unfortunately, Eighth Air Force bombers were already in flight and approached the target from a perpendicular direction, causing bombs to fall short of the target and into the 30th Infantry Division, killing 25 and wounding 131. With the attack postponed and the surprise lost, an infuriated Bradley was informed that another attack would follow the next day.

On July 25, bombers dropped 4,400 tons of bombs. The Germans, alerted by the previous attack, had dug in. Despite this, the Panzer Lehr Division was left in shambles, with 70 percent of its soldiers suffering shock and several battalion command posts destroyed. The Americans, in exposed positions and ready to move, sustained as a consequence of shorts (bombs that fell short of their targets and landed among friendly forces) another 111 men killed, almost 500 wounded, and psychological trauma for 200 more. Among the U.S. dead was Lieutenant General Lesley J. McNair, commander of Army Ground Forces, who was visiting the front to observe the attack.

In spite of this tragedy, VII Corps immediately attacked, although strong pockets of German resistance limited the advance to only a mile or two. The next day Collins took the bold decision to commit his armored and motorized forces, even though no U.S. unit had reached its planned objectives. The disrupted German command-and-control network failed to react when U.S. armored divisions sliced through the lines on July 26. The next day, Collins's mobile units exploited their success deeper into the German rear areas, which led Bradley to order VIII Corps through the breach to seize Avranches.

According to the plan, once forces moved toward Brittany, the U.S. Third Army, commanded by Lieutenant General George S. Patton Jr., would be activated. To facilitate this transition, Bradley gave Patton immediate command of VIII Corps, which he drove hard to capture Avranches on July 31 and mark the end of COBRA. In just six days the entire German front had collapsed, enabling the Allies to carry out their own operational blitzkrieg deep into France.

Steven J. Rauch

## Further Reading

Blumenson, Martin. *Breakout and Pursuit.* Washington, DC: Center of Military History, 1961.

Carafano, James J. *After D-Day: Operation Cobra and the Normandy Breakout.* Boulder, CO: Lynne Rienner, 2000.

# Battle of Leyte Gulf

| Date | October 23–26, 1944 | |
|---|---|---|
| Location | Leyte Gulf and nearby waters, Philippine Islands | |
| Opponents (*winner) | *United States and Australia | Japan |
| Commander | Admiral William F. Halsey Jr.; Vice Admiral Thomas C. Kinkaid | Vice Admiral Kurita Takeo; Vice Admiral Ozawa Jisaburo; Vice Admiral Nishimura Shoji |
| # Ships | 216 U.S. warships (2 Australian): 8 fleet carriers, 8 light carriers, 18 escort carriers, 12 battleships, 24 cruisers, 141 destroyers and destroyer escorts; many PT boats, submarines, and fleet auxiliaries; some 1,712 aircraft | 68 Japanese warships: 1 fleet carrier, 3 light carriers, 9 battleships, 14 heavy cruisers, 6 light cruisers, and 35 destroyers; 700+ aircraft (117 embarked, rest land-based) |
| Importance | Marks the end of Japanese fleet as an effective fighting force. | |

The Battle of Leyte Gulf was history's largest naval engagement. The 282 vessels involved (216 U.S., 2 Australian, and 64 Japanese vessels) surpassed the 250 ships of the 1916 Battle of Jutland. The Battle of Leyte Gulf involved nearly 200,000 men

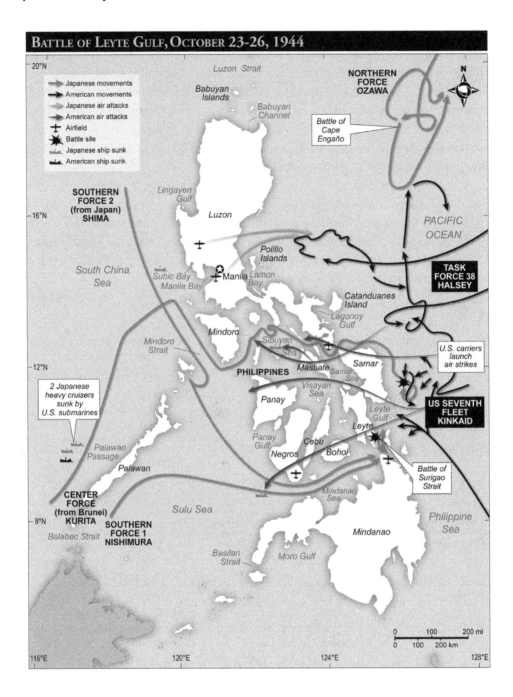

**BATTLE OF LEYTE GULF, OCTOBER 23-26, 1944**

and took place over an area of more than 100,000 square miles. The engagement saw all aspects of naval warfare as well as the use of the largest guns ever at sea, the last clash of the dreadnoughts, and the introduction of kamikaze aircraft.

In July 1944, U.S. president Franklin Roosevelt met at Honolulu with his two major Pacific theater commanders to decide on the next target after the conquest of the Mariana Islands. Commander of Southwest Pacific Forces General Douglas

A Japanese kamikaze aircraft dives toward a U.S. warship during the Battle of Leyte Gulf, which saw the first official employment of suicide aircraft by the Japanese in the war. (AP Photo)

MacArthur argued strongly for a return to the Philippines; Central Pacific commander Admiral Chester W. Nimitz, supported by chief of naval operations Ernest J. King, wanted to secure Taiwan. Both plans would place U.S. forces astride the Japanese oil lifeline from the Netherlands East Indies, but Roosevelt sided with MacArthur primarily for political reasons. The next target would be Okinawa rather than Taiwan.

On October 20, more than 132,000 men of the U.S. Sixth Army went ashore on the island of Leyte in the Philippines. Warned by the preliminary bombardment, the Japanese put into effect their contingency plan. The Naval General Staff in Tokyo had actually developed four plans under the SHO (VICTORY) code name. Operation SHO-1 covered defense of the Philippine archipelago and involved the entire Combined Fleet.

Japanese naval air strength had been severely reduced in the June 1944 Battle of the Philippine Sea, and during October 12–14 U.S. carrier planes and U.S. Army B-29 heavy bombers attacked Japanese airfields on Formosa, Okinawa, and the Philippines. These strikes wiped out much of the Japanese land-based aviation and denied the Japanese Navy badly needed support. This alone probably doomed the Japanese plan. The Japanese did add extra antiaircraft guns to their ships in an attempt to offset their lack of airpower, but offensively they had to rely on naval gunnery and some 335 land-based planes in the Luzon area.

The Japanese hoped to destroy sufficient U.S. shipping to break up the amphibious landing. The plan had four elements. A decoy force would attempt to draw the U.S. fleet north, while two elements struck from the west, on either side of Leyte, to converge on the landing area in Leyte Gulf and destroy the shipping there. At the same time, shore-based Japanese aircraft were to carry out attacks. At best the plan was a long shot.

On October 18 the Japanese intercepted American messages regarding the approaching Leyte landings, and Toyoda initiated SHO-1. The original target for the fleet engagement was October 22, but logistical difficulties delayed it to October 25.

Vice Admiral Ozawa Jisaburo's decoy Northern Force (Third Fleet), which consisted of the heavy carrier *Zuikaku,* three light carriers, two hybrid battleship-carriers, three cruisers, and eight destroyers, sortied from Japan. Ozawa had only 116 planes flown by half-trained pilots. Japanese submarines off Formosa were ordered south, toward the eastern approaches to the Philippine archipelago, and shortly before October 23 what remained of the Japanese 2nd Air Fleet began to arrive on Luzon.

The strongest element of the Japanese attack was the 1st Diversion Attack Force. It reached northwest Borneo on October 20, refueled, split into two parts, and moved toward Leyte two days later. The Center Force under Vice Admiral Kurita Takeo contained the bulk of Japanese attack strength, including the superbattleships *Musashi* and *Yamato.* With their 18.1-inch guns, these 70,000-ton behemoths were, at the time, the largest warships ever built. Kurita also had 3 older battleships, 12 cruisers, and 15 destroyers. The Center Force would pass to the north of Leyte, through San Bernardino Strait. Vice Admiral Nishimura Shoji's Southern Force (C Force) of 2 battleships, 1 heavy cruiser, and 4 destroyers struck eastward to force its way through Surigao Strait, south of Leyte and north of Mindanao. The Southern Force was trailed by the Second Diversion Attack Force, commanded by Vice Admiral Shima Kiyohide, with 2 heavy cruisers, 1 light cruiser, and 4 destroyers. Shima's force was late joining Nishimura's force and followed it into Surigao Strait.

Opposing the Japanese were two U.S. Navy fleets: Vice Admiral Thomas C. Kinkaid's Seventh Fleet, operating under General MacArthur's Southwest Pacific Command, and Admiral William F. Halsey's Third Fleet, under Nimitz at Pearl Harbor. Leyte was the first landing to involve two entire U.S. fleets and the first without unified command, which had unfortunate consequences for U.S. forces. The Seventh Fleet was split into three task groups. The first consisted of Rear Admiral Jesse Oldendorf's 6 old battleships, 16 escort carriers, 4 heavy and 4 light cruisers, 30 destroyers, and 10 destroyer escorts. The other two elements were amphibious task groups carrying out the actual invasion.

The Seventh Fleet had escorted the invasion force to Leyte and now provided broad protection for the entire landing area. Because most of Halsey's amphibious assets had been loaned to Kinkaid, the Third Fleet consisted almost entirely of Vice Admiral Marc Mitscher's Task Force (TF) 38 of 14 fast carriers (more than 1,000 aircraft) organized into four task groups containing 6 battleships, 8 heavy and 13 light cruisers, and 57 destroyers. The Third Fleet's orders called for it to secure air superiority over the Philippines, protect the landings, and maintain pressure on the Japanese. If the opportunity to destroy a major part of the Japanese fleet presented itself or could be created, this was to be the Third Fleet's primary task.

U.S. forces detected both western Japanese strike forces early on. The Battle of Leyte Gulf was actually a series of battles, the first of which was the Battle of the Sibuyan Sea (October 23–24). Early on October 23, the U.S. submarines *Darter* and *Dace* discovered Kurita's Center Force entering Palawan Passage from the South China Sea and alerted Admiral Halsey, whose Third Fleet guarded San Bernardino Strait. The submarines sank two Japanese heavy cruisers, the *Atago* (Kurita's flagship) and *Maya,* and damaged a third. Kurita transferred his flag to the *Yamato,* and his force continued east into the Sibuyan Sea, where beginning on the morning of October 24, TF-38 launched five air strikes against it.

The first wave of carrier planes concentrated on the *Musashi.* It took 19 torpedoes and nearly as many bombs before finally succumbing with the loss of half of its crew of nearly 2,200 men. The all-day air attacks also damaged several other Japanese vessels. At 2:40 p.m. on October 25, U.S. pilots reported that Kurita had reversed course and was heading back west; Halsey assumed that this part of the battle was over. He did issue a preliminary order detailing a battle line of battleships known as TF-34 to be commanded by Vice Admiral Willis A. Lee. Admiral Kinkaid was aware of that signal and assumed that TF-34 had been established.

Meanwhile, Japanese land-based aircraft from the 2nd Air Fleet harassed a portion of TF-38. Most of the Japanese planes were shot down, but they did sink the light carrier *Princeton* and badly damaged the cruiser *Birmingham.* Unknown to Halsey, however, after nightfall Kurita's force changed course again and resumed heading for San Bernardino Strait.

Warned of the approach of the Japanese Center Force, Kinkaid placed Oldendorf's 6 old Seventh Fleet fire-support battleships (all but 1 a veteran of Pearl Harbor), flanked by 8 cruisers, across the mouth of Surigao Strait to intercept Center Force. He also lined the strait with 39 patrol torpedo (PT) boats and 28 destroyers.

The Battle of Surigao Strait (October 24–25) was a classic example of crossing the T in naval warfare. Nishimura's force was annihilated. While the battleships often get the credit for the Surigao Strait victory, it was U.S. destroyers that inflicted most of the damage. Two converging torpedo attacks sank the battleship *Fuso* and three destroyers. The Japanese then encountered Oldendorf's battle line, whereupon all Japanese warships except the destroyer *Shigure* were sunk. Nishimura went down with his flagship, the battleship *Yamashiro.*

Shima's force, bringing up the rear, was attacked 30 minutes later by PT boats, which crippled a light cruiser. Shima attempted an attack, but his flagship collided with one of Nishimura's sinking vessels. Oldendorf's ships pursued the retreating Japanese. Another Japanese cruiser succumbed to attacks by land-based planes and those of Rear Admiral Thomas L. Sprague's escort carriers. The rest of Shima's force escaped when Oldendorf, knowing that his ships might be needed later, turned back.

During the night of October 24–25, Kurita's force, hoping to join that of Nishimura in Leyte Gulf, moved through San Bernardino Strait and turned south. In the most controversial aspect of the battle, near midnight Halsey had left San Bernardino Strait unprotected to rush with all available Third Fleet ships after Admiral Ozawa's decoy fleet, which had been sighted far to the north. Several of Halsey's subordinates registered reservations about his decision, but the admiral would not be deterred. Compounding the error, Halsey failed to inform Kinkaid, who assumed that TF-34 was protecting the strait.

Halsey's decision left the landing beaches guarded only by the Seventh Fleet's Taffy 3 escort carrier group, commanded by Rear Admiral Clifton A. F. Sprague. Taffy 3 was one of three such support groups operating off Samar. Sprague had six light escort carriers, three destroyers, and four destroyer escorts.

Fighting off Samar erupted at about 6:30 a.m. on October 24, as Taffy 3 found itself opposing Kurita's 4 battleships, including the giant *Yamato;* 6 heavy cruisers; and 10 destroyers. The aircraft from all three Taffy groups now attacked the Japanese. Unfortunately, the planes carried only fragmentation bombs for use against land targets; the planes put up a strong fight nonetheless, dropping bombs, strafing, and generally harassing the powerful Japanese warships. Sprague's destroyers and destroyer escorts also joined the fight. Their crews skillfully and courageously attacked the much more powerful Japanese warships, launching torpedoes and laying down a smokescreen to try to obscure the escort carriers. These combined attacks forced several Japanese cruisers to drop out of the battle.

Kurita basically lost his nerve. By 9:10 a.m., Kurita's warships sank the escort carrier *Gambier Bay,* the only U.S. carrier ever lost to gunfire, and also sank the destroyers *Hoel* and *Johnston* and the destroyer escort *Samuel B. Roberts.* Kurita believed that he was being attacked by aircraft from TF-38, and just when he might have had a crushing victory, at 9:11 he ordered his forces to break off the attack, his decision strengthened by the fact that the southern attacking force had been destroyed. Kurita hoped to join Ozawa's force to the north but changed his mind and exited through San Bernardino Strait. The four ships lost by Taffy 3 were the only U.S. warships sunk by Japanese surface ships in the Battle of Leyte Gulf.

At 9:40 p.m., Kurita's ships reentered San Bernardino Strait. As the Japanese withdrew, they were attacked by aircraft from Vice Admiral John S. McCain Sr.'s task force from Halsey's fleet, which sank a destroyer. Meanwhile, Admiral Sprague's escort carriers and Oldendorf's force returning from the Battle of Surigao Strait came under attack from land-based suicide kamikaze aircraft. Named for the Divine Wind (Kamikaze), a 13th-century typhoon that saved Japan from invasion by Kublai Khan's fleet, these were the first such attacks of the war. They sank the escort carrier *St. Lo* and damaged several other ships.

Earlier, at about 2:20 a.m. on October 25, Mitscher's search planes from Halsey's force located Ozawa's northern decoy force. At dawn, the first of three strikes was launched in what became known as the Battle of Cape Engaño. Ozawa had sent most of his planes to operate from bases ashore and thus had only antiaircraft fire with which to oppose the attack. While engaging Ozawa, Halsey learned of the action off Samar when a signal came in from Kinkaid at 8:22, followed by an urgent request eight minutes later for fast battleships.

At 8:48 Halsey ordered Vice Admiral McCain's Task Group (TG) 38.1 to make "best possible speed" to engage Kurita's Center Force. TG-38.1 was en route from the Ulithi to rejoin the other elements of TF-38. Since TG-38.1 had more carriers and planes than any of the three other task groups in Halsey's force, detaching it made good sense. Several minutes later Halsey was infuriated by a query from Nimitz at Pearl Harbor: "WHERE IS RPT WHERE IS TASK FORCE THIRTY-FOUR RR THE WORLD WONDERS." At 10:55, Halsey ordered all six fast battleships and TG-38.2 to turn south and steam at flank speed, but they missed the battle. After the war, Kurita admitted his error in judgment; Halsey never did. In fact, Halsey said that his decision to send the battleships south to Samar was "the greatest error I committed during the Battle of Leyte Gulf."

By nightfall, U.S. aircraft, a submarine, and surface ships had sunk all 4 of Ozawa's carriers as well as 5 other ships. In effect, this blow ended Japanese carrier aviation. But the battle of annihilation that would have been possible with the fast battleships had slipped from Halsey's grasp. Still, of Ozawa's force, only 2 battleships, 2 light cruisers, and 1 destroyer escaped. Including retiring vessels sunk on October 26 and 27, Japanese losses in the battle were 29 warships (4 carriers, 3 battleships, 6 heavy and 4 light cruisers, 11 destroyers, and 1 submarine) and more than 500 aircraft. Japanese personnel losses were some 10,500 seamen and aviators dead. The U.S. Navy lost only 6 ships (1 light carrier, 2 escort carriers, 2 destroyers, and 1 destroyer escort) and more than 200 aircraft. About 2,800 Americans were killed and another 1,000 wounded.

The Battle of Leyte Gulf ended the Japanese fleet as an organized fighting force.

Spencer C. Tucker

## Further Reading

Cutler, Thomas J. *The Battle of Leyte Gulf, 23–26 October 1944.* New York: HarperCollins, 1994.

Field, James A., Jr. *The Japanese at Leyte Gulf: The Shō Operation.* Princeton, NJ: Princeton University Press, 1947.

Morison, Samuel Eliot. *History of United States Naval Operations in World War II*, Vol. 12, *Leyte*. Boston: Little, Brown, 1975.

Potter, E. B. *Bull Halsey*. Annapolis, MD: Naval Institute Press, 1985.

Willmott, H. P. *The Battle of Leyte Gulf: The Last Fleet Action*. Bloomington: Indiana University Press, 2006.

## Battle of the Bulge

| Date | December 16, 1944–January 16, 1945 | |
|------|-----------------------------------|---|
| Location | Ardennes Forest region of northeastern France and southern Belgium | |
| Opponents (*winner) | *United States and United Kingdom | Germany |
| Approx. # Troops | 600,000 Americans, 55,000 British; 1,300 tanks, 394 artillery pieces | Initial force of 410,000 men (later some 500,000), 1,420 tanks and assault guns, 2,600 artillery pieces and rocket launchers, 1,000+ combat aircraft |
| Importance | The largest battle ever in terms of men engaged for U.S. forces and a temporary setback for the Allies in the West that actually speeds up the German defeat. | |

By the autumn of 1944, Germany's fate was largely sealed. The Western Allies were driving on Germany from the west, and the Soviets were closing from the east. German chancellor Adolf Hitler, however, rejected the rational course for his people of surrender. Deaf to all reason, his alternative was a desperate gamble. The resulting monthlong German Ardennes Offensive, popularly known as the Battle of the Bulge, only speeded the German military defeat.

With the Eastern Front static for several months and the Allied offensive on the Western Front gaining ground, in September 1944 Hitler conceived of a sudden offensive in the Ardennes region to take the Western Allies by surprise, break their front, and recapture the Belgian port of Antwerp. Hitler hoped at the least that such an attack would purchase three to four months to deal with the advancing Soviets. Commander of German forces in the west Generalfeldmarschall Gerd von Rundstedt thought that the plan was unrealistic, as did other high-ranking officers. However, Hitler refused to budge, and substantial German forces were transferred from the Eastern Front for what turned out to be the largest battle fought on the Western Front in the war and the largest single engagement ever for the U.S. Army.

Hitler could not have selected a better location for his attack. Allied forces in the Ardennes were weak because General Dwight D. Eisenhower, Allied Expeditionary

U.S. soldiers of the 289th Infantry Regiment on their way to cut off the St. Vith-Houffalize Road in Belgium in January 1945. The Battle of the Bulge in the Ardennes Forest was the largest battle on the Western Front in World War II and the largest engagement ever involving U.S. troops. (National Archives)

Force supreme commander, had deployed most of his strength northward and southward. The timing could not have been better for the Germans either, as poor weather initially restricted the use of Allied airpower. German security was excellent, as Hitler had restricted all communication to secure land lines, which Allied Ultra radio intercepts could not pick up.

The Western Allies were complacent because Ultra revealed nothing of the German plans and because they believed that only they could launch an offensive. Telltale signs were ignored. In an exceptional achievement, the Germans secretly marshaled 410,000 men, 1,420 tanks and assault guns, 2,600 artillery pieces and rocket launchers, and some 1,000 combat aircraft. While this force was considerably greater than the Allied forces in the Ardennes, it was also dwarfed by what the Allies could ultimately bring to bear.

The German offensive began in the predawn darkness and fog of December 16, 1944, catching the Allies by surprise. Initially, 12th Army Group commander General Omar N. Bradley and his subordinate, Third Army commander Lieutenant

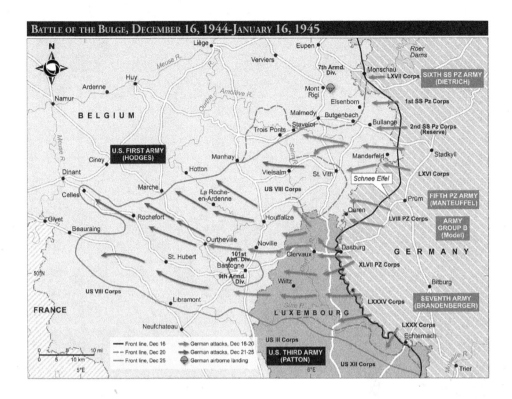

General George S. Patton, did not believe it to be a major operation. Eisenhower did, and on its second day he ordered the battle-weary 82nd and 101st Airborne Divisions to the front from a reconstitution camp in France. Traveling in trucks, the 101st Airborne Division arrived at midnight on December 18 near the important road hub of Bastogne. This small Belgian town would play a key role in the battle.

The attacking German force of 24 divisions, moving against three divisions of Lieutenant General Courtney Hodges's First Army, soon drove a bulge in the American lines, which gave the battle its name. The Battle of the Bulge is more a campaign of a series of smaller battles, each lasting a week or more, with the whole extending for more than four weeks. The German penetration eventually extended some 50 miles deep and 70 miles wide.

On December 22, four German soldiers under a white flag walked toward an American outpost near Bastogne. They carried an ultimatum addressed to "the U.S.A. commander of the encircled town of Bastogne." The message called on the American commander (Brigadier General Anthony McAuliffe, in the absence of Major General Maxwell D. Taylor) to save his troops with an "honorable surrender." McAuliffe's response to the Germans was one of the most memorable statements of the war: "To the German Commander: Nuts. The American commander."

German forces flowed around Bastogne, heading northwest toward the Meuse. Generalfeldmarschall Walther Model, commander of Army Group B and charged with carrying out the offensive, sought to have the Fifth Panzer Army make the main effort. Hitler, ignorant of the situation on the ground, insisted that this be done by SS Oberstgruppenführer Josef "Sepp" Dietrich's Sixth Panzer Army.

On the north shoulder of the bulge, the U.S. 1st Infantry Division dug in. The Americans massed 348 artillery pieces that shattered the German attack. In the center, units fighting mostly in isolated formations stood firm, impeding the German advance. Patton's Third Army rushed to the rescue from the south. Patton had ordered his staff to prepare for just such a contingency, and he assured an unbelieving Eisenhower that he could wheel his army 90 degrees and strike north into the bulge with three divisions in only two days. Patton accomplished this feat in what was one of the most memorable mass maneuvers of the war.

Other Allied resources were also diverted to the Ardennes fighting. Then on December 23 the weather changed along the front, clearing the sky, freezing the ground, and making the terrain passable for armor. Allied aircraft filled the skies, and transports parachuted supplies into Bastogne, where the defenders were down to only 10 rounds per gun. On Christmas Day the German tanks ground to a halt, out of fuel, while U.S. 2nd Armored Division gunners had a turkey shoot at Celles, almost at the German objective of the Meuse, in which the Americans destroyed 82 German tanks. On December 26 the 4th Armored Division of Patton's Third Army lifted the siege of Bastogne.

Unfortunately, 21st Army Group commander British field marshal Bernard L. Montgomery had elected to remain on the defensive, overruling U.S. VII Corps commander Major General J. Lawton Collins's plan to cut off the bulge by striking from each shoulder. Finally, though, the Allies attacked midway up the salient, although this obviated the chance to surround the Germans. Patton held that timidity on the part of Eisenhower and Montgomery allowed the bulk of the German attackers to escape.

On January 1, 1945, as part of the offensive, the Germans mounted an air attack on Allied air bases in Belgium. Operation BODENPLATTE (BASE PLATE) destroyed 500–800 Allied aircraft, most of them on the ground, but also saw about 300 German aircraft shot down and 214 trained pilots lost, many to Allied antiaircraft fire.

On the ground, the Battle of the Bulge dragged on to the middle of January. Hitler had already ordered part of the participating Panzer divisions transferred east, but before these resources could arrive, the Soviets began their last great offensive. By the end of January, the U.S. First Army and Third Army had reached the German frontier and reestablished the line of six weeks before.

The Battle of the Bulge had been fought and won largely by American forces. Of the 600,000 U.S. troops involved, 19,000 were killed, about 47,000 were wounded, and 15,000 were taken prisoner. Of the 55,000 British engaged, casualties totaled 1,400, of whom 200 were killed. The Germans, employing nearly 500,000 men in the battle, sustained nearly 100,000 killed, wounded, or captured. Both sides suffered heavy equipment losses, about 800 tanks on each side, and the Germans lost virtually all their aircraft committed. But the Western Allies could quickly make good their losses, while the Germans could not. In effect, all Hitler had accomplished was to hasten the end of the war.

Spencer C. Tucker

**Further Reading**

Cole, Hugh M. *The United States Army in World War II: The European Theater of Operations; The Ardennes: Battle of the Bulge.* Washington, DC: U.S. Government Printing Office, 1965.

Dupuy, Trevor N. *Hitler's Last Gamble: The Battle of the Bulge, December 1944–January 1945.* New York: HarperCollins, 1944.

Eisenhower, John S. D. *The Bitter Woods.* New York: Putnam, 1969.

Forty, George. *The Reich's Last Gamble: The Ardennes Offensive, December 1944.* London: Cassell, 2000.

MacDonald, Charles B. *A Time for Trumpets: The Untold Story of the Battle of the Bulge.* New York: William Morrow, 1985.

## Tokyo Raid

| Date | March 9–10, 1945 | |
|---|---|---|
| Location | Tokyo, Japan | |
| Opponents (*winner) | *United States | Japan |
| Commander | Major General Curtis LeMay | Unknown |
| # Aircraft | 334 B-29 heavy bombers | Numbers of antiaircraft guns and aircraft unknown |
| Importance | The single most destructive air raid in history, its success leads to similar attacks on most major Japanese cities, a significant factor in the Japanese decision to surrender in August 1945. | |

U.S. Army Air Forces (USAAF) strategic bombing of the Japanese home islands began in June 1944, when the four-engine Boeing B-29 Superfortress entered service flying from bases in China. Basing the B-29s there proved unsatisfactory for a number of reasons. All supplies for the planes, including bombs and even fuel, had to be flown in from India over the so-called Hump of the Himalayas, an extremely difficult and time-consuming operation. Then too, Chinese Nationalist troops were unable to protect the B-29 airfields. No sooner were the fields in operation than Japanese troops attacked and took them.

Another solution was at hand. In July and August 1944, U.S. forces captured Saipan, Guam, and Tinian in the Mariana Islands. Even as these were being cleared of their last Japanese defenders, naval construction brigades (CBs, or Seabees) were at work building runways and support facilities for Brigadier General Haywood S. "Possum" Hansell's XXI Bomber Command. Soon the XXI Bomber Command's B-29s were striking Japan.

The initial B-29 raids from the Marianas were of 150–200 planes per strike, with the 1,200-mile flight to and from Tokyo taking up to 16 hours in the air. USAAF planners had called for precision bombing, but this proved impossible from 30,000 feet. Jet streams threw the planes off course, and ice forming on windshields and wings reduced aircraft performance. The B-29s also flew unescorted and had to pass twice over the Japanese island of Iwo Jima. By December 1944, the B-29 loss rate per mission was averaging 6 percent (the maximum permissible was 5 percent), lowering both morale and crew efficiency.

The raids did have an effect on Japan, however. The strain of frequent air alerts reduced Japanese worker efficiency and lowered the morale of the entire population. The concentration of U.S. bombing attacks on aircraft factories also forced their dispersal, bringing about a decline in actual production.

XXI Bomber Group, nominally under Lieutenant General Nathan Twining's Twentieth Air Force, actually answered to USAAF commander General Henry H. "Hap" Arnold and the Joint Chiefs of Staff in Washington, D.C., and Arnold was displeased with the unit's progress. In January 1945 Arnold replaced Hansell with Major General Curtis LeMay, who had enjoyed success commanding XX Bomber Command in India. LeMay was determined to repeat his performance in the Marianas.

Having been instructed to give priority to attacks on cities rather than industrial targets, in February and March 1945 LeMay developed new tactics. He decided to replicate British air chief marshal and head of Bomber Command Sir Arthur "Bomber" Harris's strategy of area bombing at night. This would take advantage of the Japanese failure to develop an effective night fighter. The B-29s were to fly low, stripped of all armament except the tail gun to increase payloads. They would be loaded with incendiary rather than high-explosive bombs and would drop their loads from only 5,000–8,000 feet. These plans resulted in considerable apprehension among the aircrews involved.

LeMay's first great firebombing raid was against the Japanese capital of Tokyo on the night of March 9–10. In the single most destructive raid in the history of warfare, a total of 334 B-29s flying at 7,000 feet dropped 1,667 tons of incendiary bombs on a city that largely consisted of wooden structures. Widespread firestorms destroyed 15 square miles of central Tokyo, including 267,171 houses. Japanese sources cite 83,793 confirmed dead and 40,918 injured, while more than 100,000 people were rendered homeless. The success of the Tokyo Raid was repeated four times during the next 10 nights.

During the next months, B-29s hit the largest Japanese cities. Of 64 major cities, 63 were struck. Only the cultural center of Kyoto was spared. Up to 300,000 Japanese died in these attacks. B-29 losses dropped dramatically, to 1.4 percent, in part because of the U.S. capture of Iwo Jima and its use as a fighter field and emergency landing point for crippled B-29s. By August 1945, Japan's cities were burned-out shells. Targets were so scarce that the big U.S. bombers were used to drop mines in the Inland Sea, shutting down what was left of Japanese shipping and helping bring the Japanese nation to starvation levels. Under these conditions and with the dropping of the atomic bombs on Hiroshima and Nagasaki, Japanese leaders decided to surrender.

Spencer C. Tucker

## Further Reading

Coffey, Thomas M. *Iron Eagle: The Turbulent Life of General Curtis LeMay.* New York: Crown, 1986.

Hata Ikuhiko, Sase Morimasa, and Tuneishi Keiichi, eds. *Sekai Senso Hanzai Jiten* [Encyclopedia of Crimes in Modern History]. Tokyo: Bungei-Shunju, 2002.

Johoji Asami. *Nihon Boku Shi* [History of Japanese Air Defense]. Tokyo: Hara Shobo, 1981.

Kerr, E. Bartlett. *Flames over Tokyo: The U.S. Army Air Forces' Incendiary Campaign against Japan, 1944–1945.* New York: Donald I. Fine, 1991.

## Battle of Okinawa

| Date | April 1–June 21, 1945 | |
|---|---|---|
| Location | Okinawa in the Ryukyu Islands | |
| Opponents (*winner) | *United States and United Kingdom | Japan |
| Commander | Lieutenant General Simon B. Buckner; Major General Roy S. Geiger | Lieutenant General Ushijima Mitsuru |
| Approx. # Troops | 183,000 troops | 117,000 troops |
| Importance | At great cost, U.S. forces secure a staging area for the planned invasion of the Japanese home islands, which, however, is rendered moot by the Japanese decision to surrender. | |

Located in the Ryukyu group of islands between Kyūshū, the southernmost island of Japan, and Taiwan (Formosa), Okinawa is about 60 miles long and at most 18 miles wide. Taken by Japan in 1875, Okinawa is mountainous in the north and south and level and cultivated in the central portion. If the United States could take the island, it would sever Japanese communications with southern China, but the principal reason was to secure a staging area for the projected invasion of Japan. Okinawa offered suitable air bases, anchorages, and staging areas for such a vast undertaking.

The operation, code-named ICEBERG, fell to Admiral Raymond Spruance's Fifth Fleet. The lifting force consisted of 1,213 vessels of 45 different classes and types in Vice Admiral Richmond Kelly Turner's Task Force (TF) 51. They ranged from 179 attack transports and cargo ships to 187 landing ship tanks. This did not include the covering force of 88 ships of Vice Admiral Marc Mitscher's TF-58 or the 22 ships of TF-57, a British component commanded by Vice Admiral H. B. Rawlings.

The land assault force for what would be the Pacific theater's largest and most complicated amphibious operation was U.S. Army lieutenant general Simon Bolivar

U.S. landing area on the Japanese island of Okinawa on April 13, 1945, during Operation ICEBERG. Okinawa was to be the staging area for a U.S. invasion of the Japanese home islands. (National Archives)

Buckner's Tenth Army of some 180,000 men. It consisted of Major General Roy S. Geiger's III Marine Amphibious Corps (1st, 2nd, and 6th Marine Divisions) and Major General John R. Hodge's XXIV Army Corps (7th, 27th, 77th, and 96th Infantry Divisions).

Tokyo had begun strengthening Okinawa at the end of March 1944 with the activation of the Thirty-Second Army. By October 1944 it contained four divisions (9th, 24th, 62nd, and 28th Divisions on Sakishima) plus other units. Altogether, Japanese commander on Okinawa Lieutenant General Ushijima Mitsuru commanded about 130,000 men, including the 20,000-man Okinawan Home Guard. The Japanese constructed a formidable defensive system, particularly on the southern part of the island.

In the second half of March 1945, U.S. forces sought to isolate Okinawa by striking Japanese air bases on Kyumshum and the Sakishima island group between Formosa and Okinawa. Army heavy bombers also hit Formosa and the Japanese home island of Honshu. During these operations, the ships, especially the aircraft carriers, came under heavy Japanese kamikaze attacks.

During March 18–19, 1945, Allied ships off Okinawa came under a heavy kamikaze attack. The carrier *Franklin* took two bomb hits on its flight deck that nearly incinerated the upper decks. Heroic efforts by the crew saved the carrier, but the attacks led to the loss of 724 members of its crew, the highest casualty rate of any surviving U.S. Navy vessel in any war. The carrier *Wasp* was also hit by a kamikaze but was saved, thanks only to new firefighting techniques.

During March 14–31, air attacks and naval shelling proceeded against Okinawa. Beginning on March 23, the 77th Infantry Division secured the outlying Kerama

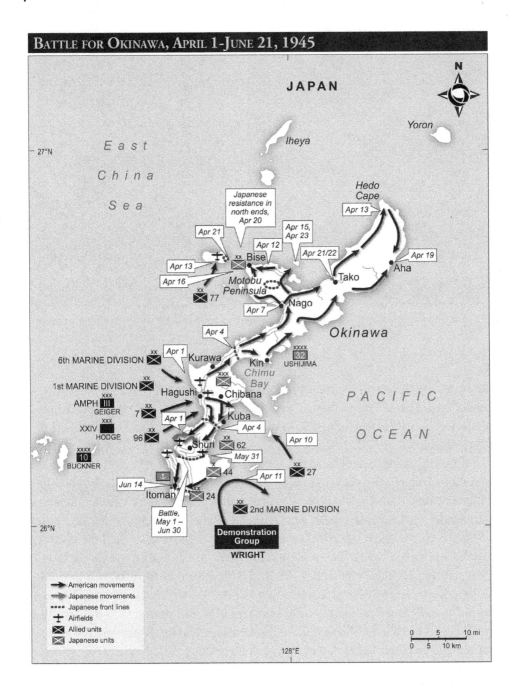

**BATTLE FOR OKINAWA, APRIL 1-JUNE 21, 1945**

Islands. This step provided anchorages and artillery positions for the invasion force and led to the destruction of some 300 small Japanese suicide boats.

On the morning of Easter Sunday, April 1, the Americans went ashore on Okinawa proper, landing on the western coast Kadena beaches. Some 16,000 troops came ashore in the first hour, and 50,000 had come ashore by the end of the day. The initial assault was deceptively easy, as the Japanese again did not contest the beaches but instead chose to fight in the more populous interior.

The U.S. Marine Corps III Amphibious Corps on the left (1st and 6th Divisions) now turned north. It met relatively little opposition in clearing the northern area by April 13 and nearby Ie Shima Island during April 16–20. The U.S. Army XXIV Corps swung south. The main landing was facilitated by a demonstration against the southern end of the island by the U.S. Marine Corps 2nd Division. The 27th and 77th Infantry Divisions were held in reserve. Ushijima now had the majority of his 24th and 62nd Divisions in the rugged southern end of the island, where they could mount a determined defense.

It was at this point, beginning on April 7, that the Japanese launched their first major kamikaze assault, aimed at driving the Allied fleet from Okinawa. Some 121 kamikazes and 117 additional orthodox aircraft swept in on the amphibious force. The Americans claimed 383 of the attackers shot down, but 2 U.S. destroyers and 4 smaller ships were sunk, and 24 other vessels were damaged.

The Allies countered by extending their destroyer screen to 95 miles from Okinawa. The destroyers provided early warning of the attacks but also became easy targets for the kamikazes. From April 6 until July 29, Japanese suicide attacks pounded the destroyer screen, and 14 of the ships were sunk. Through June 10, the Japanese had launched nearly a dozen mass kamikaze raids of between 50 and 300 planes each against the invasion fleet. During the two months that the U.S. Navy was off Okinawa, it underwent 2,482 kamikaze attacks. The kamikazes were eventually defeated by new defensive formations that provided maximum antiaircraft fire protection to the carriers and by crushing Allied air superiority.

The largest kamikaze was actually a battleship, the *Yamato*. Departing Japan on April 6 on a one-way mission to Okinawa to attack the invasion fleet and then be beached as a stationary fort, the giant battleship and its escort force of one light cruiser and eight destroyers were intercepted on April 7 by 180 U.S. carrier aircraft 200 miles from Okinawa and sunk in a furious assault of nearly four hours. Only 269 Japanese were rescued; 3,063 aboard the *Yamato* died. U.S. planes also sank the cruiser and four of the escorting destroyers, killing another 1,187 officers and men. U.S. losses in the attack came to 10 aircraft and 12 men.

Meanwhile, in fighting on land, XXIV Corps met stiff resistance in the south. Japanese defenders were well dug in along a series of east-west ridgelines across the island, and they incorporated Okinawan burial caves in their successive, mutually supporting positions. The U.S. advance soon ground to a halt.

On April 22 the 1st Marine Division took up position on the right of the line; it was joined there later by the 6th Marine Division. The marines then came up against the main Japanese defensive line, with the heart of its defense at Shuri Castle. On May 4 the Japanese mounted a desperate counterattack that made some headway before it was blunted. On May 18 the marines took Sugar Loaf Hill, the western portion of the Shuri Line. Four days later the Japanese withdrew seven miles south to a new line.

On June 18 Buckner was killed by a Japanese shell while at a forward observation post, the highest-ranking U.S. officer lost to hostile fire in the war. Geiger then took command. The only U.S. marine ever to command a field army, he directed the final fighting.

Although pockets of resistance remained, Geiger declared the island secure on June 21. The Americans took only 7,400 Japanese prisoners. General Ushijima committed ritual suicide. The Japanese suffered 92,000–94,000 military dead. They also lost to all causes 6,810 aircraft. Okinawa was also the costliest battle for the Americans in the Pacific theater. The army lost 12,520 dead and 36,631 wounded. The marines suffered 2,938 dead and 13,708 wounded. The navy lost 4,907 men killed and 4,874 wounded and was the only service in the battle for which dead exceeded wounded; this was a higher casualty toll than all the other wars fought by the U.S. Navy put together. The navy also lost 38 ships sunk and 368 damaged. Civilians on Okinawa especially suffered. Of the preinvasion population of 450,000, perhaps 94,000 died. At great cost, the United States had, however, secured the staging base for its planned invasion of Japan.

Spencer C. Tucker

### Further Reading

Gow, Ian. *Okinawa, 1945: Gateway to Japan.* Garden City, NY: Doubleday, 1985.

Inoguchi Rikihei and Nakajima Tadashi, with Roger Pineau. *The Divine Wind: Japan's Kamikaze Force in World War II.* New York: Bantam, 1978.

Leckie, Robert. *Okinawa: The Last Battle of World War II.* New York: Viking, 1995.

Millot, Bernard. *Divine Thunder: The Life and Death of the Kamikazes.* Translated by Lowell Blair. New York: McCall, 1970.

## Hiroshima and Nagasaki Bombings

| Date | August 6 and 9, 1945 | |
| --- | --- | --- |
| Location | Cities of Hiroshima and Nagasaki, Japan | |
| Opponents (*winner) | *United States | Japan |
| Commander | Lieutenant Colonel Paul W. Tibbets Jr.; Major Charles W. Sweeney | Unknown |
| # Aircraft | B-29 bombers of the 509th Composite Group, dropping one atomic bomb on each city | Unknown number of Japanese antiaircraft defenses |
| Importance | The first employment of atomic weapons in history (and the last to date), the blasts hasten the Japanese decision to surrender. | |

In light of heavy U.S. casualties in the capture of the islands of Iwo Jima and Okinawa (26,500 and 75,600 killed or wounded, respectively), it is easy to see why members of the U.S. Joint Chiefs of Staff (JCS) were reluctant to invade the Japanese home islands, which the Japanese planned to defend with 1 million troops,

3,000 kamikaze aircraft, and 5,000 suicide boats. With the invasion scheduled for November 1, 1945, and well aware of the probable high cost, the JCS pressed President Franklin D. Roosevelt at the February 1945 Yalta Conference to get the Soviet Union into the war against Japan.

Following the successful test-firing of an atomic bomb at Alamogordo, New Mexico, on July 16, 1945, sharp debate occurred among advisers to U.S. president Harry S. Truman over employing the new weapon. Although some key advisers, including de facto JCS chairman Admiral of the Fleet William Leahy, were opposed, most favored its use. Employing the bomb was not then seen as the threat to world peace that it is today. The terror threshold had probably already been passed in

The atomic bomb cloud over the Japanese city of Hiroshima, August 6, 1945, just two minutes after the 12.5 million kiloton explosion obliterated much of the city. (Corel)

the firebombing of Japanese cities. By 1945 it was total war, and the assumption was always that the bomb would be used if it became available.

Proponents of employing the atomic bomb argued that it would in all likelihood bring the war to a speedy end and save many American lives. If this occurred, the United States would not have to share occupation of Japan with the Soviet Union. The atomic bomb was thus seen as essentially a psychological weapon to influence Japanese political leaders rather than as a military tool. The bomb might also deter Soviet leader Joseph Stalin from future aggression. Truman said that he never regretted his decision to employ the bomb, which was in any case strongly supported by the great majority of the American people.

Revisionist historians hold that the Japanese government was trying desperately to leave the war and that employing the bomb was therefore unnecessary, but Tokyo had not yet reached the decision to surrender when the first bomb was dropped. Emperor Hirohito and his chief advisers still hoped for a negotiated settlement, and a last decisive battle might force the Allies to grant more favorable peace terms. Historian Ray Skates concluded that the first phase of the invasion of Japan, the conquest of the island of Kyūshū planned for November 1945, would have taken two months and resulted in 75,000–100,000 U.S. casualties. Such losses would not have affected the outcome of the war, but they might indeed have brought the political goals sought by the Japanese leaders.

Even if the bomb had not been employed, an invasion of Japan might not have been necessary. The United States would have continued the strategic bombing campaign, which by August 1945 had largely burned out the Japanese cities. The nation was close to starvation, with caloric intake at an average of only 1,680 daily, and even this reduced food supply was highly dependent on railroad distribution. Destruction of the Japanese railroads might have been the final straw bringing a decision for peace even without the bomb.

Yet not employing the atomic bomb would in all likelihood have delayed the Japanese surrender and brought a significantly higher cost in Japanese lives. One estimate is that during the war the Japanese lost 323,495 dead on the home front, the vast majority of these to air attack. Continued strategic bombing would have sharply increased this total, and many others would simply have died of starvation. In effect, dropping the bomb resulted in a net saving of lives, both Japanese and American.

Following Japanese rejection of the Potsdam Proclamation on July 26 that threatened total destruction if unconditional surrender was not accepted, President Truman authorized use of the atomic bomb. The bomb would be carried in the Boeing B-29 Superfortress *Enola Gay* of the specially trained 509th Composite Group of the Twentieth Army Air Force. Lieutenant Colonel Paul Tibbets was the aircraft commander. The bomb consisted of a core of uranium isotope 235 shielded by several hundred pounds of lead, all encased in explosives designed to condense the uranium and initiate a fission reaction. Nicknamed "Little Boy," it possessed a force equivalent to 12,500 tons (12.5 kilotons) of TNT.

The *Enola Gay* departed Tinian at 2:45 a.m. on August 6. Two B-29s assigned as observer aircraft accompanied it. The bomb was armed in the air shortly after 6:30. The flight to Japan was uneventful. Weather planes informed Tibbets that the primary target, Hiroshima, was clear.

The port city of Hiroshima is located in southern Honshu and in August 1945 served as the headquarters of the Japanese Second Army. Hiroshima was also a major supply depot. This city of some 250,000 people had not yet suffered heavily in the American bombing offensive.

The *Enola Gay* arrived over Hiroshima at an altitude of 31,600 feet. An air-raid alert had sounded, and most people in the city had taken cover. Realizing that there were only a few planes overhead, many people then came back out in the open and were thus without protection when the bomb detonated. The *Enola Gay* dropped the bomb at 8:15:17 a.m. local time. After a descent of nearly six miles, it detonated 43 seconds later, some 1,890 feet over a clinic and about 800 feet from the aiming point, Aioi Bridge.

The initial fireball expanded to 110 yards in diameter and generated heat in excess of 300,000 degrees Centigrade. Core temperatures reached more than 50 million degrees. At the clinic directly beneath the explosion, the temperature was several thousand degrees.

The immediate blast destroyed almost everything within two miles of ground zero. The resultant mushroom cloud rose to 50,000 feet and was observed by B-29s more than 360 miles away. After 15 minutes, the atmosphere dropped radioactive black rain, adding to the death and destruction.

Four square miles of Hiroshima disappeared in seconds, including 62,000 buildings. Approximately 100,000 Japanese died outright, another 40,000 were injured, and 171,000 were left homeless. About one-third of those killed instantly were soldiers. Most elements of the Japanese Second General Army were at physical training on the grounds of Hiroshima Castle when the bomb exploded. Barely 900 yards from the explosion's epicenter, the castle and the people there were vaporized. Radiation sickness added to the death toll over several years. This was, however, less carnage than inflicted in the March firebombing of Tokyo.

The bombing mission changed the nature of warfare but did not end the war. Truman released a statement on August 7 describing the weapon and calling on Japan to surrender but without result. On August 8 the Soviet Union declared war on Japan, with Stalin honoring to the day his pledge at Yalta to enter the war against Japan "two or three months after the defeat of Germany." That same day the Soviets invaded and quickly overran Manchuria. The next day, August 9, the B-29 *Bockscar,* commanded by Major Charles W. Sweeney, carried out a second atomic bomb strike. The primary target of Kokura was obscured by smoke and haze, and the bomb was dropped on the secondary target, the seaport and industrial city of Nagasaki, with a population 230,000 people. Hills protected portions of the city, so less than half of Nagasaki was destroyed. The blast there claimed about 70,000 dead, either killed outright or dying later from radiation, and injured as many more.

After prolonged meetings with his advisers, Emperor Hirohito made the decision for peace. Braving possible assassination by fanatics determined to fight to the end, Hirohito communicated the decision over the radio on August 15. On September 2 the final terms of surrender were signed aboard the battleship *Missouri* in Tokyo Bay, and the Japanese islands came under the rule of a U.S. army of occupation under General Douglas MacArthur.

Spencer C. Tucker

## Further Reading

Frank, Richard B. *Downfall: The End of the Japanese Empire.* New York: Random House, 1999.

Maddox, Robert James. *Weapons for Victory: The Hiroshima Decision Fifty Years Later.* Columbia: University of Missouri Press, 1995.

Skates, John Ray. *The Invasion of Japan: Alternative to the Bomb.* Columbia: University of South Carolina Press, 1998.

Thomas, Gordon, and Max Morgan-Witts. *Enola Gay.* New York: Stein and Day, 1977.

# U.S. Submarine Campaign against Japanese Shipping

| Date | December 1941–August 1945 | |
|---|---|---|
| Location | Pacific theater | |
| Opponents (*winner) | *United States | Japan |
| Commander | Chiefs of Naval Operations and Admirals Harold R. Stark and Ernest J. King | Commanders of the Imperial Japanese Navy Combined Fleet Admiral Yamamoto Isoroku, Admiral Koga Mineichi, Admiral Toyoda Soemu, and Vice Admiral Ozawa Jisaburō |
| # Submarines | 314 submarines | Unknown number of Japanese surface warships and aircraft |
| Importance | The only campaign of its type in naval history to register success, it cut off the importation of key natural resources such as oil, ruined the Japanese economy, and brought that nation to the brink of starvation. | |

One day after the Japanese attack on Pearl Harbor on December 7, 1941, Admiral Harold R. Stark, chief of naval operations, declared unrestricted submarine warfare against Japan. When the United States entered World War II, the U.S. Navy's Asiatic and Pacific Fleet submarine forces included 55 large boats and 18 medium-sized ones (out of a total of 111). Some 73 submarines were under construction.

Yet until April 1, 1942, U.S. submarines sank only a modest 93,300 tons of Japanese shipping, less than 10 percent of what an average of 100 operational German submarines sank in the same period. At this stage of the war, U.S. submarine operations suffered from the early loss of the Philippines, for which the poorly developed Australian submarine bases could not compensate. In addition, the campaign was hobbled by a doctrine that required submarines to concentrate on enemy heavy warships and by the chronic problems of the Mark XIV torpedoes.

Following the erratic performance in 1942 that yielded a total of 620,616 tons of Japanese merchant shipping, the U.S. submarine campaign gathered pace in 1943.

The smaller S-class coastal submarine and the T-class fleet submarines were gradually replaced by the larger and more capable submarines of the Gato, Balao, and Tench classes. Beginning in mid-1942, the U.S. Navy began installing the first SJ surface search radars in the submarines, which further enhanced their combat value (German submarines, by comparison, only received radars in mid-1944), and in October 1943 the torpedo problems were finally resolved.

The Japanese mercantile fleet amounted to 6.4 million tons at the time of Pearl Harbor. Following the cessation of neutral shipping to Japan, this volume was barely sufficient to cover the needs for industrial and civilian imports (3 million tons) and the movement of troops and supplies across the sea. The situation was briefly alleviated by the capture of 1 million tons of merchant ships during the Japanese advance in early 1942. By mid-1943, however, the U.S. submarine campaign had already eaten up these small gains made by captures and new construction.

In 1943 the U.S. submarine service was fully committed to the war against the Japanese sea lines of communications, even though an operational order issued by Pacific Fleet commander Admiral Chester W. Nimitz in June 1943 still listed aircraft carriers and battleships as prime targets. Key traffic patterns of Japanese shipping had been identified, and U.S. submarines operating from Pearl Harbor and Australian bases conducted systematic patrols of such choke points as the Luzon bottleneck.

Because the Japanese Navy failed to respond to the increasing threat and organize valuable transports and cargo vessels into convoys, Japan lost 1.668 million tons of merchant shipping in 1943, with submarines accounting for 1.34 million tons of the total. The volume of imports into Japan fell from 35 million tons in 1942 (already down from a peacetime level of 67 million tons) to 27 million in 1943. In late 1943 the Japanese Navy reluctantly committed itself to convoying some of the more valuable transports and cargo ships, but the assets assigned remained woefully short of what was necessary to stem or even reduce the bloodletting. In addition, Japanese escort ships possessed neither active sonars nor radars, and their depth charges were ineffective. Nonetheless, U.S. submarine losses were substantial.

In response to the Japanese convoys, the U.S. Navy introduced the Coordinated Submarine Attack Groups—small ad hoc wolf packs. Throughout 1944, U.S. submarines continued to inflict crippling losses on the Japanese merchant marine, amounting to 2.43 million tons. In 1944, Japanese imports dropped to a mere 16 million tons. Figures for the key materials were even more alarming. Oil imports fell from 1.75 million barrels per month in August 1943 to 360,000 barrels in July 1944. After September 1943, at best only 28 percent of the petroleum shipped from the southern regions actually made it to the home islands, and during the last 15 months of the war, only an average of 9 percent did. By the time the massive strategic air attacks began to lay waste to Japan's cities, a substantial part of the industry located therein was already idle due to the lack of materials. The destruction of more than 3 million tons of Japanese merchant shipping in 1944 left barely enough tonnage to cover the basic military requirements of Japan's army and navy, much less those of the civilian sector.

During this phase of intensive war on the enemy's sea lines of communications, the U.S. submarines also achieved some remarkable successes against Japanese warships. In the Battle of the Philippine Sea (June 19–20, 1944), U.S. submarines claimed two Japanese carriers (*Taihō* and *Shōkaku*), and on the first day of the Battle of Leyte Gulf (October 23–26, 1944), for which no less than 29 submarines had been deployed, U.S. submarines sank two heavy cruisers and fatally damaged a third.

Toward the end of 1944, the diminutive Japanese escort force was raised to the status of an escort fleet and provided with somewhat better means, including aircraft, simple radar sets, and useful depth charges. Thus, in the last quarter of 1944, the Japanese antisubmarine forces reached their peak efficiency (as did the U.S. submarines), sinking four U.S. submarines in October and another four in November. Thereafter, crushing Allied naval and air superiority and the lack of fuel oil put an end to most organized Japanese naval activities, although not before U.S. submarines had scored further spectacular successes against the Japanese fleet. In November, the U.S. submarine *Archerfish* sank the giant carrier *Shinano* on its shakedown cruise, and the *Sealion* dispatched the battleship *Kongō;* in December, *Redfish*'s torpedoes claimed the new carrier *Unryō* in the East China Sea.

The number of U.S. submarine successes of any kind declined steeply in 1945 for want of suitable targets and because of a highly successful mining campaign in the Japanese home waters that year, which claimed the lion's share of the 1.6 million tons of Japanese shipping lost in 1945. U.S. submarines entered the last sanctuaries of Japanese shipping in the Sea of Japan in June 1945 to ravage the remnants of the Japanese merchant fleet but thereafter found targets exceedingly scarce. During the last months of the war, the submarines were confined to seeking what little coastal traffic had managed to escape the mine barrages and the attention of U.S. aircraft. When the war was over, Japan's merchant fleet had been reduced to 12 percent of its prewar size, and only half of the surviving ships—a paltry 312,000 tons of mostly minor vessels—were in operation due to fuel shortages.

In addition to their economic impact, the U.S. submarines played a decisive role in paralyzing Japan's maritime empire in the western and southwestern Pacific by denying the Japanese the use of their interior lines of communications for the movement of troops and equipment by sea. Thus, U.S. submarines facilitated the advance of the U.S. amphibious forces, which could safely bypass the immobilized and isolated Japanese island garrisons.

The U.S. submarine service began the war with 111 boats and during the war added 203 and lost 52 (50 of them in the Pacific). Of the 16,000 submariners who sailed on war patrols, 3,506 did not return—a casualty rate of 22 percent, the highest of all arms in the U.S. services during the war. Nevertheless, the U.S. submarine campaign in World War II was the only campaign of its type in the history of naval warfare that can be rated a complete success. The submarines played a decisive role in the war by incapacitating Japan's economy. Of the 7.8 million tons of Japanese merchant shipping lost between 1941 and 1945, nearly two-thirds (4.8 million tons) was sunk by U.S. submarines, which were also responsible for one-third of the Japanese warship losses.

Dirk Steffen

**Further Reading**

Blair, Clay. *Silent Victory: The U.S. Submarine War against Japan.* Philadelphia: Lippincott, 1975.

Parillo, Mark P. *The Japanese Merchant Marine in World War II.* Annapolis, MD: Naval Institute Press, 1993.

Van Der Vat, Dan. *The Pacific Campaign: The U.S.-Japanese Naval War, 1941–1945.* New York: Simon and Schuster, 1992.

## Pusan Perimeter Defense and Breakout

| Date | August 5–September 23, 1950 | |
|------|------|------|
| Location | Port of Pusan (present-day Busan) in far southeastern Korea | |
| Opponents (*winner) | *United Nations Command | North Korea |
| Commander | Lieutenant General Walton Walker | Lieutenant General Kang Kon; General Kim Chaek |
| Approx. # Troops | 156,500 men (92,000 combat troops) | Perhaps 98,000 men (80,000 combat) |
| Importance | Perhaps the outstanding example of a mobile defense in U.S. military history, it prevented UNC forces from being driven into the sea and enabled the Inchon Invasion. | |

On June 25, 1950, the Korean People's Army (KPA, North Korean Army) of the Democratic People's Republic of Korea (DPRK, North Korea) invaded the Republic of Korea (ROK, South Korea). This began the Korean War (1950–1953). North Korean leader Kim Il Sung's goal was to conquer South Korea in a matter of weeks before the United States, if it should choose to intervene, could influence the outcome. He almost succeeded.

U.S. president Harry S. Truman committed U.S. forces, however. On June 27, with the Soviet Union boycotting its sessions, the Security Council of the United Nations (UN) voted to ask UN member states to furnish "every assistance" to South Korea. On June 30 Truman authorized U.S. Far Eastern commander General Douglas MacArthur to employ all available forces in Korea.

The four U.S. divisions in Japan comprising Lieutenant General Walton H. Walker's Eighth Army were all below authorized strength. Training levels were low, equipment was worn and dated, and there were serious shortages in weapons. By cannibalizing the 7th Division, however, MacArthur was able to get first the 24th Infantry Division and then the 25th Infantry Division and 1st Cavalry Division to Korea within two weeks.

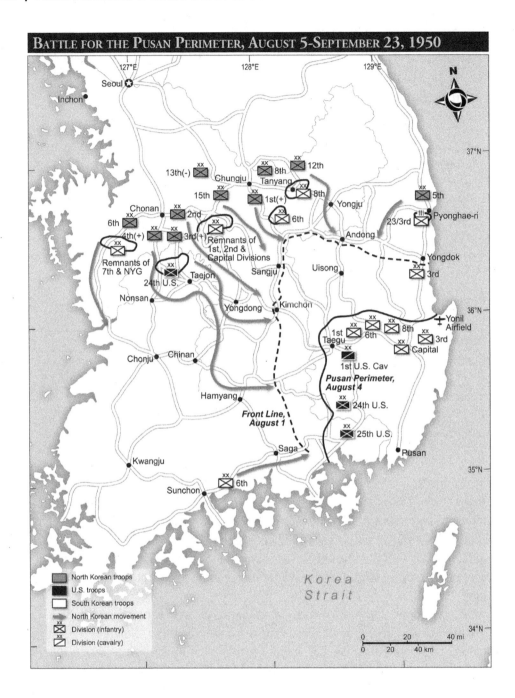

BATTLE FOR THE PUSAN PERIMETER, AUGUST 5-SEPTEMBER 23, 1950

Meanwhile, the war was going badly for the outnumbered and outgunned Republic of Korea Army (ROKA, South Korean Army) and its 500 U.S. military advisers. Seoul fell on June 28, with South Korean troops forced to abandon most of their equipment north of the Han River when bridges on the southern edge of that city were blown prematurely. On July 5, U.S. Task Force Smith went into battle at Osan, 50 miles south of Seoul. Numbering only 540 U.S. troops, the task force was expected to stop an entire KPA division spearheaded by T-34 tanks but was speedily overwhelmed. Meanwhile, the United Nations Command (UNC) came into being. Truman insisted on a U.S. commander and on July 10 named MacArthur to head the new UNC.

U.S. troops did not perform well initially. Poor training and faulty equipment and shortages impacted morale and fighting ability. Difficult terrain, primitive logistics, poor communication, and refugees choking the roads probably did more to delay the KPA advance than did American infantry. From the Battle of Osan, South Korean and U.S. 24th Division forces suffered an unbroken string of reverses. Slowly but surely the defenders were driven south toward the port of Pusan (present-day Busan).

Walker sought to trade space for time to build up his forces and hold until the UNC could build up its strength. By the end of July, however, Eighth Army was out of space, and on July 29 Walker issued his famous "Stand or Die" order. Holding Pusan was critical, but if Walker's forces withdrew too far, they would have insufficient depth in which to maneuver and mass forces for an eventual breakout. Walker ordered his forces behind the Naktong River and by August 4 had established what became known as the Pusan Perimeter (also known as the Naktong Perimeter), a rectangle, approximately 100 by 50 miles, in the southeastern corner of Korea around Pusan.

Over the next month, Eighth Army was reinforced with the 5th Regimental Combat Team (RCT), the 1st Marine Provisional Brigade, regiments of the 2nd Infantry Division, and the British 27th Infantry Brigade. Walker also had the five surviving ROKA divisions. On the west, his defensive line ran along the Naktong River except for the southernmost 15 miles, where the river turned east away from the line. The northern boundary ran through the mountains from Naktong-ni to Yonngdong on the east coast and the sea.

Walker enjoyed the advantage of interior lines and an effective logistics network. Pusan was key. Korea's chief seaport, Pusan boasted modern facilities capable of handling 30 oceangoing vessels simultaneously with a daily discharge capacity of up to 45,000 tons. Walker also had the advantage of rail lines linking Pusan with Miryang, Taegu, and Pohang. Walker positioned his U.S. divisions and five ROKA divisions along the perimeter. U.S. Army doctrine called for an infantry division to hold no more than a 9-mile-wide front, but frontages along the Pusan Perimeter ran 20–40 miles.

By mid-August, Walker could call on more than 500 tanks, a 5 to 1 advantage over the KPA. Walker also had the U.S. Navy and the U.S. Air Force, key elements in the ultimate victory. Ships close offshore provided accurate and highly effective gunfire support on the perimeter's flanks. The U.S. Fifth Air Force enjoyed complete air supremacy, meaning that Walker could move assets within the perimeter without regard to cover and concealment. This enhanced the UNC's mobility advantage, while the KPA was also prey to regular air attacks and was forced to move largely at night.

Initially, 11 KPA divisions, commanded by Lieutenant General Kang Kon, faced UNC forces. In mid-August, two additional divisions and elements of a third joined the battle. While intelligence estimates at the time gave a different picture, the UNC actually held a slight numerical advantage of some 92,000 to 70,000 men, although many of Walker's troops were manning the logistics infrastructure.

Between August 5 and September 9, KPA forces attacked the Pusan Perimeter along four widely separated axes, all of which followed natural approach corridors. KPA forces had the initiative and could concentrate superior numbers at the selected points of attack, while Walker was obliged to spread his troops across the entire front, shifting individual regiments as required. None of his divisional commanders had ever commanded divisions in combat, so Walker had to train them on the job.

On August 9 Walker launched a division-sized limited-objective attack (Task Force Kean) on his southern flank, but stubborn KPA resistance blocked it. Between August 5 and 18, the KPA launched a series of attacks along the other three avenues. Although the attackers registered gains, all the drives were halted thanks to Walker's skillful shifting of assets and the arrival of reinforcements.

On August 27 the KPA launched its second offensive in the same avenues. This time the attacks were well coordinated and hit simultaneously. By September 3, Walker was fighting in five different locations at the same time. American casualties during the first two weeks of September 1950 were the heaviest of the war, yet Walker was able to shift his reserves inside the ever-shrinking perimeter and prevent any major breakthroughs. On September 9 General Kang Kon was killed in a land mine explosion and was replaced by General Kim Chaek as commander of KPA forces. On September 12 the KPA offensive reached its culminating point and stalled. Eighth Army now numbered about 84,500 troops, while the ROKA totaled some 72,000.

When the U.S. X Corps of two divisions landed at the port of Inchon (present-day Incheon) on September 15, well behind the bulk of the KPA, UNC forces were still locked in battle along the Pusan Perimeter. The next day Eighth Army began its attempt to break out. Hampered by insufficient river-crossing equipment and a severe shortage of artillery ammunition, the breakout was not achieved until September 23, when KPA forces began a withdrawal. The allies followed, and late on September 26 just north of Osan, lead elements of Eighth Army linked up with the U.S. 31st Infantry Regiment of the 7th Infantry Division of X Corps.

The battle for the Pusan Perimeter was one of history's great mobile defensive operations. It was certainly the longest, largest, and most complex mobile defense in U.S. military history. The single biggest flaw for the KPA in the battle was its inability to achieve the necessary mass at a decisive point. Its only hope had been to achieve overwhelming mass at one point, punch through the thinly held UNC lines, and drive on Pusan, but the KPA had failed to do this. Only 20,000 to 30,000 of KPA troops along the Pusan Perimeter ever returned to North Korea. The defenders paid a high price as well. Between July 5 and September 16, Eighth Army casualties totaled 4,280 killed in action, 12,377 wounded, 2,107 missing, and 401 confirmed captured.

Spencer C. Tucker

## Further Reading

Appleman, Roy E. *South to the Nakong, North to the Yalu.* Washington, DC: Office of the Chief of Military History, 1961.

Ent, Uzal W. *Fighting on the Brink: Defense of the Pusan Perimeter.* Paducah, KY: Turner Publishing, 1996.

Hoyt, Edwin P. *The Pusan Perimeter.* New York: Stein and Day, 1984.

Robertson, William G. *Counterattack on the Naktong, 1950.* Fort Leavenworth, KS: Combat Studies Institute, 1985.

# Inchon Landing

| Date | September 15, 1950 | |
| --- | --- | --- |
| Location | Port of Inchon (present-day Incheon), west of Seoul, South Korea | |
| Opponents (*winner) | *United Nations Command | North Korea |
| Commander | General Douglas MacArthur; Major General Edward M. Almond | General Choi Yong Kun |
| Approx. # Troops | 70,000 men (total invasion force); more than 230 ships | 8,500 men (initially) |
| Importance | Secures a major port, cuts the North Korean supply line south to the Pusan Perimeter, and leads to the recapture of Seoul. | |

The amphibious assault at Inchon (present-day Incheon) by U.S. forces was General Douglas MacArthur's masterstroke that turned the tide of the Korean War (1950–1953). By mid-July 1950, even as Republic of Korea Army (ROKA, South Korean Army) and U.S. troops were fighting to defend the vital port of Pusan against the Korean People's Army (KPA, North Korean Army), United Nations Command (UNC) commander General MacArthur prepared to present the Democratic People's Republic of Korea (DPRK, North Korea) with a two-front war. Confident that Eighth Army could hold the Pusan Perimeter, MacArthur began diverting resources for an invasion force.

MacArthur selected Inchon. Korea's second-largest port, it was only 15 miles from Seoul, the capital of the Republic of Korea (ROK, South Korea). This area was the most important road and rail hub in Korea and a vital link in the main KPA supply line south. Cutting it would starve KPA forces facing Eighth Army. Kimpo Airfield near Inchon was one of the few hard-surface airfields, and the capture of Seoul would be a serious psychological blow for the North Koreans. Planning for the invasion, code-named Operation CHROMITE, began on August 12.

In one of the best known photographs of the Korean War, 1st Division marines use scaling ladders to climb over the sea wall during the September 15, 1950, Inchon invasion. (National Archives)

Only MacArthur favored Inchon. The Joint Chiefs of Staff (JCS) and most of MacArthur's subordinate commanders opposed it. Tidal shifts there were among the highest in the world. At ebb tide the harbor turned into mudflats, and the navy would have only a three-hour period on each tide to enter or leave the port. The channel was narrow and winding; one sunken ship would block all traffic. There were no beaches, only 12-foot seawalls that would have to be scaled.

MacArthur rejected suggestions for other sites and on August 28 received formal JCS approval for the landing, to be carried out by X Corps. Activated on August 26 and commanded by Major General Edward M. Almond, X Corps consisted principally of Major General Oliver P. Smith's 1st Marine Division and Major General David G. Barr's 7th Army Division. Vice Admiral A. D. Struble commanded Joint Task Force (JTF) 7 for the landing; Rear Admiral James Doyle, who developed the landing plan, was second-in-command.

More than 230 ships took part in the operation. The armada, carrying nearly 70,000 men, was a makeshift affair and included ships from many countries. Thirty-seven of 47 landing ship tanks in the invasion were hastily recalled from Japanese merchant service and manned by Japanese crews. Planes from four carriers provided air support over the landing area.

Although loading was delayed by Typhoon Jane on September 3, deadlines were met. On September 13, JTF-7 was hit at sea by Typhoon Kezia, although no serious damage resulted. JTF-7 reached the Inchon narrows just before dawn on September 15, the fifth day of air and naval bombardment by four cruisers and six destroyers.

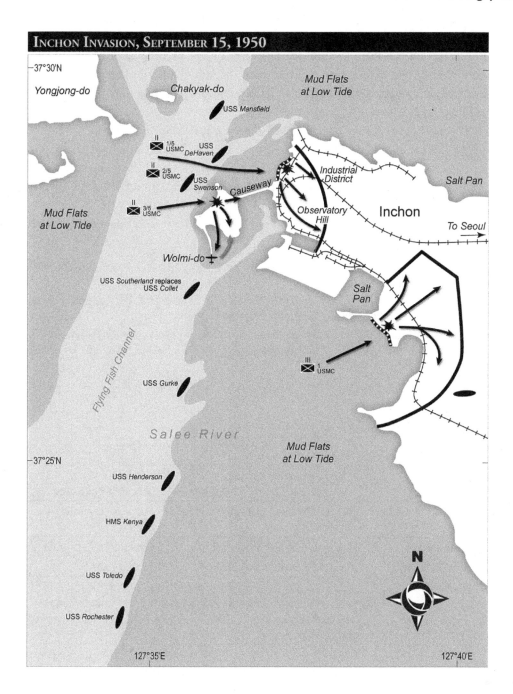

INCHON INVASION, SEPTEMBER 15, 1950

37°30'N

Yongjong-do

Chakyak-do

Mud Flats
at Low Tide

USS Mansfield

1/5
USMC
USS
DeHaven

2/5
USMC
USS
Swenson

Causeway

Industrial
District

Observatory
Hill

Salt Pan

Inchon

To Seoul

3/5
USMC

Mud Flats
at Low Tide

Wolmi-do

USS Southerland replaces
USS Collet

Salt
Pan

Flying Fish Channel

USS Gurke

1
USMC

Salee River

Mud Flats
at Low Tide

37°25'N

USS Henderson

HMS Kenya

USS Toledo

N

USS Rochester

127°35'E

127°40'E

At 6:33 a.m. as MacArthur observed events from the bridge of the *Mount McKinley*, the 5th Marines went ashore to capture Wolmi-do, the island controlling access to the harbor. Resistance was light. At 2:30 p.m. cruisers and destroyers began a shore bombardment of Inchon, and at 5:31 the first Americans climbed up ladders onto the seawall. On D-Day the marines sustained casualties of 20 dead, 1 missing, and 174 wounded. The next day as they drove on Seoul, Eighth

Army began a breakout along the Pusan Perimeter in extreme southeastern Korea. On September 18 the 7th Infantry Division began landing at Inchon, and on September 21 a remaining marine regiment disembarked. The Inchon and Pusan forces made contact north of Osan at 10:26 p.m. on September 26. Seoul fell the next day.

UNC forces were now poised to cross the 38th Parallel into North Korea and reunite the country. Certainly, victory in the Inchon-Seoul Campaign greatly increased MacArthur's self-confidence. The KPA was so badly beaten that he was certain that the war for Korea had been won and that the conflict was just a matter of mopping up. This assessment proved to be incorrect.

Spencer C. Tucker

## Further Reading

Field, James A., Jr. *History of United States Naval Operations: Korea.* Washington, DC: Naval History Division, 1962.

Heil, Robert Debs, Jr. *Victory at High Tide: The Inchon-Seoul Campaign.* Baltimore: Nautical and Aviation Publishing Company of America, 1979.

Montross, Lynn, and Nicholas Canzona. *U.S. Marine Corps Operations in Korea,* Vol. 2, *The Inchon-Seoul Operation.* Washington, DC: United States Marine Corps Historical Branch, 1955.

## Battle of Chipyong-ni

| Date | February 13–15, 1951 | |
|---|---|---|
| Location | Chipyuong-ni (Present-day Jipyeong-ri) in Jije-myeon, Yangpyeong County, Gyeonggi-do Province, South Korea | |
| Opponents (*winner) | *United Nations Command: United States and France | People's Republic of China |
| Commander | Colonel Paul L. Freeman Jr. | General Peng Dehuai |
| Approx. # Troops | 4,500 U.S. and French troops | 25,000 men |
| Importance | Regarded as a major turning point in the Korean War, it marked the end of Chinese forces holding the initiative in the war and proved that UNC forces could hold their own against the Chinese Army. | |

In late November 1950 as United Nations Command (UNC) forces drove into the Democratic People's Republic of Korea (DPRK, North Korea) toward the Yalu River, Chinese troops, known as the Chinese People's Volunteer Army (CPVA), intervened in the war in force. UNC forces pulled back below the 38th Parallel and gave up Seoul, the capital of the Republic of Korea (ROK, South Korea). Large stocks of UNC supplies were destroyed to prevent their capture, and plans were even prepared for the total evacuation of the Korean Peninsula should that prove necessary. Fighting in mid-February 1951 at the small village of Chipyong-ni (present-day Jipyeong-ri) and at Wonju settled the question of whether U.S. and other UNC forces could prevail against the CPVA.

Chipyong-ni, located about 50 miles east of Seoul, was a key transportation hub. Here a railroad line traversed the juncture of several roads. The village was held by Colonel Paul Freeman's 23rd Regimental Combat Team (RCT) of the U.S. 2nd Infantry Division. The 23rd RCT included the regiment's three infantry battalions, the French Infantry Battalion, a ranger company, and attached artillery, tank, and engineer elements. The division's other two regiments—the 9th and 38th Regiments—were at Wonju.

On February 11–12, two CPVA armies and a Korean People's Army (KPA, North Korean Army) corps struck the central UNC front. They scattered three Republic of Korea Army (ROKA, South Korean Army) divisions and forced other UNC troops in the sector to withdraw southward. The attack was concentrated on the communication centers of Wonju and Chipyong-ni. Colonel Freeman soon received word of the withdrawal of friendly units on his flanks and noted the ominous buildup of several communist divisions to his front.

Knowing that he was greatly outnumbered, Freeman asked 2nd Division commander Major General Nick Ruffner when he too could commence withdrawal. To Freeman's surprise, Ruffner refused permission. Instead, he informed Freeman that new Eighth Army commander General Matthew B. Ridgway wanted a test of strength; Chipyong-ni and Wonju were to be defended and held. Ruffner ordered Freeman to form a tight perimeter defense pocket, dig in deeply, and lay in supplies of food, ammunition, and other items. Freeman was informed that if he was attacked and surrounded, he would be resupplied by airdrops and a relief column from the 5th Cavalry Regiment of the 1st Cavalry Division, driving up from Yoju to the south.

Freeman promptly complied with his orders while at the same time carrying out vigorous patrols for up to three miles in front of all forward positions. Freeman's 1st Battalion was located to the north sector of the perimeter, the 3rd Battalion was to the east, the 2nd Battalion was to the south, and the French Battalion was to the south and southwest. Freeman held his B Company and the ranger company in reserve in the center of the perimeter near his regimental command post.

During the afternoon of February 13, the CPVA Thirty-ninth Army and elements of the Forty-first and Forty-second Armies had taken up position around the 23rd RCT's perimeter. Some 25,000 Chinese troops now faced 4,500 UNC defenders. Freeman informed his battalion commanders to expect a major assault that night.

Shortly after dusk, the Chinese commenced shelling the perimeter center and some forward positions. Around 11:00 p.m., the 1st Battalion came under attack. The Chinese were driven off by intense artillery and mortar fire. Whistles, bugles, and other noise-making devices indicated that a wider attack was imminent, and by midnight all perimeter units except the 3rd Battalion were engaged.

By daylight the entire 23rd RCT's perimeter was under Chinese assault, which continued unabated over the next several days. Freeman's forward companies held off CPVA efforts to overrun the town and killed thousands of the attackers. Freeman himself was slightly wounded in the leg by a shell fragment, but he refused to be evacuated while fighting continued.

Around 3:15 a.m. on February 14, a large number of communist troops forced most of F and G Companies of the 2nd Battalion from their positions on the southern rim of the perimeter and occupied the high ground there. A serious threat to the very existence of the perimeter, this exposed the flank of the remainder of the 2nd Battalion to the east and the French Battalion to the west and gave communist forces full and unobstructed observation of and allowed them to directly fire upon the entire center of the perimeter. The CPVA also held a pathway through which forces could be channeled into the perimeter.

Freeman recognized that the gap had to be closed if his command was to survive. He immediately ordered a counterattack by the ranger company and surviving elements of F and G Companies. This commenced at daylight on February 14 but was repulsed with heavy losses.

Freeman then ordered B Company, his regimental reserve, to retake the ground lost and restore the integrity of the perimeter. B Company launched its attack around 12:00 p.m. on February 15. The attack occurred across open ground on a sunny day, in full view of communist forces and under intense communist fire. Mortar and machine-gun fire rained on the attacking troops, who took heavy casualties. By 4:00 p.m., with help from a napalm air strike and the realization by communist forces that a UNC armored relief column was approaching from the south, B Company finally routed the enemy and closed the breach in the perimeter. Fighting ended when the perimeter was secured.

In its attack, B Company suffered more than 50 percent casualties, and all of its platoon sergeants were killed or wounded. These casualties are in sharp contrast with the half dozen or so casualties incurred by other companies of the regiment that were on line, which had the advantage of occupying well-prepared, deeply dug, textbook-designed and -constructed positions. At dusk on February 15, the leading elements of the 5th Cavalry Regiment entered the perimeter through the road from Yoju that passed between and marked the boundaries of the 2nd Battalion and French Battalion positions.

UNC casualties in the fighting at Chipyong-ni were 51 killed, 250 wounded, and 42 missing. Confirmed communist casualties totaled some 2,000 killed and 3,000 wounded, although their actual losses are assumed to be much higher.

The Chipyong-ni fighting signaled a change in U.S. battlefield tactics in Korea. Before it and the Wonju engagement, UNC forces had followed the practice of rolling with the punch when attacked. Instead of standing and fighting, units would withdraw to avoid anticipated encirclement. The fighting at Chipyong-ni and at Wonju to the east has been called the Gettysburg, or high-water mark, for the

CPVA in Korea. The battle was a major turning point in the Korean War in that it marked the end of the CPVA holding the initiative. The battle established that U.S. and UN forces could withstand anything and everything that the communists could throw at them. The CPVA never again held the clear strategic initiative in the war.

Sherman W. Pratt

**Further Reading**

Blair, Clay. *The Forgotten War: America in Korea, 1950–1953.* New York: Times Books, 1987.

Hamburger, Kenneth E. *Leadership in the Crucible: The Korean War Battles of Twin Tunnels & Chipyong-ni.* College Station: Texas A&M University Press, 2003.

Munroe, Clark C. *The Second United States Infantry Division in Korea, 1950–1951.* Tokyo: Toppan Printing, n.d. [1952].

Pratt, Sherman W. *Decisive Battles of the Korean War: An Infantry Company Commander's View of the War's Most Critical Engagements.* New York: Vantage, 1992.

## Ia Drang Valley Campaign

| Date | October 19–November 20, 1965 | |
| --- | --- | --- |
| Location | Ia Drang Valley of west-central Vietnam | |
| Opponents (*winner) | *United States | North Vietnam |
| Commander | Lieutenant Colonels Harold G. Moore, Robert Tully, and Robert McDade | Colonel Nguyen Huu An |
| Approx. # Troops | 3 infantry battalions | 5 infantry battalions |
| Importance | U.S. military leaders believe that they have prevented a major communist military victory and that the war can be won through an attrition strategy. | |

By June 1965, the U.S.-backed Army of the Republic of Vietnam (ARVN, South Vietnamese Army) was in desperate straits, losing the equivalent of an infantry battalion a week. Military Assistance Command Vietnam (MACV) commander General William Westmoreland, who had charge of U.S. forces in Vietnam, therefore decided to hit People's Army of Vietnam (PAVN, North Vietnamese Army) forces first, always his preferred strategy. To carry this out, he committed to battle an entirely new formation, the 1st Air Cavalry Division (known as the 1st Cav).

The 1st Cav relied on the helicopter. This seemed ideally suited to Vietnam, which had few roads and an abundance of jungle. Although it would take a number of lifts to move the entire 1st Cav, all of its 16,000 men and equipment, including artillery, could be transported by its 435 helicopters.

When the 1st Cav arrived in Vietnam in August 1965, Westmoreland considered breaking up the division into its component brigades and stationing them at various locations around South Vietnam. Division commander Major General Harry W. O.

Second Lieutenant C. R. Rescorla of the 1st Cavalry Division (Airmobile) moves against People's Army of Vietnam (PAVN, North Vietnamese Army) snipers on November 17, 1965, during the Battle of the Ia Drang Valley. This running engagement was the first major clash between U.S. and PAVN troops of the Vietnam War and one of its bloodiest battles. (AP Photo)

Kinnard strongly objected, and Westmoreland agreed to assign the 1st Cav intact to a base area just north of Route 19 where the road passed through the village of An Khe in September 1965.

Meanwhile, U.S. intelligence had identified a PAVN troop concentration in South Vietnam's western Central Highlands. PAVN forces there had been operating out of Cambodia to attack U.S. Special Forces camps in the Central Highlands and seize them prior to a drive to the sea down Route 19 that would split South Vietnam in two. PAVN brigadier general Chu Huy Man, commander of PAVN units on the western plateau, planned to lay siege to the Special Forces camp at Plei Mei with its 12 Americans and some 400 indigenous mountain people, known as Montagnards. Man hoped thereby to provoke a reaction by a road-bound ARVN relief force, which he would then ambush and destroy. Once he had accomplished this, Man planned to assault Pleiku City, permitting an advance down Route 19 toward the city of Qui Nhon and the coast.

Man positioned his three regiments around the 2,500-foot-high Chu Pong massif on the Cambodian border and then on October 19 attacked the Plei Mei camp. Following a weeklong battle, the attack and resulting ambush of an ARVN relief force both failed thanks in large part to U.S. air support and air-lifted artillery, and Westmoreland decided on a spoiling attack.

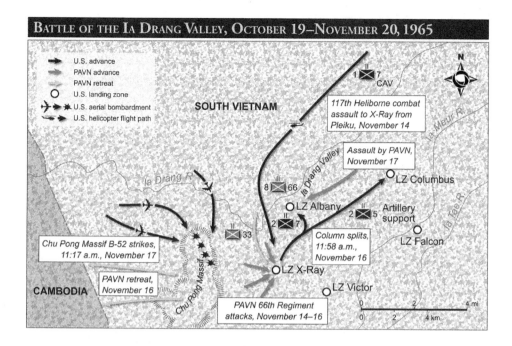

This decision resulted in the battle in the Ia Drang Valley, a forested area just east of the Chu Pong massif. The Battle of Ia Drang was the first major battle of the war between PAVN and U.S. Army units and one of the war's bloodiest encounters.

On October 27 Westmoreland committed a brigade of the 1st Cav to a search-and-destroy operation. For two weeks there was sporadic but light contact between the opposing sides. This changed dramatically on November 14, and during the next four days savage fighting erupted over landing zones (LZs) X-Ray and Albany.

The battle began when the first troopers of some 450 men comprising Lieutenant Colonel Harold G. Moore's 1st Battalion of the 7th Cavalry Regiment landed at LZ X-Ray almost on top of two PAVN regiments of 2,000 men. Outnumbered and in unfamiliar terrain, the Americans fought desperately. Elephant grass, tall anthills, and small trees all obstructed fields of fire.

PAVN political commissar La Ngoc Chau, temporarily commanding the PAVN 66th Regiment, under intense U.S. artillery fire and air bombardment tried to outflank the U.S. forces at X-Ray to the south. Moore was able to get his men in line just in time, although one of his platoons advanced too far, and PAVN forces cut off and almost destroyed it. Moore requested assistance and received B Company of the 2nd Battalion of the 7th Cavalry Regiment, employing it in reserve that night.

Chau resumed the attack at dawn on November 15, and Lieutenant Colonel Robert Tully's 2nd Battalion of the 5th Cavalry Regiment marched overland to provide much-needed support. In bitter and sometimes hand-to-hand combat, the Americans drove back all the PAVN attacks. The Americans also rescued the survivors of the cutoff platoon as 15 B-52 bombers from Guam initiated six days of air strikes on the Chu Pong massif, the first time in the war that B-52s were employed in a tactical role in support of ground troops.

Two additional batteries of artillery meanwhile arrived at LZ Columbus, bringing to 24 the number of guns providing support to the beleaguered Americans at X-Ray. That night the PAVN 66th Regiment withdrew.

Early on November 16 Chau launched a last attack, which the Americans easily repulsed. Lieutenant Colonel Robert McDade's 2nd Battalion of the 7th Cavalry Regiment arrived that day, and the Americans retrieved their own dead and counted those of the PAVN 66th Regiment. The Americans tallied PAVN losses at 634 killed, but estimates placed the total number at 1,215 killed, or 10 times the 1st Cav losses. That same day, Moore's battalion was lifted to Camp Holloway at Pleiku. Tully's 2nd Battalion of the 5th Cavalry Regiment and McDade's 2nd Battalion of the 7th Cavalry Regiment remained at X-Ray.

On November 17 McDade's battalion, with A Company of the 1st Battalion of the 7th Cavalry Regiment attached, was ordered to march two miles toward LZ Albany and reestablish contact with PAVN units. At the same time, Tully's battalion was to march overland to the fire base at LZ Columbus. McDade's men were moving to LZ Albany, strung out in a 500-yard column in high elephant grass and jungle, when they walked into a three-battalion PAVN ambush.

Chau ordered his men to get as close to the Americans as possible in order to avoid U.S. artillery fire and air support. The ensuing two-hour firefight devolved into a series of small combats in which all unit cohesion was lost. In late afternoon, B Company of the 1st Battalion of the 5th Cavalry Regiment arrived overland from LZ Columbus and fought its way into LZ Albany to assist McDade's troopers. At dusk, B Company of the 2nd Battalion of the 7th Cavalry Regiment also arrived. Early on November 18, Chau withdrew across the border into Cambodia. PAVN losses are unknown, but the Americans sustained 155 killed and another 124 wounded.

The monthlong Ia Drang Valley Campaign, which the PAVN official history of the war refers to as the Plei Me Campaign, ended on November 20. During that period, the 1st Cav lost 305 killed (the PAVN claimed that 1,700 Americans and 1,370 "puppet troops" had been "eliminated from the field of combat"). The PAVN official history gives no casualty figures for its side in the campaign, but the Americans estimated total PAVN losses at 3,561, fewer than half of these confirmed.

Both sides claimed victory. The PAVN learned that it could survive high-tech American weapons and the new helicopter tactics and also learned that it could minimize casualties by keeping its troops close to U.S. positions. The North Vietnamese leadership was not unduly concerned about the lopsided casualty totals, believing that even with losses of 10 to 1 they would eventually wear down American resolve.

The Americans believed that they had prevented a decisive PAVN success before the U.S. deployment could be completed and that they had successfully demonstrated the air mobility concept. Westmoreland saw the impressive kill ratio advantage as proof that the war could be won through attrition by carrying the conflict to the PAVN in search-and-destroy operations. *Time* magazine selected him as its Man of the Year for 1965.

Spencer C. Tucker

## Further Reading

Coleman, J. D. *Pleiku: The Dawn of Helicopter Warfare in Vietnam.* New York: St. Martin's, 1988.

Davidson, Philip B. *Vietnam at War: The History, 1946–1975.* New York: Oxford University Press, 1988.

Military History Institute of Vietnam. *Victory in Vietnam: The Official History of the People's Army of Vietnam, 1954–1975.* Translated by Merle L. Pribbenow. Lawrence: University Press of Kansas, 2002.

Moore, Harold G., and Joseph L. Galloway. *We Were Soldiers Once . . . and Young.* New York: Random House, 1992.

## Tet Offensive

| Date | January 30–March 28, 1968 | |
|---|---|---|
| **Location** | South Vietnam | |
| **Opponents (*winner)** | *United States and Republic of Vietnam (South Vietnam) | Democratic Republic of Vietnam (North Vietnam) and South Vietnamese Communists (Viet Cong [VC]) |
| **Commander** | General William Westmoreland | Lieutenant General Tran Van Tra; General Hoang Van Thai |
| **Approx. # Troops** | 1 million troops | 600,000 troops |
| **Importance** | Communist forces incur massive casualties (the VC is all but wiped out), but the American public now turns against the war, forcing the U.S. political leadership to seek a way out. | |

The Tet Offensive was a decisive turning point in the Vietnam War. On July 6, 1967, the leadership of the Democratic Republic of Vietnam (DRV, North Vietnam) met in Hanoi to consider plans to bring the Vietnam War to a speedy and successful conclusion. Militarily, the war had not been going well for the Viet Cong (VC) and the People's Army of Vietnam (PAVN, North Vietnamese army), who were unable to compete with U.S. military firepower and mobility. North Vietnamese defense minister General Vo Nguyen Giap favored a strategy of scaling back operations in South Vietnam and conducting an even more protracted war to wear the Americans down, but the DRV leadership was determined to try to end the war in one master stroke. In essence, they sought to repeat the triumph over the French at Dien Bien Phu in 1954. The plan has been attributed to Giap, but he was in fact in Eastern Europe for medical treatment during the time the plan was drafted and implemented.

The plan borrowed from Chinese communist doctrine and was based on the concept of the general offensive. Accompanying the general offensive would be the general uprising, during which the people of South Vietnam would rally to the communist cause and overthrow the Saigon government. The general uprising was a distinctly Vietnamese element of revolutionary dogma.

Success depended on three key assumptions: the Army of the Republic of Vietnam (ARVN, South Vietnamese Army) would not fight and would in fact collapse under the impact of the general offensive; the people of South Vietnam would carry out the general uprising; and American will to continue the war would crack in the face of the overwhelming shock.

The general offensive was set for Tet 1968, the beginning of the Lunar New Year and the most important holiday in the Vietnamese year. The plans, however, were a tightly held secret, and the exact timing and objectives of the attack were withheld from field commanders until the last possible moment. The communist military buildup and staging for the Tet Offensive was a masterpiece of deception. Beginning in the autumn of 1967, VC and PAVN forces mounted a series of bloody but seemingly pointless battles in the border regions and the northern part of South Vietnam near the demilitarized zone (DMZ).

The battles at Loc Ninh and Dak To were part of the communist peripheral campaign designed to draw U.S. combat units from the urban areas and toward the borders. The operations also were designed to give communist forces experience in larger-scale conventional attack formations. In January 1968, several PAVN divisions began to converge on the isolated U.S. Marine Corps outpost at Khe Sanh in the northern I Corps Tactical Zone, near the DMZ.

Khe Sanh was a classic deception, and the North Vietnamese depended on the Americans misreading history and seeing another Dien Bien Phu in the making, although the North Vietnamese were not averse to taking the base there if this proved feasible. From January 21, 1968, until the point at which the countrywide attacks erupted during Tet, the attention of most of the U.S. military and the national command structure was riveted on Khe Sanh. The battle became an obsession for President Lyndon Johnson.

Meanwhile, the communists used the Christmas 1967 cease-fire to move their forces into position, while senior commanders gathered reconnaissance on their assigned objectives. In November 1967, troops of the 101st Airborne Division had captured a communist document calling for the general offensive and general uprising, but U.S. intelligence analysts dismissed it as mere propaganda. Such a bold stroke seemed too fantastic, because U.S. intelligence did not believe that the communists had the capability to attempt it.

Lieutenant General Frederick C. Weyand, commander of U.S. II Field Forces headquartered in Long Binh some 15 miles east of Saigon, was concerned about the pattern of increased communist radio traffic around the capital in addition to a strangely low number of contacts made by his units in the border regions. On

January 10, 1968, Weyand convinced General William Westmoreland, commander of the Military Assistance Command, Vietnam (MACV), to let him pull more U.S. combat battalions back in around Saigon. As a result, there were 27 battalions (instead of the planned 14) in the Saigon area when the attack came. Weyand's foresight would prove critical.

The countrywide communist attacks were set to commence on January 31, but the secrecy of their buildup cost them in terms of coordination. At 12:15 a.m. on January 30, Da Nang, Pleiku, Nha Trang, and nine other cities in central South Vietnam came under attack. Commanders in Viet Cong Region 5 had started 24 hours too early. This was apparently because they were following the lunar calendar in effect in South Vietnam rather than a new lunar calendar proclaimed by the DRV leadership for all of Vietnam.

As a result of this premature attack, the Tet holiday cease-fire was canceled, ARVN troops were called back to their units, and U.S. forces went on alert and moved to blocking positions in key areas. Communist forces had largely lost the element of surprise.

At 1:30 a.m. on January 31, the Presidential Palace in Saigon came under attack. By 3:40 a.m. the city of Hue was also under attack, and the Tet Offensive was in full swing. Before the day was over, 5 of 6 autonomous cities, 36 of 44 provincial capitals, and 64 of 245 district capitals were under attack.

With the exception of Khe Sanh, the ancient capital of Hue, and the area around Saigon, the fighting was over in a few days. Hue was only retaken on February 25, and the Cho Lon area of Saigon was finally cleared on March 7. By March 20, PAVN units around Khe Sanh began to melt away in the face of overwhelming American firepower.

Militarily, the Tet Offensive was a tactical disaster for the communists. By the end of March 1968, they had not achieved a single one of their objectives. More than 58,000 VC and PAVN troops died in the offensive, with the Americans suffering 3,895 dead and the ARVN losing 4,954. Non-U.S. Allies lost 214. More than 14,300 South Vietnamese civilians also died.

Communist forces had achieved significant surprise in both the timing and the scale of their offensive, but they were unable to exploit it; they had violated the principle of mass. By attacking everywhere, they had superior strength nowhere. The attack had been launched piecemeal across the country and was repulsed piecemeal. The DRV leadership had also been wrong in two of its three key assumptions. The people of South Vietnam did not rally to the communist cause, and the general uprising never took place—even in Hue, where Communist forces held the city for the longest time. Nor did the ARVN fold. The ARVN required significant stiffening in certain areas but on the whole fought well.

The biggest loser in the Tet Offensive was the VC. Although a large portion of the PAVN conducted the feint at Khe Sanh, VC guerrilla forces had led the most attacks in South Vietnam and suffered the heaviest casualties. The guerrilla infrastructure developed over so many years was wiped out. After Tet 1968, the war was run entirely by North Vietnam. The VC were never again a significant force on the battlefield. When Saigon fell in 1975, it was to four PAVN corps.

The South Vietnamese government took steps to bolster the ARVN by drafting 18- and 19-year-olds. But the government faced staggering problems after the Tet Offensive, particularly in caring for what official figures admitted to be some 627,000 newly homeless people. Pacification efforts had also suffered a serious blow in the withdrawal of troops from the countryside to defend the cities.

The North Vietnamese leadership had been absolutely correct in their third major assumption. Their primary enemy did not have the will. While the United States had delivered the communists a crushing tactical defeat, the American public perceived the Tet Offensive very differently. Early reporting of a smashing communist victory went largely uncorrected in the media. Also, many of those who shaped public opinion now came out forcefully against the war. After the Tet Offensive, U.S. policy focused not on winning the war but instead on seeking a way out. Thus, the Tet Offensive is one of the most paradoxical of history's decisive battles and marks the psychological turning point of the Vietnam War.

David T. Zabecki

**Further Reading**

Military History Institute of Vietnam. *Tap Chi Lich Su Quan Su: So Dac Biet 20 Nam Tet Mau Than* [Military History Magazine: 20th Anniversary of the 1968 Tet Offensive Special Issue], Issue 2, 1988.

Pribbenow, Merle L. "General Vo Nguyen Giap and the Mysterious Evolution of the Plan for the 1968 Tet Offensive." *Journal of Vietnamese Studies* (Summer 2008): 1–33.

Oberdorfer, Don. *Tet!* New York: Doubleday, 1971.

Willbanks, James H. *The Tet Offensive: A Concise History.* New York: Columbia University Press, 2007.

## Cambodian Incursion

| Date | April 29–July 22, 1970 | |
| --- | --- | --- |
| **Location** | Eastern Cambodia west and northwest of Saigon, South Vietnam | |
| **Opponents (*winner)** | *United States and Republic of Vietnam (South Vietnam) | Democratic Republic of Vietnam (North Vietnam) and Viet Cong (VC) |
| **Commander** | Lieutenant General Michael S. Davison; Lieutenant General Do Cao Tri | General Hoang Van Thai |
| **Approx. # Troops** | 50,000 Army of the Republic of Vietnam; 30,000 U.S. troops | 40,000 North Vietnamese and VC |
| **Importance** | The operation destroys immense communist military stockpiles and buys time for Vietnamization but reignites anti–Vietnam War sentiment in the United States. | |

On March 18, 1970, pro-U.S. prime minister General Lon Nol seized power in Cambodia from neutralist leader Prince Norodom Sihanouk. Lon Nol closed the port of Sihanoukville and sent his small army, the Forces Armées Nationale Khmer (FANK, Khmer National Armed Forces), against an estimated 60,000 Vietnamese communist troops entrenched in three Cambodian border provinces. On April 4, 1970, the Vietnamese Communist Party's politburo directed People's Army of Vietnam (PAVN, North Vietnamese Army) troops to seize control of the 10 Cambodian provinces bordering South Vietnam. PAVN and VC forces then occupied additional Cambodian provinces and threatened Phnom Penh itself.

U.S. president Richard Nixon, searching for some means to show Hanoi that he was serious about "our commitment in Vietnam," seized on the situation and granted the long-standing request from the Military

A U.S. armored personnel carrier passes by dead civilians as it pushes into Cambodia on May 9, 1970. Although Cambodia was supposed to be a neutral country, it had long served as a sanctuary for Communist forces fighting in Vietnam, and Army of the Republic of Vietnam (ARVN) and U.S. forces invaded the country that spring to destroy the Communist base areas and buy time for "Vietnamization." (Hulton Archive/Getty Images)

Assistance Command, Vietnam (MACV), to attack the communist sanctuaries in Cambodia. During April 14–20, the Army of the Republic of Vietnam (ARVN, South Vietnamese Army) mounted a number of multibattalion operations, without U.S. military advisers, just across the border and seized major communist supply caches. Surprised PAVN and VC forces merely withdrew into the Cambodian interior.

Nixon then authorized the employment of U.S. ground forces up to 19 miles in Cambodia, while ARVN could proceed up to 37 miles. He took this step despite

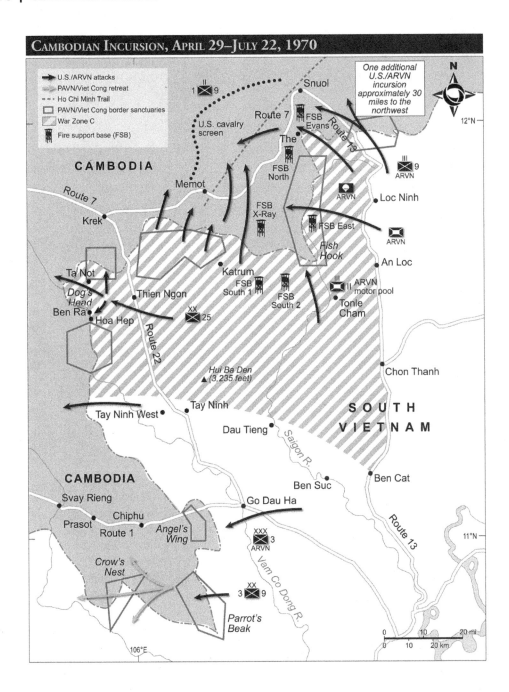

CAMBODIAN INCURSION, APRIL 29–JULY 22, 1970

the opposition of Secretary of Defense Melvin Laird and Secretary of State William Rogers. The operation ultimately involved some 50,000 ARVN and 30,000 U.S. troops. U.S. Army lieutenant general Michael S. Davison, II Field Force commander, and Lieutenant General Do Cao Tri, ARVN III Corps commander, directed the operations that saw ARVN forces invading the so-called Parrot's Beak west of Saigon, while U.S. forces moved into the Fishhook northwest of Saigon. Lon Nol was not consulted.

A flotilla of 40 U.S. river patrol boats entered Cambodia on the Kham Span River on May 6, and two days later another 100 U.S. and Republic of Vietnam Navy (VNN, South Vietnamese Navy) patrol boats moved up the Mekong River but only to the distances inside Cambodia specified earlier by Nixon. U.S. and VNN ships also established a naval blockade in the Gulf of Thailand to prevent communist aid from reaching Cambodia by sea.

Apart from buying time for Vietnamization and additional U.S. troop withdrawals, Nixon hoped that the invasion would relieve pressure by communist forces on the FANK, destroy communist base areas and the communist command center known as COSVN (Central Office for South Vietnam), and break the stalemate in the Paris negotiations.

At the same time, the United States provided equipment to the Cambodian Army, which soon grew to more than 100,000 men but proved to be no match for the seasoned communist forces, which drove the poorly trained Cambodian forces into the urban areas and even threatened Phnom Penh itself. Meanwhile, ARVN forces in Cambodia, outraged by Cambodian Army murders of hundreds of ethnic Vietnamese, looted several Cambodian towns. Later, ARVN forces evacuated some 20,000 ethnic Vietnamese from Cambodia.

U.S. ground forces departed Cambodia by June 30, but ARVN forces remained into 1971, creating several hundred thousand new refugees while being supported by U.S. long-range artillery, tactical air support, and Boeing B-52 Stratofortress strikes.

The Cambodian Incursion saw the capture or destruction of immense communist stockpiles, including 22,892 individual weapons, 2,509 crew-served weapons, and tens of millions of rounds of ammunition, some 45,000 rockets, 435 vehicles, 6 tons of medical supplies, and 700 tons of rice. This was 10 times the amount captured inside Vietnam during the previous year and in small arms alone was sufficient to supply 55 communist main force battalions for one year. MACV reported communist casualties as 11,349 killed and 3,328 captured or defected. ARVN losses were 638 killed, 4,009 wounded, and 35 missing. U.S. casualties totaled 338 killed, 1,525 wounded, and 13 missing.

The Cambodian Incursion did purchase additional time for Vietnamization and gave the ARVN the initiative on all battlefields in South Vietnam during 1970 and 1971. But the incursion also revealed the ARVN's major problems and complete dependence on U.S. air support. In any case, the gains were short-lived. The communists soon reclaimed their sanctuaries and reestablished control in eastern Cambodia, and they substantially improved the Ho Chi Minh Trail network through eastern Laos.

Cambodia was left the most devastated nation in the region. To avoid massive bombings, communist forces moved into the Cambodian interior as Lon Nol's army, receiving only minimal U.S. assistance, struggled for the next five years against both the PAVN and the Cambodian communists, known as the Khmer Rouge (Red Khmer), who now received substantial PAVN aid.

The Cambodian Incursion also rejuvenated the antiwar movement in the United States and led to the killing of protesting students and nonprotesting bystanders at Kent State University and Jackson State College in May 1970. Angry congressmen also restricted presidential war making by passing the Cooper-Church Amendment. In addition, the communist side at the Paris peace talks refused to negotiate until U.S. troops departed Cambodia.

Spencer C. Tucker

## Further Reading

Military History Institute of Vietnam. *Victory in Vietnam: The Official History of the People's Army of Vietnam, 1954–1975*. Translated by Merle L. Pribbenow. Lawrence: University Press of Kansas, 2002.

Nolan, Keith William. *Into Cambodia: Spring Campaign, Summer Offensive, 1970*. Novato, CA: Presidio, 1990.

Shaw, John M. *The Cambodian Campaign: The 1970 Offensive and America's Vietnam War*. Lawrence: University of Kansas Press, 2005.

Stanton, Shelby L. *The Rise and Fall of an American Army: The U.S. Ground Forces in Vietnam, 1965–1975*. Novato, CA: Presidio, 1985.

Tran Dinh Tho. *The Cambodian Incursion*. Washington, DC: U.S. Army Center of Military History, 1979.

## Operation LINEBACKER II

| Date | December 18–29, 1972 | |
|---|---|---|
| Location | Targets in the vicinity of Hanoi and Haiphong, North Vietnam | |
| Opponents (*winner) | *United States | North Vietnam |
| Commander | General John M. Vogt Jr. | Unknown |
| # Aircraft | 207 B-52 bombers; a large number of U.S. Air Force and U.S. Navy fighter-bombers | Some 50 MiG aircraft; more than 1,242 SAMs; antiaircraft guns |
| Importance | Brings North Vietnamese leaders back to the negotiating table in Paris. | |

On December 13, 1972, negotiations at Paris to end the Vietnam War, which had resumed in early November, collapsed. Nguyen Van Thieu, president of the Republic of Vietnam (RVN, South Vietnam), rejected the original terms agreed to in Paris, and the government of the Democratic Republic of Vietnam (DRV, North Vietnam) refused to make significant changes in a document already signed and indeed published the peace terms agreed to. When negotiations resumed and reached an impasse, U.S. president Richard M. Nixon chose to blame the North Vietnamese rather than Thieu and issued an ultimatum for DRV representatives to return to the conference table within 72 hours "or else." When Hanoi rejected the demand, Nixon turned to airpower to enforce his ultimatum.

Wintry skies over North Vietnam were overcast with drizzle, and the only aircraft in the U.S. inventory capable of all-weather bombing operations were the U.S. Air Force's Boeing B-52 Stratofortresses and General Dynamics F-111 Aardvark fighter-bombers and the U.S. Navy's Grumman A-6 Intruders. Although the A-6s and F-111s were capable of bombing almost any target with relative precision, there were not sufficient numbers of them to continue the bombing of North Vietnam at the desired intensity.

On December 14 Nixon ordered mines resown in Haiphong Harbor, and on December 18 Operation LINEBACKER II, originally conceived as a three-day maximum-effort strategic bombing campaign, commenced. By that time more than half of the Strategic Air Command (SAC) B-52 force was in theater with 150 bombers at Andersen Air Force Base, Guam, and 60 B-52s at U-Tapao Royal Thai Air Force Base, Thailand.

Flying in three-ship cells, the B-52s carried the brunt of what airmen dubbed the "Eleven-Day War" and peace activists called the "Christmas Bombings." The B-52s attacked area targets such as airfields, petroleum-storage facilities, warehouse complexes, railroad marshaling yards, and power plants. On the night of December 18–19, 129 B-52 sorties were flown, with 3 bombers lost to surface-to-air missiles (SAMs). The 3 percent loss rate, while regrettable, was also predictable and acceptable.

The second night saw 93 B-52s bomb North Vietnamese targets. Although SAMs damaged 2 bombers, there were no losses. The old saying "If it ain't broke don't fix it" seemed to apply, and on the night of December 21 the same basic attack plan was used when three waves of 33 B-52s each returned to strike previously attacked targets as well as oil storage facilities. This time 6 B-52s were lost and another was heavily damaged.

Although a 6 percent loss rate was acceptable for World War II B-17 missions over Germany, such a loss rate could not be sustained for long given the relatively small number of B-52s in the SAC inventory. The fault lay squarely with poor SAC mission planning. B-52 bomber streams during those first three nights were up to 70 miles long, and the three-plane cells lumbered along toward their targets at more or less the same altitude, speed, and heading. The turn points were uniform and predictable, and the losses were inevitable.

SAC now revamped its planning, with a switch in both force packaging and strategy. During the next two nights, the number of bombers scheduled dropped from the 100-plus of the first three nights to 33. On the night of December 21, the air-defense support system took top priority. But because 2 more B-52s were lost on December 21, missions in the immediate vicinity of Hanoi were curtailed. On the following night, B-52s pounded petroleum-storage areas and rail yards around the port of Haiphong. There were no losses. One B-52 was shot down on raids over each of the next two nights before bombing was suspended for a 36-hour period to mark Christmas. At that point, 11 B-52s had been shot down.

Most legitimate targets in North Vietnam had already been reduced to rubble. In fact, it was the sustained bombing of North Vietnam of LINEBACKER I (May 9–October 23, 1972) during the communist Spring Offensive (Easter Offensive) that had devastated North Vietnam. The so-called Christmas Bombings mostly just rearranged the rubble. The differences in the two campaigns were their objectives and their intensity. During LINEBACKER I the primary objective was to stop a massive, conventional invasion. LINEBACKER I was an interdiction campaign that had the strategic effect of compelling North Vietnam to negotiate seriously for the first time in the war. LINEBACKER II, on the other hand, was a strategic bombing campaign aimed at the will of the North Vietnamese leadership. Its sole objective was to force the Hanoi government to quickly come to an agreement on a cease-fire. The fact that most of the targets constituted parts of the transportation system was simply because these targets, along with airfields and storage complexes, were suitable for area bombing. Furthermore, other than the Thai Nguyen steelworks, North Vietnam had no war-making industries.

Most of the destruction wreaked on North Vietnam during LINEBACKER I had been inflicted by fighter-bombers, and while the bombing was substantial, it had taken place over a period of several months. North Vietnam had plenty of time to adjust and to get used to the bombing. LINEBACKER II was much more focused and intensive, meaning that more bombs fell on North Vietnam in a shorter period of time. The attacks by the B-52s were therefore psychologically more devastating if for no other reason than that a three-plane cell of B-52s could drop more than 300 bombs into an area the size of a railroad marshaling yard or an airfield in less than a minute.

With Hanoi having given no indication that it was ready to negotiate seriously, the bombing resumed at dawn the day after Christmas. The objective now was to render North Vietnam defenseless.

At dawn on December 26, "Ironhand" Republic F-105 Thunderchief and McDonnell Douglas F-4 Phantom fighter-bombers, planes specially modified to attack SAM sites and their guidance radars, pummeled North Vietnam's air-defense system. Sixteen U.S. Air Force F-4 Phantoms employed the long-range electronic navigation (LORAN) bombing technique to blast the main SAM assembly area in Hanoi. When the remaining operational SAM sites fired the missiles they had on hand, there would be no resupply. At dusk, U.S. Air Force General Dynamics F-111 Aardvark swing-wing fighter-bombers swooped in low over the major airfields to crater the runways so that MiG interceptors could not take off. By dark, North Vietnam lay almost defenseless.

That night's B-52 assault was overwhelming. Instead of bombing throughout the night, 120 B-52s struck 10 different targets in a 15-minute period. Surviving SAM sites still had missiles, and 2 B-52s were lost. But the 1.66 percent loss rate was acceptable.

Hanoi now cabled Washington asking if January 8, 1973, would be an acceptable date to reopen negotiations. Nixon replied that negotiations must begin on January 2 and that there would a time limit for reaching an acceptable agreement. Until Hanoi acknowledged and accepted these terms, the bombing would continue.

On December 27, 60 B-52s struck airfields and warehouses around Hanoi and Vinh. A number of B-52s bombed the Lang Dang rail yard near the Chinese border. SAMs shot down 2 more B-52s, but returning pilots noted that missile firings were more random and that the entire North Vietnamese defense effort seemed uncoordinated and sporadic. No more B-52s were lost during LINEBACKER II. Sixty B-52 sorties were flown during each of the next two nights. Virtually no SAM firings were recorded, and B-52 crews were confident that they could fly over North Vietnam with impunity. On December 28 Hanoi agreed to all of President Nixon's provisions for reopening negotiations. The next day Nixon limited the bombing to targets south of the 20th Parallel, and LINEBACKER II came to an end.

Even though Operation LINEBACKER II ended, the bombing did not. B-52s and fighter-bombers continued to pound North Vietnamese troops, supply lines, roads, bridges, and other military facilities in North Vietnam's southern panhandle. This continued bombing was meant to encourage the North Vietnamese to negotiate quickly, seriously, and in good faith.

For airmen, the so-called Eleven-Day War took on special meaning. Airpower enthusiasts claimed that if given the opportunity, bombing on the scale of LINEBACKER II could have ended the war just as quickly at any time. It became an article of faith within the U.S. Air Force that LINEBACKER II had forced the enemy to capitulate. Antiwar activists, however, held that the raids constituted another Dresden or Tokyo, referencing the destruction of those cities by Allied bombers in February 1945. Both interpretations were incorrect.

During LINEBACKER II, 739 B-52 sorties struck North Vietnam, dropping 15,237 tons of bombs. U.S. Air Force and U.S. Navy fighter-bombers added another 5,000 tons. The North Vietnamese launched virtually every SAM in their inventory to shoot down 15 B-52s and 11 other aircraft, including a rescue helicopter. Damage inflicted on targets inside North Vietnam was significant, but the country was far from devastated. Although spent SAMs falling back to earth, crashing B-52s, and an occasional stray bomb caused some damage to neighborhoods in Hanoi, Haiphong, Vinh, and elsewhere, most were left virtually unscathed. According to Hanoi's own figures, 1,312 people perished in the capital, and 300 more were killed in Haiphong. This is hardly comparable to the heavy civilian casualties in the area bombing of German and Japanese cities during World War II. What

LINEBACKER II did was to have a psychological effect on Hanoi's leaders. With their air defense in shambles and virtually all the military targets left in rubble, they did not need to take the risk that the neighborhoods and the dike system might be next.

Accordingly, peace talks moved ahead expeditiously until January 23, 1973, when the United States, North Vietnam, South Vietnam, and the Viet Cong signed a cease-fire agreement, little different from its predecessor, that took effect five days later.

Earl H. Tilford Jr.

### Further Reading

Clodfelter, Mark. *The Limits of Air Power: The American Bombing of North Vietnam.* New York: Free Press, 1989.

Eschmann, Karl J. *Linebacker: The Untold Story of the Air Raids over North Vietnam.* New York: Ivy Books, 1989.

Michel, Marshall L., III. *The Eleven Days of Christmas: America's Last Vietnam Battle.* San Francisco: Encounter Books, 2002.

Tilford, Earl H., Jr. *Crosswinds: The Air Force's Setup in Vietnam.* College Station: Texas A&M University Press, 1993.

## Operation DESERT SHIELD, Air Campaign

| Date | January 17–February 28, 1991 | |
|---|---|---|
| Location | Iraq and Kuwait | |
| Opponents (*winner) | *United States | Iraq |
| Commander | Lieutenant General Charles A. Horner | General Khaldoun Khattab |
| # Aircraft | 2,614 aircraft | Almost 1,000 aircraft |
| Importance | Secures total air supremacy over Kuwait and Iraq and sharply degrades Iraqi command and control facilities and ground forces, greatly easing the way for the subsequent coalition ground campaign. | |

Following the Iraqi occupation of Kuwait on August 2, 1990, Iraqi president Saddam Hussein rejected demands from the world community that he withdraw his troops. Acting under the authority of United Nations resolutions, U.S. president George H. W. Bush then assembled a grand coalition, including Arab states, to oust the Iraqi Army from Kuwait by force.

The buildup of U.S. forces, first to protect Saudi Arabia and then to allow offensive operations against Iraq and known as Operation DESERT SHIELD, began on August 7, 1990, with the dispatch of 48 U.S. Air Force McDonnell F-15C/D Eagles from Langley Air Force Base, Virginia, to Dhahran, Saudi Arabia. The longest operational fighter deployment in history, this nonstop flight required about 17 hours and seven en route in-flight refuelings and marked the beginning of the largest buildup of airpower in the history of the Middle East. By September 2 more than 600 aircraft were in place, buttressed by U.S. Navy and U.S. Marine Corps forces and by the deployed ground forces of Great Britain, France, and Arab coalition nations. Iraq was effectively ringed by airpower, with two carrier battle groups operating in the Red Sea and four others operating in the Persian Gulf.

Despite this show of force, coalition forces did not arrive in the Persian Gulf with an air-war plan in hand. Colonel John Warden III, author of *The Air Campaign: Planning for Combat* (1988), was called upon to furnish an air-war plan to Lieutenant General Charles A. Horner, commander of both U.S. Central Command (CENTCOM) Air Forces and the Joint Force Air Component. Warden and 20 colleagues in the Pentagon put forward what they called Operation INSTANT THUNDER (so-named to signal its difference from the attenuated and ineffective Operation ROLLING THUNDER of the Vietnam War). Believing the plan to be insufficiently detailed, Horner called on Brigadier General Buster C. Glosson to transform it into a usable document, but the final plan followed the broad outlines of Warden's ideas. The plan called for securing and maintaining air superiority; attacking the Iraqi political and military leadership by destroying command and control networks; severing Iraqi supply lines; destroying Iraqi chemical, biological, and nuclear capabilities; and destroying the elite Republican Guard units. The plan represented history's most intensive air battlefield preparation prior to a land offensive.

Iraq, with its Soviet-style integrated air-defense system, appeared to be a formidable opponent. The system included almost 1,000 aircraft, many of them flown by pilots with combat experience gained in the 1980–1988 war with Iran; 7,000 anti-aircraft guns; 16,000 surface-to-air missiles; and a modern command, control, and communications system.

The United States and its coalition allies assembled a powerful strike force of 2,614 aircraft. The countries represented in the air war and the number of aircraft they supplied were as follows: United States, 1,990; Saudi Arabia, 339; Great Britain, 73; France, 66; Kuwait, 43; Canada, 28; Bahrain, 24; Qatar, 20; United Arab Emirates, 20; Italy, 8; and New Zealand, 3. Of the total, 1,838 were fighters, bombers, or attack aircraft, and 312 were tankers.

Military operations against Iraq, known as Operation DESERT STORM, commenced on January 17, 1991. Air operations actually began on the morning of January 16 when seven Boeing B-52Gs departed Barksdale Air Force Base, Louisiana, carrying cruise missiles. These were reinforced by some 100 TLAM Tomahawk cruise missiles launched by battleships, cruisers, and destroyers stationed in the Red Sea and the Persian Gulf. The missile combination coincided with a stealthy but piloted attack force. The latter consisted first of 10 Lockheed F-117A stealth fighters flying from southern Saudi Arabia. They dropped laser-guided bombs that crippled Iraq's air-defense system. Also in action were the sophisticated U.S. Air Force MH-53J Pave Low and U.S. Army AH-64 Apache helicopters, the latter mounting a direct attack on Iraqi early-warning radar systems. A lethal array of bombers, fighters, tankers, electronic warfare aircraft, and Wild Weasels (suppression of enemy air-defense aircraft) were soon airborne in an attack that completely overwhelmed Iraqi defenses.

The air campaign proceeded flawlessly. Every one of coalition commander U.S. Army general H. Norman Schwarzkopf's requirements and every feature of General Glosson's plan was met. Large numbers of Iraqi aircraft were destroyed on the ground, whereupon Hussein ordered remaining aircraft to fly to Iran. The coalition forces scored 41 air-to-air victories during the war and 2 more in the following month. The United States suffered 35 losses in combat, while coalition forces lost 8 aircraft, 6 of the latter being Royal Air Force Tornados lost in low-level attacks on heavily defended airfields. Twenty-two U.S. aircraft were also lost to noncombat accidents.

Sandstorms proved to be a significant deterrent to air operations, but the single most important factor that distracted planners from executing the air-war plan as originally conceived was the emphasis given to the elimination of the Iraqi Scud threat. The Scud was a Soviet-developed tactical ballistic missile widely sold abroad. Iraq possessed some 600 Scuds, which had the great advantage of being easily dispersed. Many were on mobile missile launchers. The principal coalition worry was an Iraqi Scud attack on Israel and a military response by the Jewish state that would unhinge the coalition.

The United States applied great pressure on Israel not to intervene in the war, but if Scuds caused significant damage in the Jewish state, it would be difficult for the Israeli government to resist public pressure for retaliation. Iraq fired two Scuds against Israel on January 17 and seven more the next day. In return for Israeli restraint, the United States supplied U.S. Army Patriot PAC-2 missiles and carried out an intensive Scud hunt that consumed an immense amount of time and resources. Iraq also fired Scuds against Saudi Arabia. Ultimately the coalition flew some 2,500 sorties against the Scuds and their missile launchers, detracting from the other aerial effort but diminishing the Scud threat to firings of one or less per day.

The coalition air campaign gutted the Iraqi forces. In the 43-day war, the coalition flew some 110,000 sorties. This effort placed an immense demand on aerial refueling capacity, with air force tankers refueling just under 46,000 aircraft and off-loading an incredible 110 million gallons of aviation fuel.

The coalition flew more than 44,000 combat sorties and dropped more than 84,000 tons of bombs. Of this amount, some 7,400 tons were precision-guided munitions (PGMs). Although less than 10 percent of the total tonnage was expended, PGMs accounted for more than 75 percent of the damage inflicted on key Iraqi targets.

The air campaign had a catastrophic effect on the Iraqi military's ability to resist. Intelligence estimates claimed that before the ground attack occurred, one-third of the Iraqi divisions were at 50 percent or lower strength, one-third were at 50–75 percent strength, and one-third were at full strength. The Iraqi armored force was decimated by tank plinking by Fairchild A-10 Warthogs and helicopters. The Warthog's performance rescued it from retirement and launched an entirely new career in air force service.

On February 24, 1991, the ground campaign began, its key component being a massive armor attack on the western flank of the Iraqi Army with the goal of cutting off and destroying Iraqi Republican Guard divisions in Kuwait. The ground forces were able to accomplish this assembly and execution in complete security, for Iraqi forces were bereft of airpower, had no insight into coalition action, and were for the most part immobile. American and coalition forces were thus able to achieve a ground victory with only minor losses.

Walter J. Boyne

### Further Reading

Boyne, Walter J. *Operation Iraqi Freedom: What Went Right, What Went Wrong and Why.* New York: Forge Books, 2003.

Hallion, Richard P. *Storm over Iraq: Air Power and the Gulf War.* Washington, DC: Smithsonian Institution Press, 1992.

Warden, John A., III. *The Air Campaign: Planning for Combat.* Washington, DC: National Defense University Press, 1988.

## Operation DESERT STORM, Ground Campaign

| Date | February 24–28, 1991 | |
|---|---|---|
| Location | Kuwait and Iraq | |
| Opponents (*winner) | *U.S.-led coalition of the United States, Britain, France, Saudi Arabia, Egypt, Syria, and other states | Iraq |
| Commander | General H. Norman Schwarzkopf | President Saddam Hussein |
| Approx. # Troops | 665,000 men; 3,318 tanks | 546,700 men; 4,280 tanks |
| Importance | A brilliant campaign, achieving its goals with minimal losses in a very short time, it demonstrates the remarkable U.S. military renaissance from the low point after the Vietnam War. | |

On August 7, 1990, following the refusal of Iraqi president Saddam Hussein to withdraw his forces from Kuwait, U.S. president George H. W. Bush ordered the deployment of forces to Saudi Arabia in Operation DESERT SHIELD. U.S. air, ground, and naval units were sent to bolster the Saudis and to demonstrate U.S. resolve in support of diplomacy.

U.S. Army general H. Norman Schwarzkopf, commander of the U.S. Central Command (CENTCOM), directed the effort. The army provided the bulk of the forces, including armor, infantry, and airborne units from the United States and Europe. The U.S. Marine Corps contributed two divisions, while offshore there were two carrier battle groups with full complements of aircraft and a marine fleet force. The U.S. Air Force deployed several wings of combat aircraft as well as transports and support units.

Coalition ground support arrived in the form of an armored division and two armored brigades from the United Kingdom and a light armored division from France. Saudi Arabia, Syria, and Egypt also provided troops, and Czechoslovakia sent a chemical decontamination and detection unit. Altogether, the in-theater coalition ground force numbered some 540,000 men from 31 countries with 3,318 tanks and 3,850 artillery pieces and supported by some 1,800 combat aircraft from 12 nations and a large naval force in the Persian Gulf and the Red Sea. Although Iraq had on paper an army of nearly 1 million men, opposing coalition forces in Kuwait totaled no more than 540,000 men, while some postwar analyses put the total at perhaps 336,000. The Iraqis also had some 4,200 tanks, 2,800 armored personnel carriers, and 3,100 artillery pieces.

Hussein remained recalcitrant, and the air campaign, dubbed Operation INSTANT THUNDER, began early on the morning of January 17, 1991. The operation took out the Iraqi air-defense network and destroyed large numbers of Iraqi aircraft, whereupon Hussein ordered remaining aircraft to fly to Iran. In retaliation, he launched Scud missiles against targets in Saudi Arabia and Israel in an attempt to draw the Jewish state into the war and split the coalition of Arab states against him. Washington applied pressure on Israel not to intervene and dispatched Patriot missile batteries to help defend the Jewish state.

With his forces now being seriously degraded by coalition airpower, Hussein, determined to begin what he threatened would be "the mother of all battles," ordered his commanders to attack across the Saudi border. Only at Khafji did such a battle occur, but during January 29–31 it was beaten back by Saudi and Qatari forces and U.S. marines supported by artillery and aircraft.

When Hussein rejected President Bush's ultimatum that he immediately evacuate Kuwait or face invasion, at 4:00 a.m. on February 24 Iraqi time (February 23 in the United States), Schwarzkopf began the ground war, Operation DESERT STORM. Coalition forces executed simultaneous drives along the coast and broke the western edge of the Iraqi flank, rolling up Hussein's troops into a pocket along the Euphrates River and the Red Sea. As the marines moved up along the coast toward Kuwait City, they were hit in the flank by Iraqi armor. In the largest tank battle in U.S. Marine Corps history, the marines, supported by aircraft, easily defeated this force in a battle that was fought in a surrealist day-into-night atmosphere caused by the smoke of burning oil wells set afire by the retreating Iraqis.

As the marines prepared to enter Kuwait City preceded by a light Arab force, Iraqi forces laden with booty fled north in whatever they could steal. Thousands of vehicles and personnel were caught in the open and pummeled by aircraft and artillery along what became known as the "Highway of Death." However, Schwarzkopf was upset by the slow pace of VII Corps (140,000 men in five divisions, 32,000 wheeled vehicles, and 6,600 tracked vehicles), the inner left-flank hook. Its commander, Lieutenant General Frederick Franks Jr., pled a lack of adequate intelligence information on Iraqi dispositions and the need to maintain supply lines. Instead of pushing forward as quickly as possible, as Schwarzkopf had urged, Franks insisted on hitting the Iraqis with the maximum strength of his armor divisions in position.

When the fist struck, it was with devastating effect. In the major opening engagement, VII Corps came up against an Iraqi rear guard of 300 tanks covering the withdrawal north toward Basra of four Republican Guard divisions. The Soviet-supplied Iraqi T-72 tank main guns were inaccurate at more than 0.9 mile (1,500 meters), while the U.S. M-1 Abrams could bring the Iraqi tanks under fire at 1.8 miles (3,000 meters). The Iraqis were wiped out at a cost of 1 American dead. As VII Corps closed to the sea, Lieutenant General Gay E. Luck's XVIII Airborne Corps (115,000 men, 21,000 wheeled vehicles, and 4,300 tracked vehicles) to its left, which had a much larger distance to travel, raced to reach the fleeing elite Iraqi Republican Guard divisions before they could escape the trap to Baghdad.

The war was then stopped. President Bush wanted to keep Iraq intact against a resurgent Iran, and chairman of the Joint Chiefs of Staff General Colin Powell had no taste for the further slaughter of Iraqis, especially given the images of the Highway of Death. Iraq thus escaped with its best Republican Guard troops largely intact. With Kuwait now liberated, hostilities were declared at an end at 8:01 a.m. on February 28 local time. The ground war had lasted 100 hours.

Schwarzkopf, who at the time declared himself satisfied with the decision to end the fighting, entered into a cease-fire agreement on March 3 that allowed the beaten Iraqis to fly their armed helicopters. The cease-fire established a no-fly zone for Iraqi fixed-wing aircraft north of the 36th Parallel to protect the Kurds, but no such prohibition protected the Shiite Muslims in southern Iraq, who now came under savage attack for having risen up against Hussein.

The Persian Gulf War, including the air portion, had lasted 43 days and was among the most lopsided conflicts in military history. Iraq lost 3,700 tanks, more than 1,000 other armored vehicles, and 3,000 artillery pieces. The coalition lost 4 tanks, 9 other combat vehicles, and 1 artillery piece. The coalition sustained 500 casualties (150 dead), many of these from accidents and friendly fire. Iraqi casualties totaled between 25,000 and 100,000 dead, with the best estimates being around 60,000. The coalition also took 80,000 Iraqis prisoner. Perhaps an equal number simply deserted.

The Persian Gulf War was a remarkable renaissance of American forces from the so-called Vietnam Syndrome of the 1970s, yet predictions that Hussein would soon be overthrown proved unfounded, paving the way for a new and more costly conflict, the Iraq War, in 2003.

Spencer C. Tucker

**Further Reading**

Gordon, Michael R., and Bernard E. Trainor. *The Generals' War.* Boston: Little, Brown, 1995.

Scales, Robert H., Jr. *Certain Victory: The U.S. Army in the Gulf War.* Washington, DC: Brassey's, 1997.

Schwarzkopf, H. Norman. *It Doesn't Take a Hero.* New York: Bantam, 1992.

## Battle of 73 Easting

| Date | February 26, 1991 | |
|---|---|---|
| Location | Southern Iraq | |
| Opponents (*winner) | *United States | Iraq |
| Commander | Colonel Don Holder; Captain H. R. McMaster | Salah Aboud Mahmoud |
| Approx. # Troops | Three troops of the 2nd Armored Cavalry Regimen, totaling: 360 men; 60–90 armored vehicles (initial combat consists of Eagle Troop of 9 M1A1 Abrams tanks and 12 Bradley infantry fighting vehicles) | As many as 3,000 men; the number of tanks and other armored vehicles present is somewhat greater than those given as destroyed, below |
| Importance | This totally lopsided battle demonstrates the tremendous superiority in training and equipment for U.S. forces over those of Iraq during the Persian Gulf War. | |

During Operation DESERT STORM, the ground portion of the Persian Gulf War, the U.S. VII and VIII Corps undertook a left hook into the western Iraqi desert in which they skirted the western limit of Iraqi frontier defenses, the so-called Saddam Line. Both corps then made a great right turn with the intention of cutting off Iraqi forces remaining in Kuwait. On February 26 Lieutenant General Frederick M. Franks Jr.'s VII Corps came into contact with Iraqi major general Salah Aboud Mahmoud's Republican Guard Tawakalnah Division.

The Iraqis had been hastily redeployed to take up improvised defensive positions along the western side of the Wadi al-Batin, which marked the Kuwaiti-Iraqi border. The Iraqis hoped to delay VII Corps long enough to allow their forces in Kuwait to escape. The Battle of Wadi al-Batin refers to VII Corps' attack on the Tawakalnah Division, while the Battle of 73 Easting was a part of the larger overall Battle of Wadi al-Batin. The term "73 Easting" simply refers to a Global Positioning System coordinate. The Battle of 73 Easting was notable for the fact that it was one of the few engagements during the war in which an outnumbered American force faced a larger Iraqi force in a stationary defensive position.

The main American force involved in the battle was the 2nd Armored Cavalry Regiment (ACR), commanded by Colonel Don Holder. It consisted of eight troops, each of about 120 soldiers in 20–30 armored vehicles. Three troops of the 2nd ACR were most involved in the 73 Easting actions. Eagle Troop, commanded by Captain H. R. McMaster, took the lead and did most of the fighting, followed by Ghost Troop and Iron Troop.

Eagle Troop was acting as a reconnaissance unit for VII Corps when it ran into the 18th Brigade of the Tawakalnah Division late in the afternoon on February 26. The Iraqis had deployed T-72M1 tanks supported by BMP (Boevaia Mashina Pekhoti, or Combat Vehicle Infantry) infantry fighting vehicles, while the Americans had M1A1 Abrams tanks and M4 Bradley armored fighting vehicles. Weather conditions at the time were poor, with a heavy storm limiting visibility, and the Americans could not call in air strikes because of this. However, the Abrams tanks and Bradley vehicles had the advantage of thermal sights, while the Abrams' gun far outranged that of the T-72s. American tanks could also fire on the move, while the Iraqis could not.

Eagle Troop found itself in a seam between the Iraqi 18th Brigade and the adjacent Iraqi 12th Armored Division. The surprised Iraqis quickly opened fire. Normal procedure called for the reconnaissance units to wait for heavier supporting units to catch up, but Iraqi fire was so intense that McMaster had no choice but to engage. At the start of the fighting, Eagle Troop consisted of just 9 Abrams tanks and 12 Bradleys.

The tank-versus-tank battle was over quickly, with 37 T-72s and 32 other vehicles destroyed in just 40 minutes. Ghost and Iron Troops moved up to join in the battle. However, Iraqi resistance at 73 Easting proved to be unexpectedly determined. Iraqi tanks made attempts to maneuver and outflank American tanks rather than remaining in stationary defensive positions, as was their normal operating procedure. Iraqi troops typically surrendered or broke and fled when their tanks were knocked out, but the infantry of the Tawakalnah Division continued to resist, employing rocket-propelled grenades. Ghost Troop was heavily counterattacked after nightfall and had to call in an artillery bombardment of 2,000 howitzer rounds and 12 rockets. Iraqi opposition finally ended about six hours after the battle first began.

The U.S. 1st Infantry Division arrived later that night to pass through the battle scene and continue the unrelenting U.S. advance. American losses in the battle were minimal, with the Iraqis destroying only one Bradley. A second Bradley was hit by friendly fire. Despite the ferocity of their resistance, the Iraqis proved ultimately ineffective in countering the American advance. Altogether, the Iraqis lost 113 armored vehicles and suffered 600 casualties.

The first defeat for the Iraqi Republican Guard in the war, the Battle of 73 Easting allowed the 1st Infantry Division to move into the heart of the Iraqi defenses and then into Kuwait. The battle generated controversy after the war as commentators tried to explain how three troops of an armored cavalry regiment could destroy an entire Iraqi brigade. Some stressed the superiority of American technology and the woeful state of the Iraqi army in which even the elite Republican Guard units fought unsuccessfully. Others pointed to the skill level of the American soldiers, arguing that their proficiency rather than the disparity in technology explained the battle's one-sided outcome. Still others thought that the air campaign that had preceded the ground phase of Operation DESERT STORM had been decisive in disorganizing the Iraqis' defense and their will to fight.

Paul W. Doerr

### Further Reading

Gordon, Michael R., and Bernard E. Trainor. *The General's War: The Inside Story of the Conflict in the Gulf.* New York: Little, Brown, 1995.

Macgregor, Douglas. *Warrior's Rage: The Great Tank Battle of 73 Easting.* Annapolis, MD: Naval Institute Press, 2012.

Pollack, Kenneth M. *Arabs at War: Military Effectiveness, 1948–1991.* Lincoln: University of Nebraska Press, 2002.

Scales, Robert H., Jr. *Certain Victory: The U.S. Army in the Gulf War.* Washington, DC: Brassey's, 1997.

## Battle of Mogadishu

| Date | October 3, 1993 | |
| --- | --- | --- |
| Location | Mogadishu, Somalia | |
| Opponents (*winner) | *Somali National Alliance | United States |
| Commander | Mohammed Farrah Aidid | Major General William F. Garrison |
| Approx. # Troops | 4,000–6,000 men | 160 men; 19 aircraft, 12 vehicles |
| Importance | Leads to the U.S. withdrawal from the humanitarian mission in Somalia. | |

On August 22, 1993, new U.S. secretary of defense Les Aspin authorized the deployment to Somalia of the Joint Special Operations Task Force. This step came in response to attacks by Mohammed Farrah Aidid's Somali National Alliance (SNA) fighters on U.S. and United Nations (UN) personnel operating in Somalia during Operation UNOSOM II (Operation CONTINUE HOPE) forces and installations providing humanitarian assistance to Somalis during the civil war that had begun there in

1991. Aidid went underground following air and ground assaults on his strongholds in June and July, and U.S. Task Force Ranger was assigned the mission of capturing Aidid and his key lieutenants and turning them over to UNOSOM II forces. Unfortunately, Aspin scrapped the original plan to send tanks.

On October 3–4 in Operation GOTHIC SERPENT, Task Force Ranger launched its third attack into the area of Mogadishu held by Aidid's followers. Rocket-propelled grenades brought down two U.S. Sikorsky UH-60 Black Hawk helicopters, however. A 15-hour firefight then ensued between the lightly armed U.S. forces on the ground and Aidid's militia. A relief force spearheaded by Pakistani tanks was slow to reach the fighting area but finally rescued the surviving rangers and Delta Force members trapped in the city.

The battle claimed 18 U.S. dead and 79 wounded. Chief Warrant Officer Mike Durant was wounded and captured, but under intense pressure, Aidid released him on October 14. Two Malaysian soldiers were also killed, and 7 were wounded; the Pakistanis suffered 2 wounded. Somali casualties were estimated at 500–1,500. Delta Force snipers Master Sergeant Gary Gordon and Sergeant First Class Randall Shugart were awarded posthumous Medals of Honor for their part in the battle, the first U.S. military personnel to be so honored since the Vietnam War.

The fighting in Mogadishu prompted U.S. president William J. Clinton on October 7 to send in an additional 1,700 army troops, but the high U.S. death toll in the October 3–4 battle and images of the bodies of U.S. soldiers being dragged through the streets of Mogadishu led to a backlash in the United States against the mission, and Clinton announced that all U.S. troops in Somalia would be withdrawn within six months. The last troops departed on March 25, 1994, although 55 marines remained behind to guard the U.S. embassy until it closed that September.

Operations RESTORE HOPE and CONTINUE HOPE in Somalia claimed 27 Americans killed in action, 4 dead from accidents, and more than 100 wounded. This, the continued internal strife in Somalia, and the strong opposition of the SNA toward the UN brought a total UN withdrawal in March 1995. This carefully planned U.S.-UN action was carried out without casualties. Meanwhile, the American military deaths in Somalia prompted a renewal of the debate in the United States and a hesitancy to employ U.S. military force in regions of the world in which the risks were high and the United States did not have vital national interests, including the concurrent humanitarian crisis in Bosnia.

Spencer C. Tucker

**Further Reading**

Bowden, Mark. *Black Hawk Down: A Story of Modern War.* New York: Atlantic Monthly Press, 1999.

Clarke, Walter S., and Jeffrey Ira Herbst. *Learning from Somalia: The Lessons of Armed Humanitarian Intervention.* Boulder, CO: Westview, 1997.

## Operation ENDURING FREEDOM

| Date | October 7–December 17, 2001 | |
|---|---|---|
| Location | Afghanistan | |
| Opponents (*winner) | *United States and NATO; Afghan Northern Alliance | Taliban and Al Qaeda |
| Commander | General Tommy Franks; Colonel John Mulholland; Mohammad Fahim Khan; Mohammad Ismail Khan; Abdul Rashid Dostum; Kharim Khalili | Osama bin Laden; Mullah Mohammad Omar |
| Approx. # troops | Initially 200–300 special operations personnel, rising to some 5,200 troops (U.S.) and as many as 20,000 Afghans | As many as 40,000 Taliban and Al Qaeda |
| Importance | Topples the Taliban government of Afghanistan and forces much of the Taliban and Al Qaeda to relocate to Pakistan. | |

Following the September 11, 2001, attacks by the Al Qaeda terrorist organization that left nearly 3,000 Americans dead in New York City, Pennsylvania, and Virginia, U.S. president George W. Bush announced a campaign to root out the perpetrators. This effort became known as the Global War on Terror. Bush singled out Al Qaeda and its leader, Osama bin Laden, as well as "every terrorist group of global reach" in countries that had given it sanctuary. Operation ENDURING FREEDOM (OEF) was the specific effort of the Global War on Terror to strike Al Qaeda in Afghanistan.

OEF viewed Al Qaeda and its affiliates as combatants who had declared war against the United States rather than as criminals. As such, the United States received the support of the North Atlantic Treaty Organization (NATO) under its Article V, which asserts that an armed attack against one NATO country is an attack against all.

Although there were initially seven theaters of OEF, OEF-Afghanistan (OEF-A) was the main effort. OEF-A called for military intervention with regime change and was a joint, combined, and interagency operation. The operation drew considerable international support, ranging from battlefield preparation to humanitarian assistance. The governments of the United Kingdom, Canada, France, Turkey, and Japan all committed military assets, including warships, aircraft, troops, Special Forces, and disaster response teams. NATO deployed nine ships and several Airborne Warning and Control Systems aircraft to the United States to free up American assets to deploy to Afghanistan, while diplomatic efforts secured the support of neighboring Central Asian states and, critically, Pakistan. Planning for OEF-A took four weeks and was carried out by the U.S. Central Command (CENTCOM), commanded by U.S. Army general Tommy Franks.

Afghan anti-Taliban fighters pray in front of their tank overlooking the White Mountains of Tora Bora in northeastern Afghanistan on December 10, 2001. (AP Photo/David Guttenfelder)

The 5th Special Operations Group (Airborne) constituted the bulk of the Special Forces effort under Joint Special Operations Task Force–North (JSOTF-N). JSOTF-N included Special Forces teams (Operational Detachment Alpha) from the United States and allied nations, Central Intelligence Agency (CIA) paramilitaries of the Special Activities Division, and aviation, logistics, and U.S. Army and Marine Corps conventional troop assets. Already on September 26, CIA agents had been inserted into the Panjshir Valley to identify indigenous commanders to partner against the Taliban government of Afghanistan and Al Qaeda.

After the Taliban government of Afghanistan rejected weeks of demands by President Bush that it hand over bin Laden and members of Al Qaeda, air operations commenced on October 7, 2001. This took the form of bombing and cruise missile attacks on air-defense and communications infrastructure.

As the air attacks went forward, Special Forces and CIA teams deployed as ground-support elements for the Northern Alliance fighters, the indigenous anti-Taliban forces predominantly in northern Afghanistan. The U.S. forces were inserted into Mazar-e Sharif and Bagram, followed by Kunduz-Taloqan, Kandahar City, and finally Tora Bora. One of the most important advantages brought by the Special Forces teams was close air support, a game changer for the indigenous forces. Close air support took the form of B-1 and B-52 bombers; F-14, F-15, F-16, and F-18 fighter aircraft; and AH-44, AH-64, MH-53, and CH-47 Chinook helicopters. The ground teams also oversaw the delivery of humanitarian assistance to the civilian population, conducted psychological warfare, provided medical evacuations, and furnished intelligence prior to ground deployments.

On October 19, the first 12-man Special Forces team conducted a night insertion near Mazar-e Sharif by helicopter. The 12-man team then trekked through the mountains on horseback to meet with Northern Alliance leaders Rashid Dostum, Atta Mohammad, and Bismullah Khan and Hazara commander Karim Khalili. Dostum's cavalry and Atta Mohammad's forces then fought their way into Mazar-e Sharif, crushing the Taliban defenders and taking the city on November 10, thanks in large part to U.S. air support. This first victory of OEF-A provided a strategic base for coalition and Afghan forces.

Special Forces in the Shamali Plains around Bagram then linked with Afghan forces in the defensive stronghold of Ahmad Shah Massoud, the Northern Alliance commander who had been assassinated by Al Qaeda the previous September. Tajik Northern Alliance commanders Fahim Khan and Bismullah Khan were instrumental in retaking Bagram Airfield and the Afghan capital of Kabul. During October 19–20, Special Forces personnel were inserted around Bagram. Although both Bagram and Kabul were fortified, Special Forces–directed close air support killed hundreds of the Taliban and Al Qaeda defenders. On November 13, Fahim Khan led the assault into Kabul, taking it that day.

After these early victories, Afghan forces and the Special Forces moved against Taloqan and Kunduz, two key cities near the northern border that were held by some 5,000 Taliban and Al Qaeda fighters. Tajik Northern Alliance commander Daoud first took Taloqan and then Kunduz, greatly aided by Special Forces–directed close air support. The Taliban put up a stiff fight in Khanabad west of Taloqan, employing both direct-fire heavy weapons and indirect tank fire. Daoud entrenched outside the city, while close air support degraded the defenses by destroying tanks, trucks, and bunkers. Khanabad fell on November 23 after 11 days of fighting; 3,500 Taliban surrendered.

The prisoners taken at Khanabad posed a serious logistical problem, and they were transferred to Dostum's Qali Jangi fortress prison near Mazar-e Sharif, where 600 of them managed to disarm the guard force on November 25. U.S. Special Forces personnel then conducted an operation to retake the prison and free friendly forces. Charlie Company, 1st Battalion, 87th Infantry of the 10th Mountain Division, served as a quick reaction force as well as provided perimeter security and medical assistance. The five-day battle here resulted in the deaths of 500 of the prisoners, along with 1 American officer, Johnny Michael Spann, the first American casualty to hostile fire in the war.

Taking Kandahar was a challenge. The city was far from the northern supply lines, and the population was not a natural ally of the U.S. forces, as had been the case with the Tajiks, Uzbeks, and Hazaras. The Special Forces teams found a key ally in Popalzai tribal leader Hamid Karzai, later the president of Afghanistan. His father had been killed by the Taliban, and Karzai was pro-Western, educated, and a Popalzai Pashtun. Although a recognized and respected political figure, Karzai lacked martial credentials and initially had only 35 fighters loyal to him. Barakzai leader and warlord Gul Agha Sherzai was also critical in helping to organize anti-Taliban forces in Kandahar.

On October 20 prior to the Special Forces–indigenous partnership against the Taliban, 200 U.S. Army rangers from the 3rd Battalion, 75th Regiment, seized a small airfield outside Kandahar. The airfield served as a logistical and refueling hub for the southern Special Forces teams and was held by Marine Expeditionary Unit 15. Another operation was directed against a compound southwest of Kandahar City that was believed to house Mullah Mohammad Omar. These two operations threw the Taliban and Al Qaeda off balance and demonstrated that the U.S.-led coalition could go anywhere.

Two Special Forces teams supported by two command and control elements—a total of 27 men—were sent in to support operations in southern Afghanistan. The first was inserted into Tarin Kot to meet Karzai, who arrived in Afghanistan from Pakistan on October 9 and then spent several weeks assembling a force of anti-Taliban fighters. By the time Karzai and his 150 fighters arrived there, the people of Tarin Kot had already displaced the Taliban. The Taliban sent in reinforcements in mid-November, but U.S. supplies of weapons, ammunition, and food reinforced Karzai's fighters. Close air support, called in by the Special Forces teams, pounded the Taliban convoys. Tarin Kot was declared secure by November 18; this was a critical political and military victory.

Another Special Forces team linked with local Barakzai commander Gul Agha Sherzai, who moved on Kandahar from the south with 800 tribesmen. The Taliban ambushed Sherzai's forces in Takhta Pol, but a Special Forces team on a nearby ridge called in air strikes to break up the Taliban's machine-gun and rocket-propelled grenade fire. Takhta Pol fell on November 24, severing the connection between Kandahar and the key Pakistani border town of Chaman. Several days of air strikes followed. On December 5, however, a mistaken attack on the Special Forces position in Arghandab killed 3 Americans and wounded every member of the team and also wounded 65 Afghan militiamen. Sherzai and his men moved against Kandahar Airfield on December 7 but found it deserted; Mullah Omar and the Taliban leadership had fled Kandahar the day before. As Karzai negotiated the surrender of the Taliban, Sherzai was confirmed as governor of Kandahar on December 8.

One of the toughest Special Forces battles of OEF took place in the Tora Bora region in the rugged eastern mountains south of Jalalabad at elevations of 10,000–12,000 feet during December 2–17. Here Al Qaeda and Taliban fighters had established training camps and fortified cave complexes with concealed bunkers and ammunition and weapons caches. Intelligence also indicated that bin Laden was probably in the area. There were too few U.S. forces in country to launch a conventional assault, and indigenous forces were also lacking relative to previous battles. The initial U.S. partner here was Hazrat Ali, a Pashai militia commander who maintained a force of ethnic Pashai and loyal Northern Alliance soldiers.

U.S. AC-130 Spectre gunships struck the area around the clock as Special Forces teams and Ali's men positioned themselves on Tora Bora's eastern and western ridgelines. The Special Forces teams remained on the ridges while Ali's men battled below. More than a week of air strikes destroyed organized resistance. Several hundred Al Qaeda fighters were captured or killed, but many more escaped to Pakistan, bin Laden among them.

The initial phase of the liberation of Afghanistan ended with the Tora Bora operation. It was militarily remarkable from the standpoint that a small number of U.S. and allied forces (several hundred on the ground) were able to topple the Taliban regime and kill thousands of Taliban and Al Qaeda fighters throughout the country while only incurring a dozen U.S. casualties. The partnership with indigenous forces proved decisive. American bombing, specifically close air support, was crucial. It significantly degraded the Taliban and Al Qaeda forces.

Although Operation ENDURING FREEDOM enjoyed great success initially and is considered one of the most impressive special operations missions in history, it proved indecisive in the long run. The U.S. military was soon forced to shift attention and resources to Iraq with the beginning of the war there, and this allowed the Taliban and Al Qaeda new life and forced a protracted struggle in Afghanistan that is ongoing.

Larissa Mihalisko

**Further Reading**

Biddle, Stephen. *Afghanistan and the Future of Warfare.* Carlisle Barracks, PA: Strategic Studies Institute, U.S. Army War College, 2002.

Boaz, John, ed. *The U.S. Attack on Afghanistan.* Detroit: Thompson/Gale, 2005.

Schroen, Gary. *First In: An Insider's Account of How the CIA Spearheaded the War on Terror in Afghanistan.* New York: Presidio/Ballantine, 2005.

Stewart, Richard W. *Operation Enduring Freedom: The United States Army in Afghanistan, October 2001–March 2002.* Washington, DC: U.S. Army Center of Military History, 2003.

Wright, Donald P. *A Different Kind of War: The United States Army in Operation Enduring Freedom (OEF), October 2001–September 2005.* Fort Leavenworth, KS: Combat Studies Institute Press, U.S. Army, 2010.

# Battle of Baghdad

| Date | April 5–10, 2003 | |
| --- | --- | --- |
| Location | Baghdad, Iraq | |
| Opponents (*winner) | *United States | Iraq |
| Commander | Major General Buford Blount | President Saddam Hussein |
| Approx. # Troops | 30,000 troops | 45,000 troops |
| Importance | Topples the government of Saddam Hussein. | |

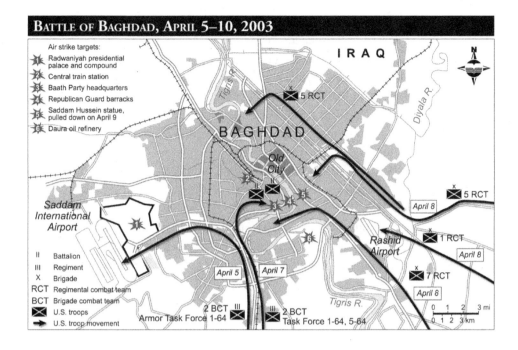

On March 20, 2003, a coalition invasion ground force of 100,000 U.S., British, and Australian troops moved into southern Iraq from Kuwait in what became known as Operation IRAQI FREEDOM. The ultimate U.S. military goal was the capture of the Iraqi capital of Baghdad, a city of 5 million people 300 miles to the north. Before the Iraq War, American planners operated under the assumption that removing Iraqi dictator Saddam Hussein from power would very likely require a ground attack on Baghdad. What everyone from U.S. president George W. Bush on down wanted to avoid, however, was grueling urban warfare that would devastate the city and lead to heavy casualties on all sides, the civilian populace included. To prevent costly urban combat, the U.S. Army developed a plan to isolate Baghdad first, with the 3rd Infantry Division encircling the city from the west and the I Marine Expeditionary Force enveloping it from the east. Once a rough cordon had been established around Baghdad, the Americans intended to employ a combination of air strikes, armored and mechanized infantry raids, special forces incursions, and other small-scale operations to whittle away at the city's defenses and Baath Party control of the government, ideally reducing one or both to the breaking point.

The army never got the opportunity to test its operational concept for taking Baghdad, however, as the plan was scrapped once elements of the 3rd Infantry Division reached the outskirts of Baghdad just a little over two weeks into the campaign. By April 4, 2003, the division had secured two of the three objectives on its half of the cordon west of the Tigris River: Saddam International Airport, codenamed LIONS, and the crucial highway junction just south of the city, referred to as

SAINTS. The third area, TITANS, controlled the roads heading northwest out of Baghdad and remained in Iraqi hands. Meanwhile, the 1st Marine Division, which had a more difficult approach to the capital through the populated center of the country, was involved in fierce fighting with Republican Guard armor, Iraqi militia, and foreign irregulars and had yet to reach either of the two objectives on its side of the Tigris. Rather than wait for the encirclement of Baghdad to be completed, the 3rd Infantry Division commander, Major General Buford Blount, decided to begin probing the city's defenses immediately.

The battles on the approach to Baghdad suggested to Blount that Iraqi resistance was beginning to crumble, while the latest intelligence reports indicated that Baghdad was not the heavily fortified, stoutly defended death trap that some were expecting. In fact, the opposite proved to be true, as Hussein's paranoia had played directly into American hands. His fears of a coup had prevented him from undertaking military preparations of any kind in Baghdad, and he had entrusted defense of the capital to a relatively small cadre of loyal troops—the three brigades of the Special Republican Guard—supported by the irregulars known as Fedayeen Saddam.

Blount launched his first foray into Baghdad on April 5, sending an armored battalion from the 2nd Brigade Combat Team on a thunder run (or reconnaissance in force) from SAINTS into the city center and then out to the airport. The column of 29 Abrams tanks, 14 Bradley fighting vehicles, and assorted other vehicles met with a hail of small-arms fire, rocket-propelled grenades, and mortar fire from the many hundreds of Iraqi fighters who took up positions along its route. A lucky shot from a rocket-propelled grenade disabled one of the American tanks, and it had to be abandoned. Otherwise, the thickly armored Abrams and Bradleys were able to withstand multiple hits, and while the crews were exhausted at the end of the 140-minute-long mission, the vehicles themselves needed only minor repairs before again being ready for action.

The outcome of the April 5 thunder run confirmed Blount's suspicion that Baghdad's defenses were brittle. While the members of the 2nd Brigade Combat Team battalion received a day to catch their breath, Blount employed the 3rd Brigade Combat Team to tighten his grip on the city perimeter. On April 6 the brigade advanced to take control of objective TITANS, an area that included the Highway 1 bridge across the Tigris, a crucial point of entry and exit from the capital. This move triggered an intense battle with Iraqi tanks and infantry seeking to regain control of the crossing. The Iraqi attack began on the evening of April 6 and continued into the next morning before it was finally broken up by a combination of concentrated artillery fire, direct fire, and low-level strafing attacks by Fairchild-Republic A-10 Thunderbolt Warthog ground-support aircraft.

The conclusion of the battle for the Tigris bridge to the northwest coincided with the launching of the second thunder run. Intended to be a limited raid much like the first, the April 7 operation developed into something altogether different, an armored strike into the heart of downtown Baghdad. Colonel Dave Perkins, commander of the 2nd Brigade Combat Team, took all three of his maneuver battalions on the mission. Blount and his superiors up the chain of command expected Perkins to pull back to the city's edge at the end of the thunder run. Instead, Perkins made the daring decision to lead his two armored battalions into the center of Baghdad and remain there. The battalions met with strong resistance on their drive into the city and afterward had to fend off repeated attacks by small bands of Iraqi fighters once they established their defensive perimeters in the downtown area. But it was the trailing infantry battalion, assigned the vital task of protecting the brigade's supply line into Baghdad, that found itself engaged in some of the heaviest and most desperate fighting. The battalion was assailed not only by Republican Guard and Fedayeen Saddam but also by hundreds of Syrian volunteers who had arrived in Iraq only days earlier. Despite some tense moments, the battalion kept the roadway open so that supply vehicles could reach the units parked downtown.

The thunder run of April 7 struck the decisive blow in the Battle of Baghdad. On the same day, the marines breached the Iraqi defenses along the Diyala River and began their advance into eastern Baghdad. Fighting continued on April 8, especially in the downtown area and in the 3rd Brigade Combat Team's sector at TITANS. By April 9, however, resistance within the city had become generally disorganized and sporadic, as increasing numbers of Iraqi fighters put down their weapons and melted into the general populace. The Baathist regime also dissolved, and some governing officials returned home. Others, most notably Hussein and his two sons, Uday and Qusay, slipped out of the capital and sought refuge elsewhere, leaving Baghdad to the U.S. Army and marines. Baghdad was considered secured by April 10. Two days later, the 101st Airborne Division relieved the marines and the 3rd Infantry Division in Baghdad, allowing them to deploy northwest to Hussein's ancestral home of Tikrit.

Casualty figures for the Battle of Baghdad are not terribly reliable, but it is believed that the coalition suffered 34 dead, and at least 250 wounded. Iraqi dead have been given as 2,300 killed, but the actual figure is undoubtedly much higher. There is no estimate of Iraqi wounded.

Jeff Seiken

## Further Reading

Fontenot, Gregory. *On Point: The United States Army in Operation Iraqi Freedom.* Fort Leavenworth, KS: Combat Studies Institute Press, 2004.

Gordon, Michael R., and General Bernard Gordon. *Cobra II: The Inside Story of the Invasion and Occupation of Iraq.* New York: Pantheon Books, 2006.

Zucchino, David. *Thunder Run: The Armored Strike to Capture Baghdad.* New York: Grove, 2004.

## Second Battle of Fallujah

| Date | November 7–December 23, 2004 | |
|---|---|---|
| Location | Fallujah, Iraq | |
| Opponents (*winner) | *United States, United Kingdom, and Iraq | Mujahideen Shura and Al Qaeda in Iraq |
| Commander | U.S. Marine Corps major generals Richard F. Natonski and James Mattis | Abdullah al-Janabi; Omar Hussein Hadid |
| Approx. # Troops | 10,000 U.S. marines and soldiers, 2,000 Iraqi Army personnel, 850 Royal Marines | 3,000 insurgents |
| Importance | Demonstrates great U.S. tactical skill in urban warfare, but the damage in the city plays itself out in ongoing sectarian violence and Iraqi political upheaval. | |

The city of Fallujah is located some 42 miles west of Baghdad in Iraq. Following the decision to halt the coalition assault on Fallujah in Operation VIGILANT RESOLVE (the First Battle of Fallujah) during April–May 2004, the U.S. Marine Corps had withdrawn from the city and turned over security to the so-called Fallujah Brigade, an ad hoc force of local men who had formerly served in the Iraqi Army. The Fallujah Brigade failed dismally in this task, giving the insurgents another chance to claim victory and attract additional recruits. During the summer and autumn months, the Fallujah police turned a blind eye as the insurgents fortified positions inside Fallujah and stockpiled supplies. The Iraqi Interim Government, formed on June 28, 2004, then requested a new effort to capture and secure the city.

In preparation for the ground assault, coalition artillery and aircraft began selective strikes on Fallujah on October 30, 2004. Coalition ground forces (American, Iraqi, and British) cut off electric power to the city on November 5 and distributed leaflets warning residents to stay in their homes and not use their cars. The latter was a response to insurgent suicide bombers who had been detonating cars packed with explosives. On November 7, the Iraqi government announced a 60-day state of emergency throughout most of Iraq. Because of all these warnings, 75–90 percent of Fallujah's civilian population abandoned the city before the coalition ground offensive began. Many fled to Syria.

The Americans initially labeled the assault Operation PHANTOM FURY. Iraqi prime minister Ayad Allawi, however, renamed it AL-FAJR (NEW DAWN). The operation's main objective was to bolster Iraqi government prestige by demonstrating the government's ability to control its own territory. The American military focused on the important secondary objective of killing as many insurgents as possible while keeping coalition casualties low. Approximately 10,000 American soldiers and marines and 2,000 Iraqi troops participated, along with some Royal Marines troops. American forces involved had considerable experience in urban combat.

The assault plan called for a concentration of forces north of Fallujah. Spearheaded by heavy armor, army and marine units would attack due south along precisely defined sectors. The infantry would methodically clear buildings, leaving the trailing Iraqi forces to search for insurgents and assault the city's 200 mosques, which coalition tacticians suspected would be used as defensive insurgent strong points. Intelligence estimates suggested that some 3,000 insurgents defended the city, one-fifth of whom were foreign jihadists. Intelligence estimates also predicted fanatical resistance.

Ground operations associated with the Second Battle of Fallujah commenced on November 7, 2004, when an Iraqi commando unit and the U.S. Marine Corps 3rd Light Armored Reconnaissance Battalion conducted a preliminary

U.S. Marine Corps artillery outside of Fallujah, Iraq, firing against an insurgent position on November 11, 2004, during the Second Battle of Fallujah (November 7–December 23, 2004). (Department of Defense)

assault. The objective was to secure the Fallujah General Hospital west of the city and capture two bridges over the Euphrates River, thereby isolating the insurgent forces inside the city. This preliminary assault was successful, allowing the main assault to commence after dark the following evening. The American military chose this time because its various night-vision devices would provide a tactical advantage over the insurgents. Four marine infantry and two army mechanized battalions attacked in the first wave. M-1A2 Abrams tanks and M-2A3 Bradley infantry fighting vehicles provided mobile firepower for which the insurgents had no answer, enabling the American soldiers to drive deep into Fallujah. Iraqi forces also performed surprisingly well. After four days of operations, coalition forces had secured about half the city.

By November 11, the methodical American advance had driven most of the insurgents into the southern part of Fallujah. Three days of intense street fighting ensued, during which the Americans reached the southern limits of the city. On

November 15 the Americans reversed direction and attacked north to eliminate any insurgents who had been missed in the first pass and to search more thoroughly for insurgent weapons and supplies. For this part of the operation, the ground forces were broken into squad-sized elements to conduct their searches. By November 16, American commanders judged Fallujah secured, although the operation would not end officially until December 23, by which time many residents had been allowed to return to their homes.

U.S. casualties in the battle were 95 killed and 560 wounded; Iraqi Army losses were 11 killed and 43 wounded. Insurgent losses were estimated at between 1,200 and 2,000 killed with another 1,000 to 1,500 captured. The disparity in the casualties indicated the extent of the coalition's tactical advantage. Indeed, postbattle army and marine assessments lauded the tremendous tactical skill in urban warfare displayed by American forces. However, the intense house-to-house fighting had caused the destruction of an estimated 20 percent of the city's buildings, while another 60 percent of the city's structures were damaged. The tremendous damage, including that to 60 mosques, enraged Iraq's Sunni minority. Widespread civilian demonstrations and increased insurgent attacks followed. Although the 2005 Iraqi elections were held on schedule, Sunni participation was very low, partially because of the Sunnis' sense of grievance over the destruction in Fallujah.

James Arnold

**Further Reading**

Ballard, John R. *Fighting for Fallujah: A New Dawn for Iraq.* Westport, CT: Praeger Security International, 2006.

Bellavia, David. *House to House: An Epic Memoir of War.* New York: Free Press, 2007.

Gott, Kendall D., ed. *Eyewitness to War: The U.S. Army in Operation Al Fajr; An Oral History.* 2 vols. Fort Leavenworth, KS: Combat Studies Institute Press, 2006.

# Bibliography

Aitchison, Robert. *A British Eyewitness at the Battle of New Orleans: The Memoir of Royal Navy Admiral Robert Aitchison, 1808–1827*. Edited by Gene A. Smith. New Orleans: Historic New Orleans Collection, 2004.

Alexander, Joseph H. *Utmost Savagery: The Three Days of Tarawa*. Annapolis, MD: Naval Institute Press, 1995.

Allen, Gardner W. *A Naval History of the American Revolution,* Vol. 1. Cambridge, MA: Houghton Mifflin, 1913.

Allen, Thomas B. *Tories: Fighting for the King in America's First Civil War.* New York: HarperCollins, 2010.

Alsop, J. D. "The Age of the Projectors: British Imperial Strategy in the North Atlantic in the War of the Spanish Succession." *Acadiensis* 21(1) (1991): 30–53.

Anderson, Fred. *Crucible of War: The Seven Years' War and the Fate of the Empire in British North America, 1754–1766*. New York: Knopf, 2000.

Antal, Sandor. *A Wampum Denied: Procter's War of 1812*. Ottawa: Carleton University Press, 1997.

Appleman, Roy E. *South to the Nakong, North to the Yalu*. Washington, DC: Office of the Chief of Military History, 1961.

Arnold, James R. *Grant Wins the War: Decision at Vicksburg*. New York: Wiley, 1997.

Atkinson, Rick. *An Army at Dawn: The War in North Africa, 1942–1943*. New York: Henry Holt, 2002.

Axtell, James. *After Columbus: Essays in the Ethnohistory of Colonial North America*. New York: Oxford University Press, 1988.

Azoy, A. C. M. *Charge! The Story of the Battle of San Juan Hill*. New York: Longmans, 1961.

Babits, Lawrence E. *A Devil of a Whipping: The Battle of Cowpens*. Chapel Hill: University of North Carolina Press, 1998.

Babits, Lawrence E., and Joshua B. Howard. *Long, Obstinate, and Bloody: The Battle of Guilford Courthouse*. Chapel Hill: University of North Carolina Press, 2009.

Ballard, John R. *Fighting for Fallujah: A New Dawn for Iraq*. Westport, CT: Praeger Security International, 2006.

Ballard, Michael B. *Pemberton: A Biography*. Jackson: University Press of Mississippi, 1991.

Bannon, John Francis. *The Spanish Borderlands Frontier, 1513–1821*. Albuquerque: University of New Mexico Press, 1974.

Barbuto, Richard V. *Niagara, 1814: America Invades Canada.* Lawrence: University Press of Kansas, 2000.

Bauer, K. Jack. *The Mexican War, 1846–1848.* New York: Macmillan, 1974.

Bauer, K. Jack. *Surfboats and Horse Marines: U.S. Naval Operations in the Mexican War, 1846–48.* Annapolis, MD: U.S. Naval Institute, 1969.

Bearss, Edwin C. *The Vicksburg Campaign.* 3 vols. Dayton, OH: Morningside, 1995.

Beatie, Russel H. *Army of the Potomac: Birth of Command, November 1860–September 1861.* New York: Da Capo, 2002.

Bell, William G. "Winning the West: The Army in the Indian Wars, 1865–1890." In *American Military History,* edited by Maurice Matloff, 300–318. Washington, DC: Office of the Chief of Military History, 1973.

Bellavia, David. *House to House: An Epic Memoir of War.* New York: Free Press, 2007.

Bender, Mark L. "The Failure of General William Hull at Detroit in 1812 and Its Effects on the State of Ohio." Unpublished master's thesis, Kent State University, 1971.

Beninato, Stephanie. "Popé, Pose-yema, and Naranjo: A New Look at the Leadership in the Pueblo Revolt of 1680." *New Mexico Historical Review* 65 (October 1990): 417–435.

Biddle, Stephen. *Afghanistan and the Future of Warfare.* Carlisle Barracks, PA: Strategic Studies Institute, U.S. Army War College, 2002.

Black, Jeremy. *War for America: The Fight for Independence, 1775–1783.* Stroud, Gloucestershire, UK: Alan Sutton, 1991.

Blair, Clay. *The Forgotten War: America in Korea, 1950–1953.* New York: Times Books, 1987.

Blair, Clay. *Ridgway's Paratroopers: The American Airborne in World War II.* Garden City, NY: Dial, 1985.

Blair, Clay. *Silent Victory: The U.S. Submarine War against Japan.* Philadelphia: Lippincott, 1975.

Blumenson, Martin. *Breakout and Pursuit.* Washington, DC: Center of Military History, 1961.

Boaz, John, ed. *The U.S. Attack on Afghanistan.* Detroit: Thompson/Gale, 2005.

Bodge, George Madison. *Soldiers in King Philip's War.* Baltimore: Genealogical Publishing, 1967.

Bonk, David. *St. Mihiel 1918: The American Expeditionary Forces' Trial by Fire.* London: Osprey, 2011.

Bowden, Henry Warner. "Spanish Missions, Cultural Conflict, and the Pueblo Revolt of 1680." *Church History* 44 (June 1975): 217–228.

Bowden, Mark. *Black Hawk Down: A Story of Modern War.* New York: Atlantic Monthly Press, 1999.

Boyne, Walter J. *Operation Iraqi Freedom: What Went Right, What Went Wrong and Why.* New York: Forge Books, 2003.

Braim, Paul F. *The Test of Battle: The American Expeditionary Forces in the Meuse-Argonne Campaign.* Shippensburg, PA: White Mane, 1998.

Breuer, William B. *Operation Torch: The Allied Gamble to Invade North Africa.* New York: St. Martin's, 1985.

Brooks, Victor. *The Boston Campaign.* Conshohocken, PA: Combined Publishing, 1999.

Brown, Dee. *Bury My Heart at Wounded Knee.* New York: Holt, Rinehart and Winston, 1970.

Buchanan, John. *The Road to Guilford Court House: The American Revolution in the Carolinas.* New York: Wiley, 1997.

Burstein, Andrew. *The Passions of Andrew Jackson.* New York: Knopf, 2003.

Burton, Brian. *Extraordinary Circumstances: The Seven Days Battles.* Bloomington: Indiana University Press, 2001.

Carafano, James J. *After D-Day: Operation Cobra and the Normandy Breakout.* Boulder, CO: Lynne Rienner, 2000.

Carter-Edwards, Dennis. "The War of 1812 along the Detroit Frontier: A Canadian Perspective." *Michigan Historical Review* 13(2) (Fall 1987): 25–49.

Castel, Albert. *Decision in the West: The Atlanta Campaign of 1864.* Lawrence: University Press of Kansas, 1992.

Cave, Alfred. *The Pequot War.* Amherst: University of Massachusetts Press, 1996.

Cave, Alfred. "The Shawnee Prophet, Tecumseh, and Tippecanoe." *Journal of the Early Republic* 22(4) (Winter 2002): 637–673.

Champlain, Samuel de. *The Works of Samuel de Champlain,* Vol. 6, *1629–1632.* Toronto: Champlain Society, 1936.

Chapelle, Howard I. *The History of the American Sailing Navy: The Ships and Their Development.* New York: Norton, 1949.

Chet, Guy. *Conquering the American Wilderness: The Triumph of European Warfare in Colonial Northeast.* Amherst: University of Massachusetts Press, 2003.

Chidsey, Donald Barr. *The Siege of Boston.* Boston: Crown, 1966.

Clarke, Walter S., and Jeffrey Ira Herbst. *Learning from Somalia: The Lessons of Armed Humanitarian Intervention.* Boulder, CO: Westview, 1997.

Clary, David A. *Eagles and Empire: The United States, Mexico, and the Struggle for a Continent.* New York: Bantam, 2009.

Clodfelter, Mark. *The Limits of Air Power: The American Bombing of North Vietnam.* New York: Free Press, 1989.

Coburn, Frank Warren. *The Battle of April 19, 1775: In Lexington, Concord, Lincoln, Arlington, Cambridge, Somerville, and Charlestown, Massachusetts.* Lexington, MA: Lexington Historical Society, 1922.

Coddington, Edwin B. *The Gettysburg Campaign: A Study in Command.* New York: Scribner, 1984.

Coffey, Thomas M. *Iron Eagle: The Turbulent Life of General Curtis LeMay.* New York: Crown, 1986.

Coffman, Edward M. *The War to End All Wars: The American Military Experience in World War I.* 1968; reprint, Lexington: University Press of Kentucky, 1998.

Cohen, Felix S. *Handbook of Federal Indian Law.* Washington, DC: U.S. Department of the Interior, Office of the Solicitor, 1945.

Cole, Hugh M. *The United States Army in World War II: The European Theater of Operations; The Ardennes: Battle of the Bulge.* Washington, DC: U.S. Government Printing Office, 1965.

Coleman, J. D. *Pleiku: The Dawn of Helicopter Warfare in Vietnam.* New York: St. Martin's, 1988.

Connell, Evan S. *Son of the Morning Star: Custer and the Little Bighorn.* New York: North Point, 1984.

Conroy, Robert. *The Battle of Manila Bay: The Spanish-American War in the Philippines.* New York: Macmillan, 1968.

Corkran, David H. *The Carolina Indian Frontier.* Columbia: University of South Carolina Press, 1970.

Cozzens, Peter. *Shenandoah 1862: Stonewall Jackson's Valley Campaign.* Chapel Hill: University of North Carolina Press, 2008.

Cummings, Edward B. "E Pluribus Unum: The American Battle Line at New Orleans, 8 January 1815." *On Point: Journal of Army History* 14(3) (December 2008): 6–12.

Cutler, Thomas J. *The Battle of Leyte Gulf, 23–26 October 1944.* New York: HarperCollins, 1994.

Dameron, J. David. *Kings Mountain: The Defeat of the Loyalists, October 7, 1780.* Cambridge, MA: Da Capo, 2003.

Dana, Elizabeth Ellery. *The British in Boston: Being the Diary of Lieutenant John Barker of the King's Own Regiment from November 15, 1774 to May 31, 1776.* Cambridge, MA: Harvard University Press, 1924.

Daniel, Larry J. *Shiloh: The Battle That Changed the Civil War.* New York: Simon and Schuster, 1997.

Daniels, James B. "The Battle of Chippewa." *American History* 42(4) (October 2007): 46–53.

Davidson, Philip B. *Vietnam at War: The History, 1946–1975.* New York: Oxford University Press, 1988.

Davis, Burke. *The Campaign That Won America: The Story of Yorktown.* New York: Dial, 1970.

Davis, Burke. *The Cowpens–Guilford Courthouse Campaign.* Philadelphia: University of Pennsylvania Press, 2002.

DeKay, James Tertius. *Monitor.* New York: Walker, 1997.

D'Este, Carlo. *Bitter Victory: The Battle for Sicily, 1943.* New York: E. P. Dutton, 1988.

Detzer, David R. *Allegiance: Fort Sumter, Charleston and the Beginning of the Civil War.* New York: Harcourt, 2001.

Detzer, David. *Donnybrook: The Battle of Bull Run, 1861.* New York: Harcourt Books, 2004.

Dewey, George. *The Autobiography of George Dewey.* 1913; reprint, Annapolis, MD: Naval Institute Press, 1987.

Donaldson, Gordon. *Battle for a Continent: Quebec 1759.* Garden City, NY: Doubleday, 1973.

Dull, Paul S. *A Battle History of the Imperial Japanese Navy, 1941–1945.* Annapolis, MD: Naval Institute Press, 1978.

Duncan, David Ewing. *Hernando de Soto: A Savage Quest in the Americas.* New York: Crown, 1995.

Dunnigan, Brian L. "'The Prettiest Settlement in America': A Select Bibliography of Early Detroit through the War of 1812." *Michigan History* 27(1) (March 2001): 1–20.

Dupuy, Trevor N. *Hitler's Last Gamble: The Battle of the Bulge, December 1944–January 1945.* New York: HarperCollins, 1944.

Eccles, W. J. "The Battle of Quebec: A Reappraisal." *French Colonial Historical Society Proceedings* 3 (1978): 70–81.

Eccles, William J. *The Canadian Frontier, 1534–1760.* Albuquerque: University of New Mexico Press, 1984.

Eccles, William J. *The Ordeal of New France.* Toronto: Hunter Rose, 1979.

Eisenhower, John S. D. *The Bitter Woods.* New York: Putnam, 1969.

Eisenhower, John S. D. *So Far from God: The U.S. War with Mexico, 1846–1848.* New York: Random House, 1989.

Ent, Uzal W. *Fighting on the Brink: Defense of the Pusan Perimeter.* Paducah, KY: Turner Publishing, 1996.

Eschmann, Karl J. *Linebacker: The Untold Story of the Air Raids over North Vietnam.* New York: Ivy Books, 1989.

Essame, Hubert. *The Battle for Europe, 1918.* London: Batsford, 1972.

Everest, Allan S. *The War of 1812 in the Champlain Valley.* Syracuse, NY: Syracuse University Press, 1981.

Faragher, John M. *A Great and Noble Scheme: The Tragic Story of the Expulsion of the French Acadians from Their American Homeland.* New York: Norton, 2005.

Field, James A., Jr. *History of United States Naval Operations: Korea.* Washington, DC: Naval History Division, 1962.

Field, James A., Jr. *The Japanese at Leyte Gulf: The Shō Operation.* Princeton, NJ: Princeton University Press, 1947.

Fischer, David Hackett. *Washington's Crossing.* New York: Oxford University Press, 2004.

Fitz-Enz, David G. *Plattsburg, the Final Invasion: The Decisive Battle of the War of 1812.* New York: Cooper Square, 2001.

Fontenot, Gregory. *On Point: The United States Army in Operation Iraqi Freedom.* Fort Leavenworth, KS: Combat Studies Institute Press, 2004.

Forty, George. *The Reich's Last Gamble: The Ardennes Offensive, December 1944.* London: Cassell, 2000.

Frank, Richard B. *Downfall: The End of the Japanese Empire.* New York: Random House, 1999.

Frank, Richard B. *Guadalcanal: The Definitive Account of the Landmark Battle.* New York: Random House, 1990.

Frégault, Guy. *Canada: The War of the Conquest.* Translated by Margaret M. Cameron. London: Oxford University Press, 1969.

French, Allen. *The Siege of Boston.* Spartanburg, SC: Reprint Co., 1969.

Fuchida, Mitsuo, and Masatake Okumiya. *Midway, the Battle That Doomed Japan: The Japanese Navy's Story.* Annapolis, MD: Naval Institute Press, 1955.

Furguson, Ernest B. *Chancellorsville, 1863: The Souls of the Brave.* New York: Knopf, 1992.

Gabriel, Michael P. *Major General Richard Montgomery: The Making of an American Hero.* Madison, NJ: Fairleigh Dickinson University Press, 2002.

Gallagher, Gary W., ed. *Antietam: Essays on the 1862 Maryland Campaign.* Chapel Hill: University of North Carolina Press, 1999.

Gallagher, Gary W., ed. *The Shenandoah Valley Campaign of 1862.* Chapel Hill: University of North Carolina Press, 2003.

Gallagher, Gary W., Stephen D. Engle, Robert K. Krick, and Joseph T. Glatthaar. *The American Civil War: This Mighty Scourge of War.* Oxford, UK: Osprey, 2003.

Gilpin, Alec R. *The War of 1812 in the Old Northwest.* East Lansing: Michigan State University Press, 1958.

Gordon, Michael R., and General Bernard Gordon. *Cobra II: The Inside Story of the Invasion and Occupation of Iraq.* New York: Pantheon Books, 2006.

Gordon, Michael R., and Bernard E. Trainor. *The General's War: The Inside Story of the Conflict in the Gulf.* New York: Little, Brown, 1995.

Gott, Kendall D., ed. *Eyewitness to War: The U.S. Army in Operation Al Fajr; An Oral History.* 2 vols. Fort Leavenworth, KS: Combat Studies Institute Press, 2006.

Gow, Ian. *Okinawa, 1945: Gateway to Japan.* Garden City, NY: Doubleday, 1985.

Graham, Gerald S., ed. *The Walker Expedition to Quebec, 1711.* Toronto: Champlain Society, 1953.

Graham, Michael B. *Mantle of Heroism: Tarawa and the Struggle for the Gilberts, November, 1943.* Novato, CA: Presidio, 1993.

Granados, Luis Fernando. *Sueñan las piedras: Alzamiento ocurrido en la ciudad de México, 14, 15, y 16 de septiembre de 1847* [Dream of Stones: The Mexico City Uprising, 14, 15, and 16 September 1847]. Mexico City: Ediciones Era, 2003.

Graves, Donald E. *Red Coats & Grey Jackets: The Battle of Chippawa, 5 July 1814.* Toronto: Dundurn, 1994.

Greene, A. Wilson. *The Final Battles of the Petersburg Campaign: Breaking the Backbone of the Rebellion.* Knoxville: University of Tennessee Press, 2008.

Gregg, Charles T. *Tarawa.* New York: Stein and Day, 1984.

Grimsley, Mark. *And Keep Moving On: The Virginia Campaign, May–June 1864.* Lincoln: University of Nebraska Press, 2005.

Guthman, William H. *March to Massacre: A History of the First Seven Years of the United States Army, 1784–1791.* New York: McGraw-Hill, 1970.

Haan, Richard L. "'The Trade Does Not Flourish as Formerly': The Ecological Origins of the Yamassee War of 1715." *Ethnohistory* 28 (1982): 341–358.

Haley, James L. *The Buffalo War: The History of the Red River Indian Uprising of 1874.* Norman: University of Oklahoma Press, 1985.

Hallas, James H. *Squandered Victory: The American First Army at St. Mihiel.* Westport, CT: Praeger, 1995.

Hallion, Richard P. *Storm over Iraq: Air Power and the Gulf War.* Washington, DC: Smithsonian Institution Press, 1992.

Hamburger, Kenneth E. *Leadership in the Crucible: The Korean War Battles of Twin Tunnels & Chipyong-ni.* College Station: Texas A&M University Press, 2003.

Hammel, Eric. *Guadalcanal, Decision at Sea: The Naval Battle of Guadalcanal, November 13–15, 1942.* Pacifica, CA: Pacifica Press, 1988.

Hansen, Todd, ed. *The Alamo Reader: A Study in History.* Mechanicsburg, PA: Stackpole, 2003.

Hardin, Stephen L. *Texian Iliad: A Military History of the Texas Revolution.* Austin: University of Texas Press, 1994.

Harrison, Lowell H. *George Rogers Clark and the War in the West.* Lexington: University of Kentucky Press, 2001.

Hartcup, Guy. *Code Name Mulberry: The Planning, Building and Operation of the Normandy Harbours.* London: David and Charles, 1977.

Hata Ikuhiko, Sase Morimasa, and Tuneishi Keiichi, eds. *Sekai Senso Hanzai Jiten* [Encyclopedia of Crimes in Modern History]. Tokyo: Bungei-Shunju, 2002.

Heidler, David S., and Jeanne T. Heidler. *Old Hickory's War: Andrew Jackson and the Quest for Empire.* Mechanicsburg, PA: Stackpole, 1996.

Heil, Robert Debs, Jr. *Victory at High Tide: The Inchon-Seoul Campaign.* Baltimore: Nautical and Aviation Publishing Company of America, 1979.

Hesketh, Roger. *Fortitude: The D-Day Deception Campaign.* New York: Overlook, 2000.

Hess, Earl J. *Pickett's Charge: The Last Attack at Gettysburg.* Chapel Hill: University of North Carolina Press, 2001.

Hess, Earl J. *Trench Warfare under Grant and Lee: Field Fortifications in the Overland Campaign.* Chapel Hill: University of North Carolina Press, 2007.

Hirsch, Adam J. "The Collision of Military Cultures in Seventeenth-Century New England." *Journal of American History* 74 (1988): 1187–1212.

Holmes, Richard. *The Western Front.* New York: TV Books, 2000.

Holzer, Harold, and Tim Mulligan. *The Battle of Hampton Roads: New Perspectives on the USS* Monitor *and CSS* Virginia. New York: Fordham University Press, 2006.

Horn, John. *The Petersburg Campaign, June 1864–April 1865.* Conshohocken, PA: Combined Books, 1993.

Horn, Stanley F. *The Decisive Battle of Nashville.* Baton Rouge: Louisiana State University Press, 1984.

Howe, George F. *The United States Army in World War II: Northwest Africa; Seizing the Initiative in the West.* Washington, DC: U.S. Government Printing Office, 1957.

Hoyt, Edwin P. *Blue Skies and Blood: The Battle of the Coral Sea.* New York: S. Eriksson, 1975.

Hoyt, Edwin P. *The Pusan Perimeter.* New York: Stein and Day, 1984.

Hudson, Charles. *Knights of Spain, Warriors of the Sun: Hernando de Soto and the South's Ancient Chiefdoms.* Athens: University of Georgia Press, 1997.

Inoguchi Rikihei and Nakajima Tadashi, with Roger Pineau. *The Divine Wind: Japan's Kamikaze Force in World War II.* New York: Bantam, 1978.

Ivers, Larry E. *British Drums on the Southern Frontier: The Military Colonization of Georgia, 1733–1749.* Chapel Hill: University of North Carolina Press, 1974.

James, D. Clayton. *The Years of MacArthur,* Vol. 2, *1941–1945.* Boston: Houghton Mifflin, 1975.

Jennings, Francis. *Empire of Fortune: Crowns, Colonies, and Tribes in the Seven Years' War in America.* New York: Norton, 1990.

Johnson, David L. "The Yamasee War." Master's thesis, University of South Carolina, 1980.

Johnson, Timothy D. *A Gallant Little Army: The Mexico City Campaign.* Lawrence: University Press of Kansas, 2007.

Johnston, Joseph E. *Narrative of Military Operations, Directed, during the Late War between the States.* New York: D. Appleton, 1874.

Johoji Asami. *Nihon Boku Shi* [History of Japanese Air Defense]. Tokyo: Hara Shobo, 1981.

Jortner, Adam J. *The Gods of Prophetstown: The Battle of Tippecanoe and the Holy War for the American Frontier.* New York: Oxford University Press, 2011.

Josephy, Alvin M. *500 Nations: An Illustrated History of North American Indians.* New York: Knopf, 1994.

Kanon, Tom. "'A Slow, Laborious Slaughter': The Battle of Horsehoe Bend." *Tennessee Historical Quarterly* 58(1) (March 1999): 2–15.

Karr, Ronald Dale. "'Why Should You Be So Furious?': The Violence of the Pequot War." *Journal of American History* 85 (1998): 876–909.

Keegan, John. *Six Armies in Normandy: From D-Day to the Liberation of Paris, June 6th–August 25th, 1944.* New York: Viking, 1982.

Kernan, Alvin. *The Unknown Battle of Midway.* New Haven, CT: Yale University Press, 2005.

Kerr, E. Bartlett. *Flames over Tokyo: The U.S. Army Air Forces' Incendiary Campaign against Japan, 1944–1945.* New York: Donald I. Fine, 1991.

Ketchum, Richard M. *Decisive Day: The Battle for Bunker Hill.* Garden City, NY: Doubleday, 1974.

Ketchum, Richard M. *Saratoga: Turning Point of America's Revolutionary War.* New York: Henry Holt, 1997.

Ketchum, Richard M. *The Winter Soldiers: The Battles for Trenton and Princeton.* New York: Anchor Books, 1975.

Key, William. *The Battle of Atlanta and the Georgia Campaign.* Atlanta: Peachtree Publishers, 1981.

Knaut, Andrew L. *The Pueblo Revolt of 1680: Conquest and Resistance in Seventeenth-Century New Mexico.* Norman: University of Oklahoma Press, 1995.

Knight, James R. *The Battle of Franklin: When the Devil Had Full Possession of the Earth.* Charleston, SC: History Press, 2009.

Konstam, Angus. *San Juan Hill, 1898: America's Emergence as a World Power.* Westport, CT: Praeger, 2004.

Krick, Robert K. *Conquering the Valley: Stonewall Jackson at Port Republic.* New York: William Morrow, 1996.

Lanctot, Gustave. *Canada and the American Revolution, 1774–1783.* Translated by Margaret M. Cameron. Cambridge, MA: Harvard University Press, 1967.

La Pierre, Laurer L. *1759: The Battle for Canada.* Toronto: McClelland and Stewart, 1990.

Larrabee, Harold A. *Decision at the Chesapeake.* London: William Kimber, 1965.

Latimer, Jon. *Niagara, 1814: Final Invasion.* Oxford, UK: Osprey, 2010.

Lavender, David. *Climax at Buena Vista: The American Campaigns in Northeastern Mexico, 1846–47.* Philadelphia: Lippincott, 1966.

Leach, Douglas Edward. *Arms for Empire: A Military History of the British Colonies in North America.* New York: Macmillan, 1973.

Leach, Douglas Edward. *Flintlock and Tomahawk: New England in King Philip's War.* East Orleans, MA: Parnassus Imprints, 1992.

Leach, Douglas Edward. *Roots of Conflict: British Armed Forces and Colonial Americans, 1677–1763.* Chapel Hill: University of North Carolina Press, 1986.

Leckie, Robert. *Okinawa: The Last Battle of World War II.* New York: Viking, 1995.

Leduc, Gilbert F. *Washington and "the Murder of Jumonville."* Boston: Société Historique Franco-Americaine, 1943.

Lewis, Adrian R. *Omaha Beach: A Flawed Victory.* Chapel Hill: University of North Carolina Press, 2001.

Lister, Jeremy. *Concord Fight.* Cambridge, MA: Harvard University Press, 1931.

Lloyd, Christopher. *The Capture of Quebec.* New York: Macmillan, 1959.

Lord, Walter. *The Dawn's Early Light.* New York: Norton, 1972.

Lumpkin, Henry. *From Savannah to Yorktown: The American Revolution in the South.* Columbia: University of South Carolina Press, 1981.

Lundstrom, John. *The First Team: Pacific Naval Air Combat from Pearl Harbor to Midway.* Annapolis, MD: Naval Institute Press, 1990.

Lunt, James. *John Burgoyne of Saratoga.* New York: Harcourt, Brace, Jovanovich, 1975.

Lyon, Eugene. *The Enterprise of Florida: Pedro Menéndez de Avilés and the Spanish Conquest of 1565–1568.* Gainesville: University Press of Florida, 1976.

Lytle, Richard. *The Soldiers of America's First Army: 1791.* Lanham, MD: Scarecrow, 2004.

MacDonald, Charles B. *A Time for Trumpets: The Untold Story of the Battle of the Bulge.* New York: William Morrow, 1985.

Macgregor, Douglas. *Warrior's Rage: The Great Tank Battle of 73 Easting.* Annapolis, MD: Naval Institute Press, 2012.

Maddox, Robert James. *Weapons for Victory: The Hiroshima Decision Fifty Years Later.* Columbia: University of Missouri Press, 1995.

Mallonée, Richard. *Battle for Bataan: An Eyewitness Account.* New York: I Books, 2003.

Malone, Patrick M. *The Skulking Way of War: Technology and Tactics among the New England Indians.* Baltimore: Johns Hopkins University Press, 1993.

Marquis, Christopher G. "Reckoning at Horseshoe Bend." *Military Heritage* 12(1) (August 2010): 42–49.

Marshall, George C. *Memoirs of My Services in the World War, 1917–1918.* Boston: Houghton Mifflin, 1976.

Masterman, J. C. *The Double-Cross System in the War of 1939–1945.* New Haven, CT: Yale University Press, 1972.

Matovina, Timothy M. *The Alamo Remembered: Tejano Accounts and Perspectives.* Austin: University of Texas Press, 1995.

Mattes, Merrill J. *Fort Laramie Park History, 1834–1977.* Washington, DC: U.S. Department of the Interior, 1980.

Mauer, Mauer. *The U.S. Air Service in World War I,* Vol. 3, *The Battle of St. Mihiel.* Washington, DC: Office of Air Force History, 1979.

McHenry, Herbert L. *As a Private Saw It: My Memories of the First Division, World War I.* Indiana, PA: A. G. Halldin, 1988.

McPherson, James. *Battle Cry of Freedom: The Civil War Era.* New York: Oxford University Press, 1988.

McPherson, James M. *Crossroads of Freedom: Antietam.* New York: Oxford University Press, 2002.

McPhillips, Martin. *The Battle of Trenton.* Parsippany, NJ: Silver Burdett, 1984.

Michel, Marshall L., III. *The Eleven Days of Christmas: America's Last Vietnam Battle.* San Francisco: Encounter Books, 2002.

Middlebrook, Martin. *The Schweinfurt-Regensburg Mission.* New York: Scribner, 1983.

Military History Institute of Vietnam. *Tap Chi Lich Su Quan Su: So Dac Biet 20 Nam Tet Mau Than* [Military History Magazine: 20th Anniversary of the 1968 Tet Offensive Special Issue], Issue 2, 1988.

Military History Institute of Vietnam. *Victory in Vietnam: The Official History of the People's Army of Vietnam, 1954–1975.* Translated by Merle L. Pribbenow. Lawrence: University Press of Kansas, 2002.

Miller, David H. *Custer's Fall: The Native American Side of the Story.* Norman: University of Nebraska Press, 1985.

Millet, Bernard. *The Battle of the Coral Sea.* Annapolis, MD: Naval Institute Press, 1974.

Millett, Allan R. "Caesar and the Conquest of the Northwest Territory: The Wayne Campaign, 1792–95." *Timeline: A Publication of the Ohio Historical Society* 14 (1997): 2–21.

Millot, Bernard. *Divine Thunder: The Life and Death of the Kamikazes.* Translated by Lowell Blair. New York: McCall, 1970.

Montross, Lynn, and Nicholas Canzona. *U.S. Marine Corps Operations in Korea,* Vol. 2, *The Inchon-Seoul Operation.* Washington, DC: United States Marine Corps Historical Branch, 1955.

Moore, Harold G., and Joseph L. Galloway. *We Were Soldiers Once . . . and Young.* New York: Random House, 1992.

Moore, Stephen L. *Eighteen Minutes: The Battle of San Jacinto and the Texas Independence Campaign.* Plano: Republic of Texas Press, 2004.

Moorehead, Alan. *The March to Tunis: The North African War, 1940–1943.* New York: Harper and Row, 1967.

Morison, Samuel Eliot. *History of United States Naval Operations in World War II,* Vol. 1, *The Rising Sun in the Pacific, 1931–April 1942.* Boston: Little, Brown, 1948.

Morison, Samuel Eliot. *History of United States Naval Operation in World War II,* Vol. 4, *Coral Sea, Midway and Submarine Actions, May 1942–August 1942.* Boston: Little, Brown, 1949.

Morison, Samuel Eliot. *History of United States Naval Operations in World War II,* Vol. 8, *New Guinea and the Marianas, March 1944–August 1944.* Boston: Little, Brown, 1953.

Morison, Samuel Eliot. *History of United States Naval Operations in World War II,* Vol. 9, *Sicily-Salerno-Anzio, January 1943–June 1944.* Boston: Little, Brown, 1954.

Morison, Samuel Eliot. *History of United States Naval Operations in World War II,* Vol. 12, *Leyte.* Boston: Little, Brown, 1975.

Morrissey, Brendan. *Quebec 1775: The American Invasion of Canada.* Translated by Adam Hook. Oxford, UK: Osprey, 2003.

Morrissey, Brendan. *Yorktown, 1781: The World Turned Upside Down.* London: Osprey, 1997.

Morton, Louis. *United States Army in World War II: The War in the Pacific; Fall of the Philippines.* Washington, DC: Office of the Chief of Military History, United States Army, U.S. Government Printing Office, 1953.

Munroe, Clark C. *The Second United States Infantry Division in Korea, 1950–1951.* Tokyo: Toppan Printing, n.d. [1952].

Murfin, James V. *The Gleam of Bayonets: The Battle of Antietam and Robert E. Lee's Maryland Campaign, September 1862.* Baton Rouge: Louisiana State University Press, 2004.

Neillands, Robin. *The Bomber War: The Allied Air Offensive against Nazi Germany.* New York: Overlook, 2001.

Nelson, James L. *Benedict Arnold's Navy: The Ragtag Fleet That Lost the Battle of Lake Champlain but Won the American Revolution.* New York: McGraw-Hill, 2006.

Nester, William R. *The Great Frontier War: Britain, France, and the Imperial Struggle for North America, 1607–1755.* Westport, CT: Praeger, 2000.

Nichols, Edward J. *Zach Taylor's Little Army.* Garden City, NY: Doubleday, 1963.

Nolan, Keith William. *Into Cambodia: Spring Campaign, Summer Offensive, 1970.* Novato, CA: Presidio, 1990.

Oatis, Steven J. *A Colonial Complex: South Carolina's Frontiers in the Era of the Yamasee War, 1680–1730.* Lincoln: University of Nebraska Press, 2004.

Oberdorfer, Don. *Tet!* New York: Doubleday, 1971.

Orr, Charles. *History of the Pequot War: The Contemporary Accounts of Mason, Underhill, Vincent and Gardener.* Cleveland, OH: Helman-Taylor, 1897.

Palmer, Dave R. *1794: America, Its Army, and the Birth of the Nation.* Novato, CA: Presidio, 1994.

Palmer, Frederick. *Clark of the Ohio: A Life of George Rogers Clark.* Whitefish, MT: Kessinger, 2004.

Palmer, Michael A. "A Failure of Command, Control, and Communications: Oliver Hazard Perry and the Battle of Lake Erie." *Journal of Erie Studies* 17 (Fall 1988): 7–26.

Pargellis, Stanley. "Braddock's Defeat." *American Historical Review* 41(2) (January 1936): 253–269.

Parillo, Mark P. *The Japanese Merchant Marine in World War II.* Annapolis, MD: Naval Institute Press, 1993.

Parkman, Francis. *Montcalm and Wolfe.* New York: Atheneum, 1984.

Parshall, Johnathan, and Anthony Tully. *Shattered Sword: The Untold Story of the Battle of Midway.* Washington, DC: Potomac Books, 2005.

Paschall, Rod. *The Defeat of Imperial Germany, 1917–1918.* Chapel Hill, NC: Algonquin, 1989.

Paul, R. Kay. "Death at the Horseshoe—Birth of a Legend: Andrew Jackson's Campaign against the Creek Indians." Unpublished master's thesis, California State University, Dominquez Hills, 2007.

Pfanz, Harry W. *Gettysburg: Culp's Hill and Cemetery Hill.* Chapel Hill: University of North Carolina Press, 1993.

Pfanz, Harry W. *Gettysburg: The Second Day.* Chapel Hill: University of North Carolina Press, 1987.

Pierce, Michael D. *The Most Promising Young Officer: A Life of Ranald Slidell Mackenzie.* Norman: University of Oklahoma Press, 1993.

Pitch, Anthony. *The Burning of Washington: The British Invasion of 1814.* Annapolis, MD: Naval Institute Press, 1998.

Pitt, Barrie. *1918: The Last Act.* New York: Ballantine, 1963.

Plank, Geoffrey G. *An Unsettled Conquest: The British Campaign against the Peoples of Acadia.* Philadelphia: University of Pennsylvania Press, 2001.

Pohl, James W. *The Battle of San Jacinto.* Austin: Texas State Historical Association, 1989.

Pollack, Kenneth M. *Arabs at War: Military Effectiveness, 1948–1991.* Lincoln: University of Nebraska Press, 2002.

Potter, E. B. *Bull Halsey.* Annapolis, MD: Naval Institute Press, 1985.

Prange, Gordon W., with Donald M. Goldstein and Katherine V. Dillon. *At Dawn We Slept: The Untold Story of Pearl Harbor.* New York: McGraw-Hill, 1981.

Prange, Gordon W., with Donald M. Goldstein and Katherine V. Dillon. *Miracle at Midway.* New York: McGraw-Hill, 1982.

Prange, Gordon W., with Donald M. Goldstein and Katherine V. Dillon. *Pearl Harbor: The Verdict of History.* New York: McGraw-Hill, 1986.

Pratt, Sherman W. *Decisive Battles of the Korean War: An Infantry Company Commander's View of the War's Most Critical Engagements.* New York: Vantage, 1992.

Pribbenow, Merle L. "General Vo Nguyen Giap and the Mysterious Evolution of the Plan for the 1968 Tet Offensive." *Journal of Vietnamese Studies* (Summer 2008): 1–33.

Priest, John M. *Antietam: The Soldier's Battle.* New York: Oxford University Press, 1994.

Reid, John G., ed. *The "Conquest" of Acadia, 1710: Imperial, Colonial, and Aboriginal Constructions.* Toronto: University of Toronto Press, 2004.

Reid, Stuart, and Gerry Embleton. *Quebec 1759: The Battle That Won Canada.* London: Osprey, 2003.

Reilly, Robin. *The British at the Gates: The New Orleans Campaign and the War of 1812.* New York: Putnam, 1974.

Remini, Robert V. *The Battle of New Orleans.* New York: Penguin, 1999.

Roberts, David. *The Pueblo Revolt: The Secret Rebellion That Drove the Spanish Out of the Southwest.* New York: Simon and Schuster, 2004.

Roberts, Kenneth. *The Battle of Cowpens: The Great Morale-Builder.* Garden City, NY: Doubleday, 1958.

Robertson, James I., Jr. *Stonewall Jackson: The Man, the Soldier, the Legend.* New York: Macmillan, 1997.

Robertson, William G. *Counterattack on the Naktong, 1950.* Fort Leavenworth, KS: Combat Studies Institute, 1985.

Roland, Charles Pierce. *Albert Sidney Johnston: Soldier of Three Republics.* Austin: University of Texas Press, 1964.

Rountree, Helen C., ed. *Powhatan Foreign Relations, 1500–1722.* Charlottesville: University Press of Virginia, 1993.

Rountree, Helen C., and E. Randolph Turner III. *Before and After Jamestown: Virginia's Powhatans and Their Predecessors.* Gainesville: University Press of Florida, 2002.

Samuels, Peggy, and Harold Samuels. *Teddy Roosevelt at San Juan: The Making of a President.* College Station: Texas A&M University Press, 1997.

Sarf, Wayne Michael. *The Little Bighorn Campaign, March–September 1876.* Conshohocken, PA: Combined Books, 1993.

Scales, Robert H., Jr. *Certain Victory: The U.S. Army in the Gulf War.* Washington, DC: Brassey's, 1997.

Schroen, Gary. *First In: An Insider's Account of How the CIA Spearheaded the War on Terror in Afghanistan.* New York: Presidio/Ballantine, 2005.

Schuetz, Janice E. *Episodes in the Rhetoric of Government-Indian Relations.* Westport, CT: Greenwood, 2002.

Schwarzkopf, H. Norman. *It Doesn't Take a Hero.* New York: Bantam, 1992.

Scott, Leonard. "The Surrender of Detroit." *American History Illustrated* 12(3) (March 1977): 28–36.

Sears, Stephen W. *Chancellorsville.* Boston: Houghton Mifflin, 1996.

Sears, Stephen W. *Landscape Turned Red: The Battle of Antietam.* New York: Ticknor and Fields, 1983.

Sears, Stephen W. *To the Gates of Richmond.* New York: Ticknor and Fields, 1992.

Shaw, John M. *The Cambodian Campaign: The 1970 Offensive and America's Vietnam War.* Lawrence: University of Kansas Press, 2005.

Sherman, William T. *Memoirs of General W. T. Sherman.* New York: Library of America, 1990.

Simmons, Marc. *The Last Conquistador: Juan de Oñate and the Settling of the Far Southwest.* Norman: University of Oklahoma Press, 1991.

Skaggs, David. "River Raisin Redeemed: William Henry Harrison, Oliver Hazard Perry, and the Midwestern Campaign, 1813." *Northwest Ohio History* 77 (Spring 2010): 67–84.

Skaggs, David Curtis. *Oliver Hazard Perry: Honor, Courage and Patriotism in the Early U.S. Navy.* Annapolis, MD: Naval Institute Press, 2006.

Skaggs, David Curtis. *Thomas Macdonough: Master of Command in the Early U.S. Navy.* Annapolis, MD: Naval Institute Press, 2003.

Skates, John Ray. *The Invasion of Japan: Alternative to the Bomb.* Columbia: University of South Carolina Press, 1998.

Sklenar, Larry. *To Hell with Honor: Custer and the Little Big Horn.* Norman: University of Oklahoma Press, 2000.

Smith, Gene A. *Iron and Heavy Guns: Duel between the* Monitor *and* Merrimac. Abilene, TX: McWhiney Foundation Press, 1998.

Smith, Peter C. *Midway, Dauntless Victory: Fresh Perspectives on America's Seminal Naval Victory of 1942*. Barnsley, UK: Pen and Sword Maritime, 2007.

Smith, Timothy B. *The Untold Story of Shiloh: The Battle and the Battlefield*. Knoxville: University of Tennessee Press, 2006.

Smyth, Howard McGraw, and Albert N. Garland. *Sicily and the Surrender of Italy*. Washington, DC: U.S. Government Printing Office, 1965.

Sommers, Richard J. *Richmond Redeemed: The Siege at Petersburg*. Garden City, NY: Doubleday, 1981.

Spector, Ronald. *Admiral of the New Empire: The Life and Career of George Dewey*. Baton Rouge: Louisiana State University Press, 1974.

Spector, Ronald H. *Eagle against the Sun: The American War with Japan*. New York: Free Press, 1985.

Stacey, C. P., and Donald E. Graves, eds. *Quebec, 1759: The Siege and the Battle*. Revised ed. London: Robin Brass Studio, 2002.

Stanley, George. *Canada Invaded, 1775–1776*. Toronto: Hakkert, 1973.

Stanley, George F. G. *War of 1812: Land Operations*. Ottawa: National Museums of Canada and Macmillan, 1983.

Stanton, Shelby L. *The Rise and Fall of an American Army: The U.S. Ground Forces in Vietnam, 1965–1975*. Novato, CA: Presidio, 1985.

Stewart, Richard W. *Operation Enduring Freedom: The United States Army in Afghanistan, October 2001–March 2002*. Washington, DC: U.S. Army Center of Military History, 2003.

Sudgen, John. *Tecumseh's Last Stand*. Norman: University of Oklahoma Press, 1985.

Sutherland, Daniel E. *Fredericksburg & Chancellorsville: The Dare Mark Campaign*. Lincoln: University of Nebraska Press, 1998.

Sword, Wiley. *The Confederacy's Last Hoorah: Spring Hill, Franklin, & Nashville*. New York: HarperCollins for the University of Kansas Press, 1992.

Sword, Wiley. *President Washington's Indian War: The Struggle for the Old Northwest, 1790–1795*. Norman: University of Oklahoma Press, 1985.

Symonds, Craig. *Decision at Sea: Five Naval Battles That Shaped American History*. New York: Oxford University Press, 2005.

Syrett, David. *The Royal Navy in American Waters, 1775–1783*. Aldershot, UK: Scolar, 1989.

Takushiro Hatsutori. *Daitoa Senso Zenshi* [Complete History of the Greater East Asian War]. Tokyo: Hara Shobo, 1965.

Taylor, Blaine. "Shaky Stand at Bladensburg." *Military Heritage* 6 (5) (April 2005): 66–71, 83.

Tebbel, John W. *The Battle of Fallen Timbers, August 20, 1794*. New York: Franklin Watts, 1972.

Thomas, Gordon, and Max Morgan-Witts. *Enola Gay*. New York: Stein and Day, 1977.

Tilford, Earl H., Jr. *Crosswinds: The Air Force's Setup in Vietnam*. College Station: Texas A&M University Press, 1993.

Tilley, John A. *The British Navy and the American Revolution*. Columbia: University of South Carolina Press, 1987.

Tourtellot, Arthur B. *Lexington and Concord*. New York: Norton, 1959.

Tran Dinh Tho. *The Cambodian Incursion*. Washington, DC: U.S. Army Center of Military History, 1979.

Trask, David F. *The War with Spain in 1898*. Lincoln: University of Nebraska Press, 1996.

Tregaskis, Richard. *Guadalcanal Diary*. New York: Random House, 1943.

Trigger, Bruce G. *Natives and Newcomers: Canada's "Heroic Age" Reconsidered*. Kingston, ON: McGill-Queen's University Press, 1985.

Trudeau, Noah Andre. *The Last Citadel: Petersburg, Virginia, June 1864–April 1865*. Baton Rouge: Louisiana State University Press, 1991.

Tucker, Spencer C. *Blue and Gray Navies: The Civil War Afloat*. Annapolis, MD: Naval Institute Press, 2006.

Tucker, Spencer C. *Rise and Fight Again: The Life of General Nathanael Greene*. Wilmington, DE: ISI Books, 2009.

Tunnell, Harry D. *To Compel with Armed Force: A Staff Ride Handbook for the Battle of Tippecanoe*. Fort Leavenworth, KS: Combat Studies Institute, U.S. Command and General Staff College, 2000.

Turner, Jonathan S. "Horseshoe Bend: Epic Battle on the Southern Frontier." Unpublished master's thesis, Georgia Southern University, 1996.

Utley, Robert M. *Frontier Regulars: The United States and the American Indian, 1866–1891*. New York: Macmillan, 1973.

Van Der Vat, Dan. *The Pacific Campaign: The U.S.-Japanese Naval War, 1941–1945*. New York: Simon and Schuster, 1992.

Verrier, Anthony. *The Bomber Offensive*. New York: Macmillan, 1969.

Walker, Dale L. *The Boys of '98: Theodore Roosevelt and the Rough Riders*. New York: Forge, 1999.

Waller, George M. *Samuel Vetch: Colonial Enterpriser*. Chapel Hill: University of North Carolina Press, 1960.

Ward, Christopher. *The War of the Revolution*. 2 vols. New York: Macmillan, 1952.

Warden, John A., III. *The Air Campaign: Planning for Combat*. Washington, DC: National Defense University Press, 1988.

Wheeler, Richard. *Sword over Richmond*. New York: Harper and Row, 1986.

Whitman, John W. *Bataan: Our Last Ditch: The Bataan Campaign, 1942*. New York: Hippocrene Books, 1990.

Willbanks, James H. *The Tet Offensive: A Concise Hist*ory. New York: Columbia University Press, 2007.

Williams, Amelia W., and Eugene C. Barker, eds. *The Writings of Sam Houston, 1813–1863*. 8 vols. Austin: University of Texas Press, 1938–1943.

Willmott, H. P. *The Battle of Leyte Gulf: The Last Fleet Action*. Bloomington: Indiana University Press, 2006.

Willmott, H. P., with Tohmatsu Haruo and W. Spencer Johnson. *Pearl Harbor*. London: Cassell, 2001.

Winders, Richard Bruce. *Mr. Polk's Army: The American Military Experience in the Mexican War*. College Station: Texas A&M University Press, 1997.

Winders, Richard Bruce. *Sacrificed at the Alamo: Tragedy and Triumph in the Texas Revolution*. Abilene, TX: State House Press, 2003.

Winschel, Terrence J. *Vicksburg: Fall of the Confederate Gibraltar*. Abilene, TX: McWhiney Foundation Press, 1999.

Winschel, Terrence J., ed. *Triumph and Defeat: The Vicksburg Campaign*. Campbell, CA: Savas, 1998.

Wise, Stephen R. *Gate of Hell: Campaign for Charleston Harbor, 1863.* Columbia: University of South Carolina Press, 1994.

Woodworth, Steven E. *Beneath a Northern Sky: A Short History of the Gettysburg Campaign.* Wilmington, DE: Scholarly Resources, 2003.

Wooster, Robert. *The Military and United States Indian Policy, 1865–1903.* New Haven, CT: Yale University Press, 1988.

Wright, Derrick. *A Hell of a Way to Die: Tarawa Atoll, 20–23 November 1943.* London: Windrow and Greene, 1997.

Wright, Donald P. *A Different Kind of War: The United States Army in Operation Enduring Freedom (OEF), October 2001–September 2005.* Fort Leavenworth, KS: Combat Studies Institute Press, U.S. Army, 2010.

Wynne, Graeme. *If Germany Attacks: The Battle in Depth in the West.* London: Faber and Faber, 1940.

Y'Blood, William T. *Red Sun Setting: The Battle of the Philippine Sea.* Annapolis, MD: Naval Institute Press, 1980.

Zabecki, David T. *The German 1918 Offensives: A Case Study in the Operational Art of War.* New York: Routledge, 2006.

Zabecki, David T. *Steel Wind: Colonel Georg Bruchmüller and the Birth of Modern Artillery.* Westport, CT: Praeger, 1994.

Zucchino, David. *Thunder Run: The Armored Strike to Capture Baghdad.* New York: Grove, 2004.

# Index

# About the Author

**SPENCER C. TUCKER**, PhD, held the John Biggs Chair of Military History at his alma mater, the Virginia Military Institute in Lexington, for 6 years until his retirement from teaching in 2003. Before that, he was professor of history for 30 years at Texas Christian University, Fort Worth. He has also been a Fulbright Scholar and, as a U.S. Army captain, an intelligence analyst in the Pentagon. Currently the senior fellow of military history at ABC-CLIO, he has written or edited 46 books, including the comprehensive six-volume *A Global Chronology of Conflict*, the four-volume *Almanac of American Military History*, and *Battles That Have Changed History*, all published by ABC-CLIO.